JOHN WILLIS'

DANCE

WORLD

1976

Volume 11

1975-1976 SEASON

CROWN PUBLISHERS, INC.
One Park Avenue
New York, N.Y. 10016

TO

KATHERINE DUNHAM

dancer, choreographer, actress, director, teacher, ethnologist, and anthropologist. Her research and expertise in every type of dance from primitive to ballet made her one of the most eminent and influential exponents of ethnic dance in America.

CONTENTS

EDITOR: JOHN WILLIS

Assistant Editor: Don Nute

Staff: Alberto Cabrera, Scott Chelius, Jack Moore, Fred Ortiz, Stanley
Reeves, William Schelble, Paul Woodson

Staff Photographers: Ron Reagan, Lyn Smith, Van Williams

Opposite Page: Mikhail Baryshnikov, Natalia Makarova in American Ballet Theatre's "Sleeping Beauty"

DANCE PROGRAMS ON BROADWAY

LYCEUM THEATRE
Opened Tuesday, June 10, 1975*

PAUL TAYLOR DANCE COMPANY

Artistic Director-Choreographer, Paul Taylor; Administrator, Neil S. Fleckman; Musical Director, John Herbert McDowell; Wardrobe Supervisor, Carla Messina; Rehearsal Mistress, Bettie deJong; Administrative Assistant, Emily Leinster

COMPANY

Bettie deJong	Greg Reynolds
Carolyn Adams	Lila York
Eileen Cropley	Ruth Andrien
Nicholas Gunn	Linda Kent
Elie Chaib	Robert Kahn
Monica Morris	Michael Deane

PROGRAM

"Sports and Follies" (Eric Satie, Paul Taylor), "3 Epitaphs" (American Folk Music, Taylor), "Duet" (Joseph Haydn, Taylor), "Private Domain" (Iannis Xenakis, Taylor), and *New York Premiere* of "Esplanade" (J. S. Bach, Paul Taylor; Costumes, John Rawlings; Lighting, Jennifer Tipton) danced by the company

Company Manager: Michael Kasdan
Press: Howard Atlee, Meg Gordean
Stage Manager: Perry Cline

* Closed June 15, 1975 after limited engagement of 8 performances. Returned to the Mark Hellinger Theatre Tuesday, January 13, 1976 for 8 additional performances, closing Jan. 18, 1976. Lila York was on leave. The program consisted of "From Sea to Shining Sea" (John Herbert McDowell, Paul Taylor), "Esplanade" (Bach, Taylor), and the *New York Premiere* of "Runes" (Gerald Busby, Paul Taylor Costumes, George Tacit; Lighting, Jennifer Tipton) on Jan. 13, 1976 performed by the company and Gerald Busby playing his composition.

Ron Reagan, Kenn Duncan Photos

Right: Paul Taylor (top) and company

Nicholas Gunn, Carolyn Adams in "Duet"

Carolyn Adams in "Sports and Follies"

"Three Epitaphs" Above and Top: "Runes"

Robert Kahn, Eileen Cropley, Nicholas Gunn, Ruth Andrien, Elie Chaib, Monica Morris in "Esplanade" (also above)

PAUL TAYLOR DANCE COMPANY

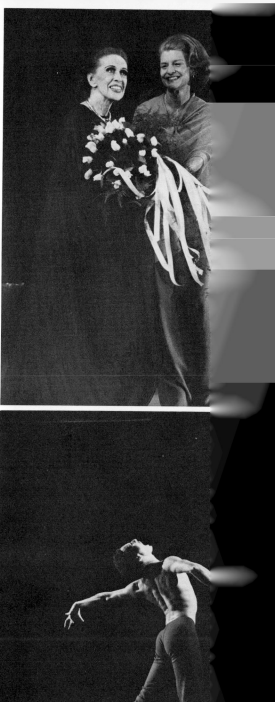

MARTHA GRAHAM
DANCE COMPANY

Artistic Director-Choreographer, Martha Graham; Conductor, Robert Irving; Music Adviser, Eugene Lester; Rehearsal Directors, Ross Parkes, Patricia Birch, Carol Fried, Diane Gray; Settings, Isamu Noguchi, Leandro Locsin; Lighting, Jean Rosenthal, William H. Batchelder, Ronald Bates; Costumes, Halston; General Manager, Cynthia Parker; Company Manager, Frank Lackner; Costumer, Ursula Reed; Management Consultant-Press Representative, Tom Kerrigan; Producer, Ron Protas

COMPANY

Takako Asakawa, Phyllis Gutelius, Ross Parkes, David Hatch Walker, Diane Gray, Janet Eilber, Peggy Lyman, Tim Wengerd, Mario Delamo, Daniel Maloney, Peter Sparling, Lucinda Mitchell, Diana Hart, Bonnie Oda Homsey, Eric Newton, Elisa Monte, Susan McGuire, Shelley Washington, David Chase

PROGRAM

FANFARES composed by Eugene Lester

MESSENGER OF FATE excerpted from the Prologue of "Clytemnestra" (Halim El-Dabh; Vocalist, John Ostendorf) danced by Mario Delamo

SERAPHIC DIALOGUE (Norman Dello Joio) danced by Takako Asakawa, Diane Gray, Elisa Monte, Phyllis Gutelius, David Hatch Walker, Peggy Lyman, Susan McGuire

LAMENTATION (Zoltan Kodaly) danced by Peggy Lyman

DIVERSION OF ANGELS (Norman Dello Joio) danced by Janet Eilber, Takako Asakawa, Shelly Washington, Peter Sparling, David Hatch Walker, Tim Wengerd, Bonnie Oda Homsey, Lucinda Mitchell, Eric Newton, Susan McGuire, Elisa Monte

PAS DE DEUX FROM SWAN LAKE ACT II (Tchaikovsky, Petipa/Ivanov) danced by Margot Fonteyn and Rudolf Nureyev

World Premiere of LUCIFER (Halim El-Dabh, Martha Graham; Setting, Leandro Locsin; Costumes, Halston; Lighting, Ronald Bates) danced by Rudolf Nureyev (Lucifer), Margot Fonteyn (Night) and the company

Martha Swope Photos

**Top Right: First Lady Betty Ford and Martha Graham
at curtain call in celebration of the
Graham company's fiftieth
anniversary**

Peggy Lyman in "Lamentation"

Mario Delamo in "Messenger of Fate" from "

Margot Fonteyn, Rudolf Nureyev (also above) in
"Lucifer" Top: Takako Asakawa, Peter Sparling,
Janet Eilber in "Diversion of Angels"

Rudolf Nureyev in "Lucifer" Top: Elisa Monte,
David Hatch Walker in "Seraphic Dialogue"

10

MARTHA GRAHAM DANCE COMPANY

MAJESTIC THEATRE
Monday, October 6, 1975
Linda Mann Reed presents:

CHARLES WEIDMAN
—A CELEBRATION

Staged by Donald Saddler; Commentator, Walter Terry; Lighting, Richard Winkler; Stage Managers, Craig Jacobs, Judy Olsen; Sound, Paul Spong, Richard Miller; Wardrobe, Anthony Karniewich; Hairstylist, Masarone; Production Assistant, Stuart Rekant; Press, Donald Smith

PROGRAM

CHARLES WEIDMAN THEATRE DANCE COMPANY (Beatrice Seckler, Artistic Director): Barry Barychko, Carol-Geneve, Deborah Carr, Joanne Edelmann, Joanne Kaczynsky, Robert Kosinski, V. Keith Martin, Joenine Roberts, Max Shufer, Janet Towner, Paul Wilson, Janice Wodynski, dancing "Lynchtown" (Engel, Weidman), "Brahms Waltzes, Op. 39" (Brahms, Weidman), "Visualization or From a Farm in New Jersey" (Saint-Saens, Weidman)

JOSE LIMON DANCE COMPANY (Ruth Currier, Artistic Director): Carla Maxwell, Robyn Cutler, Laura Glenn, Marjorie Philpot, Tonia Shimin, Risa Steinberg, Ann Vachon, Mark Ammerman, Bill Cratty, Christopher Gillis, Gary Masters, Fred Mathews, Louis Solino, dancing "The Shakers" (Traditional, Doris Humphrey)

MARY ANTHONY DANCE THEATRE (Mary Anthony, Artistic Director): Daniel Maloney, Gwendolyn Bye, Tonia Shimin, Erick Hodges, Michael Burg (Narrator), performing "The Unicorn in the Garden" from "Fables for Our Time" (Freda Miller, Weidman)

ALVIN AILEY REPERTORY WORKSHOP members Daniela Malusardi and John Young dancing "Fix Me, Jesus" from "Revelations"

KATHERINE LITZ dancing "The Glyph"

DANIEL NAGRIN dancing "Strange Hero"

**Right: Gary Masters, Carla Maxwell,
Risa Steinberg in "The Shakers"**

Charles Weidman Theatre Dance Company in "Lynchtown"
(Ron Reagan Photo)

URIS THEATRE
Opened Tuesday, November 4, 1975.*
Ballet Theatre Foundation, Inc. presents:

AMERICAN BALLET THEATRE

Directors, Lucia Chase, Oliver Smith; Associate Director, Antony Tudor; General Manager, Daryl Dodson; Music Director-Conductor, Akira Endo; Assistant Director, Enrique Martinez; Regisseur, Dimitri Romanoff; Conductor, Tibor Pusztai; Ballet Master, Michael Lland; Lighting, Nananne Porcher; Ballet Mistress, Fiorella Keane; Production Associate, Marian Kinsella; Production Assistant, Dana Bruce

COMPANY

PRINCIPALS: Karena Brock, Erik Bruhn, Fernando Bujones, Eleanor D'Antuono, Vladimir Gelvan, Cynthia Gregory, Gelsey Kirkland, Ted Kivitt, Bonnie Mathis, Ivan Nagy, Rudolf Nureyev, Terry Orr, Marcos Paredes, John Prinz, Martine Van Hamel, Sallie Wilson, Gayle Young

SOLOISTS: Buddy Balough, William Carter, Warren Conover, Kristine Elliott, Nanette Glushak, Jolinda Menendez, Hilda Morales, Frank Smith, Marianna Tcherkassky, Clark Tippet, Charles Ward, Dennis Wayne

CORPS: Christopher Aponte, Elizabeth Ashton, Victor Barbee, Carmen Barth, Amy Blaisdell, Nina Brzorad, Miguel Campaneria, George de la Pena, Susan Frazer, Paul Gifford, Rodney Gustafson, Melissa Hale, Aurea Hammerli, Cynthia Harvey, Kenneth Hughes, Janne Jackson, Marie Johansson, Susan Jones, Francia Kovak, Linda Kuchera, Elaine Kudo, Charles Maple, Dennis Marshall, Sara Maule, Ruth Mayer, Christine O'Neal, Gregory Osborne, Michael Owen, Kirk Peterson, Janet Popeleski, Berthica Prieto, Leigh Provancha, Cathryn Rhodes, Richard Schafer, Raymond Serrano, Janet Shibata, Christine Spizzo, Denise Warner, Patricia Wesche, Sandall Whitaker

REPERTOIRE

"Raymonda" (Alexandre Glazounov, Marius Petipa; Re-staged with additional choreography by Rudolf Nureyev; Based on original Libretto by Pashkova, Vsevolojsky and Petipa; Scenery and Costumes, Nicholas Georgiadis; Lighting, Nicholas Cernovitch)

Company Manager: Herbert Scholder
Press: Virginia Hymes, Joan Ehrlich-White, Fran Michelman, Charles France
Stage Managers: Dan Butt, Jerry Rice, Peggy Gardner

* Closed November 16, 1975 after limited engagement of 16 performances. Returned in repertory Monday, December 22, 1975 through February 1, 1976 for 48 performances. Additional Principal Dancers who appeared were Mikhail Baryshnikov, Paolo Bortoluzzi, Carla Fracci, Marcia Haydee, Natalia Makarova, Yoko Morishita. Cynthia Gregory, Dennis Wayne and Rudolf Nureyev did not dance during this engagement.

REPERTOIRE

"Giselle" (Adam, Blair), "The Leaves Are Fading" (Dvorak, Tudor), "At Midnight" (Mahler, Feld), "Les Patineurs" (Meyerbeer, Ashton), "Le Spectre de la Rose" (Weber, Fokine), "Coppelia" (Delibes, Martinez), "Brahms Quintet" (Brahms, Nahat), "Le Baiser de la Fee" (Stravinsky/Tchaikovsky, Neumeier), "The River" (Ellington, Ailey), "Fall River Legend" (Gould de Mille), "Las Hermanas" (Martin, MacMillan), "Jardin aux Lilas" (Chausson, Tudor), "Fancy Free" (Bernstein, Robbins), "Tales of Hoffman" (Offenbach, Darrell), "Shadowplay" (Koechlin, Tudor), "Les Sylphides" (Chopin, Fokine), "The Maids" (Milhaud, Ross), "Gemini" (Henze, Tetley), "La Sylphide" (Lovenskjold, Bruhn after Bournonville), "Epilogue" (Mahler, Neumeier), "La Ventana" (Lumbye, Bruhn after Bournonville), "Medea" (Barber, Butler)

PREMIERES: "Hamlet: Connotations" (Aaron Copland, John Neumeier; Sets, Robin Wagner; Costumes, Theoni V. Aldredge) on Tuesday, Jan. 6, 1976; "Push Comes to Shove" (Haydn, Twyla Tharp; Designs, Santo Loquasto; Lighting, Jennifer Tipton) on Friday, Jan. 9, 1976; "Awakening" (Craig Steven Shuler, Robert Weiss Costumes, Susan Tammany) on Tuesday, Dec. 30, 1975 danced by Gelsey Kirkland and Mikhail Baryshnikov.

Martha Swope Photos

Gelsey Kirkland, Ivan Nagy

Top Left: Rudolf Nureyev,
Gelsey Kirkland in "Raymonda"

Marcia Haydee, Mikhail Baryshnikov in "Hamlet: Connotations" Top: (L) Mikhail Baryshnikov in "Medea" (R) Natalia Makarova in "Coppelia"

Left: Clark Tippet, Martine Van Hamel, Mikhail Baryshnikov Top: (L) Mikhail Baryshnikov (R) Martine Van Hamel, Clark Tippet in "Push Comes to Shove"

AMERICAN BALLET THEATRE

Zhandra Rodriguez, Terry Orr, Karena Brock in "Les Patineurs" Top: (L) Martine Van Hamel in "The River" (R) Fernando Bujones, Terry Orr, Buddy Balough in "Fancy Free"

URIS THEATRE

Opened Tuesday, November 18, 1975.*

Hurok Concerts presents:

MARGOT FONTEYN
& RUDOLF NUREYEV

with Leslie Edwards, Daniel Lommel, and Michael Ballard, Richard Haisma, Jerry Pearson, Robert Small, Alexander Minz, John DeVilliers, David Jackson, Larry Leritz, Daniel Murphy, Mark Trares, Gary Cordial, Gregory Ismailov, Joe McClung, Charles McAdams, David Wallach, Caroline Todd

PROGRAM

"Marguerite and Armand" (Franz Liszt, Frederick Ashton; Costumes, Cecil Beaton; Decor, William Chappell), "Songs of a Wayfarer" (Gustav Mahler, Maurice Bejart; New York Premiere), "Le Corsaire Pas de Deux" (Riccardo Drigo/Leon Minkus, Marius Petipa), and *AMERICAN PREMIERES* of "Moments" (Maurice Ravel, Murray Louis; Costumes and Lighting, Barrow), "Amazon Forest Final Pas de Deux" (Villa-Lobos, Frederick Ashton; Sung by Karen Lundry)

Press: Sheila Porter, Lilliam Libman
Stage Manager: William Hammond

* Closed Nov. 29, 1975 after limited engagement of 13 performances.

Margot Fonteyn, Rudolf Nureyev in "Marguerite and Armand" Top Left in "Le Corsaire"

Margot Fonteyn, Rudolf Nureyev in "Marguerite and Armand" (also top right) Top Left: Rudolf Nureyev in "Le Corsaire"

MARK HELLINGER THEATRE
Opened Monday, December 8, 1975.*
Martha Graham Center for Contemporary Danc, Inc., presents the Fiftieth Anniversary Season of:

MARTHA GRAHAM
DANCE COMPANY

Artistic Director-Choreographer, Martha Graham; Producer, Ron Protas; Associate Artistic Directors, Ross Parkes, Robert Powell; Conductors, Aaron Copland, Robert Irving, Stanley Sussman; Composers, Hunter Johnson, Mordecai Seter; Rehearsal Directors, Carol Fried, Linda Hodes, Ross Parkes, Robert Powell; Settings, Isamu Noguchi, Arch Lauterer, Leandro Locsin, Marisol; Lighting, Jean Rosenthal, Ronald Bates; Costumes, Halston; Hairstylist, Ian Harrington; General Manager, Cynthia Parker; Production Supervisor, Ronald Bates

COMPANY

Takako Asakawa, Jean Erdman, Diane Gray, Linda Hodes, Yuriko Kimura, Pearl Lang, Rudolf Nureyev, Ross Parkes, David Hatch Walker

David Chase, Mario Delamo, Janet Eilber, Eivind Harum, Bonnie Oda Homsey, Peggy Lyman, Susan McGuire, Daniel Maloney, Lucinda Mitchell, Elisa Monte, Pater Sparling, Armgaard von Bardeleben, Tim Wengerd

Jessica Chao, Linda Hayes, Ohad Naharin, Barry Smith, Keiko Takeye Henry Yu

OPENING NIGHT GALA: Introduction by Martha Graham; *World Premiere* of "Adorations" (Set, Leandro Locsin; Lighting, Ronald Bates; Costumes, Halston; Choreography, Martha Graham; Accompanist, Reed Hanson), *World Premiere* of "Point of Crossing" (Mordecai Seter, Martha Graham), "Lamentation" (Zoltan Kodaly, Graham), "Diversion of Angels" (Norman Dello Joio, Graham), "Lucifer" (Halim El-Dabh, Graham)

REPERTOIRE

"Acrobats of God" (Carlos Surinach), "Cave of the Heart" (Samuel Barber), "Clytemnestra" (Halim El-Dabh), "Cave of the Heart" (Samuel Barber), "Appalachian Spring" (Aaron Copland), "Herodiade" (Paul Hindemith), "Night Journey" (William Schuman), "Frontier" (Louis Horst), "Letter to the World" (Hunter Johnson), "Circe" (Alan Hovhaness), "Errand into the Maze" (Gian-Carlo Menotti), "Seraphic Dialogue" (Norman Dello Joio), "Dark Meadow" (Carlos Chavez), and *World Premiere* of "The Scarlet Letter" (Hunter Johnson, Martha Graham; Set, Marisol; Costumes, Halston; Lighting, Ronald Bates; Conductor, Robert Irving) with Rudolf Nureyev as Dimmesdale, Janet Eilber as Hester, and Tim Wengerd as Hester's Husband.

Company Manager: Frank Lackner
Press: Tom Kerrigan
Stage Managers: Perry Silvey, Walter Kaiser

* Closed January 3, 1976 after 32 performances

Martha Swope Photos

Top Left: Susan McGuire, Daniel Maloney in "Adorations"
Below: Rudolf Nureyev, Janet Eilber in "The Scarlet Letter"

Ross Parkes, Diane Gray, Janet Eilber,
Tim Wengerd in "Point of Crossing"

David Hatch Walker, Takako Asakawa in "Adorations" Top: Ross Parkes, Yuriko Kimura in "Point of Crossing"

Pearl Lang in "Herodiade" Top: Peggy Lyman in "Frontier"

MARTHA GRAHAM DANCE COMPANY

Takako Asakawa, David Hatch Walker in "Diversion of Angels" Above: Ross Parkes, Diane Gray in "Night Journey" Top: Rudolf Nureyev, Janet Eilber in "Lucifer"

Linda Hodes in "Acrobats of God" Above: Takako Asakawa "Clytemnestra" Top: Asakawa, David Hatch Walker in "Seraphic Dialogue"

URIS THEATRE
Opened Wednesday, February 25, 1976.*

DANCE THEATRE OF HARLEM

Directors, Arthur Mitchell, Karel Shook; Conductor, Tania Leon; General Manager, Theatre Now, Inc., Norman E. Rothstein; Technical Director-Lighting, Gary Fails; Costumes, Zelda Wynn; Assistant Musical Director, David Gagne; Ballet Master, William Scott; Ballet Mistress, Gayle McKinney; Wardrobe Master, Lawrence Taylor; Coordinators, Herbert Smith, Lorenzo James

COMPANY

Lydia Abarca, Karen Brown, M. Elena Carter, Stephanie Dabney, Brenda Garrett, Yvonne Hall, Virginia Johnson, Susan Lovelle, Gayle McKinney, Melva Murray-White, Sheila Rohan, Karen Wright, Roman Brooks, Homer Bryant, Ronald Perry, Paul Russell, Allen Sampson, Samuel Smalls, Keith Saunders, William Scott, Eddie Shellman, Mel Tomlinson, Derek Williams, Joseph Wyatt

REPERTOIRE

"Fete Noire" (Shostakovich, Arthur Mitchell), "Forces of Rhythm" (Traditional/Contemporary, Louis Johnson), "Holberg Suite" (Greig, Mitchell), "Le Corsaire Pas de Deux" (Drigo, Karel Shook), "Every Now and Then" (Quincy Jones, William Scott), "Biosfera" (Marlos Nobre, Mitchell), "Douglas" (Geoffrey Holder, Holder), "Rhythmetron" (Nobre, Mitchell), "Allegro Brillante" (Tchaikovsky, Balanchine), "Bugaku" (Mayuzumi, Balanchine), "Concerto Barocco" (Bach, Balanchine), "Caravansarai" (Santana, Talley Beatty), "Agon" (Stravinsky, Balanchine), "Don Quixote Pas de Deux" (Minkus, Karol Shook), "Design for Strongs" (Tchaikovsky, Taras), "Afternoon of a Faun" (Debussy, Robbins), "The Beloved" (Hamilton, Truitte/Horton), "The Combat" (DeBanfield, Dollar), "Carmen" (Bizet, Ruth Page)

PREMIERES: "Manifestations" (Primous Fountain III, Arthur Mitchell; Costumes, Zelda Wynn) danced by Homer Bryant, Susan Lovelle, Mel Tomlinson on Wednesday, Feb. 25, 1976; "Concerto" (Mendelssohn, William Dollar; Costumes, Zelda Wynn) debuted Tuesday, March 2, 1976; "Romeo and Juliet Pas de Deux" (Prokofiev, Gabriella Taub-Darvish; Costumes, Zelda Wynn) opened Thursday, March 4, 1976, danced by Lydia Abarca and Paul Russell

Company Manager: Robert Frissell
Press: Merle Debuskey, Susan L. Schulman, Lorenzo James
Stage Managers: Gary Fails, Richard Gonsalves

* Closed March 28, 1976 after limited engagement of 39 performances.

Ron Reagan, Marbeth, Anthony Crickmay Photos

Mel Tomlinson, Susan Lovelle in "Manifestations"
Top Right: Roman Brooks, Virginia Johnson, William Scott in "Caravansarai"

Susan Lovelle, Homer Bryant, Mel Tomlinson in "Manifestations"

21

"Fete Noire" Top: Roman Brooks, Gayle McKinney in "The Beloved" Right: Sheila Rohan in "Dougla"

"Every Now and Then" Above: Lydia Abarca, Roman Brooks, William Scott in "Carmen and Jose"

22

DANCE THEATRE OF HARLEM

ginia Johnson in "Forces of Rhythm" Above: Ronald Perry,
Lydia Abarca in "Bugaku" Top: Virginia Johnson,
Ronald Perry in "Allegro Brillante"

Elena Carter, Paul Russell in
"Le Corsaire" Top: "Le Combat"

DANCE PROGRAMS AT LINCOLN CENTER

NEW YORK STATE THEATER
Opened Tuesday, July 1, 1975.*
Ballet Theatre Foundation in association with City Center of Music and
Drama presents:

AMERICAN BALLET THEATRE

Directors, Lucia Chase, Oliver Smith; Associate Director, Antony
Tudor; General Manager, Daryl Dodson; Principal Conductor, David Gilbert; Guest Conductor, Akira Endo; Assistant to Directors,
Enrique Martinez; Regisseur, Dimitri Romanoff; Ballet Masters,
Scott Douglas, Michael Lland; Ballet Mistress, Fiorella Keane; Assistant Conductor, Tibor Pusztai; Lighting, Nananne Porcher;
Wardrobe, Robert Holloway, May Ishimoto, Robert Boehm; Production Associate, Marian Kinsella; Production Assistant, Dana
Bruce

COMPANY

PRINCIPALS: Mikhail Baryshnikov, Karena Brock, Erik Bruhn,
Fernando Bujones, Eleavor D'Antuono, Cynthia Gregory, Jonas
Kage, Gelsey Kirkland, Ted Kivitt, Natalia Makarova, Bonnie Mathis, Ivan Nagy, Rudolf Nureyev, Terry Orr, Marcos Paredes, John
Prinz, Martine Van Hamel, Sallie Wilson, Gayle Young

SOLOISTS: Buddy Balough, William Carter, David Coll, Warren
Conover, Deborah Dobson, Nanette Glushak, Kim Highton, Keith
Lee, Jolinda Menendez, Hilda Morales, Marianna Tcherkassky,
Charles Ward, Dennis Wayne, Maria Youskevitch

CORPS: Elizabeth Ashton, Victor Barbee, Carmen Barth, Amy
Blaisdell, Nina Brzorad, George de la Pena, Kristine Elliott, Susan
Frazer, Paul Gifford, Rodney Gustafson, Kevin Haigen, Melissa
Hale, Cynthia Harvey, Kenneth Hughes, Janne Jackson, Marie Johansson, Susan Jones, Francia Kovak, Linda Kuchera, Charles Maple, Dennis Marshall, Sara Maule, Ruth Mayer, Christine O'Neal,
Gregg Osborne, Michael Owen, Kirk Peterson, Janet Popeleski,
Berthica Prieto, Leigh Provancha, Cathryn Rhodes, Giselle Roberge, Richard Schafer, Kevin Self, Raymond Serrano, Janet
Shibata, Frank Smith, Christine Spizzo, Clark Tippet, Denise
Warner, Patricia Wesche, Sandall Whitaker

REPERTOIRE

"Giselle" (Adam, Blair), "Swan Lake" (Tchaikovsky, Blair). "La
Sylphide" (Lovenskjold, Bournonville), "La Bayadere" (Minkus,
Petipa), "Etudes" (Riisager, Lander, "Concerto" (Shostakovich,
MacMillan), "Gemini" (Henze, Tetley), "Le Jeune Homme et la
Mort" (Bach, Petit), "Les Noches" (Stravinsky, Robbins), "Pillar of
Fire" (Schoenberg, Tudor), "The River" (Ellington, Ailey) "Les
Sylphides (Chopin, Fokine), "Theme and Variations" (Tchaikovsky,
Balanchine), "Undertow" (Schuman, Tudor), *New Productions* of
"Raymonda" (Glazounov, Nureyev), and "Shadowplay" (Koechlin,
Tudor), *WORLD PREMIERES* of "The Leaves Are Fading" (Antonin Dvorak, Antony Tudor; Sets, Ming Cho Lee; Costumes, Patricia Zipprodt) on July 17, 1975; "Epilogue" (Gustav Mahler, John
Neumeier; Lighting, Nicholas Cernovitch) danced by Natalia
Makarova and Erik Bruhn on Tuesday, July 8, 1975.

Company Manager: Herbert Scholder
Press: Virginia Hymes, Joan Ehrlich-White
Stage Managers: Dan Butt, Jerry Rice, Bentley Roton

* Closed Aug. 9, 1975 after limited engagement of 40 performances,
and a gala benefit on Monday, July 28, 1975.

Martha Swope Photos

Top Right: Ivan Nagy, Natalia Makarova in "Giselle"

Gelsey Kirkland, Mikhail Baryshnikov in "Giselle"

Carla Fracci, Gayle Young in "Jardin aux Lilas" Top: (L) Lucia Chase, Gayle Young, Sallie Wilson in "Fall River Legend" (R) Natalia Makarova, Fernando Bujones in "Don Quixote"

Ivan Nagy, Natalia Makarova
Above: Mikhail Baryshnikov, Gelsey Kirkland in
"La Fille Mal Gardee"

Natalia Makarova, Enrique Martinez, Ivan Nagy in
"La Fille Mal Gardee" Top: Marianna Tcherkassky,
Fernando Bujones in "The Nutcracker"

Gelsey Kirkland, Mikhail Baryshnikov in "Coppelia"
Top: Natalia Makarova, Ted Kivitt in "Coppelia"

Natalia Makarova in "Coppelia"
AMERICAN BALLET THEATRE

METROPOLITAN OPERA HOUSE
Opened Tuesday, July 22, 1975.*
Hurok Concerts present:

NATIONAL BALLET OF CANADA
with
RUDOLF NUREYEV

Artistic Director, David Haber; Producer, Erik Bruhn; Musical Director-Conductor, George Crum; Ballet Mistress, Joanne Nisbet; Ballet Master, David Scott; General Manager, Gerry Eldred; Assistant Conductor, John Goss; Conductor, Aubrey Bowman; Concert Master, Isabell Vila; Production Director, Mary Jolliffe; Assistant General Manager, Jacques Mizne; Wardrobe Supervisor, James Ronaldson; Resident Scenic Artist, Georg Schogl; Assistant to Artistic Director, David Walker; Technical Coordinator, Mario De Maria

COMPANY

PRINCIPALS: Vanessa Harwood, Mary Jago, Karen Kain, Nadia Potts, Veronica Tennant, Frank Augustyn, Gary Norman, Tomas Schramek, Sergui Stefanschi, Hazaros Surmeyan

SOLOISTS: Victoria Bertram, Colleen Cool, Linda Maybarduk, Sonia Perusse, Wendy Reiser, Gailene Stock, Jacques Gorrissen, Charles Kirby: Clinton Rothwell, Gloria Luoma, Mavis Staines, Daniel Capouch, Stephen Greenston, James Kudelka, David Roxander

CORPS: Yolande Auger, Susan Bodie, Carina Bomers, Anne Byrnes, Glenda Carhart, Ann Ditchburn, Lorna Geddes, Susan Keen, Jennifer Laird, Daphne Loomis, Cynthia Lucas, Karin Mawson, Esther Murillo, Patricia Oney, Jennifer Orr, Heather Ronald, Katherine Scheidegger, Barbara Szablowski, Karen Tessmer, Charmain Turner, Valerie Wilder, Gizella Witkowsky, Jane Wooding

REPERTOIRE

"The Sleeping Beauty" (P. I. Tchaikovsky, Rudolf Nureyev after Petipa; Scenery and Costumes, Nicholas Georgiadis), "Coppelia" (Leo Delibes, Erik Bruhn after Arthur Saint-Leon; Scenery and Costumes, Maurice Strike), "Swan Lake" (Tchaikovsky, Erik Bruhn after Petipa), "La Sylphide" (Loewenskijold, Erik Bruhn after Bournonville), "Don Juan" (Gluck Thomas Luis de Victoria, John Neumeier; Decor and Costumes, Filippo Sanjust)

Company Manager: Hamish Robertson
Press: Sheila Porter, Rima Corben, Robert Weiss
Stage Managers: Norm Dyson, Ernest Abogov, Lawrence Beevers

* Closed August 10, 1975 after limited engagement of 23 performances.

Ken Bell Photos

**Left: "Coppelia" Top: Karen Kain,
Rudolf Nureyev in "Don Juan"**

Vanessa Harwood, Constantin Patsalas in "Coppelia"

Karen Kain in "Swan Lake"

**Karen Kain, Rudolf Nureyev in
"Swan Lake" (also above and top)**

**Rudolf Nureyev Above: Nadia Potts
Top: Karen Kain, Nureyev in "Swan Lake"**

Sergiu Stefanschi, Veronica Tennant Top: Stefanschi,
Tomas Schramek, Wendy Reiser in "La Sylphide"

Rudolf Nureyev, Veronica Tennant (also top)
Above: Frank Augustyn in "The Sleeping Beauty"

30

NATIONAL BALLET OF CANADA

NEW YORK STATE THEATER
Opened Tuesday, August 12, 1975.*
City Center of Music and Drama Inc. presents:

ALVIN AILEY CITY CENTER DANCE THEATER

Artistic Director-Choreographer, Alvin Ailey; General Manager, Ivy Clarke; Associate Artistic Director-Ballet Master, Ali Pourfarrokh; Musical Director-Conductor, Howard Roberts; Associate Conductor, Robert Rogers; Administrative Assistant, Lois Framhein; Lighting Supervisor, Chenault Spence; Sound, Abe Jacob, Gerald Krulewicz; Wardrobe Supervisor, Donna Barry; Wardrobe Mistress, Gloria Scott; Wardrobe Master, Duane Talley; Assistant Ballet Mistress, Mari Kajiwara; Production Manager, Ralph McWilliams

COMPANY

Charles Adams, Sarita Allen, Christopher Aponte, Nerissa Barnes, Fred Bratcher, Enid Britten, Sergio Cal, Masazumi Chaya, Ulysses Dove, Valerie Feit, Meg Gordon, Judith Jamison, Melvin Jones, Mari Kajiwara, Jodi Moccia, Delila Moseley, Michihiko Oka, Carl Paris, Cynthia Penn, Kelvin Rotardier, Beth Shorter, Warren Spears, Estelle Spurlock, Clive Thompson, Elbert Watson, Dudley Williams, Donna Wood, Peter Woodin, Sara Yarborough, Tina Yuan, and *GUEST ARTISTS* Brother John Sellers, Bernard Thacker

REPERTOIRE

"Rainbow 'Round My Shoulder" (arranged by Robert de Cormier and Milton Okun, Donald McKayle), "The Mooche" (Duke Ellington, Ailey), "Blues Suite" (Traditional, Ailey), "Cry" (Coltrane/-Nyro/Voices of East Harlem, Ailey), "Carmina Burana" (Carl Orff, John Butler), "Revelations" (Traditional, Ailey), "Road of the Phoebe Snow" (Ellington/Strayhorn, Talley Beatty), "Night Creature" (Ellington, Ailey), "Dance for Six" (Vivaldi, Trisler), "Love Songs" (Russel/Wind/Bleecher/Scott, Ailey), "After Eden" (Hoiby, Butler), "A Song for You," "Portrait of Billie" (Songs of Billie Holiday, Butler)

Company Manager: Richard Grayson
Press: Howard Atlee, Meg Gordean
Stage Managers: William Burd, Donald Moss

* Closed August 24, 1975 after limited engagement of 16 performances.

John Elbers, Randy Masser, Donald Moss, Fred Fehl, Alan Bergman, Rosemary Winckley Photos

**Right: Michihiko Oka, Tina Yuan in
"After Eden" Top: Judith Jamison in "Cry"**

Judith Jamison, Clive Thompson in "Liberian Suite"

**Elbert Watson, Melvin Jones, Michihiko Oka,
Ulysses Dove in "Rainbow 'Round my Shoulder"**

**Clive Thompson, Tina Yuan in "Hidden Rites" also top
in "Lark Ascending" Above: "Night Creature"**

**Clive Thompson, Tina Yuan in "Carmina Burana" Above:
"The Mooche" with Sarita Allen Top: Carl Paris,
Mari Kajiwara, Warren Spears in "Echoes in Blue"**

Dudley Williams in "A Song for You"

"Revelations" (also above) Top: Ulysses Dove,
Enid Britten in "Road of the Phoebe Snow"

Mari Kajiwara, Melvin Jones, Judith Jamison in
"Revelations" Above: Estelle Spurlock, Judith Jamison,
Sarita Allen, Sara Yarborough in "The Mooche"

NEW YORK STATE THEATER
Opened Tuesday, November 11, 1975.*
City Center of Music and Drama, Inc. presents the sixty-third New York season of:

NEW YORK CITY BALLET

General Director, Lincoln Kirstein; Ballet Masters, George Balanchine, Jerome Robbins, John Taras; Assistant Ballet Masters, Tom Abbott, Rosemary Dunleavy; Music Director-Principal Conductor, Robert Irving; Associate Conductor, Hugo Fiorato; Costumer, Karinska; Wardrobe Supervisors, Sophie Pourmel, Leslie Copeland; Wardrobe Mistress, Dorothy Fugate; Wardrobe Master, Larry Calvert; Hairstylist, James Brusock; General Manager, Betty Cage; Assistant Manager, Edward Bigelow

COMPANY

Muriel Aasen, Merrill Ashley, Debra Austin, Tracy Bennett, Anthony Blum, Jean-Pierre Bonnefous, Bonita Borne, Elyse Borne, Leslie Brown, Jilise Bushling, Victoria Bromberg, Maria Calegari, Stephen Caras, Victor Castelli, Hermes Conde, Bart Cook, Gail Crisa, Jacques d'Amboise, Richard Dryden, Daniel Duell, Joseph Duell, Gerard Ebitz, Renee Estopinal, Suzanne Farrell, Nina Fedorova, Elise Flagg, Laura Flagg, Wilhelmina Frankfurt, Susan Freedman, Jean-Pierre Frohlich, Judith Fugate, John Grensback, Lauren Hauser, Susan Hendl, Lisa Hess, Nichol Hilinka, Linda Homek, Richard Hoskinson, Dolores Houston, Kipling Houston, Elise Ingalls, Sandra Jennings, William Johnson, Jay Jolley, Allegra Kent, Deborah Koolish, Deni Lamont, Sara Leland, Lourdes Lopez, Adam Luders, Robert Maiorano, Peter Martins, Laurence Matthews, Kay Mazzo, Patricia McBride, Teena McConnell, Francisco Moncion, Catherine Morris, Marnee Morris, Peter Naumann, Colleen Neary, Kyra Nichols, Shaun O'Brien, Frank Ohman, Delia Peters, Susan Pillarre, Bryan Pitts, Terri Lee Port, Christine Redpath, Lisa de Ribere, David Richardson, Francis Sackett, Paul Sackett, Stephanie Saland, Lilly Samuels, Peter Schaufuss, Marjorie Spohn, Carol-Marie Strizak, Carol Sumner, Richard Tanner, Helgi Tomasson, Nolan T'Sani, Violette Verdy, Karin von Aroldingen, Sheryl Ware, Heather Watts, Robert Weiss, Garielle Whittle, Sandra Zigars

REPERTOIRE

(All choreography by George Balanchine except where noted) "Agon" (Stravinsky), "Allegro Brillante" (Tchaikovsky), "Brahms-Schoenberg Quartet" "Chansons Madecasses" (Ravel, Jerome Robbins), "The Concert" (Chopin, Robbins), "Concerto Barocco" (Bach), "Coppelia" (Delibes), "Cortege Hongrois" (Glazounov), "Danses Concertantes" (Stravinsky), "Daphnis et Chloe" (Ravel, John Taras), "Divertimento from Le Baiser de la Fee" (Stravinsky), "Donizetti Variations", "Don Quixote" (Nabokov), "Duo Concertant" (Stravinsky), "Dybbuk Variations" (Bernstein, Robbins,' "Episodes" (Webern) "Fanfare" (Britten, Robbins), "Firebird" (Stravinsky, Balanchine/Robbins), "Four Temperaments" (Hindemith), "Gaspard de la Nuitt" (Ravel), "Goldberg Variations" (Bach, Robbins), "Harlequinade" (Drigo), "Illuminations" (Britten, Ashton), "In G Major" (Ravel, Robbins), "In the Night" (Chopin, Robbins), "Ivesiana" (Ives), "Jewels: Emeralds (Faure), Rubies (Stravinsky), Diamonds" (Tchaikovsky), "Ma Mere L'Oye" (Ravel, Robbins), "Nutcracker" (Tchaikovsky), "Meditation" (Tchaikovsky), "Tarantella" (Gottschalk/Kay), "Tchaikovsky Pas de Deux," "Valse-Fantasie" (Glinka), "Prodigal Son" (Prokofiev), "Rapsodie Espagnole" (Ravel), "Raymonda Variations" (Glazounov), "Scherzo Fantastique" (Stravinsky), "Scotch Symphony" (Mendelssohn), "Serenade" (Tchaikovsky), "Sonatine" (Ravel), "Stars & Stripes" (Sousa/Kay), "Stravinsky Violin Concerto," "Swan Lake" (Tchaikovsky), "Symphony in C" (Bizet), "Symphony in Three Movements" (Stravinsky), "Le Tombeau de Couperin" (Ravel), "Tschaikovsky Piano Concerto No. 2," "Tchaikovsky Suite No. 3," "Tzigane" (Ravel), *NY PREMIERES* of "The Steadfast Tin Soldier" (Georges Bizet, George Balanchine; Scenery and Costumes, David Mitchell; Lighting, Ronald Bates), and "Chaconne" (Christoph Willibald Gluck, George Balanchine; Lighting, Ronald Bates; Conductor, Robert Irving) on Thursday, Jan. 22, 1976.

Company Manager: Zelda Dorfman
Press: Virginia Donaldson, Larry Strichman, Leslie Bailey
Stage Managers: Ronald Bates, Kevin Tyler, Roland Vazquez

Martha Swope Photos

**Top Right: Robert Weiss, Patricia McBride in
"The Steadfast Tin Soldier" (also below)**

* Closed Feb. 15, 1976 after 106 performances. Returned for Spring Season (April 27—June 27, 1976) of 71 performances. John Bass joined the company. Added to the repertoire were "Afternoon of a Faun" (Debussy), "An Evening's Waltzes" (Serge Prokofiev, Robbins), "Bugaku" (Mayuzumi), "The Cage" (Stravinsky), "Dances at a Gathering" (Chopin, Robbins), "Four Bagatelles" (Beethoven), "Irish Fantasy" "Camille Saint-Saens, d'Amboise), "A Midsummer Night's Dream" (Mendelssohn), "Monumentum pro Gesualdo" (Stravinsky), "Movements for Piano and Orchestra" (Stravinsky), "La Sonnambula" (Vittorio Rieti), "Valse Fantaisie" (Michael Glinka), "Variations pour une Porte et un Soupir" (Pierre Henry), "Watermill" (Ito, Robbins), "Western Symphony" (Sousa/Kay), "Who Cares?" (Gershwin/Kay), *WORLD PREMIERE* Thursday, May 13, 1976 of "Union Jack" (Hershy Kay, adapted from traditional British music; George Balanchine; Scenery and Costumes, Rouben Ter-Arutunian; Lighting, Ronald Bates) for the entire company. On Thursday, May 20, 1976 a new revised version of "Square Dance" (Corelli-Vivaldi, Balanchine) was performed.

Karin von Aroldingen (R) Above: Suzanne Farrell
Top: Jean-Pierre Bonnefous,
Patricia McBride in "Union Jack"

Bart Cook, Karen von Aroldingen, Victor Castelli Above:
Peter Martins Top: Helgi Tomasson in "Union Jack"

35

Peter Martins, Suzanne Farrell (also top) in "Chaconne"   Daniel Duell, Muriel Aasen in "The Nutcracker"

Kay Mazzo, Bart Cook (also top) in "Square Dance"

Colleen Neary, Peter Martins in "The Nutcracker"

NEW YORK CITY BALLET

"Le Tombeau de Couperin" Top: (L) Kay Mazzo, Peter Schaufuss in "Cortege Hongrois" (R) Stephanie Saland, Shaun O'Brien in "Coppelia"

Suzanne Farrell, Peter Martins in "In G Major" Top: (L) Suzanne Farrell in "Ivesiana" (R) Sheryl Ware, Jacques d'Amboise in "Scotch Symphony"

NEW YORK CITY BALLET

Colleen Neary (C) in "Fanfare" Top: Robert Weiss, Violette Verdy in "Donizetti Variations"

Merrill Ashley, Robert Weiss in "Stars and Stripes" Top: Adam Luders, Colleen Neary in "Brahms-Schoenberg Quartet"

NEW YORK CITY BALLET

METROPOLITAN OPERA HOUSE
Opened Monday, April 19, 1976.*
Hurok presents:

THE ROYAL BALLET

Founder, Ninette de Valois; Founder-Choreographer, Frederick Ashton; Director, Kenneth MacMillan; Administrator, John Hart; Music Director, Ashley Lawrence; Ballet Master, Donald MacLeary; Conductors, Anthony Twiner, Emanuel Young; Ballet Mistress, Jill Gregory; Regisseur, Henry Legerton; Principal Repetiteur, Michael Somes; Technical Director, Tom McCarthur; Michael Brown, Joyce Wells

COMPANY

PRINCIPALS: David Ashmole, Michael Coleman, Lesley Collier, Laura Connor, Vergie Derman, Anthony Dowell, David Drew, Wayne Eagling, Leslie Edwards, Alexander Grant, Ann Jenner, Gerd Larsen, Monica Mason, Merle Park, Jennifer Penney, Ria Peri, Derek Rencher, Brian Shaw, Wayne Sleep, Alfreda Thorogood, David Wall

SOLOISTS: David Adams, Christopher Carr, Sandra Conley, Wendy Ellis, Rosalind Eyre, Adrian Grater, Carl Myers, Marguerite Porter, Rosemary Taylor, Anita Young

CORYPHEES: Sally Ashby, Belinda Corken, Peter Fairweather, Graham Fletcher, Garry Grant, Dennis Griffith, Sally Inkin, Jennifer Jackson, Susan Lockwood, Anthony Molyneux, Suzanna Raymond, Mark Silver, Jacqueline Tallis, Hilary Tickner, Julie Wood, Christine Woodward

CORPS: Joanna Allnatt, Michael Batchelor, Stephen Beagley, Amanda Beck, Anthony Conway, Susan Crow, Bess Dales, Derek Deane, Jane Devine, Nicolas Dixon, Antony Dowson, Jacqueline Elliott, Lynn Hollamby, Judith Howe, Robert Jude, Christine Keith, Gillian Kingsley, Barbara Lower, Ross MacGibbon, Vanessa Millar, Andrew Moore, Linda Moran, Lorna Murray, Denise Nunn, William Perrie, Katharine Pianoff, Gail Taphouse, Heather Walker, Rosalyn Whitten, Nicholas Whittle, Pippa Wylde

GUEST ARTISTS: Natalia Makarova, Rudolf Nureyev, Lynn Seymour

REPERTOIRE

"Romeo and Juliet" (Prokofiev, MacMillan), "Swan Lake" (Tchaikovsky, Petipa/Ivanov/Ashton/de Valois), "La Bayadere" (Minkus, Petipa/Nureyev), "La Fille Mal Gardee" (Ferdinand Herold/Lanchbery, Ashton), "Manon" (Massenet, MacMillan), "The Dream" (Mendelssohn, Ashton), "Song of the Earth" (Mahler, MacMillan)

NEW YORK PREMIERES: "A Month in the Country" (Chopin/Lanchbery, Ashton), "Rituals" (Bartok, MacMillan), "Elite Syncopations" (Scott Joplin/Selected, MacMillan)

General Manager: John H. Wilson
Company Manager: Vernon Clarke
Press: Sheila Porter, Norman Lombino, Peter Brownlee
Stage Managers: Armand Gerrard, Andis Marton

* Closed May 15, 1976 after limited engagement of 32 performances.

Philip Gammon, Judith Howe in "Elite Syncopations"

Lynn Seymour, Derek Rencher, Top Left: Lynn Seymour, Anthony Dowell in "A Month in the Country"

Rudolf Nureyev, Merle Park in "Romeo and Juliet"
bove: Lynn Seymour, Monica Mason in "Rituals" Top: Lynn
Seymour in "A Month in the Country"

Alexander Grant in "La Fille Mal Gardee"
Top: Natalia Makarova, Anthony Dowell in
"Romeo and Juliet"

"Swan Lake" Top: (L) Rudolf Nureyev, Merle Park (R) Natalia Makarova, Anthony Dowell in "Swan Lake"

Anthony Dowell in "The Dream" above with Monica Mason
in "Song of the Earth" Top: "La Bayadere"

Merle Park, Rudolf Nureyev in "Manon"
Top: Natalia Makarova, Anthony Dowell in "Manon"

THE ROYAL BALLET

45

METROPOLITAN OPERA HOUSE
Opened Tuesday, May 12, 1976.*
Hurok presents:

ROYAL DANISH BALLET

Director, Flemming Flindt; Assistant Artistic Directors, Lizzie Rode, Henning Kronstam; Producers, Kirsten Ralov, Lizzie Rode, Hans Brenaa, Fleming Flindt, Henning Kronstam, Niels Bjorn Larsen; Conductors, Peter Ernst Lassen, Tamas Veto; Technical Director, Jorgen Mydtskov; Wardrobe Supervisor, Stephanie Cheretun; Dance Coordinator, Simon Semenoff

COMPANY

PRINCIPALS: Sorella Englund, Vivi Flindt, Mette Honningen, Anna Laerkesen, Solveig Ostergaard, Kirsten Simone, Ib Andersen, Johnny Eliasen, Flemming Flindt, Palle Jacobsen, Niels Kehlet, Henning Kronstam, Aage Poulsen, Flemming Ryberg, And Guest Artist: Peter Martins

CORPS: Dinna Bjorn, Jette Buchwald, Therese Boving, Lise la Cour, Gabi Dissmann, Annemarie Dybdal, Susan Folkenberg, Ingrid Glindemann, Ann Kristin Hauge, Nina Herlov, Linda Hindberg, Inge Jensen, Lillian Jensen, Mona Jensen, Lis Jeppesen, Anne Lise Johnsen, Winnie Johnsen, Mette-Ida Kirk, Eva Kloborg, Sussi Marcell, Benedikte Paaske, Lizzie Rode, Vibeke Roland, Heidi Ryom, Liselotte Sand, Birthe Schmahr, Lene Schroder, Agneta Segerskog, Nina Siiger, Ulla Skow, Anne Sonnerup, Lise Stripp, Anita Soby, Eva Soemod, Anne Marie Vessel, Annemari Vingard, Arlette Weinreich, Kirsten Wulff, Frank Andersen, Michael Bastian, Arne Bech, Thomas Berentzen, Mogens Boesen, Rene Endrup, Tommy Frishoi, Morten Hansen, Poul Erik Hesselkilde, Poul-Rene Hjorth, Ib Jeppesen, Hans Jakob Kolgard, Kim Nielsen, Kjeld Noack, Claus Schroder, Ole Suhr, Ulrik Trojaborg, Arne Villumsen, Tage Wendt

CHILDREN: Dennie Frank, Ulla Frederiksen, Marianne Hansen, Anja Strom, Jannie Thomsen, Nila Weinreich, Mike Andersen, Niels Balle, Allan Nielsen, Jacob Sparso, Ole Steffensen, Aage Thordal

REPERTOIRE

"Napoli Act III" (Gade/Helsted/Paulli/Lumbye, August Bournonville), "La Sylphide" (Herman Lovenskjold, Bournonville), "The Lesson" (Georges Delerue, Flemming Flindt), "Carmen" (Georges Bizet, Roland Petit after Prosper Merimee), "Etudes" (Knudage Riisager/Carl Czerny, Harald Lander)
U. S. PREMIERES: Thursday May 20, "Romeo and Juliet" (Serge Prokofiev, John Neumeier), Thursday May 27, "Triumph of Death" Thomas Koppel, Flemming Flindt after Eugene Ionesco), Thursday June 3, "The Guards of Amager" (V. C. Holm, Bournonville), May 17, "Four Seasons" (Antonio Vivaldi, Flemming Flindt)

General Manager: John H. Wilson
Company Managers: Lee Walter, Julie Kocich
Press: Sheila Porter, Rima Corben, Norman Lombino
Stage Manager: Arne Bech

* Closed June 5, 1976 after limited engagement of 23 performances.

"Triumph of Death" also above with Flemming Flindt

Vivi Flindt in "Triumph of Death"
Top Left: Mette-Ida Kirk, Ib Andersen in
"Romeo and Juliet"

Vivi Flindt, Henning Kronstam in "The Volunteers of Amager" Top: "The Four Seasons"

47

Niels Kehlet, Mette Honnigen, Flemming Ryberg in "Etudes" Top: (L) Flemming Flindt, Sorella Englund in "Carmen" (R) Neils Kehlet, Sorella Englund in "La Sylphide"

"Napoli" Top: (L) Peter Martins in "La Sylphide" (R) Flemming Flindt, Anne Marie Vessel in "The Lesson"

THE ROYAL DANISH BALLET

DANCE PROGRAMS AT NEW YORK CITY CENTER

CITY CENTER DOWNSTAIRS
June 3–7, 1975*
Modern Dance Artists, Inc., presents:

SANASARDO DANCE COMPANY

Artistic Director-Choreographer, Paul Sanasardo; Stage Manager, Judy Kayser; Associate Director, Diane Germaine; Executive Director, William Weaver; Press, John Udry; Video Director, David Devanney

COMPANY

Diane Germaine, Joan Lombardi, Janet Panetta, Michele Rebeaud, Anne-Marie Hackett, Elyssa Paternoster, Robin Shimel, Jeri McAndrews, Bert Terborgh, Douglas Nielsen, Harry Laird, Jose Meier, Alex Dolcemascolo

PROGRAM

WORLD PREMIERE of "A Consort for Dancers" produced, directed, choreographed and designed by Paul Sanasardo; Music composed and performed by Gwendolyn Watson; Poems of Anne Sexton read by Marian Winters and William Weaver. Part I: All My Pretty Ones, Part II: The Death Notebooks

* Company returned for 14 additional performances Dec. 2 - 14, 1975. On Dec. 9, 1975 "A Memory Suite" (Virgil Thompson/Herbert L. Clarke/Frank Simon/Carl Hohne, Paul Sanasardo; Costumes, Ida Ruskin) had its *World Premiere.* Added to the repertoire were "Shadows" (Satie/Scarlatti/Bach, Sanasardo), and "The Path" (Steve Drews, Sanasardo). This program was repeated April 22 - 25, 1976 at Playwrights Horizons Queens Theatre-in-the-Park.

Lois Greenfield Photos

Jose Meier, Harry Laird, Douglas Nielsen
Top Right: Joan Lombardi, Nielsen in
"A Consort for Dancers"

Joan Lombardi, Diane Germaine, Janet Panetta in
"A Consort for Dancers" (also above)

50

Paul Sanasardo in "A Memory Suite"
Above: Douglas Nielsen, Diane Germaine in
"The Path" Top: Joan Lombardi in "Shadows"

Marianne Folin, Harry Laird in "A Memory Suite"
Top: Janet Panetta, Bert Terborgh in
"A Consort for Dancers"

51

CITY CENTER DOWNSTAIRS

September 2–7, 1975
Hi Enterprises presents:

DANCERS

Artistic Director, Dennis Wayne; Lighting, Edward Greenburgh;/Press, John Udry; David Murin, Betty Williams, David Allen, John Dayger

Dennis Wayne
Martine Van Hamel
Bonnie Mathis
Janet Popeleski
Elaine Kudo
Buddy Balough
Kenneth Hughes
Arvind Harum

REPERTOIRE: "Lazarus" (Lubos Fiser, Norman Walker), "Murder of George Keuter" (Ratter, Cliff Keuter), "Still Point" (Debussy, Todd Bolander), "Musete di Taverni" (Couperin, Keuter), "Pàvane for Solo Dancer" (Gabriel Faure, Norman Walker), "After Eden" (Lee Hoiby, John Butler)

PREMIERES: "Caught in the Quiet" (Erik Satie, Buddy Balough), "Quickening" (Lutoslawski, Elina Mooney), "Of Us Two" (Stravinsky, Cliff Keuter), "Prussina Officer" (Bartok, Norman Walker), "Solo for Martine van Hamel" (Ravel, Jorge Samaniego)

Right: Bonnie Mathis, Dennis Wayne

Bonnie Mathis, Dennis Wayne

Opened Wednesday, October 1, 1975.*
Foundation for American Dance in association with City Center of Music and Drama, Inc. presents:

CITY CENTER JOFFREY BALLET

Artistic Director, Robert Joffrey; Associate Director, Gerald Arpino; Music Director, Seymour Lipkin; General Administrator, Peter S. Diggins; Ballet Master, Basil Thompson; Lighting, Jennifer Tipton; Associate Conductor, Sung Kwak; Assistant Ballet Master, Scott Barnard; Production Coordinator, Penelope Curry; Production Assistant, Tom Bucher; Costume Supervisor, John Allen; Wardrobe Supervisor, Dorothy Coscia

COMPANY

Charthel Arthur, Diana Cartier, Francesca Corkle, Donna Cowen, Starr Danias, Ann Marie De Angelo, Ingrid Fraley, Erika Goodman, Jan Hanniford, Alaine Haubert, Denise Jackson, Krystyna Jurkowski, Miyoko Kato, Jean McCabe, Carol Messmer, Pamela Nearhoof, Diane Orio, Beatriz Rodriguez, Trinette Singleton, Jodi Wintz, Rebecca Wright, Sara Yarborough, Dermot Burke, Adix Carman, Gary Chryst, Richard Colton, Donn Edwards, Robert Estner, Tom Fowler, Larry Grenier, Jerel Hilding, Christian Holder, Jeffrey Hughes, Chris Jensen, Philip Jerry, Kevin McKenzie, Russell Sultzbach, Paul Sutherland, Burton Taylor, Robert Thomas, Edward Verso, Glenn White, William Whitener

REPERTOIRE

"Viva Vivaldi!" (Vivaldi, Gerald Arpino), "Deuce Coupe II" (Beach Boys, Twyla Tharp), "The Dream" (Mendelssohn, Ashton), "The Big City" (Tansman, Jooss), "Monotones" (Satie, Ashton), "Valentine" (Druckman, Arpino), "Jeu de Cartes" (Stravinsky, Cranko), "Opus I" (Webern, Cranko), "Offenbach in the Underworld" (Offenbach, Tudor), "N.Y. Export, Op. Jazz" (Prince, Robbins), "Kettentanz" (Strauss, Arpino), "As Time Goes By" (Haydn, Tharp), "Interplay" (Gould, Robbins), "The Green Table" (Cohen, Jooss), "Moves" (Silence, Robbins), "Parade" (Satie, Massine), "Remembrances" (Wagner, Joffrey), "Trinity" (Alan Raph/Lee Holdridge, Arpino), "Pas des Deesses" (Field, Joffrey), "The Relativity of Icarus" (Samual, Arpino), "Petrouchka" (Stravinsky, Fokine), "Confetti" (Rossini, Arpino), "Reflections" (Tchaikovsky, Arpino), "The Moor's Pavane" (Purcell, Limon), and *WORLD PRE-MIERES* of "Drums, Dreams and Banjos" (Stephen Foster, Gerald Arpino) on Thursday, Oct. 9, 1975, and "Five Dances" (Sergei Rachmaninoff, Christian Holder) on Thursday, Oct. 16, 1975.

Company Managers: Hans Hortig, Stan Ware
Press: Robert Larkin, Ruth Hedrick
Stage Managers: Richard Thorkelson, Alan Gerberg

* Closed Nov. 2, 1975 after limited engagement of 39 performances. Returned March 10, 1976 for Spring season of 39 performances ending Apr. 11, 1976. Additions to the company were Lisa Bradley, Rachel Ganteaume, Charlene Gehm, Donna Ross, Carole Valleskey, Darrell Barnett, Luis Fuente, Gregory Huffman, Andrew Levinson, Roberto Medina, Dennis Poole, Craig Williams. Additions to the repertoire were "Weewis" (Walden, Sappington), "Secret Places" (Mozart, Arpino), "Fanfarita" (Chapi, Arpino), and *PREMIERES* of "Pavane on the Death of an Infanta" (Ravel, Jooss), "A Ball in Old Vienna" (Lanner, Jooss), and "Face Dancers" (Michael Kamen, Margo Sappington) on March 23, 1976.

**Top Right: Luis Fuente,
Ann Marie De Angelo in "Fanfarita"**

Lisa Bradley, Dermot Burke in "Secret Places"

"Drums, Dreams and Banjos" Top: (L) Pamela Nearhoof, Robert Estner (R) Charthel Arthur, Robert Thomas in "Drums, Dreams and Banjos"

Gary Chryst in "Parade" Top: Denise Jackson,
Russell Sultzbach in "Five Dances"

Paul Sutherland in "A Ball in Old Vienna"
Top: "Pavane on the Death of an Infanta"

CITY CENTER JOFFREY BALLET

Donna Cowen, Gary Chryst in "The Big City"

"Face Dancers" Top: Jan Hanniford,
Darrell Barnett in "Face Dancers"

"Moves" Top: "Offenbach in the Underworld"
CITY CENTER JOFFREY BALLET

Christian Holder, Burton Taylor, Beatriz Rodriguez,
Jan Hanniford in "The Moor's Pavane"

Rebecca Wright, Christian Holder in "Valentine"
Top: Charthel Arthur, Diane Orio, Donna Cowen,
Pamela Nearhoof in "Viva Vivaldi!"

Charthel Arthur, Denise Jackson, Francesca Corkle, Burton Taylor in "Pas des Deesses" Top: "Jeu de Cartes"

CITY CENTER JOFFREY BALLET

CITY CENTER 55 STREET THEATER
Opened Tuesday, November 25, 1975.*
City Center of Music and Drama Inc. presents:

ALVIN AILEY CITY CENTER DANCE THEATER

Artistic Director-Choreographer, Alvin Ailey; Associate Artisti
Director-Ballet Master, Ali Pourfarrokh; Conductor, Joyce Brow
Production Manager, Ralph McWilliams; Lighting Supervisor, Che
nault Spence; Sound, Robert Weeden; Wardrobe Supervisor, Rut
Norton; Administrative Assistant, Lois Framhein

COMPANY

Charles Adams, Sarita Allen, Enid Britten, Sergio Cal, Mazazur
Chaya, Ulysses Dove, Valerie Feit, Meg Gordon, Judith Jamison
Melvin Jones, Mari Kajiwara, Jodi Moccia, Michihiko Oka, Ca
Paris, Beth Shorter, Warren Spears, Estelle Spurlock, Clive Thomp
son, Elbert Watson, Dudley Williams, Donna Wood, Peter Woodi
Tina Yuan, and *Guest Artists* Brother John Sellers, Bernard Thacke

REPERTOIRE

"Night Creature" (Duke Ellington, Alvin Ailey), "Love Songs
(Russell/Wind/Bleecher/Scott, Ailey), "Hidden Rites" (Sciortin
Ailey), "The Mooche" (Ellington, Ailey), "Streams" (Milosla
Kabelac, Ailey), "Cry" (Coltrane/Nyro/Voices of East Harlem, A
ley), "The Road of the Phoebe Snow" (Ellington/ Strahorn, Talle
Beatty), "Revelations" (Traditional, Ailey), "The Lark Ascending
(Williams, Ailey), "Feast of Ashes" (Surinach, Ailey), "After Eden
(Hoiby, Butler), "Carmina Burana" (Orff, Butler), "According t
Eve" (Crumb, Butler)

PREMIERES: "Echoes in Blue" (Duke Ellington, Milton Myer
Costumes, Normand Maxon; Lighting, William Burd) on Sunday
Dec. 7, 1975; "Liberian Suite" (Duke Ellington, James Truitte; Re
staged and adapted from original by Lester Horton; Costumes, Sa
vatore Tagliarino; Lighting, Chenault Spence) on Friday, Nob. 2
1975.

Company Manager: R. Robert Lussier
Press: Howard Atlee, Meg Gordean
Stage Managers: William Burd, Donald Moss

* Closed Dec. 14, 1975 after limited engagement of 24 perfor
mances. Returned Tuesday, May 4, 1976 for 24 performance
closing May 23, 1976. Anita Littleman was an addition to th
company Added to the repertoire were "Reflections in D" (Elling
ton, Ailey), "Hermit Songs" (Barber, Ailey)

WORLD PREMIERES of "Black, Brown and Beige" (Duke Elling
ton, Alvin Ailey; Costumes, Randy Barcelo; Lighting, Chenau
Spence) on May 12, 1976; "Pas de Duke" (Duke Ellington, Alvi
Ailey; Designed by Rouben Ter-Arutunian; Lighting, Chenau
Spence) on Tuesday, May 11, 1976; "Caravan" (Michael Kame
based on Duke Ellington Themes, Louis Falco; Decor and Cos
tumes, William Katz; Lighting, Richard Nelson; Conductor, Joyc
Brown) on Thursday, May 6, 1976.

Ron Reagan, Donald Moss, Johan Elbers Photos

Top Left: Clive Thompson, Tina Yuan in "Streams"

Judith Jamison in "The Mooche"

Mikhail Baryshnikov, Judith Jamison in "Pas de Duke"

"Black, Brown and Beige" Top: Judith Jamison, Mikhail Baryshnikov in "Pas de Duke"
Ron Reagan Photos

Elbert Watson, Donna Wood in
"Road of the Phoebe Snow"

Estelle Spurlock in "The Mooche"
Top: Judith Jamison in "Caravan"

"Caravan" also Top with Dudley Williams

ALVIN AILEY CITY CENTER DANCE THEATER

BROOKLYN ACADEMY DANCE PROGRAMS

Harvey Lichtenstein, Executive Director
Judith Daykin, General Manager

BROOKLYN ACADEMY OF MUSIC
November 14, 15, 16, 1975.*
The Brooklyn Academy of Music presents:

PENNSYLVANIA BALLET

Executive Artistic Director, Barbare Weisberger; Artistic Director, Benjamin Harkarvy; Ballet Mistress, Fiona Fuerstner; Music Director, Maurice Kaplow; Ballet Masters, William Thompson Robert Rodham; Lighting, Nicholas Cernovitch; President, Bernard S. Weiss; General Manager, Timothy Duncan; Wardrobe Mistress, Lillian Avery; Company Coordinator, Judith von Scheven; Costume Supervisor, E. Huntington Parker; Assistant Conductor, Daniel Forlano

COMPANY

Sandra Applebaum, Dana Arey, Karen Brown, Alba Calzada, Joanne Danto, Marcia Darhower, William DeGregory, Gregory Drotar, Tamara Hadley, Mark Hochman, David Jordan Linda Karash, David Kloss, Dane LaFontsee, Barry Leon, Sherry Lowenthal, Michelle Lucci, James Mercer, Edward Myers, Anya Patton, Robin Preiss, Lawrence Rhodes, Constance Ross, Barbara Sandonato (on leave), Janek Schergen, Jerry Schwender, Gretchen Warren, Missy Yancey, Linda Zettle

REPERTOIRE

"Raymonda Variations" (Alexander Glazounov, George Balanchine), "In Retrospect" (Benjamin Britten, Robert Rodham), "Carmina Burana" (Carl Orff, John Butler), and *New York Premieres* of "Grosse Fugue" (Ludwig van Beethoven, Hans van Manen), and "Symphony in C" (Bizet, Balanchine)

Company Manager: Stephen P. Wagner
Press: David C. Speedie, Charles Ziff, Kate MacIntyre
Stage Managers: Jane Clegg, Lawrence E. Sterner

* Company returned for 4 additional performances April 8–11, 1976, performing "Opus Lemaitre" (Bach, Hans van Manen), "Nutcracker Grand Pas de Deux" (Tchaikovsky, Ivanov), *New York Premiere* "Continuum" (Jan Krzywicki, Benjamin Harkarvy), "Les Sylphides" (Frederick Chopin, Michael Fokine), "Madrigalesco" (Vivaldi, Harkarvy), "Septet Extra" (Saint-Saens, van Manen), "The Four Temperaments" (Hindemith, Balanchine)

Ron Reagan, Richard L Bitner, Roger Greenawalt Photos

**Right: "Symphony in C" Above: "Septet Extra"
Top Right: "Opus le Maitre" Below: Edward Myers,
Michelle Lucci in "Raymonda Variations"**

**Tamara Hadley, David Kloss, Gretchen Warren,
Sherry Lowenthal in "Continuum"**

"The Four Temperaments"

BROOKLYN ACADEMY OF MUSIC
March 5, 6, 7, 1976
The Brooklyn Academy of Music presents:

PILOBOLUS DANCE THEATRE

Founders-Directors, Moses Pendleton, Jonathan Wolken; Choographers, The Company; General Manager, Chris Ashe

COMPANY

Alison Chase   Moses Pendleton
Martha Clarke   Michael Tracy
Robert Morgan Barnett   Jonathan Wolken

REPERTOIRE: "Untitled" (Robert Dennis), "Pseudopodia" (Jonathan Wolken/Moses Pendleton, Wolken), "Alraune" (Dennis, Pendleton), "Walklyndon," "Vagabond" (Martha Clarke), "Ocellus" (Pendleton/Wolken), "Monkshood's Farewell," "Ciona" (Jon Appleton), "Lost in Fauna" (Dennis, Alison Chase/Pendleton), "Terra Cotta" (Peter Schickele, Barnett/Clarke), "Paggliaccio" (Martha Clarke), "Ocellus," "Vagabond" (Martha Clarke)

Right and Below: Pilobolus Dance Theatre

BROOKLYN ACADEMY OF MUSIC/LEPERCQ SPACE
January 8–11, 1976
The Brooklyn Academy of Music presents:

TRISHA BROWN DANCE COMPANY

Artistic Director-Choreographer, Trisha Brown; Lighting Design, Edward Effron; Stage Manager, Julia Gillette; Management, Art Services

COMPANY

Trisha Brown
Elizabeth Garren
Wendy Perron
Judith Ragir
Mona Sultzman

PROGRAM: "4321234," "Locus," "Sticks," "Solo Olos," "Pyramid"

Babette Mangolte Photos

**Trisha Brown Dance Company in
"Locus" Left Center: "Sticks"**

BROOKLYN ACADEMY OPERA HOUSE
March 25 - April 4, 1976 (10 performances)
The Brooklyn Academy of Music presents:

TWYLA THARP AND DANCERS

Director-Choreographer, Twyla Tharp; Administrators, Christine Estes, Arthur O'Connor; Assistant to Miss Tharp, Sharon Kinney; Production Assistant, Bernice Rubin; Stage Managers, Marv Kapell, Ellen Raphael; Costumes, Santo Loquasto; Lighting, Jennifer Tipton; Wardrobe Mistress, Virginia Magee; Press, The Merle Group, Sandra Manley

COMPANY

Twyla Tharp	Jennifer W.
Rose Marie Wright	Shelley Washington
Kenneth Rinker	Sharon Kinn
Tom Rawe	Kristin Draud

REPERTOIRE: "Give and Take" (Werner/Sousa/Franko/Meacham/Ronell, Twyla Tharp), "The Fugue," "Eight Jelly Rolls" (Jelly Roll Morton, Tharp), "The Rags Suite from The Raggedy Dances" (Joplin/Mozart, Tharp), "Bach Duet" (Bach, Tharp), "Sue's Leg" (Fats Waller, Tharp)

Tom Berthiaume Photos
Left: Tom Rawe, Twyla Tharp, Rose Marie Wright, Kenneth Rinker in "Sue's Leg" Below: Rose Marie Wright, Kenneth Rinker

"Sue's Leg"

Twyla Tharp in "Sue's Leg"

"Session"

BROOKLYN ACADEMY/PLAYHOUSE
April 23, 24, 25, 1976
Brooklyn Academy of Music presents:

LAR LUBOVITCH DANCE COMPANY

Artistic Director-Choreographer, Lar Lubovitch; Lighting Design, Tony Tucci; Administration, Performing Art Services; Guest Choreographer, Sara Rudner

COMPANY

Marie Ono, Susan Weber, Gerrie Houlihan, Aaron Osborne, Lar Lubovitch, Rob Besserer, Janet Wong, Rebecca Slifkin, Laura Gates, Charles Martin, Deborah Zalkind

PROGRAM

"Whirligogs: (Luciano Berio, Lubovitch), "Prelude in C Minor" (Bach, Lubovitch), "Girl on Fire" (Britten, Lubovitch), and *PREMIERES* of "One Good Turn" (choreographed by Sara Rudner,) and "Session" by Lar Lubovitch

Jack Mitchell Photos

**Top: Rob Besserer, Susan Weber,
Gerri Houlihan in "Avalanche"**

**Susan Weber, Lar Lubovitch in "Girl on Fire"
Top: Rob Besserer in "Avalanche"**

THE CUBICULO

Artistic Director, Philip Meister; Managing Director, Elaine Sulka; General Manager, Albert Schoemann; Technical Directors, Bill Lambert, Bradley G. Richart; Business Manager, Barbara Crow; Program Coordinators, John Dudich, Dinah Carlson

THE CUBICULO

Monday & Tuesday, June 2–3, 1975
WASHINGTON SQUARE REPERTORY DANCE COMPANY: (Laura Brittain, Artistic Director) Maxine Lee Booth, Laurie Kane, Elaine Perlmutter, Sue Mandel, Marie Pintauro, Leslie Seaman, Victorianne Pizzuto, daicing "Disengage" (Villa Lobos, Laura Brittain), "Four Squares" (Paul Russell, Kathy Duncan), "Dance in Four Short Parts for Numerous Dancers" (Bach, Brittain)

MARGARITA BANOS with AMERICAN BALLET THEATRE SCHOOL STUDENTS: Nanci Brogan, Patricia Brown, Gary Cordial, Peter Fonseca, Jane Hickey, Deborah Hood, Sally Kingery, Maia Moser, Anna Myer, Gary Cordial, Peter Fonseca, Jane Hickey, Deborah Hood, Sally Kingery, Maia Moser, Anna Myer, Vesna Nikitovich, Catherine Nussbaumer, Risa Oganesoff, Jamie Paranicas, Richard Prewitt, dancing "Prayer to Man" (Beethoven, Kathy Ross), "Chansons Madecasses" (Ravel, Ross), "Burnt Dreams" (Bohuslav Martinu, Margarita Banos), "Piedra y Campanas" (Bartok, Banos), "Creatures" (Bjorn Fongaard Galaxy, Banos), "Echoes" (Ecos de Granada Sabicas, Margarita)

Monday & Tuesday, June 9–10, 1975
MARTHA RZASA AND DANCERS: Leslie Innis, Paula Killinger, Marina Pricci, Gail Kachadurian, Tom Wetmore, Louise Rogers, Martha Rzasa, dancing "Scherzo for Five Mad Birds" (Shostakovitch, Mzasa), "Joints" (Stockhausen, Rzasa), "Agaue" (Dixie Piver, Rzasa), "The Edge" (Webern, Rzasa)

CROSSROADS: Martha Bowers, Richard Caceres, Hsueh-Tung Chen, Dian Dong, Nancy Mapother, Colette Yglesias (Artistic Adviser, Doris Rudko), dancing "One Plus 1," "Trio" (Dian Dong), "Broadcast" (Noah Creshevsky, Nancy Mapother), "One and Two" (Nancy Mapother), "Focus"

Friday & Saturday, June 13–14, 1975
PHOEBE NEVILLE with Anthony LaGiglia and Philip Hipwell in "Memory," "Triptych," "Solo"

Monday & Tuesday, June 16–17, 1975
DANCES BY ALICE TEIRSTEIN assisted by Valerie Bergman, Mei Hsueh Buobis, Linda Caruso Haviland, Marilyn Mazur, Kathy Robens, Jeffrey Strum, Andrew Quinlan-Krichels, Kathleen Quinlan-Krichels, dancing "Curtain-Raiser" (Vivaldi), "Nexus" (Donald Sosin), "Babi Yar" "Leisure Dances" (John Lewis/Sergei Natia/Ruth White/Gwendolyn Watson)

Monday, June 30, 1975
RITHA DEVI dancing "Kuchipudi," "Mahari Nrirya"

Thursday, Friday, Saturday, July 10, 11, 12, 1975
DANCES BY VIRGINIA LAIDLAW with Nina Cohen, Robert Diaz, Jill Feinberg, Kathleen Heath, Elissa Kirtzman, Edward Marsan, Frank Pistritto, Fred Shay, and Guest Artist Ira Jaffe, dancing "Circadian" (Nonesuch), "Just Ira" (Leo Sayer), "Then" (Glenn Miller), "Sentinels" (Web Terhune)

THOMAS HOLT DANCE ENSEMBLE: Kristine Bader, Betsy Baron, Lucinda, Gehrke, Thomas Holt, David McComb, Ann Moser, Allan Seward, Paulette Taylor, Philip Tietz, Alatha Winter, dancing "Duet of Summer" (Lee Holdridge, Thomas Holt), "Arienata" (Vivaldi, Holt), "Afterhours in Wonderland" (Collage, Holt), "Second Avenue Scrapbook" (Laura Nyro, Holt)

Saturday & Sunday, July 14–15, 1975
DANCE THEATRE VII, PART I: "Eagle" by Rolando Jorif danced by Dyane Harvey, "Prayer to Man" (Beethoven) choreographed and danced by Margarita Banos; "Duet for Summer" (Lee Holdridge, Thomas Holt) danced by Betsy Baron, Thomas Holt; "Vase" by Rolando Jorif danced by Maria Bueno; "Burnt Dreams" (Martinu) choreographed and danced by Margarita Banos; "Timewarp" (Schwartz/M. Wodynski, Jan Wodynski) danced by John Kelly, Robert Kosinski, Mike Wodynski; "Scherzo for 5 Mad Birds" (Shostakovitch, Martha Rzasa) danced by Leslie Innis, Paula Killinger, Marina Pricci, Louise Rogers, Martha Rzasa; "The End of Time" (Messiaen, Peggy Cicierska) danced by Maris Wolff; "Joints" (Stockhausen, Martha Rzasa) danced by Martha Rzasa, Kail Kachadurian, Tom Wetmore

Anthony LaGiglia in "Memory"

Jose Coronado in "Rose Wound"
Above: Alice Teirstein Dance Projects in "Nexus"
(Lois Greenfield Photo)

Wednesday & Thursday, July 18–19, 1975

DANCE THEATRE VII, PART II: "Horizon" (Bill Zien, Betty Salamun) danced by Joe McClung, David HB Drake, Betty Salamun; "Babi Yar" (Yevtushendo, Alice Teirstein) danced by Seth Walsh, Kathleen Quinlan-Krichels, Jerome Sarnat, Diane Chavan; "Disengage" (Villa Lobos, Laura Brittain) danced by Laurie Kane, Elaine Perlmutter, Marie Pintauro; "Since You Asked" (Collage, Sue Barnes-Moore), "Josephine Bracken" (Stockhausen, Ronnie Alejandro) danced by Betty Salamun; "In a Bed of Faded Roses" (Reynolds/Ives, Jose Coronado) danced by Icona Copen, Jose Coronado

Monday & Tuesday, October 13–14, 1975

SOLOS FOR MALE DANCERS BY JOSE CORONADO: "O Beautiful Dreamer" (Ives, Sokolow) danced by Jose Meyer, "The Eagles Are Dying" (Ives) and "Rose Wound" (Max Olivas) danced by Jose Coronado, "From the Steeples and the Mountains" (Ives) and "Silence" (Messiaen) danced by Marc Beckermen; "The Arena" (Karl-Birger Blomdahl) danced by Harry Laird, "Solo from Almas" (Kazuo Fukushima) danced by Micardo Mercado, "Corrido" (Revueltas) danced by Miguel Lopez

Thursday, Friday, Saturday, October 16, 17, 18, 1975

MARLEEN PENNISON and Dancers: Karen Berley, Kathy Dumesnil, Jay Siegel, Thomas Wilkinson, dancing "A Little Bit of Honey's," "Don't Step on the Pavement Cracks", "Bethena" (Joplin), "One Dance in the Shape of a Couple," "The Keeper," "All for the Best" (Stephen Schwartz)

Monday & Tuesday, October 20–21, 1975

VALERIE BERGMAN's "Seven Shifts" (Vivaldi/Bach), and "Eleventh Gear" (Bach/Vivaldi) danced by Valerie Bergman, Jan Brecht, Mary Van Vort; JOYA GRANBERY HOYT's "Tones" (John Holmsen Brainard) danced by Ms. Hoyt, Gail Ziaks, Valerie Farias; KATHERINE LIEPE's "Disonant Interval" (Joseph Schwantner) and "Beneath the Tip of an Iceberg" (Handel/Lolay)

Friday & Saturday, October 24–25, 1975

SERENA with Helen Adams, Sheila Kaminsky, Barbara Salmon performing Neo-Eastern dances.

Monday & Tuesday, October 27–28, 1975

GAEL STEPANEK AND COMPANY: Jamis Brenner, Whit Carman, Deborah Glaser, Kendal Klingbeil, Carol Pellegrini dancing "By Tomorrow ... Subject to Change without Notice" (Corelli, Stepanek), "Upon a Time Once" (Rossini/Beethoven/Bach/Manini, Stepanek)

SHEILA SOBEL's MWC DANCE COMPANY: Geraldine Burke, Sheila Mason, Eileen Millius, Sheila Sobel dancing "Moving Road Song, Part I and Part II"

Friday & Saturday, October 31–November 1, 1975

LOUINES LOUIS ETHNIC DANCE ENSEMBLE dancing Haitian, African, Afro-Caribbean, Jazz (No other details submitted)

Tuesday & Wednesday, November 25–26, 1976

BOB BOWYER & JO-ANN BRUGGEMANN in five dances to music by contemporary artists (No other details submitted)

Monday & Tuesday, December 1–2, 1975

ANDREA BORAK's "Crackerjacks," CANDY CHRISTAKOS' "Firefly" and "Castle Building," PEGGY SPINA's "Mango and You"

CHOREOGRAPHY BY ANNE MARIE RIDGWAY & SUSAN CREITZ: "Turnabout" (Takemitsu, Creitz), "Just One Movement, Please" (Mozart, Creitz), "A Creature Feature Piece" (Arranged, Creitz) danced by Susan Creitz, Richard Biles, Georgia Connors, Cherylle Edwards, Mark Esposito, Anne Marie Ridgway, Lorraine Persson, Janis Brenner; "Volantis" (Arranged, Ridgway) and "AHTRAM ½ MV2" (Arranged, Ridgway) danced by Janis Brenner, Timothy Crafts, Susan Creitz, Carlo Pelligrini, Anne Marie Ridgway

Monday & Tuesday, December 8–9, 1975

DANCES BY KENT BAKER and DONNA EVANS: with Donna Evans, Patrice Evans, Tom Evert, Lidia Kotarski, Suzanne Renner, Kent Baker, Richard Biles, David Corash, Dorian Petri, Dale Thompson, dancing "Baroque Suite" (Frescobaldi/Handel/Fasch, Evans), "Ichthyosauria" (Peter Klausmeyer, Baker), "Tetrauq" (Barron/Scarlatti/Lateef, Evans), "The Quickies" (Bach/A.P. Carter/Rose, Baker), "Hasten Slowly" (Balada/Feldman, Evans), "Male Model" (Bernard Herrman, Baker), "Wintershape" (Baker)

Top Right: Serena Below: Janis Brenner, Susan Creitz, Timothy Crafts, Carlo Pelligrini in "AHTRAM ½MV2"
(Don Goldstein Photo)

Donna Evans in "Hasten Slowly"
Above: Kent Baker in "Ichthyosauria"
(W. E. Berg Photos) 69

THE CUBICULO

Thursday, Friday, Saturday, December 11–13, 1975

PETER LOBDELL in the new mime works "Tales Told to the Sphinx"

Friday & Saturday, December 19–20, 1975

JAN WODYNSKI DANCE COMPANY: Bill Bass, Valerie Bergman, Joanne Edelman, John Kelly, David Malamut, Madeleine Perrone, Jan Wodynski, Mike Wodynski performing "extended vizhun," "changeover," "outing," "yeast"

THE CUBICULO

Monday & Tuesday, January 26–27, 1976

GUS SOLOMONS COMPANY/DANCE: Santa Aloi, Jack Apffel, Ruedi Brack, Gus Solomons, Jr., Katherine Galligan, JoAnn Jansen, Carl Thomsen, dancing NY Premiere of "Footnotes to an Appendix," Part II of "Statements of Nameless Root," "Molehill," "Book"

Friday & Saturday, January 30–31, 1976

NEW WORKS BY DAVID VARNEY & STEVEN WITT: danced by Livia Blankman, Janet Frachtenberg, D. Stanton Miranda, Vic Stornant, Steven Witt, Tom Brown, Karen Masaki, Fritz McKamey, Jeffrey Urban, David Varney: "with malice aforethought" (Dave Elias, Steven Witt), "an instrument to measure Spring with" (American Traditional, David Varney), "a single sparrow should fly swiftly into . . ." (Steven Witt)

Monday & Tuesday, February 2–3, 1976

BEGAM NAJMA AYASHAH in a performance of classical North India Kathak dance and gypsy dances with narration by Sabah Nissan

Friday & Saturday, February 6–7, 1976

WORKS BY MAURENE LINDEN and BETTY MARTYN: "Energy" (Paul Horn, Martyn), "Dialogue with Myself" (Luciano Berio, Martyn), "Face Dance" (Chieftans 5/Martyn) danced by Betty Martyn; "Then the Rooster Crows" (Paul Horn, Linden), "Just One More Time" (Roy Buchannan, Linden), "Flow's Lounge" (Collage, Linden) danced by Maurene Linden, Nancy Kammer, Christine Eccleston

Monday & Tuesday, February 9–10, 1976

DANCES BY FRANCIS PATRELLE & RANDOLYN ZINN: performed by Barry Weiss, Deborah Allton, Revel Paul, Sam Berman, Joyce Herring, Marcus Brown, Randolyn Zinn, Charles Potter, Adriana Keathley; "Journey: Beginning and Beginning" (Bruce G. Thompson, Francis J. Patrelle), "Song Cycle" (Justin Dello Joio, Patrelle), "The Winter Calligraphy of Ustad Selim" (Liz Swados, Randolyn Zinn), "Relationship" (Bruce G. Thompson, Patrelle), "Ardent Passage" (Oliver Messiaen, Jeff Duncan)

Friday & Saturday, February 13–14, 1976

REYNALDO ALEJANDRO DANCE THEATRE in "Sayaw Silangan III" danced by Alice Attie, Priscilla Brownlee, Rika Burnham, Asha Coorlawala, Michael Dadap, Lei-Lynne Doo, Luis Gonzalez, Ric Ornelles, Bo Lawergren, Debbie Peleo, Petal Ensemble, Sarah Petlin, Cecile Guidore, Ching Valdes

Friday & Saturday, April 2–3, 1976

CHEY NUON BORA in Orissi Indian Temple Dances

Friday & Saturday, May 7–8, 1976

WASHINGTON SQUARE REPERTORY DANCE COMPANY: Nancy Bain, Michelle Berne, Laura Brittain (Director), Leon Felder, Ann Fogelsanger, Mary Gambardella, Amy Kaplan, Rochelle Levine, Mara Lewis, Elaine Perlmutter, Naomi Schaeffer, Leslie Seaman, Barbara Sherman, Roberta Wein, Jill Wender, Michelle Whitty, Richard Cagezas (guest), dancing "Comforts" (Lynn-/Haggard/Williams), Laura Brittain), "On a Scarlatti Sonata" (Lucas Foss, Michelle Berne), "Loss (My Dance for Leslie)" (Robert Sallier, Tom Wetmore), "Joints" (Stockhausen, Martha Rzasa), "Portraits" (John Gilbert, Laura Brittain), "Disengage" (Villa Lobos, Brittain), "Today as Yesterday" (John Abercrombie, Michelle Berne), "Recycle" (Hammer/DeJohnette, Michele Berne)

Friday & Saturday, May 21–22, 1976

DANCES BY DIANNE HULBURT and NANCY MAPOTHER: with Susan Osberg, Catherine Sullivan, Terri Weksler, Nancy Hill, Sari Hornstein, Bruce Pacot, Martha Wiseman, Pierre Barreau, Jessica Fogel, Jane Comfort, Betsy Fisher, Jane Hedal, Yael Barash, Helen Castillo, Audrey Jansen, Andrea Morris, Valencia Ondes, Ayala Rimon, Laurie Reese, Rosemary Newton, dancing "Sea Songs" (Tape, Dianne Hulburt), "One and Two" (Nancy Mapother), "Broadcasts" (Tape, Nancy Mapother), "Street Scene" (Bartok, Dianne Hulburt), "Womensports" (Tape, Dianne Hulburt)

Top Right: Peter Lobdell in "Tales Told to the Sphinx"
(Pictures of People)
Below: Jan Wodynski in "Outing"
(Chuck Saaf Photo)

Karen Giombetti, Leon Felder in "Portraits"
(Elaine Perlmutter Photo)
Above: Chey Nuon Bora

70

DANCE UMBRELLA

Roundabout Theatre
November 12–December 7, 1975
Administrator, Michael Kasdan; Administrative Associate, Michael O'Rand; Production Supervisor, Bruce A. Hoover; Technical Consultant, Jon Knudsen; Press, Howard Atlee, Meg Gordean, Clarence Allsopp, Becky Flora, Arnim Johnson

ROUNDABOUT STAGE ONE
November 12–16, 1975

VIOLA FARBER DANCE COMPANY

Artistic Director-Choreographer, Viola Farber; Musical Director, Alvin Lucier; Lighting Design, Beverly Emmons; Stage Manager, T. L. Boston; Administrator, Margery Simkin

COMPANY

Viola Farber	Anne Koren
Larry Clark	Susan Matheke
Willi Feuer	Ande Peck
June Finch	Jeff Slayton

REPERTOIRE: "Poor Eddie" (Alvin Lucier, Viola Farber), "Spare Change" (Lucier, Farber), "Willi I" (Lucier, Farber), *New York Premieres* of "Duet for Susan and Willi" (Lucier, Farber), "House Guest" (Lucier, Farber), "Motorcycle/Boat" (Lucier, Farber), "Some Things I Can Remember" (Pat Richter, Farber), *WORLD PREMIERE* of "Night Shade" (Ludwig van Beethoven Viola Farber)

**Top Right: Viola Farber, Jeff Slayton,
Ande Peck, Anne Koren in "Poor Eddie"**
(Mary Lucier Photo)

**Below: Elina Mooney in "Voice"
(Cliff Keuter Dance Company) Right: Ellen Kogan,
Joan Finkelstein in Cliff Keuter's
"Of Us Two"**

ROUNDABOUT STAGE ONE
November 18, 19, 22, 23, 1975

CLIFF KEUTER DANCE COMPANY

Artistic Director-Choreographer, Cliff Keuter; Costumes and Sets, Walter Nobbe; Lighting Design, Nicholas Wolff Lyndon; Musical Direction, John Herbert McDowell; Stage Manager, Jon Knudsen

COMPANY
Cliff Keuter

Karla Wolfangle	Elina Mooney
Ellen Kogan	Ernest Pagnano
Joan Finkelstein	Michael Tipton
Ellen Jacob	John Dayger

Guest Artists: Martine van Hamel, Bonnie Mathis

PROGRAM: "Voice" (Ravel/Bach/Shostakovich, Keuter), "Sunday Papers" (Ivanovitch/McDowell, Keuter), *Company Premiere* of "Of Us Two" (Lutoslawski, Keuter), *New York Premiere* of "Table" (Ravel, Keuter), and *WORLD PREMIERE* of "Field" (Mahler, Keuter)

Cliff Keuter, Karla Wolfangle in "Table"

71

Lauren Persichetti, James Cunningham
(Ted Wester Photo)

ROUNDABOUT STAGE ONE
November 20, 21, 23, 1975

JAMES CUNNINGHAM AND THE ACME DANCE CONPANY

Artistic Director-Choreographer, James Cunningham; Lightin
Design, Raymond Dooley

COMPANY

Barbara Ellmann
William Holcomb
Lauren Persichetti
Candice Prior
Ted Striggles

PROGRAM: "Dancing with Maisie Paradocks" (Film, Jon Atkir
Choreography, James Cunningham), and *WORLD PREMIERE* o
"The 4 A.M. Show: Isis and Osiris" (Howie Harris, James Cunning
ham/Lauren Persichetti; Costumes, Michael Bottari, Ron Case)

ROUNDABOUT STAGE ONE
November 25–30, 1975

LAR LUBOVITCH COMPANY

Artistic Director-Choreographer, Lar Lubovitch; Lighting Designer, Beverly Emmons; Stage Manager, Maxine Glorsky; Administration, Performing Artservices, Inc.

COMPANY

Mari Ono, Susan Weber, Gerrie Houlihan, Aaron Osborne, Lar
Lubovitch, Rob Besserer, Janet Wong, Rebecca Slifkin, Laura
Gates, Charles Martin, Deborah Zalkind, and Guest Artists Sara
Rudner and John Daygar

REPERTOIRE

"Zig Zag" (Stravinsky, Lubovitch), "Prelude in C Minor" (Bach,
Lubovitch), "Air for a G String" (Bach, Lubovitch), "The Time
before the Time after (after the Time Before)" (Stravinsky, Lubovitch) "Whirligogs" (Luciano Berio, Lubovitch), "Statement (Stravinsky, Lubovitch), and *PREMIERES* of "Rapid Transit"
(Stravinsky, Lubovitch), "Girl on Fire" (Britten, Lubovitch), "Boa"
(Choreographed by Sara Rudner)

Susan Weber, Lar Lubovitch in "Girl on Fire"
(Jack Mitchell Photo)

Merce Cunningham and Company in "Rebus"
(Jack Mitchell Photo)

ROUNDABOUT STAGE ONE
December 2–7, 1975

MERCE CUNNINGHAM AND DANCE COMPANY

Artistic Director-Choreographer, Merce Cunningham; Lighting
Design, Mark Lancaster; Stage Manager, Charles Atlas; Music Coordinator, John Fullemann; Technical Director, Andy Tron; Administrator, Greg Tonning

COMPANY

Karole Armitage, Karen Attix, Ellen Cornfield, Merce Cunning-
ham, Morgan Ensminger, Meg Harper, Susana Hayman-Chaffey,
Cathy Kerr, Chris Komar, Robert Kovich, Raymond Kurshals,
Charlie Moulton, Julie Roess-Smith

REPERTOIRE: "Events #143 - #148"

JENNIFER MULLER & THE WORKS

Artistic Director-Choreographer, Jennifer Muller; Managing Director, Carl Hunt; Music Director, Burt Alcantara; Lighting Director, Richard Nelson; Stage Manager, Gregory Husinko

COMPANY
Jennifer Muller

John Preston   Christopher Pilafian
Carol-rae Kraus   Katherine Liepe
Matthew Diamond   Angeline Wolf

PROGRAM: "Introductory Piece/Clown," Company Premiere of "White" (Traditional Japanese, Muller), "Intermission Piece #1," *New York Premiere* of "Winter Pieces" (Burt Alcantara, Muller), "Intermission Piece #2/Oranges," "Speeds" (Alcantara, Muller)

Matthew Diamond, Jennifer Muller in "Speeds"

KATHRYN POSIN DANCE COMPANY

Artistic Director-Choreographer, Kathryn Posin; Associate Artistic Director, Lance Westergard; Producing Director, David White; Technical Director, Edward Effron; Musical Director, Kirk Nurock; Stage Manager, David Rosenberg; Press, Barbara Schwartz

COMPANY
Kathryn Posin

Dian Dong   Ricky Schussel
William Gornel   Lance Westergard
Holly Reeve   Marsha White

PROGRAM: "Waves" (Laurie Spiegel, Posin), "Days" (Kirk Nurock, Posin), "Bach Pieces" (Bach, Posin), and *WORLD PREMIERE* Feb. 24, 1976 of "Light Years" (John McLaughlin/Mahavishnu Orchestra, Kathryn Posin; Costumes, Peggy Schierholz)

Kathryn Posin Dance Company in "Waves"
(Joel Gordon Photo)

ELIZABETH KEEN DANCE COMPANY

Artistic Director-Choreographer, Elizabeth Keen; Stage Manager, Jon Knudsen; Lighting Designers, Beverly Emmons, Jon Knudsen

COMPANY

Elizabeth Keen   Patti Kozono
Michael Blue Aiken   Dalienne Majors
Donald Byrd   Candice Prior
Hannah Kahn   Ted Striggles

PROGRAM: "Line Drawing" (Gabriel Faure, Keen), "Parenthesis" (Elizabeth Keen), "Onyx" (David Jolley/Garrett List, Keen), "Polite Entertainment for Ladies and Gentlemen" (Stephen Foster, Keen), and *WORLD PREMIERE* of "Rainbow Tonight" (Keith Jarrett, Elizabeth Keen)

**Elizabeth Keen Dance Company in
"A Polite Entertainment for Ladies and Gentlemen"**
(Lois Greenfield Photo)

KAZUKO HIRABAYASHI DANCE THEATRE

Artistic Director-Choreographer, Kazuko Hirabayashi; Company Manager, Grace Sardelle; Stage Manager, Maxine Glorsky; Production Supervisor, Technical Assistance Group (TAG); Sound, Roger Jay; Assistant to Director, Ralph Farrington

COMPANY

Gerald Banks, Richard Caceres, Grazia Della-Terza, Ralph Farrington, Guillermo Gonzalez, William Holahan, Jim May, Jacqueline McKannay, Ohad Naharin, Janet Panetta, Jeanne Ruddy, Philip Salvatori, Linda Spriggs, Christopher Stocker, Robert Swinston, Teri Weksler, Christine Wright

REPERTOIRE

"Night of the Four Moons with Lone Shadow" (George Crumb, Hirabayashi), "In a Dark Grove" (Lawrence Rosenthal, Hirabayashi), "The Stone Garden" (Ryohei Hirose, Hirabayashi), "Mudai" (untitled) (Mauricio Kagel, Hirabayashi), "Mask of Night" (George Crumb, Hirabayashi)

MARGARET BEALS & IMPULSES CO.

Choreography, Margaret Beals; Lighting Design-Stage Manager, Edward M. Greenberg; Costume, Janaki

COMPANY

Margaret Beals, dance
Edward M. Greenberg, light
Janaki, voice
Dewan Motihar, sitar
Michael Rod, winds
Badal Roy, tabla
Gwendolyn Watson, cello

PROGRAM: "Wild Swans in Epitaph" (poetry of Edna St. Vincent Millay), "Improvisation," "Tulips," "Parting Monologue: Love Is a. . . ." (poetry of Carl Sandburg)

Margaret Beals and Impulses Company
Top: Kazuko Hirabayashi Dance Theatre in
"The Stone Garden"
(Ron Reagan Photos)

DAN WAGONER AND DANCERS

Artistic Director-Choreographer, Dan Wagoner; General Manager, Frank Wicks; Lighting Design, Jennifer Tipton; Stage Manager, Joan Devine

COMPANY

Dan Wagoner	George Montgomery
Christopher Banner	Regan Frey
Heidi Bunting	Sally Hess
Robert Clifford	Judith Moss

REPERTOIRE: "Taxi Dances" (Popular, Wagoner), "Broken Hearted Rag Dance" (Scott Joplin, Wagoner), *WORLD PREMIERE* March 9, 1976 of "A Dance for Grace and Elwood" (Robert Sallier/Carole Weber, Dan Wagoner; Costumes, Kae Yoshida), "Summer Rambo" (Bach, Wagoner), "Brambles" (George Montgomery, Wagoner), "Changing Your Mind" (Dan Wagoner), "Duet" (Purcell, Wagoner)

5 by 2 DANCE COMPANY

Jane Kosminsky
Bruce Becker

REPERTOIRE: "Duet" (Haydn, Paul Taylor), "Negro Spirituals" (Traditional songs/Genevieve Pitot, Helen Tamiris), "Suite Richard" (Traditional, Bruce Becker), "Song" (Mahler, Anna Sokolow), "A Cold Sunday Afternoon, a Little Later" (Donald Erb, Cliff Keuter), "Sola" (Penn-Oldham/Janis Joplin, Mario Delamo), "Meditations of Orpheus" (Hovhaness, Norman Walker), "Indeterminate Figure" (Robert Starer, Daniel Nagrin), "The Beloved" (Judith Hamilton, James Truitte/Lester Horton)

Dan Wagoner, Regan Frey in "Summer Rambo"
(Ron Reagan Photo)

PLAYWRIGHTS HORIZONS

Robert Moss, Executive Producer
Philip Himberg, Producing Director

QUEENS PLAYHOUSE-IN-THE-PARK

October 16–19, 1975
FRED BENJAMIN DANCE COMPANY performing "Mountain High," "Double Solitude," "Dealing with the Facts and Pain," "Prey," "Parallel Lines," "Our Thing," "Ceremony," "Ember," "From the Moon of the Moon"

November 6–9, 1975
MARCUS SCHULKIND DANCE COMPANY and BOB BOWYER and JO-ANN BRUGGEMANN, dancing "The Lady's Night Out," "Big Bird," "Menuetto," "Lambent," "Teen Angels," "Nite Club," "The 'Fred and Barbara' Section," "Affettuoso," "Rock 'n' Roll," "A Piece of Bach"

January 1–4, 1976
ELEO POMARE DANCE COMPANY performing "Climb," "N'Other Shade of Blue," "Passage," "Serendipity," "Narcissus Rising," "Las Desenamoradas"

January 22–25, 1976
THEATRE DANCE COLLECTION performing "Fordanak," "Mandragora," "Double Solitude," "Puppets," "Diary," "Misalliance"

February 19–22, 1976
MARIA ALBA SPANISH DANCE COMPANY dancing "Danzas Fantasticas," "Intermezzo," "Jota Navarra," "Ritmos Flamencos," "Suite Colombiana," "Baile Para Dos," "Cante y Musica," "Solo en el," "Siglo XXI," "Typically Spanish!," "Sevilla de Noche"

April 22–25, 1976
SANASARDO DANCE COMPANY performing "A Consort for Dancers," "All My Pretty Ones," "The Death Notebooks," "Shadows," "A Memory Suite," "The Path"

May 13–16, 1976
MARGARET BEALS and LEE NAGRIN performing "Stings"

May 27–30, 1976
PEARL LANG AND DANCE COMPANY performing "Prairie Steps," "Broken Dialogues," "Piece for Brass," "Shirah"

**Top Right: Marcus Schulkind, Elisa Monte in
"The Fred & Barbara Section"**
Below: Bob Bowyer, Jo-Ann Bruggemann
(Nathaniel Tileston Photo)

The Theatre Dance Collection in "Misalliance"   **Joan Lombardi, Douglas Nielsen in "A Consort for Dancers"**

RIVERSIDE THEATRE DANCE FESTIVAL

Arthur Bartow, Artistic Director

THEATRE OF THE RIVERSIDE CHURCH
November 6, 7, 8, 1975
The Riverside Theatre Dance Festival presents:

HAVA KOHAV DANCE THEATRE

Director-Choreographer, Hava Kohav; Ballet Mistress, Ilona Copen; Ballet Master, Bruce Block; Light Design, Pat Benten; Costumes, Raya Alpert, Hava Kohav; Stage Manager, Robert Wheeler; Press, Harriet Brickman

COMPANY
Hava Kohave

Ilona Copen	Dale Townsend
Bruce Block	Richard Martin
Helga Langen	Patrick McCord

PROGRAM: "Straight and Curved" (Peter Maxwell Davies, Hava Kohav), "Moments" (Herb Alpert/D. Standen, Kohav), "A Dance" (Scarlatti/Purcell, Kohav), "Carnival (nee Gwendolyn)" (Popular/-Traditional, Kohav), and *PREMIERE* of "Plaything of the Wind" (Gwendolyn Watson/Villa Lobos, Hava Kohav)

Right: Hava Kohav in "Plaything of the Wind"
(Zachary Freyman Photo)

THEATRE OF THE RIVERSIDE CHURCH
November 14, 15, 16, 1975
The Riverside Theatre Dance Festival and the Circum-Arts Foundation present:

RICHARD BILES DANCE COMPANY

Artistic Director-Choreographer, Richard Biles; Lighting Design-Stage Manager, Jon Garness; Stage Assistant, William Stivale; Production Assistant, William Campbell; Festival Coordinator, James Van Abbema; Costumes and Slides, Richard Biles

COMPANY

Richard Biles, Kathy Buchanan, Pamela Budner, Donna Evans, Kathy Kroll, Sandra Seymour, Ed Conti, David Corash, Susan Creitz, Phillip Weiner, Luise Wykell

PROGRAM

"Fluxion" (Henze/Percussion, Biles), "Celebrants" (Albinoni/-Bading/Korngold, Biles), "Harlequin-Ade" (Arranged, Biles), "Pendulum" (Arranged sounds, Biles)

Phillip Weiner, Richard Biles in
"Harlequin-Ade" Right Center: "Pendulum"
(Norman Ader Photos)

THEATRE OF THE RIVERSIDE CHURCH
Thursday & Saturday, December 4, 6, 1975
The Riverside Theatre Dance Festival presents:

JUDE BARTLETT AND DANCERS

Artistic Director-Choreographer, Jude Bartlett; Music Director, Jill B. Jaffee; Lighting, Myra Koutzen; Technical Assistant, D. Schweppe; Coordinator, James Van Abbema

COMPANY

Jude Barlett

Kathleen Quinlan-Krichels	Lauri Gitelman
Michael Kasper	Amy Berkman
Janna Jenson	Mary Benson
Nancy Scher	Ed Averse

PROGRAM: "Cotillion" (Webern), "Sunny Satie" (Satie), "Double Suicide" (Jude Bartlett), "Chives" (Charles Ives), "Memoriam" (Bach)

Right: Jude Bartlett, Nancy Scher in "Double Suicide"
(Ron Reagan Photo)

THEATRE OF THE RIVERSIDE CHURCH
Friday & Sunday, January 16–18, 1976
The Riverside Theatre Dance Festival presents:

EDITH STEPHEN DANCE COMPANY

Artistic Director-Choreographer, Edith Stephen; Arts Administrator, Barbara Davis; Administrative Assistant, Joe Garcia; Lighting Design-Stage Manager, Martin Shapiro; Management, Robert M. Gewald

COMPANY

Edith Stephen
Diana Moore
Ralph M. Thomas
Francis Maraschiello
Jacqueline West
Jeanne Suggs
Yumike Crumly

PROGRAM: "Love in Different Colors" (Michael Dreyfuss, Edith Stephen), "Dream of the Wild Horse" (Jacques Lasri), "Continu Om (Scott Joplin, Stephen), "Spaces Indescribable" Francis Bayles, Stephen)

**Right: Edith Stephen Dance Company in
"Spaces Indescribable"**
(Ron Reagan Photo)

THEATRE OF THE RIVERSIDE CHURCH
Saturday, January 17, 1976

CHAMBER DANCE GROUP

Artistic Director, Nanette Bearden; Lighting Design, Martin Shapiro; Stage Manager, Charles P. Gollnick; Ballet Director, Marian Horosko; Costumes, Anthony Basse; Technical Assistant, D. Schweppe; Festival Coordinator, James Van Abbema

COMPANY

David Gleaton, Carole Purcell, Jean Barber, Monica Diaz, Christopher Corry, John Fogarty, Antoinette Gardella, Joaquin de la Habana, Beth Kurtz, Sheila Nowosadko, Al Seward, Lois Silk, Clint Smith, Donna Sterling, Natch Taylor, and ALONSO CASTRO DANCE THEATRE COMPANY: Helen Breasted, Jeanette Hardie, Shirley Hardie, Clifton Jones, Nicole Levinson, and Guest Artists Sheila Rohan, Walter Raines

PROGRAM

"Dance for Three" (John Field, Marian Sarach), "Giselle Pas de Deux" (Bergmueller, Marian Horosko) "Journey" (Krzyszstof/Penderecki, Marvin Gordon), "110th Street" (Tito Puente/Tambo/Tim Weisberger, Gordon), "Transients" (Rod Levitt, Gordon), "The Syrinx" (Debussy, Walter Raines), "Don Quixote Pas de Deux" (Minkus, Gordon), "Coppelia Act I" (Delibes, Horosko)

**Helen Breasted, Shirley Hardie,
Jeanette Hardie in "Journey"**
(Ina Kahn Photo)

THEATRE OF THE RIVERSIDE CHURCH
February 12–15, 1976
The Riverside Theatre Dance Festival Presents:

GREENHOUSE DANCE ENSEMBLE

Choreographers, Lillo Way, Beverly Brown, Brian Webb, Carol Conway, Robert Yohn; Lighting Design, Alan Rafel; Stage Manager, Kate Elliott

COMPANY

Lillo Way, Beverly Brown, June Anderson, Carol Conway, Brian Webb, Checker Ives, Robert Yohn

PROGRAM

"Fanfare" (Gerard Schwarz, Lillo Way), "Whelk Woman" (Eleanor Hovda, Beverly Brown), "In the Center of the Night" (Linda Thomas, Brian Webb), "Romantica" (Gerard Schwarz, Way), "Together Passing" (Sergio Cervetti, Carol Conway), "Fall Down in Brown November" (Darrell L. Crim, Robert Yohn), "Glympses of When" (Frank Martin, Brown)

Right: Carol Conway in "Together Passing"
(Ron Reagan Photo)

THEATRE OF THE RIVERSIDE CHURCH
February 19–22, 1976
The Riverside Theatre Dance Festival presents:

3 CHOREOGRAPHERS

Lighting Design, Jon Garness; Costumes, Virginia Timenes, Chunghi Chu, Kathy Buchanan; Festival Coordinator, James Van Abbema

PROGRAM

"Reflections/Monet" (Hovhaness, Susan Lundberg) danced by Connie Allentuck, Cynthia Reynolds, Sara White; "Reciprocity" (Monk, Luise Wykell) danced by Gale Ormiston and Richard Biles; "Winter Poem" choreographed and danced by Susan Lundberg; "Syzygy" (Sound, Gale Ormiston) danced by Richard Biles, Susan Lundberg, Gale Ormiston, Janet Towner; "Habitat" (Marcello/Aviary/Stravinsky, Luise Wykell) danced by Denise Ferretti, Julie Bryan, Kathy Buchanan, Luise Wykell

Left: Julie Bryan, Kathy Buchanan in "Habitat"
Above: Susan Lundberg in "Winter Poem"

THEATRE OF THE RIVERSIDE CHURCH
February 26–29, 1976
The Riverside Theatre Dance Festival (Arthur Barstow, Director) presents:

MIMI GARRARD DANCE THEATRE

Artistic Director-Choreographer, Mimi Garrard; Stage Manager-Lighting Design, Bill Campbell; Special Effects, James Seawright

COMPANY

Mimi Garrard

Gale Ormiston	Jill Feinberg
Janet Towner	Robert Kosinski
Gary Davis	Gael Stepanek
Antonia Beh	Alexander Wang

PROGRAM: "Phosphones" ('Ghent, Garrard), "Brazen" (Ghent, Garrard), "Dreamspace" (Trimble, Garrard), and *PREMIERE* of "P's and Cues" (Mozart, Mimi Garrard)

Mimi Garrard Dance Theatre in "Dreamspace"
(Tom Caravaglia Photo)

THEATRE OF THE RIVERSIDE CHURCH
Sunday, January 18, 1976
The Riverside Theatre Dance Festival presents:

ARGYR LEKAS
and her
SPANISH DANCE COMPANY

Ramos De Vigil, Jorge Navarro, Ernesto Navarro, Carlotta Santana, Maria Constancia, Carolina Leon, Paco Juanas (guitarist), Domingo Alvarado (Singer), Lina Brinkerhoff (Pianist), and Special Guest Star Ramon de los Reyes

PROGRAM

"Ole De La Curra," "Zapadeado," "Verdeales," "Farucca," "Tarantos," "Caragoles" "Allegrias de Ramon," "Tambourin-Jota"

Right: Argyr Lekas (R) and company in "Tambourin-Jota"
(Ron Reagan Photo)

THEATRE OF THE RIVERSIDE CHURCH
January 28, February 1, 1976
The Riverside Theatre Dance Festival presents:

PAUL WILSON'S
THEATREDANCE ASYLUM

Artistic Director-Choreographer, Paul Wilson; Associate Director, Francis Witkowski; General Manager, Dennis Haines; Production Manager, George Bennett; Lighting Design, Edward R. Cucurello; Production Assistant, Gary Ellis; Sound, Ralph Diaz; Videotapes, David Keller

COMPANY

Whit Carman, Kathy Eaton, Joanne Edelmann, Rebecca Kelly, Joe Schwarz, Penelope Vane, Scott Volk, Paul Wilson, Francis Witkowski, Joan Witkowski, and Guest Dancers: Dale Andre, Barry Barychko, Agnes Denis, Timothy Haynes, Janet Towner

PROGRAM

"Unison" (Handel/Pachelbel, Julie Maloney), "Traditions" (Lehman Engel, Charles Weidman), "Dancing on a Grave" (Joe Schwarz, Paul Wilson), "Show 'n' Tell" (Paul Wilson), and *PREMIERES* of "Pursuits" (Walter Piston, Rebecca Kelly), "Tossed" (Lou Grassi/Oliver Nelson Orchestra, Paul Wilson)

Left: Scott Volk, Penelope Vane in "Tossed"
(Lois Greenfield Photo)

THEATRE OF THE RIVERSIDE CHURCH
January 28–February 1, 1976
The Riverside Theatre Dance Festival presents:

CONSORT DANCE ENSEMBLE

Artistic Directors-Choreographers, Myra Hushansky, Donna Mondanaro; Technical Assistant, D. Schweppe; Festival Coordinator, James Van Abbema

COMPANY

Selby Beebe
Myra Hushansky
Miriam Kenig
Margaret O'Sullivan
Rolando Policastro
Bobbie Silvera

PROGRAM: "Millenium" (Louis Mondanaro, Donna Mondanaro), "Pulses" (Otto Luening/Vladimir Ussachevsky, Myra Hushansky, "Whispers" (Ann Bass, Myra Hushansky, "Encounters" (Iannis Xenakis, Hushansky), "The Stranger" (Albert Camus, Hushansky/Mondanaro), "The Companion" (Donna Mondanaro), "Games" (Vocal Improvisation, Mondanaro), "Brahms Waltzes" (Brahms, Charles Weidman), and *PREMIERES* of "Diverge" (William Ruggiero, Myra Hushansky), "Rage" (Ann Bass, Donna Mondanaro)

Consort Dance Ensemble in "Rage"

Zsedenyi Ballet Company in "Hungarian Peasant Wedding"

THEATRE OF THE RIVERSIDE CHURCH
March 9–14, 1976

ZSEDENYI BALLET COMPANY

Director-Choreographer, Karoly Zsedenyi; Set, Charles Barnes; Costumes, Ilona Varga; Lighting, James Van Abbema; Stage Manager, Kitty Bozic; Stage Crew, Terry Bell, John Robertshaw III, Maurice Ackroyd

PROGRAM

"Solo and Pas de Deux from Sylvia" (Delibes) danced by Susann Organek and Mark Franko; "Andante Appassionata" (Enriqu Soro) danced by Linda Sloboda and Robert Chipok; "Pas de Deu from Raymonda" (Alexander Glazounov) danced by Susanna Organek and Angel Betancourt; "The Dying Swan" (Saint-Saens danced by Elizabeth Kim; "The Hungarian Peasant Wedding" (Zol tan Kodaly) performed by Elizabeth Kim, Robert Chipok, Lind Sloboda, Anke Junge, George Fein, Susanna Organek, Susan Jurick Genie Joseph, Angel Betancourt, Mark Franko

THEATRE OF THE RIVERSIDE CHURCH
March 18–21, 1976
The Riverside Theatre Dance Festival presents:

LUISE WYKELL & COMPANY

Artistic Director-Choreographer, Luise Wykell; Lighting Design, Jon Garness; Costumes, Luise Wykell; Stage Manager, Jon Garness; Production Assistant, Edward Marsan

COMPANY

Jane Alsen, Denise Ferretti, Sue Renner, Sandra Seymour, Julie Bryan, Steven Iannacone, Richard Biles, Janis Brenner, Sharon Spanner, Jane Durbin, Marjorie Myles, Valery Farias, Rosemary Newton, Luise Wykell

PROGRAM: "The Game" (Cage/Harrison/Hyman/Rameay/Roldan/Starzer/Telemann/Ussachevsky, Luise Wykell (A Premiere)

Right: Janis Brenner, Luise Wykell in "The Game"
(Norman Ader Photo)

Phyllis Lamhut in "Hearts of Palm"
(Tom Caravaglia Photo)

THEATRE OF THE RIVERSIDE CHURCH
April 1–4, 1976
The Riverside Theatre Dance Festival presents:

PHYLLIS LAMHUT
DANCE COMPANY

Artistic Director-Choreographer, Phyllis Lamhut; Lighting Design, Ruth Grauert; Technical Director, Jon Garness; Technical Assistant, Tertius Walker; Press, Judith Scott

COMPANY

Phyllis Lamhut	Patrice Evans
Kent Baker	Thomas Evert
Donald Blumenfeld	Kathleen Gaskin
Diane Boardman	Joan Gedney
Jeffrey Eichenwald	Natasha Simon
Diane Elliot	Vic Stornant

PROGRAM: "Solo with Company" (Czajkowski, Lamhut), "Conclave" (Thomas Mark Edlun, Lamhut), and *PREMIERE* of "Hearts of Palm" (Arranged Sound, Lamhut) dedicated to James Waring

RHODE ISLAND DANCE REPERTORY COMPANY

Artistic Director, Julie Adams Strandberg; Technical Director, Peter Anderson; Producer, J. Erik Hart

COMPANY

Julie Strandberg, Kathy Eberstadt, Richard Lambertson, Skip Carter, Janet Danforth, Nancy Reichley, Marilyn Cristofori, Judith Hendin, Zane Rankin, Daniel (Williams) Grossman

REPERTOIRE

"After the Fall" (Arthur Custer, Marilyn Cristofori), "Couples" Terry Riley/West African Traditional, Daniel (Williams) Grossman), "Success" (Jack Hansen/E. J. Miller, Nora Guthrie), "Duet" (Weather Report, Ted Rotante), "National Spirit" (Traditional, Daniel Grossman), "Broken Glass" (Machaut/de la Halle/Anonymous, Kathy Eberstadt)

Left: Julie Strandberg, Kathy Eberstadt, Catherine Bodner in "Broken Glass"

MIDI GARTH DANCE COMPANY

Artistic Director-Choreographer, Midi Garth; Lighting Design, Jon Garness; Press, Reginald Gay, Aubrey Tarbox; Stage Manager, Jon Garness; Costumes, Midi Garth, Douglas McLish, Margradel Hicks

COMPANY

Midi Garth	Jody Heineman
Nina Cohen	Luisa Moore
Mark De Garmo	Christine Stevens
Chris Glover	Nancy Zendora

PROGRAM: "Workout for Six" (Liszt, Garth), "Time and Memory" (Vivaldi, Garth), "Anonymous," "Prelude to Flight" (Hovhaness), "Images," "Chorale" (Varese, Garth), and *PREMIERES* of "Open Space," "Trio" (Bach)

MARIANO PARRA SPANISH DANCE COMPANY

(program and photos not submitted)

Midi Garth in "Time and Memory"

CHOREOGRAPHY BY JOAN LOMBARDI

Managing Director, Jan Michell; Designer, Robert Bayley; Technical Director, Karen De Francis; Stage Manager, Sarah E. Locke

COMPANY
Joan Lombardi

Willa Kahn	Harry Laird
Christine Strazza	Alex Dolcemascolo
Elyssa Paternoster	Douglas Boulivar
Kate Johnson	Jose Meier

PROGRAM: "Portrait" (JoanPfeiffer/Henry Colwell/John Cage), "Segaki" (Walter Carlos), and *PREMIERES* of "All the Way Around and Back" (Collage), "Ambivalence" (Collage), "Threads" (Bach)

Joan Lombardi and dancers in "Threads"

TOWN HALL PROGRAMS

TOWN HALL
Wednesday, February 18, 1976
Town Hall Interludes presents:

ROYAL TAHITIAN
DANCE COMPANY

General Manager-Artist Director, Paulette Vienot; Artistic Director-Choreographer, Turepu Turepu; Technical Director, Pierre Vincent; Company Manager, Lou Metz; Press, Marilyn Egol

COMPANY

Catherine Dexter, Claire Leverd, Edna Teriipaia, Amelie Vaatete, Chatelaine Pincemin, Moana Heyman, Emere Haoa, Marguerite Lai, Metaurea Nellie, Juliette Fong Choi, Elise Flores, Tipea Teura, Etaeta Justine, Joe Caffery, Alexis Cadousteau, Hubert Tehuiotoa, Tekotai Paratainga, Carlos Teehu, Michel Chevalier, Andre Maheahea, Clement Pito, Michel Motfat, Edwin Maihota, Gratien Mahai

PROGRAM

"Otea Tahiti Nui," "See You in Tahiti," "Diving for Mother-of-Pearl in the Tuamotu," "Aparima Tane and Vahine," "The Romance of Loti," "Memories of Tahiti," "Come and Dance with Me," "Sunset over Bora Bora"

The Royal Tahitian Dance Company

TOWN HALL
Wednesday, April 21, 1976
Town Hall Interludes presents:

JAMES CUNNINGHAM
&
THE ACME DANCE COMPANY

Artistic Director-Choreographer, James Cunningham; Associate Artistic Director, Lauren Persichetti; Lighting Design, Raymond Dooley; Costume Coordination, Paul Steinberg; Masks, Gary Finkel, Ross Klahr; Narrators, James Cunningham, Lauren Persichetti, Ted Striggles

COMPANY

James Cunningham
Lauren Persichetti
Michael Deane
Barbara Ellmann
Candice Prior
Ted Striggles

PROGRAM: "The Return of the Fox" (A collage of the company's works), and the *World Premiere* of "Aesop's Fables" (Vincent Persichetti, James Cunningham/Lauren Persichetti)

TOWN HALL
Wednesday, May 12, 1976
Town Hall Interludes presents:

ADAM DARIUS

mime artist, performing "Invocation," "The Day the Circus Closed," "The Dreamer," "The Mourners," "The Father Who Searched for His Long Lost Son," "While in the Bathtub," "Claustrophobia" "Judge Closes Sex Shop!!," "The Village Idiot," "The Lovers," "Death of a Scarecrow"

TOWN HALL
Wednesday, May 19, 1976
Town Hall Interludes presents:

KALERIA FEDICHEVA
with
Dennis Marshall

PROGRAM: "Rossini Pas de Deux" (Rossini, Fedicheva/Chernyshov), "Dying Swan" (Saint-Saens, Fokine), "Meeting" (Boris Kravchenko, Leonid Jacobson), "Bluebird Pas de Deux" (Tchaikovsky, Petipa)

James Cunningham and the Acme Dance Company in "Aesop's Fables"

Dennis Marshall, Kaleria Fedicheva
(R. J. Kumery Photo)

MISCELLANEOUS NEW YORK DANCE PROGRAMS

41 BROADWAY STUDIO
June 4–7, 11–14, 1975

TRISHA BROWN COMPANY

Trisha Brown
Judith Ragir
Mona Sulzman
Elizabeth Garren

PROGRAM: "Pamplona Stones," "Locus (a work in progress)"

"Pamplona Stones"
(Johan Elbers Photo)

ANDAM THEATRE
June 5–29, 1975

LES BALLETS TROCKADERO DE MONTE CARLO

Artistic Directors, Antony Bassae, Peter Anastos; General Director, Natch Taylor; General Manager, Eugene McDougle; Ballet Mistress, Elenita Licklider; Music Director, Pugni Minkus-Glinka; Designers, Richard Strahan, Joseph DeAngelis; State Manager, Jay Hoffman; Lighting and Technical Director, Druth McClure; Costumes, Antony Bassae

COMPANY

Tamara Karpova, Suzina LaFuzziovitch, Olga Tchikaboumskaya, Natasha Veceslova, Zamarina Zamarkova, Lyudmilla Bolshoya, Veronika-Malaise du Mer, Eugenia Repelskii, Koko Markola, Vera Namethatunova, Pagano Sissinska, Roland Deaulin, Urali Stepanopskii, Alexis Ivanovitch Lermontov, Jack d'Aniels, Fjord Tord, Boris Yetz

a.k.a. Peter Anastos, Shawn Avrae, Antony Bassae, William Gladstone, Wayne Lane, Larry Line, J. John Martin, Allen Simpson, Clinton W. Smith, Joe Stephen, Natch Taylor, Clio Young, Zamie Zamor)

REPERTOIRE

"Coppelia" (Delibes, Marian Horosko after St. Leon), "Pas de Quatre" (Pugni, Trutti Gasparinetti), "Siberiana" (Tchaikovsky, Peter Anastos), "Snowflakes" (Tchaikovsky, Antony Bassae), "Carmen" (Bizet, Antony Bassae), "Le Lac des Cygnes" (Tchaikovsky, Tamara Karpova), "Don Quixote Pas de Deux" (Minkus, Karpova), "Go for Barocco" (Bach, Anastos), "Ecole de Ballet" (Jean-Claude Pastiche, Peter Anastos), "Firebird" (Stravinsky, Marian Horosko)

Les Ballets Trockadero de Monte Carlo in "Pas de Quatre"
(John L. Murphy Photo)

AMERICAN THEATRE LABORATORY
June 6, 7, 8, 1976

MIDI GARTH DANCE THEATER

Choreography, Midi Garth; Lighting Design, John Dodd; Costumes, Midi Garth, Marilyn Mazur, Luisa Moore; Management Consultant, Bradford Lewis; Design, Leonard Levine; Press, Reginald Gay, Nathaniel Crossland

DANCERS
Midi Garth

Jacqueline Corl	Judith Ann Harmon
Lorraine Kreps	Raymond Maguire
Marilyn Mazur	Luisa Moore

PROGRAM: "Voices" (Hovhaness), "Sea Change" "This Day's Madness" (P. Schaeffer, P. Henry), all solos by Midi Garth, "Voyages" (Webern), and *PREMIERES* of "Workout for Six" (Liszt), "Chorale" (Varese)

Midi Garth (R) in "This Day's Madness"

CHOREOGROUND THEATRE
June 6, 7, 8, 1975

CONSORT DANCE ENSEMBLE

Artistic Directors, Myra Hushansky, Donna Mondanaro; Costumes, Sylvia Woods

COMPANY

Selby Beebe
Myra Hushansky
Miriam Kenig
Donna Mondanaro

Margaret O'Sullivan
Rolando Policastro
Bobbie Silvera

PROGRAM: "Milennium" (Louis Mondanaro, Donna Mondanaro), "Unescorted" (Pete Seeger, Myra Hushansky), "Verge" (Vocal Improvisation, Mondanaro), "Brahms Waltzes" (Brahms, Charles Weidman), "Portrait" (Mondanaro), "Games" (Vocal Improvisation, Mondanaro), "Pulses" (Otto Luening/Vladimir Ussachevsky, Hushansky), "Song" (Arnold Schoenberg, Mondanaro)

Chuck Wilson Photo

**Selby Beebe, Myra Hushansky,
Bobbie Silvera in "Millennium"**
(Chuck Wilson Photo)

CUNNINGHAM STUDIO

Saturday & Sunday, June 7–8, 1975

BECKY ARNOLD
AND THE DANCING MACHINE

Choreography, Becky Arnold; Lighting, Lewis Rosen, Tom Weller; Technical Director, Nancy Golloday; Sound, Mac Emshwiller; Stage Manager, George Titus; Press, John Miner

COMPANY

Becky Arnold, Denise Blanchard, Kathy Murphy, Trish Walker, Dorsey Yearley, Richard Moses, Joanne Brauman, Diana Nicholas, Tom Wellor

PROGRAM

"Journey to Within" (Santana), "Trio A" (Choreography, Yvonne Rainer), *PREMIERE* of "Blues for Two" (Charles Mingus, Becky Arnold; Costumes, Susan White), "Dancing Machine" (Jackson Five), "Motor Dance: A Movement Kaleidoscope" (F. Karl Boyle)

John Miner Photo

Selby Beebe in "Song"
(Chuck Wilson Photo)

TEARS
June 9–12, 1975
Dance Works, Inc., presents:

SIX WORKS BY BARBARA ROAN

Artistic Directors, Barbara Roan, Irene Feigenheimer; Managing Direcror, Robert Marinaccio; Lighting Designer, Nicholas Wolff Lyndon

DANCERS

Anthony LaGiglia
Ernest Pagnano
Liz Thompson
Irene Feigenheimer
Barbara Roan

Michael Kasper
Ed Aversa
Hollyce Yoken
Betty Salamun
Karen Chalom

PROGRAM: "Prefix" (Collage), "Nightwatch" (David Crosby), "Driz...zle" (Collage), "Ocean," "Range," and *PREMIERE* of "Juggler" (John McLaughlin/Mandrake Memorial)

The Dancing Machine

DONNELL LIBRARY CENTER
Tuesday, June 10, 1975
Donnell Library Center presents:

LAURA VELDHUIS
DANCE COMPANY

Director-Choreographer, Laura Veldhuis; Technical Consultant-Designer, Joop Veldhuis

COMPANY

Mark Dana
Alan D'Angerio
Diana Gregory
Pamela Kesler
Laura Veldhuis

PROGRAM: "Green Mountain Suite" (John & Peter Isaacson, Veldhuis), "The Mind's Eye (Excerpts)" (Benjamin Britten, Veldhuis), "Father and Son" (Cat Stevens, Veldhuis), "Miles from Nowhere" (Cat Stevens, Veldhuis), "Essence and Transcendence" (Alberto Ginastera, Veldhuis)

Right: Mark Dana, Laura Veldhuis in "Essence and Transcendence" Below: Laura Veldhuis, Alan D'Angerio in "The Mind's Garden"
(Mira Photos)

LIBRARY & MUSEUM OF PERFORMING ARTS
Thursday, June 12, 1975*
Performing Arts Foundation presents:

PHILIPPINE DANCE COMPANY
OF NEW YORK

Artistic Director-Choreographer, Ronnie Alejandro; Executive Director, Bruno P. Seril; Technical Director, Chuck Golden; Stage Manager, Lee Horsman; President, Ramon de Luna

COMPANY

Ronnie Alejandro, Ching Valdes, Vicky Tiangco, Kathy Serio, Dulce Valdes, Ruth Malabrigo, Vicky Valdes, Rosemarie Valdes, Tony Parel, Sonny Zapanta, Ramon de Luna, Benny Felix, Eddie Sese, Eugene Domingo

PROGRAM

SULYAP: "Jota Cavitena" (Traditional, Alejandro), "Paypay de Manila" (Traditional, Alejandro), "Tarjata Sin Kagukan" (Dadap, Alejandro after Goquingco), "Subli" (Traditional, Alejandro after Aquino), "Pandanggo sa Ilaw" (Traditional, Alejandro after Aquino)

* This program was repeated at the American Museum of Natural History on June 22, Oct. 5, 1975, Jan. 4, Feb. 22, March 14, April 11, May 9, 1976.

TEARS
June 13, 14, 15, 1975
Dance Works, Inc., presents:

WORKS BY IRENE FEIGENHEIMER

Artistic Directors, Barbara Roan, Irene Feigenheimer; Managing Director, Robert Marinaccio; Lighting, Nicholas Wolff Lyndon; Stage Manager, Mark Litvin

DANCERS

Hollyce Yoken, Jude Bartlett, Genevieve Kapuler, Laurie Gittelman, Mary Benson, Joan Schwartz, Laurie Uprichard, Michael Kasper, Janna Jensen, Ed Aversa, Robert Simpson, Connie Brunner, Ruis Woertendyke, Jim May, Barbara Roan, Jennifer Donohue, Joan Finkelstein, Jeannie Hutchins, Billy Siegenfeld, Irene Feigenheimer

PROGRAM

"Especially" (Nickelodeon), "Stages" (Charles Madden), "Dance for Four" (John Smead), and *PREMIERES* of "Travelin' Pair" (Billy Joel), "Later Dreams, Part I" (John Smead)

Philippine Dance Company of New York

NYU AUDITORIUM THEATRE
June 18–30, 1975 (24 performances)
Chimera Foundation for Dance, Inc., presents:

NIKOLAIS DANCE THEATRE

Artistic Director, Choreography, Sound Score, Costume an
Lighting Design, Alwin Nikolais; Production Coordinator, Ruth I
Grauert; Technical Director, Peter Koletzke; Stage Managers, Ror
ald M. Bundt, Anthony Micocci; Sound, John Philip Luckacovic
Costume Director, Frank Garcia; Manager, Peter Obletz; Projectio
Technician, David Williams; Press, William Schelble

COMPANY

Lisbeth Bagnold	Chris Reisne
Rob Esposito	Jessica Sayr
Bill Groves	Karen Sin
Suzanne McDermaid	James Teeter
Gerald Otte	Fred Timr

REPERTOIRE: "Tensile Involvement" from "Masks, Props an
Mobiles," "Triple Duet" from "Grotto," "Cross-Fade," Suite from
"Sanctum," "Scenario," "Alphabet" from "Allegory," "Duet" from
"Somniloquy," "Trio" from "Vaudeville of the Elements,
"Noumenon" from "Masks, Props and Mobiles," "Foreplay," an
New York Premieres of "Temple" on Wednesday, June 18, 1975, an
"Tribe" on Friday, June 20, 1975.

Tom Caravaglia Photos

"Masks, Props and Mobiles" Above: "Tribe" Top: "Temple"
(Tom Caravaglia Photos)

Top: "Scenario" Below: "Grotto"
(Oleaga Photos)

NYU SCHOOL OF ARTS THEATRE
June 24–27, 1975
The Alum Dance Foundation presents:

MANUEL ALUM DANCE COMPANY

Artistic Director-Choreographer, Manuel Alum; Producing Director, Robert Marinaccio; Lighting Designer, Gary Harris; Stage Manager, Judy Kayser; Technical Crew, David Kissel, Jig Gillespie; Costumes, Patrick Elliot

COMPANY
Manuel Alum

Felicia Norton	Michael Rivers
Martin Bland	Iris Salomon
Roberta Caplan	Kate Johnson
Jacqulyn Buglisi	Andrew Quinlan-Krichels

PROGRAM: "Yemaya" (Ira Taxin, Alum), "Era" (K. Penderecki, Alum), "East—To Nijinsky" (Joseph Tal, Alum), *New York Premiere* of "Ilanot" (Brahms, Alum)

TERRA FIRMA
Friday & Saturday, June 27–28, 1975

NEW YORK REUNION

Artistic Directors-Choreographers, Patricia Hruby, Suzanne Oliver; Lighting Design-Production Management, Mark Goodman; Costumes, Patricia Hruby, Suzanne Oliver

COMPANY

Roxanne Bartush	Laurie McKirahan
Gail Constestabile	Holly Reeve
Patricia Hruby	Lucie Signa
Rick Hood	Ralph M. Thomas

PROGRAM: "Waves" (Aaron Copland, Suzanne Oliver), "Birds" (Antonio Vivaldi, Patricia Hruby), "A Bit about Women and Others" (Debussy, Hruby), "Growing Up in Mudville" (Carly Simon/Laura Nyro/Judy Collins, Oliver), "Game: Your Play, My Move" (Vivaldi/Jig/Blues/Joplin, Hruby)

John Dady Photo

Right: Thomas Holt Dance Ensemble
(Allan Seward Photo)
Top: New York Reunion in
"A Bit about Women and Others"

ze Klavins, Felice Lesser, Richard Roistacher in "Roulette"
(Gerry Goodstein Photo)

AMERICAN THEATRE LABORATORY
June 27, 28, 29, 1975

A DANCE EVENT

THE FELICE LESSER DANCE THEATER: Melanie Adam, Ilze Klavins, Felice Lesser, Richard Roistacher, dancing "Dichterliebe" (Robert Schumann, Felice Lesser; Text, Heinrich Heine; Costumes, Sandra Kenyen, Richard Roistacher; Pianist, Constance Cooper; Baritone, Jonathan Levi), "Roulette" (Josef Suk/Richard Einhorn electronic score, Felice Lesser)

THE THOMAS HOLT DANCE ENSEMBLE: Kristine Bader, Betsy Baron, Lucinda Gehrke, Thomas Holt, David McComb, Ann Moser, Allan Seward, Paulette Taylor, Phillip Tietz, Aletha Winter, performing "Afterhours in Wonderland" (Collage, Thomas Holt), "Arienata" (Antonio Vivaldi, Thomas Holt), "Duet for Summer" (Lee Holdridge, Thomas Holt), and *PREMIERE* of "Second Avenue Scrapbook" (Laura Nyro, Thomas Holt; Lighting, Joanna Schielke; Sound, Sue Ann Willis)

Jerry Goodstein Photo

BYRD HOFFMAN STUDIO
June 27–29, 1975

CONVERGING LINES

A dialogue with music by Tom Johnson; Realised for stage by Senta Driver; Stage Manager, John Moore; Staff Assistants, Lynn Hoogenboom, Jenny Resto; Performed by members of Harry:

Marianne Bachmann
Senta Driver
Tom Johnson
Andrea Stark

Marianne Bachmann, Senta Driver in "Converging Lines"
(Willard Midgette Photo)

MERCE CUNNINGHAM STUDIO
Friday & Saturday, June 27–28, 1975

JAN WODYNSKI DANCE COMPANY

Artistic Director-Choreographer-Costumes, Jan Wodynski; Technical Director, Mike Wodynski

COMPANY

Joanne Edelmann
John Kelly
Robert Kosinski
Madeleine Perrone
Jan Wodynski
Mike Wodynski

PROGRAM: "Interspace" (Collin Walcot), "Outing" (Ralph Towner), "Timewarp" (Schwartz, M. Wodynski), and *PREMIERE* of "Extended Vizhun" (Mike Wodynski)

"Extended Vizhun"
(Chuck Saaf Photo)

NYU SCHOOL OF THE ARTS
July 7, 8, 11, 1975

PHOEBE NEVILLE DANCE COMPANY

Artistic Director-Choreographer, Phoebe Neville; Lighting, Nicholas Wolff Lyndon; Stage Manager, Lauren Barnes; Set, Edward Spena; Original Scores, Eleanor Hovda; Soloist, Rachel Lampert

COMPANY

Anthony La Giglia
Ellen Likwornik
Mareen Pennison

Rachel Lampert
Phoebe Neville
Tryntje Shapli

PROGRAM: "Ladydance" (Hovahness, Neville), "Solo" (Hovda, Neville), "Move" (Buddhist Chants, Neville), "Oracles" (Hovda, Neville)

Ellen Likwornik, Phoebe Neville,
Marleen Pennison in "Oracles"
(Philip E. Hipwell Photo)

BATTERY PARK
Tuesday, July 29, 1975

A/P IMPROV GROUP

Judith Scott (Director), with Jill Feinberg, Stephanie Jordan, Irene Kassow, Edward Marsian, Cindy Pollack, Missy Vineyard

PROGRAM: "Recharge Battery II" (David Van Tieghem, Judith Scott)

Right: Judith Scott
(S. Dewey Photo)

WASHINGTON SQUARE METHODIST CHURCH
Wednesday, July 30, 1975
The Ravi Shankar Music Circle presents:

SUNYANA

in a performance of the classical North Indian dance "Katha"

Right: Sunyana

MARYMOUNT MANHATTAN THEATRE
August 11–17, 1975 (9 performances)
American Dance Foundation, Inc. presents:

U.S. TERPSICHORE

Directors, Richard Thomas, Barbara Fallis; Artistic Consultant, Royes Fernandez; Ballet Masters, Gretchen Schumacher, Ronald Darden; Company Coordinator, Jacqueline Maskey; Pianists, Barbara Kamhi, May Sofge; Soprano, Barbara Ione Miller; Violinist, Davinagracia

COMPANY

PRINCIPALS: Kaleria Fedicheva, Daniel Levans, Bronwyn Thomas, Manuel Gomez, Marissa Benetsky, Gretchen Schumacher, and Senior Artists: David Vaughan, Dick Andros

SOLOISTS: Heather Steelman, Alba Cruz, Craig Williams, Kim Pearce, Raymond Kurshals

CORPS: Sue Admirand, Alice Avolio, Bernadette Bleuzen, Lisa Brady, Cowles Campbell, Nancy Condon, Scott Cousins, Marcos Dinnerstein, Tina Foisie, Ina Golden, Tom Laskaris, Ellen Levine, John Mallinson, Andrew Needhammer, Michael Puleo, Leslie Rubinstein, Anfredo Sanchez, Eddie Shellman, Sallie Stadlen, Peter Wandell

REPERTOIRE

"Les Sylphides" (Chopin, after Fokine), *WORLD PREMIERE* of "Canciones Amatorias" (Enrique Granados, Daniel Levans; Costumes, Stanley Simmons), "Black Swan Pas de Deux" (Tchaikovsky, Petipa), "Winter's Pleasures" (Giaccomo Meyerbeer, after "Les Patineurs" by Frederic Ashton), "Swan Lake" (Tchaikovsky, Ivanov/Petipa), "Caprice" (Stravinsky, Levans), "Graduation Ball" (Strauss, after Lichine), Company Premiere of "Giselle" (Adam, Antony Dolin after Coralli), *NY Premiere* of "Grand Pas from La Bayadere Act II" (Minkus, Fedicheva after Petipa)

Photo by Mira

U.S. Terpsichore in "Giselle"

New York Dance Theatre
(Photo by Mira)

LINCOLN CENTER OUT-OF-DOORS
Friday, August 22, 1975
Mel Howard presents:

NEW YORK DANCE THEATRE

Artistic Director-Choreographer, Frank Ohman; Lighting and Staging, George Bardyguine

COMPANY

Lynda Yourth	Robert Maiorano
Judith Shoaff	Frank Ohman
Marnee Morris	Bryan Pitts
Elizabeth Pawluk	Stephen Rockford
Pamela Mitchell	Darryl Robinson

PROGRAM: "Bacharach Medley" (Burt Bacharach, Frank Ohman), "Song" (George Gershwin, Ohman), "Melodie" (Tchaikovsky, Ohman), "Soliloquy" (Britten, Ohman), "American Raggs" (Scott Joplin, Ron Cunningham), "Lovers of Verona" (Brahms, Ohman), "Improvisation" (Genji Ito, Marnee Morris Ito), "Hoedown" (Traditional, Ohman)

LINCOLN CENTER OUT-OF-DOORS
Friday, August 29, 1975*
Performing Arts Foundation presents:

PHILIPPINE DANCE COMPANY OF NEW YORK

Artistic Director-Choreographer, Ronnie Alejandro; Assistant Director, Ching Valdes; Executive Director, Bruna P. Seril; Technical Director, Chuck Golden; Stage Manager, Lee Horsman

COMPANY

Ronnie Alejandro, Sonny Zapanta, Cesar Villaneuva, Tony Parel, Ramon de Luna, Mel Chionglo, Benny Felix, Eddie Sese, Beth Padua, Veda Agus, Ching Valdes, Rosemarie Valdes, Dulce Valdes, Vicky Valdes, Kathy Serio, Vicky Tiangco, Ruth Malabrigo, Eugene Domingo, Melen Acaac

PROGRAM

PAMANA: "Polkabal" (Traditional/Kasilag), "Timawa" (Traditional), "Panuelo de Amor" (Traditional/Kasilag), "Paypay de Manila" (Traditional/Kasilag), "Jota Cavitena" (Traditional), "Malong" (Kasilag), "Tarjata Sin Kagukan" (Dadap), "Singkil" (Traditional), "Apayao Maidens" (Traditional/Kasilag), "Kalinga Wedding Dance" (Kasilag), "Anihan" (Gonzalez), "Binasuan" (Traditional), "Itik-Itik" (Traditional), "Subli" (Traditional), "Pandanggo sa Ilaw" (Traditional), "Tinikling" (Traditional). All choreography by Ronnie Alejandro.

* Repeated Trinity School Dec. 7, 1975, and at International House April 10, 1976.

Philippine Dance Company of New York

CENTRAL PARK MALL
Thursday, September 4, 1975*
City of New York Parks, Recreation and Cultural Affairs Administration presents:

LAURA VELDHUIS DANCE COMPANY

Artistic Director-Choreographer, Laura Veldhuis; Technical Director, Joop Veldhuis; Costumes, Salvatore Guida

DANCERS

Bill Belle
Gary Davis
Diana Gregory
Pamela Kesler
Laura Veldhuis
Alan D'Angerio

PROGRAM: "Green Mountain Suite" (Peter and John Isaacson, Veldhuis), "Excerpts from 'The Mind's Garden'" (Benjamin Britten, Veldhuis), "Miles from Nowhere" (Cat Stevens, Veldhuis), "Essence and Transcendence" (Alberto Ginastera, Velhuis)

* Program was repeated Monday and Tuesday, September 22, 23, 1975 at the Library and Museum of the Performing Arts at Lincoln Center, Friday and Saturday, Dec. 12–13, 1975 at the Energy Center, and Saturday and Sunday, March 6–7, 1976 at the American Museum of Natural History.

Laura Veldhuis, Bill Belle in "From the Mind's Eye"

Nada Reagan, Carol Conway in "Classic Kite Tails"
(David Hoff Photo)

CARNEGIE HALL
Thursday & Saturday, September 11 & 13, 1975
The Foundation for Modern Dance presents:

ERICK HAWKINS DANCE COMPANY

Director-Choreographer, Erick Hawkins; Conductor, Joel Thome; Lighting Designer, Mark Goodman; General Manager, Mark Z. Alpert; Press, Tom Kerrigan; Stage Manager, Ira Rubin

COMPANY

Erick Hawkins

Robert Yohn
Cathy Ward
Natalie Richman
Nada Reagan
Cory Terry

John Wiatt
Alan Lynes
Kristen Peterson
Kevin Tobiason
Judy Davis

PROGRAM: "Classic Kite Tails" (David Diamond, Hawkins), *New York Premieres* of "Meditation on Orpheus" (Alan Hovhaness, Hawkins; Designs, Ray Sais; Costumes, Raya), "Hurrah!" (Virgil Thomson, Hawkins; Set, Ralph Dorazio; Costumes, Nancy Cope), and *WORLD PREMIERE* of "Death Is the Hunter" (Wallingford Riegger, Erick Hawkins; Masks and Sets, Ralph Lee; Costumes, Willa Kim)

Marcus Schulkind Dance Company
(Nathaniel Tileston Photo)

AMERICAN THEATRE LABORATORY
September 19, 20, 21, 1975

MARCUS SCHULKIND DANCE COMPANY

Artistic Director-Choreographer, Marcus Schulkind; Assistant Director, Elisa Monte; General Manager, Charles Moody; Lighting, Tina Charney; Costumes, Elisa Monte; Pianist, Ann Garvey

COMPANY

Elisa Monte
Keiko Takeya
Christine Wright
Rolando Jorif
Robin Lyon
Marcus Schulkind

PROGRAM: "Lambent" (Beethoven), "The Lady's Night Out" (The Beatles/Randy Newman), "Big Bird" (Scarlatti), "Affettuoso" (Telemann)—all choreography by Marcus Schulkind

PREMIERES: "The Bicentennial Salt & Pepper Rag" (Joseph Lamb, Schulkind), "The 'Fred and Barbara' Section" (Fred Coffin, Schulkind), "A Piece of Bach" (Bach/Busoni, Schulkind)

Lotte Goslar's Pantomime Circus (Lotte Goslar center)

HUNTER COLLEGE PLAYHOUSE
Saturday & Sunday, September 27–28, 1975
Sheldon Soffer presents:

LOTTE GOSLAR'S PANTOMIME CIRCUS

Choreography and Costume Design, Lotte Goslar; Props Designed and executed by Jack Lines; Pianist, Richard Mercier; Company and Stage Manager, Jack Lines

COMPANY

Lotte Goslar

Donna Baldwin
Gary Cowan
Emilietta Ettlin
Rick Hood

Jerri Lines
Kenneth MacDonald
Dale Townsend
Ray Collins

REPERTOIRE

Greetings, For Feet Only, Child Prodigy, Friendship, Sympathy, The Flying Zucchinis, Apropos Elves, Music Box, Great Waltz, Happy Washday, So-Long!, Heap of Misery, Mercyry, Lovely, Bird Fanciers, It Starts with a Step, Life of a Flower, Cupid, Valse Very Triste, La Chasse, Leggieros, Conversation with an Ant, Collector's Items, The Come-On, A Dream, Splendor in the Grass, Grandma Always Danced

JOAN MILLER
and
CHAMBER ARTS/DANCE PLAYERS

Artistic Director-Choreographer, Joan Miller; Musical Director-Composer, Gwendolyn Watson; Associate Artistic Director, Anthony LaGiglia; Artistic Adviser, Leon Danielian; Managing Director, Carol Indianer; Business Manager, Juliene Berk; Promotional Assistant, Margaret Hanks

COMPANY

Frank Ashley, Lee Connor, Donlin Foreman, Theresa Kim, Anthony LaGiglia, Lorn MacDougal, Joan Miller, Sandie Ferranti, Pamela Greene, Roy Pacheco, Sylvia Rincon, musicians Gwendolyn Watson, William Fleet, Jr., and narrator Carol Williams

PROGRAM

"Mix" (Roebuck Staples/David Coffee/Billy Preston, Joan Miller), "Under It" (Choreography, Lee Connor), "Pass Fe White" (Poetry, Joan Miller), "Fields of Passing, Part II" (Gwendolyn Watson, Anthony LaGiglia; Premiere), "Black on Black" (William Fleet, Jr., Joan Miller), "Thoroughfare" (John Mayall, Joan Miller)

Steven Friedman Photo

Joan Miller, Anthony LaGiglia in "Fields of Passing Part I"
(Philip Hipwell Photo)

Members of Burmese National Theater

BURMESE NATIONAL THEATER

A company of 15 dancers and musicians performing "Nat Votaress," "Prince Returns from Taxila," "Bow Contest," and "Ramayana"

INDRANI

with dancers V. P. Ramakrishnan, Sukanya, and Shata Nedungadi, vocalist Visalam Venkatachalam, and percussionist Shekharan; Management, Frank Wicks

PROGRAM

"Rig Veda," "Cholkettu," "Vana Varnanam," "Woman's Beauty," "Tarangam," "Manduka Shabdam," "Orissi Suite" "Episode from the Kathakali Dance Theatre," "Tillana"

DANCES

THE BOX STAYS IN THE CLOSET (Dee Kohanna, Valerie Pullman) performed by Mickie Geller, Valerie Pullman, Kathy Robens

DEEPMOUTHED FIGURE (Kabuki, Doris Ginsberg) performed by Art Berger

WHITE BREAD (Beethoven, Valerie Pullman) danced by David Malamut, Valerie Pullman

MONEY TREE (Collage by Mickie Geller) choreographed and performed by Mickie Geller

UNTITLED SOLO (Peruvian Folk) choreographed and danced by Doris Ginsberg

SCRAPERACE (Mickie Geller) Performed by Mickie Geller, Valerie Pullman; Technical Director, Susanne Joelson

Indrani

PUBLIC/NEWMAN THEATER
Opened Tuesday, October 7, 1975.*
Original Ballets Foundation in association with New York Shakespeare
Festival (Joseph Papp, Producer) presents:

ELIOT FELD BALLET

Artistic Director-Choreographer, Eliot Feld; Administrator, Cora
ahan; Pianists, Gladys Celeste Mercader, Peter Longiaru; Music
oordinator, Herbert Harris; Assistant to Administrator, Catherine
. Paull; Wardrobe Master, Jackie Carhart

COMPANY

liot Feld, Helen Douglas, Richard Fein, Richard Gilmore, Micha-
a Hughes, Cynthia Irion, Charles Kennedy, Edmund LaFosse,
lizabeth Lee, Remus Marcu, Linda Miller, George Montalbano,
nnifer Palo, Reva Pincusoff, Christine Sarry, Jeff Satinoff, Naomi
orkin, John Sowinski, Patrick Swayze

REPERTOIRE

At Midnight" (Mahler, Feld), "Tzaddik" (Copland, Feld), "The
onsort" (Dowland/Neusidler/Others/Arranged by Michael
affee, Feld), "Intermezzo" (Brahms, Feld), "Sephardic Song" (Tra-
tional, Feld), "The Real McCoy" (Gershwin, Feld), "Embrace
iger and Return to Mountain" (Subotnick, Glen Tetley), "Cortege
arisien" (Chabrier, Feld), *Company Premieres* of "Harbinger"
erge Prokofiev, Feld), "Early Songs" (Richard Strauss, Feld), and
WORLD PREMIERES of "Mazurka" (Frederic Chopin, Feld; Cos-
mes, Rouben Ter-Arutunian; Lighting, Thomas Skelton) on Sun-
ay, Oct. 12, 1975, and "Excursions" (Samuel Barber, Feld) on
aturday, Oct. 18, 1975.

Press: Merle Debuskey, Susan L. Schulman

Herbert Migdoll, Lois Greenfield Photos

Right: Michaela Hughes, Eliot Feld in "The Real McCoy"
Top: "Excursions"

Linda Miller, Edmund LaFosse in "Early Songs"   **Richard Fein, Christine Sarry in "Intermezzo"**

Raymond Johnson Dance Company in
"As the World Turns Out"
(M. B. Hunnewell Photo)

Linda Hayes, Jim Auwae, Mary Anthony,
Rick Ornellas, Gwendolyn Bye in "Gloria in G Major"

94

THE LOFT
October 10, 11, 12, 1975.*
Circum-Arts Foundation presents:

GALE ORMISTON DANCE COMPANY

Choreography, Sound Score, Costume Design by Gale Ormiston; Technical Director, Jon Garness.

COMPANY

Gale Ormiston
Luise Wykell
Richard Biles

PROGRAM

"Criteria"

* Repeated January 8–11, 1976, and May 23–26, 1976.

COLDEN CENTER FOR PERFORMING ARTS
Saturday, October 11, 1975

NEW YORK DANCE THEATRE

Artistic Director-Choreographer, Frank Ohman; Lighting and Staging, George Bardyguine; Costumes, Tar Baby Ltd.

COMPANY

Lynda Yourth	Robert Maiorano
Elizabeth Pawluk	David Anderson
Marnee Morris	Ian Walton
Judith Shoaff	Bryan Pitts
Pamela Mitchell	Darryl Robinson
Pam Kesler	Frank Ohman

PROGRAM: "Melodie" (Tchaikovsky, Ohman), "Song" (Gershwin, Ohman), "Encores" (Bach/Don Sebesky, David Anderson), "Dreams" (Richard Wagner, Ohman), *World Premiere* of "Just Poems" (Poetry and Choreography, Robert Maiorano), "Les Belles Americaines" (Jacques Offenbach, Ohman) "Winters Dreams" (Tchaikovsky, Ohman), "Hoedown" (American Traditional, Ohman)

Photo by Mira

Top Right: Gale Ormiston in "Criteria"
Below: New York Dance Theatre

ST. PETER'S EPISCOPAL CHURCH
Saturday & Sunday, October 11–12, 18–19, 1975

KATHRYN BERNSON/
STORMY MULLIS
and Dancers

CHOREOGRAPHY, Kathryn Bernson, Stormy Mullis; Musical Director, Rob Bonfiglio; Compositions, Rob Bonfiglio, Richard Einhorn; Lighting, Nancy Golladay

DANCERS

Kathryn Bernson, Stormy Mullis, Morgan Ensminger, Dana Roth, Monica Solem, Maris Wolf, Richard Einhorn, Carl Mullis, Rob Bonfiglio, Nancy Golladay, Maynard Stowe

PROGRAM

"Walking and Talking," "Real Costumes," "The Flying Zucchinis," "No Watering," "Irene and the Chicken," "Carl Takes a Bow" all choreographed by Kathryn Bernson; "Crackers," "Family Reunion," "San Diego Zoo," "If You Can Walk You Can Dance" all choreographed by Stormy Mullis

UNIVERSALIST CHURCH
October 16, 18, 25, 26, 1975
Universalist Center for the Arts presents:

NEW YORK LYRIC BALLET

Artistic Director-Choreographer, Lawrence Robert Leritz; Rehearsal Assistant, Roxanne Messina; Costumes, Joseph Davis; Lighting, Sally Small; Conductor, Mark Cleghorn; Set, David Vosburgh; Management, Griffin Enterprises

COMPANY

Rosanne Messina
Sandra Borgman
Jayn Cohodas
Lawrence Robert Leritz

PROGRAM: "Temple and Village Dances" (Bizet, Leritz), "The Nature Forces" (Bizet, Leritz), "Great Bird White Eagle" (Bizet, Leritz)

Ammon Ben Nomis Photo

Lawrence Robert Leritz in "The Nature Forces"

GREEK ART THEATRE
Monday, October 20, November 3, 1975

LAWRENCE ROBERT LERITZ
and
HIS DANCE CELEBRATION

Director, Allan Charlet; Choreographer, Lawrence Robert Leritz; Lighting, Sally Small

DANCERS
Joan Cooper
Lawrence Robert Leritz
Roxanne Messina

PROGRAM: "Les Huguenots" (Meyerbeer), a one-act ballet based on Meyerbeer's opera.

Top Right: Lawrence Robert Leritz in "Les Huguenots"

SPRING STREET
Saturday & Sunday, October 25, 26, 1975
The Soho Media Coop presents:

LAURA FOREMAN DANCE THEATRE

Director-Choreographer, Laura Foreman; Music Director, John Watts; Sound Technician, Hank O'Neal; Stage Manager, Laurel Dann

PROGRAM
"Bud" (John Watts, Laura Foreman) performed by Roxanne Bartush, David Malamut, Lucie Signa, Satoru Shimazaki

LARRY RICHARDSON'S DANCE GALLERY
Thursday, October 30, 1975

BRUCE PACOT AND DANCERS

PROGRAM: "Parting Dances" choreographed by Bruce Pacot, and danced by Ruth Alpert, Ruth Barnes, Scotti Mirviss, Daniel Press, David Malamut; "Mazurka" (Milhaud, Pacot) and "Wheatfields" (Tape Collage, Pacot) danced by Julie Roess-Smith, Bruce Pacot, Jane Comfort, Nancy Mapother, Susan Bodine

**Right Center: Roxanne Bartush,
Satoru Shimazaki, Lucie Signa in "Program"**
(Lois Greenfield Photo)

CONSTRUCTION COMPANY DANCE STUDIO
Friday, October 31, 1975

BARBARA GARDNER
FOR HALLOWEEN

"The Troublesome Fables of Achmed Flee" Chapter 2: "The Cell of Wallachia"; Choreographed and danced by Barbara Gardner; Music, Emmerich Kalman; Decor, Dorothy Podber, Jack Champlain, Dale Joe, Jacques Brouwers; Technical Director, Ted Cosbey; Lights, Linnea Pearson; Sound, Richard Michaels; Stage Manager, Jacques Brouwers

Lorraine Senna Photo

Barbara Gardner
(Bruce J. Fields Photo)

COOPER UNION GREAT HALL
Friday, October 31, 1975
Cooper Union Forum of the Performing Arts and Performing Arts Foundation, Inc., present:

PHILIPPINE DANCE COMPANY OF NEW YORK

Artistic Director-Choreographer, Ronnie Alejandro; Founder-Executive Director, Bruna P. Seril; Stage Manager, Lee Horsman; Assistant Director, Ching Valdes; Technical Director, Chuck Golden

COMPANY

Ramon de Luna, Eddie Sese, Benny Felix, Abelardo Sulit, Veda Agus, Irvi Sulit, Nina Muriel, Rosemarie Valdes, Vicky Tiangco, Kathleen Serio, Ruth Malabrigo, Melinda Acaac, Vicky Valdes, Gigi Sulit, Tessie Tablit, Micah Valdes

PROGRAM

DIWANG PILIPINO: "Bailes de Ayer Suite," "Sarimanok Suite," "Taga Bundok Suite," "Sa Kabukiran Suite"

Philippine Dance Company of New York

MARYMOUNT MANHATTAN THEATRE
October 31, November 1, 2, 1975
Marymount Manhattan College Presents:

RUDY PEREZ DANCE THEATRE

Artistic Director-Choreographer, Rudy Perez; Production Manager-Lighting Design, Kenneth F. Merkel; Technical Director, Terence Byrne; Assistant to Director, David Varney; Audio, John Moore; Administrative Director, Sandy Fowlkes

COMPANY

Tom Brown
Georges Giroud
Karen Masaki
Rudy Perez
Jeffrey Urban
David Varney

PROGRAM: "Fairplay" (American Traditional, David Varney), "Parallax" (Noah Creshevsky, Rudy Perez), "Centerbreak" (Collage, Perez), *PREMIERE* of "Colorado Ramble" (George Reinholt, Rudy Perez)

Jeffrey Urban and Rudy Perez Dance Theatre in "Colorado Ramble"
(Johan Elbers Photo)

UNITARIAN CHURCH AUDITORIUM
Thursday, November 6, 1976*

VIJA VETRA

DANCES OF INDIA: Meditation and Purification Sutra, Stotram, Shlokam, Pushpanjali and Devotional Poems, Puja, Radha, Krishna, Bharata Natyam, Alarippu, Tillana, Kathak

* Program repeated Sunday, January 25, 1976.

Vija Vetra

AMERICAN THEATRE LABORATORY
November 6–9 1975
Dance Theater Workshop presents:

JEFF DUNCAN DANCE REPERTORY COMPANY

Artistic Director-Choreographer, Jeff Duncan; Lighting, Edward Byers; Costumes, Jack Moore, Manja Todorovic, Leor C. Warner, Art Bauman, Georgia Collins; Stage Manager, Tina Charney

COMPANY

Gary Davis	Lenore Latimer
Jeff Duncan	Valerie Pullman
Peggy Hackney	Anne Sahl
Timothy Haynes	Stuart Smith

Guest Artist: James May

PROGRAM: "Songs Remembered" (Alban Berg, Jack Moore), "Bach Fifth Clavier Concerto" (Bach, Jeff Duncan; *Premiere*), "Winesburg Portraits" (Folk, Duncan), "Resonances" (Pierre Henry, Duncan), "Errands" (The Ventures/Beethoven, Art Bauman), "Phases of the Oracle" (Francois Bayle, Duncan)

V. Sladon Photo

Right: Ratilekha
Top: Valerie Pullman, Tim Haynes in "Resonances"

NYU EDUCATION AUDITORIUM
Friday, November 7, 1975
NYU Program in Educational Theatre presents:

RATILEKHA

in "Odissi Temple Dances of India": Mangalacharan, Batu Nritya, Abhinaya, Saveri Pallavi, Abhinaya, Ahe Nila Soila

WASHINGTON SQUARE METHODIST CHURCH
November 13, 14, 15, 1975

HARRY

Director-Choreographer, Senta Driver; Lighting Design, Robin Kronstadt; Staff Assistants, Tim Callaghan, Judith Field, Lynn Hoogenbloom, Sharon Kinney, Raymond Kurshals, Tim Maurer

DANCERS

Marianne Bachmann
Senta Driver
Tom Johnson
Andrea Stark

PROGRAM: "Solo from Gallery" (John Fahey), "The Kschessinska Variations from Coverging Lines" (Tom Johnson), "Anniversary" (Driver), "The Star Game" (Johnson), "Board Fade Except" (Thomas Skelton), "Tout le Monde" (Tom Johnson), "From Here to There and Back Again" (James Lindholm), "Melodrama" (Robbie Basho), "Two Steps Outside" (Lukas Foss, Vera Blaine), "Dances to This Music #1" (Robbie Basho), "Memorandum," "Lecture with Singing" (Tom Johnson)

Johan Elbers Photo

Marianne Bachmann, Timothy Driver in "Melodrama"

FELT FORUM
Friday & Sunday, November 7–9, 1975
Mel Howard presents:

PARTHENON DANCERS OF GREECE

(a company of 40)
No other details available.

AMERICAN THEATRE LABORATORY
November 13–16, 1975
Dance Theater Workshop presents:

LINDA TARNAY & DANCERS

Director-Choreographer, Linda Tarney; Set Design and Execution, Lorne Swarthout; Lighting Design-Stage Manager, Edward I. Byers

DANCERS

Linda Tarnay, Stuart Hodes, Erin Martin, Art Berger, Doris Ginsberg, Alfredo Gonzales, Holly Harbinger, David Malamut, Tryntje Shapli, Merian Soto, Deborah Dennis, Barbara Ellmann, Candy Gilles-Brown, Rachel Harms, Marilyn Klaus

PROGRAM

"Jack and Jill" (Haydn), "Bird Watch" (Hornstein), "Eight Dancing Princesses" (Louis XIII/Traditional/Country Cooking), "Prelude X 3" (Chopin), "Ocean" (Cervetti)

MERCE CUNNINGHAM STUDIO
November 14, 15, 16, 1975

DOUGLAS DUNN

performing his own choreography in a solo dance "Gestures in Red"

Top Right: Parthenon Dancers of Greece
Below: Linda Tarnay

Indra-nila

HUNTER COLLEGE PLAYHOUSE
Saturday & Sunday, November 15–16, 1975
Hunter College Concert Bureau presents:

BALLET HISPANICO OF NEW YORK

Artistic Director-Choreographer, Tina Ramirez; Press, Judi Jedlicka

COMPANY

(names not submitted)

REPERTOIRE

"Caribbean Suite" (Popular, Charles Moore/Tina Ramirez), "Congo Tango Palace" (Miles Davis, Talley Beatty), "Deer Dance" (Traditional, Jose Coronado), "Echoes of Spain" (Albeniz/Temptations/Mandrill, Louis Johnson), "Fiesta en Vera Cruz" (Jose Pablo Moncayo, Jose Coronado), "Games" (Traditional, Donald McKayle), "La Boda de Luis Alonso" (Gimenez, Paco Fernandez), "Mira Todas Esas Bellas Rosas Rojas" (Santana, Beatty), "Quintet" (Nyro, Alvin Ailey), "Sedalia" (Joplin, Lois Bewley), and *PREMIERE* of "Tres Cantos" (Revueltas/Chavez/Fernandez, Talley Beatty)

(No photos submitted)

CHRIST CHURCH UNITED METHODIST
Wednesday, November 19, 1975
The Commission on Worship and Fine Arts presents:

INDRA-NILA

Dances not choreographed by Indra-nila were choreographed and taught by Guru G. Ellappa; Music arranged and performed by Guru Ellappa and his orchestra and recorded in Madras; Production Coordinator, Estelle Elliott; Stage Manager, Geneva Helm; Lighting, Carolyn Halpert

PROGRAM

"Shiva Slokam," "Ananda Natanam," "Allarrippu," "Natanam Adinar," "Juggat Janani," "Suddha Paityakaran," "Gowri Kalyanam," "Maha Ganapati," "Kartikeya," "Kurathy," "Thillanna," "Thaye Yashoda," "Lotus Pond," "Raghu Pati," "Raghava"

WASHINGTON SQUARE METHODIST CHURCH
November 20, 21, 22, 1975

CHOREOGRAPHY BY REYNALDO ALEJANDRO

Production Manager, Lee Horsman; Lighting Director, T. Byrne; Executive Producer, Domingo Hornilla, Jr.; Stage Manager, Madeleine Abalos; Costumes, Bruna Seril, Madeleine Abalos, Sarah Petlin, Jose Coronado

DANCERS

Rika Burnham, Austin Alexis, Asha Coorlawala, Julie Laskaris, Ching Valdes, Betty Salamun, Lei-Lynne Doo, Luis Gonzalez, Sarah Petlin

PROGRAM

"Mandadawak" (Bo Lawergren), "D'Wata" (Lawergren), "Meditation for Strings" (David Clancy, Jr.), "Diwa Ng Pagkakaisa" (Creative Sound Composition), "Mater Dolorosa" (Clancy), "Pandanggo" (Michael Dadap), "Josephine Bracken" (Karlheinz Stockhausen), "Maranaw Suite" (Lucrecia Kasilag)

"Maranaw Suite" by Reynaldo Alejandro

HUNTER COLLEGE PLAYHOUSE
Thursday & Saturday, November 20 & 22, 1975

LHAMO FOLK DANCE OF TIBET

(No other details available)

Lhamo Folk Theatre of Tibet

MARYMOUNT MANHATTAN THEATRE
November 20–23, 1975

DON REDLICH DANCE COMPANY

Artistic Director-Choreographer, Don Redlich; Stage Manager, Mark Litvin; Lighting Design, Nicholas Wolff Lyndon, Mark Litvin; Costumes, Margaret Tobin, Sally Ann Parsons; Press, Robert Marinaccio; Technical Crew, Frank Kelly, Gordon Links; Technical Director, Terrence Byrne; Management, Sheldon Soffer

COMPANY

Don Redlich
Jennifer Donohue
Irene Feigenheimer
Barbara Roan
Billy Siegenfeld

PROGRAM: "Patina" (Besard/Caruso/Galilei/Gianoncelli, Don Redlich), "Three Bagatelles: (Lukas Foss, Redlich), *WORLD PREMIERES* of "Rota" (George Crumb, Hanya Holm), and "Traces" (American Folk, Don Redlich)

Don Redlich Dance Company in "Rota"
(Lois Greenfield Photo)

AMERICAN THEATRE LABORATORY
November 21, 22, 23, 1975
Dance Theater Workshop presents:

JACK MOORE & ERIN MARTIN

"Legacy" (Schutz/Shastocovitch/Stravinsky, Erin Martin) performed by Alice Cohen, Holly Harbinger, Regina Larkin, Francine Piggott, Linda Tarnay (New York Premiere)

"Songs Remembered" (Alban Berg, Jack Moore) danced by Anne Sahl and Jeff Duncan

"Daddy's Girl" (Duke Ellington, Erin Martin) danced by Erin Martin

"Love Songs for Jason Mayhew" (J. J. Cale, Jack Moore) danced by Bill Bass and David Malamut (Premiere)

Mariette Pathy Allen Photo

**Top Right: David Malamut, Bill Bass in
"Love Songs for Jason Mayhew"**

AMERICAN THEATRE LABORATORY
November 25, December 2, 9, 16, 1975
Dance Theatre Workshop presents:

CHOREOGRAPHER'S SHOWCASE

Executive Director, David R. White; Assistant Director, Doris Ginsberg; Technical Director, Tina Charney; Production Consultant, Edward I. Byers; Coordinator, Art Bauman; Stage Manager, Tina Charney

PROGRAM

"Hallelujah" (New England Hymn) choreographed and danced by Anne Sahl; "Dreams of Survival" (Humza el Din, Micki Goodman) danced by Irene O'Brien, Alimu Nitumboa, Sharon Weinstein, Peggy Hackney; "Faun" (Debussy) choreographed and danced by Gary Davis; "How's Your Father" choreographed and danced by Chris Small; "There's a Rainbow in the Sky" (James Irsay, Randolyn Zinn; Poem, Peter L. Wilson, read by Timothy Jerome) danced by Andrea Zinn, Randolyn Zinn; "Walking through Similar Orchards" (Betsy Blachly, Karen Attix) danced by Karen Attix, George Titus; "New Fall Peace" (Charles Madden, Sybil Huskey) danced by Sybil Huskey, Eva de Kievit, Diann Sichel Perrelli, Anne Woods

Right Center: Gary Davis in "Faun"
(Tom Caravaglia Photo)

AMERICAN THEATRE LABORATORY
November 28, 29, 30, 1975
Dance Theater Workshop presents:

JAN VAN DYKE & DANCERS

Artistic Director-Choreographer, Jan Van Dyke; Costumes, Valerie Shanks; Lighting, Jack Halstead; Technical Staff, Mary Conroy, Adrian Engel, Dierdre Lavrakas, Janer Thompson

DANCERS

Pat Bellman, Sybil Davis, Cynthia Fletcher, Jean Jones, Carla Perlo, Ruth Rivin, Susan Sachs, Lisa Seigman, Valerie Shanks, Lynda Spikell, Virginia Freeman, Elly Canterbury, Jan Van Dyke

PROGRAM

"Ceremony" (Leo Sayer/Dave Courtney/Hank Williams, Jan Van Dyke), "Paradise Castle" (Irving Berlin/George Crumb, Jan Van Dyke), "Ella" (Sylvia Fine, Jan Van Dyke)

Carla Perlo, Jan Van Dyke in "Ella"
(Bill Suworoff Photo)

101

HUDSON GUILD
Saturday & Sunday, November 29–30, 1975

SOUNDS IN MOTION

Artistic Director-Choreographer, Dianne McIntyre; Administrative Director, Damon Wright; Technical Director, Sandra Ross; Manager, Lonnetta Gaines

COMPANY

Dianne McIntyre	Bernardine Jennings
Lonnette Gaines	Mickey Davidson
Linda Griffin	William Donald
Clayton Strange	Kenneth McPherson

PROGRAM: "Jesus Children of America" (Stevie Wonder, Quincy Edwards), "Spirit Bird" (Babafumi Akunyun, Dorian Williams), "Smoke Clouds" (Selected, Dianne McIntyre), "A Free Thing VIII," "Memories" (Eubie Blake, McIntyre)

Top Right: Linda Griffin (on ladder), William Donald, Lonnetta Gaines, Phillip Bond in "Jesus' Children of America"

WONDERHOUSE THEATRE
December 4–7, 1975

ALONSO CASTRO DANCE COMPANY

Director-Choreographer, Alonso Castro; Lighting, Sally Small; Stage Manager, Kurt Sayblack; Costumes, Bill Ortzack; Company Manager, Ina Kahn

COMPANY

Helen Breasted, Phyllis Briley, Judith Gianadda, Jeannette Hardie, Shirley Hardie, Cecilia Hewlett, Nicole Levinson, Shirley Milgrom, Beverly Teague, Clifton Jones, Jonathan Green, Charles Karp, Leland Walsh, Miriam Kaufman, Silvia Levey, Dolores Pascucci, Martin DeMartino, Marty Feldman, Stuart Greenbaum, Doug Schwegler, Billy Toth, Alonso Castro

PROGRAM

"Drag" (Larry Lockwood, Alonso Castro), "Threshold" (Irwin Bazelon, Castro), "110th Street" (Tito Puente, Tim Weisberger, Tamboo, Marvin Gordon), "Journey" (Ernst Bloch, Castro)

Ina Kahn Photo

Helen Breasted, Shirley Hardie, Jeannette Hardie in "Journey" (Ina Kahn Photo)

AMERICAN THEATRE LABORATORY
December 5, 6, 7, 1975
Dance Theater Workshop presents:

MURIEL COHAN/PATRICK SUZEAU

PROGRAM: "Caligula" (Muriel Cohan; Lighting, Barbara Rosoff), "Poems of Lorca" (George Crumb, Cohan/Suzeau), and *PREMIERES* of "Aquarelle" (Dmitri Shostakovich, Patrick Suzeau), "La Sibylla" (Shostakovich, Paul Hindemith, Suzeau), "Dress-Up" (Shostakovich, Muriel Cohan)

John Dady Photo

Muriel Cohan, Patrick Suzeau in "Aquarelle"

AN EVENING OF DANCE THEATRE

Choreography, Claire Henry; Lighting Design and Execution, Margo Kaminsky; Stage Manager, David Markay; Tape, Lewis Rosen; Costumes and Props, Harriet Zucker

COMPANY

Jon Argon
Mary Joiner
Kas Self
John Thomas Waite
Christy Wilson
Harriet Zucker

PROGRAM: "Private Lives" (Noel Coward), "Separation" (Vanilla Fudge), "Waiting for Godot" (Samuel Beckett), "How Many Feet to the Exit?" (Maurice Bolyer), "From the Insane Asylum" (Joseph Kaufer)

**Top Right: Harriet Zucker, Christy Wilson,
Mary Joiner, Alyssa Satin in "Knots"**
(Donni Gillies Photo)

Julie Maloney
(Tom Maloney Photo)

DANCES BY JULIE MALONEY

Artistic Director-Choreographer, Julie Maloney; Stage Manager, George Bennett; Lighting Designer, Andy Tron; Sound, Jan Kamil; Tapes, Jan Kamil, Michael Wodynski; Costumes, Rebecca Kelly, Madeleine Perrone

DANCERS

Whit Carman
Joanne Edelmann
Rebecca Kelly
Julie Maloney
Madeleine Perrone
Paul Wilson

PROGRAM: "2 into 1's" (Jacques Brel, Maloney), "Conversation" (Donald Erb, Maloney), and *PREMIERES* of "Night Workers" (Environments, Maloney), "Hat Strut" (Perigeo, Maloney), and "Unison" (Handel/Pachelbel, Maloney)

Tom Maloney Photo

THE ORIGINAL HOOFERS

Staged by Larl Becham; Lighting, David Adams; Stage Design, Jun Maeda; Costumes, Robin Pennings, Nancy Steimel; Sound, Jim Jordan; Stage Manager, Tad Truesdale; Press, Howard Atlee; Technical Assistants, Les Banda, Charles Embry, Larry Steckman

COMPANY

Buster Brown, Ralph Brown, Lon Chaney, Chuch Green, Raymond Kaalund, Jimmy Slide, Tony Azito, Denise Rogers, Larl Becham, Marilyn Amaral, Sherri Brewer, Joyce Griffin, Lois Hayes, Yvette Johnson, Marcia McBroom, Valois Mickens, Terrie Taylor

PROGRAM

"Rockin in Rhythm," "Uptown Lowdown," "Mr. Melody," "Original Softshoe," "Daiquiri Cubana," "Eccentric," "Baby Bronze," "Let's Dance," "Parade of the Satin Dolls," "Digga Digga Doo," "Paddle and Roll King," "Tropic Tornado," "The Sand," "Down Beat," "Bluesette," "Challenge," Finale

Ammon Nomis Photo

Larl Becham and La Soubrettes

Saturday & Sunday, December 6–7, 1975

SATORU SHIMAZAKI

PROGRAM: "Faltering" developed and danced by Mr. Shimazaki

Ron Reagan Photo

Left: Satoru Shimazaki

THE BIG APPLE DANCE THEATRE
December 6–13, 1975

BIG APPLE DANCE THEATRE

Founder-Director-Choreographer, Kay Wylie; Lighting Designer, William Tomas Butler, Jr.

COMPANY
Kay Wylie

Maggie Bohrer
Pamela Francis
Sandy Moran

Buffy Price
Christy Wilson
Cora Woogen

PROGRAM: "Duet" (Mongo Santamaria, Christy Wilson), "Alice" (Sadistic Mika Band, Kay Wylie), "The Third Time Around" (Donald Byrd, Kay Wylie), "The World of Toulouse-Lautrec Revisited" (Satie, Wylie)

Glenn S. Treeson Photo

Left: "The World of Toulouse-Lautrec, Revisited"

CONSTRUCTION COMPANY DANCE STUDIO
Monday, December 8, 1975

BARBARA GARDNER
FOR CHANUKAH

"Chapter 4 'The Celebration' from "The Troublesome Fables of Achmed Flee"; Choreographed and danced by Barbara Gardner; Music, Christophe Willibald von Gluck; "Book II: Le Salon de Mme. Papillon/Saga of the Leotard Kid" from "Divine Comedies" Choreographed and danced by Barbara Gardner; Masks, Tom Gardner; Lights, Jenny Bell; Stage Manager, Linnea Pearson; Sound, Richard Michaels.

Bruce J. Fields Photo

Left: Barbara Gardner

HUNTER COLLEGE PLAYHOUSE
Friday & Saturday, December 12–13, 1975
Hunter Arts Concert Bureau presents:

CHIANG CHING DANCE COMPANY

Artistic Director-Choreographer, Chiang Ching; Composer, Chou Wen-Chung; Composer-Conductor, Chinary Ung; Costumes, Chiang Ching, Patrizia von Brandenstein; Lighting, David Kissel

COMPANY
Chiang Ching
Linda Dobson
Georges Giroud
Chih-Ming Lu
Shir Lee Wu
Tzi Ma

PROGRAM: "Three Folk Songs," "Yang Kuan," "Between" (Premier), "A Moment," "Flak" (Bela Bartok, Stuart Hodes), "Escape," Premiere of "All in Spring Wind"

Chiang Ching Dance Company

MERCE CUNNINGHAM STUDIO
December 12, 13, 14, 1975

JUDY PADOW & COMPANY

Artistic Director-Choreographer, Judy Padow; Lighting Designer, Dave Hulbert; Costumes, Janie Paul, Diana Rolls

COMPANY

Cynthia Hedstrom
Mary Overlie
Danny Tai
David Woodberry

PROGRAM: "Repeat," "Solo Patterning," "The Drift," "Threes," "Panorama," "Indian Summer," "Jamming," "The Snake Dance," "Panorama Repeat"

AMERICAN THEATRE LABORATORY
December 12, 13, 14, 1975

UNNATURAL ACTS
IN A PLEASANT ATMOSPHERE

Choreography, Bill Kirkpatrick; Lighting, Blu Lambert, Les Banda; Stage Manager, Howard Meadow

PROGRAM

"Pre-Fab" (Sousa/Wonder) danced by Bill Kirkpatrick, Lisa Nalven; "Retainer" (Robert DeVoe) danced by Bill Kirkpatrick; "Pennydances" (Prokofiev) danced by Bill Kirkpatrick, Lisa Nalven, Patricia Yenawind, Eva Vasquez, Art Berger; "Fit to Be Tied" (Tape), danced by Bill Kirkpatrick, Lisa Nalven, Eva Vasquez, Patricia Yenawine; "Belljar" danced by Lisa Nalven; "Dance for Six" (Olatunji) danced by Art Berger, Lisa Nalven, Eva Vasquez, Patricia Yenawine

Mary Overlie, David Woodberry,
Cynthia Hedstrom in "Threes"
(Babette Mangolte Photo)

ROBERT F. KENNEDY THEATRE
Opened Thursday, December 18, 1975.*
The Robert F. Kennedy Theatre for Children (Martin Gregg, Executive Director) and the Downtown Ballet Company (Robert Shuster, Executive Director) present:

THE CHRISTMAS DOOR

Conceived and Choreographed by Paschal Guzman; Music, Tchaikovsky's "Nutcracker"; Narrative Script, Tinsley Crowder; Costumes, John E. Dransfield; Sets and Lighting, Michael J. Hotopp, Paul de Pass

and
SOOLAIMON

A folk ballet choreographed by Paschal Guzman; Danced to Neil Diamond's "The African Trilogy." Names of company not submitted.

Press: Owen Levy

* Closed Dec. 28, 1975 after 17 performances and 2 previews.

Johan Elbers Photo

AMERICAN THEATRE LABORATORY
December 18–21, 1975

CAROL CONWAY DANCE COMPANY

Director, Carol Conway; Lighting Designer, Paul Butler; Stage Manager, Michael Liniero; General Manager, William J. Ansorge; Costumes, James Pelletier, Raya; Sets, Daryl McConnell, James Pelletier, Eric Blasenheim

COMPANY

June Anderson	Marta Renzi
Will Ansorge	Julie Salwen
Carol Conway	Sandy Sheridan
Checker Ives	Brian Webb
Debe Miller	Sara White

PROGRAM: "Duelle" (Sergio Cervetti, Carol Conway), "Aleluya Nocturne" (Lorca, Brian Webb), *WORLD PREMIERES* of "Un Peu de Gateau" (Bela Bartok, Brian Webb), "Red Right Returning" (Sergio Cervetti, Carol Conway)

Michele Moran Photo

Carol Conway, Brian Webb in "Red Right Returning"
Above: Deborah Salmirs, Paschal Guzman in
"The Christmas Door"

105

NYU AUDITORIUM THEATRE
December 19, 1975–January 10, 1976
Chimera Foundation presents:

MURRAY LOUIS DANCE COMPANY

Artistic Director-Choreographer, Murray Louis; Manager, William Bourne; Stage Manager, Anthony Micocci; Technical Directors, Peter Koletzke, Richard Talcott; Costumes, Frank Garcia; Production Coordinator, Ruth Grauert; Press, Judy Jacksina, William Schleble

COMPANY
Murray Louis

Michael Ballard
Richard Haisma
Helen Kent
Dianne Markham

Anne McLeod
Robert small
Jerry Pearson
Sara Pearson

REPERTOIRE

"Geometrics" (Alwin Nikolais, Murray Louis), "Moments" (Ravel, Louis), "Bach Suite" (Bach, Louis), "Facets" (Nikolais, Louis), "Chimera" (Nikolais, Louis), "Hoopla" (Nikolais, Louis), "Scheherezade" (Rimsky-Korsakov/Nikolais, Louis), "Porcelain Dialogues" (Tchaikovsky, Louis), "Continuum" (Corky Siegel Blues Band/Nikolais, Louis), "Index (to necessary neuroses. . . .)" (Oregon Ensemble, Louis), and *World Premiere* of "Catalogue" (Victor Herbert, Murray Louis) on Dec. 19, 1975.

Left: Murray Louis
Below: "Proximities"
(Agor, Tom Caravaglia Photos)

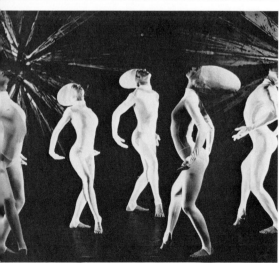

"Scheherezade"

"Hoopla"
Above: "Index"

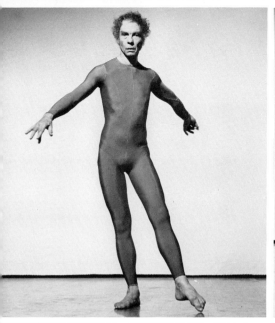

CUNNINGHAM STUDIO
December 20, 1975–January 11, 1976
(Saturdays and Sundays only)

MERCE CUNNINGHAM
AND DANCE COMPANY

Director-Choreographer, Merce Cunningham; Lighting, Mark Lancaster; Stage Manager, Charles Atlas; Music Coordinator, John Fullemann; Technical Director, Andy Tron; Administrator, Greg Tonning; Music by Jon Gison, David Behrman, Liz Phillips

COMPANY

Karole Armitage, Karen Attix, Ellen Cornfield, Merce Cunningham, Morgan Ensminger, Meg Harper, Susana Hayman-Chaffey, Cathy Kerr, Christ Komar, Robert Kovich, Raymond Kurshals, Charlie Moulton, Julie Roess-Smith

PROGRAM: Events # 149–156

Jack Mitchell Photos

Top: Merce Cunningham
Below: Meg Harper, Chris Komar,
Brynar Mehl, Cathy Kerr
Top Right: Susan Hayman-Chaffey, Brynar Mehl

Merce Cunningham, Ellen Cornfield, Charles Moulton
Above: Robert Kovich, Chris Komar

AMERICAN THEATRE LABORATORY
December 26, 27, 28, 1975

CHOREO-MUTATION

Artistic Directors-Choreographers, Shirley Ede Rushing, Thomas Pinnock, Noel Hill; Lighting Design-Stage Manager, Tina Charney

COMPANY
Thomas Pinnock
Shirley Ede Rushing
Noel Hall
Melvada Hughes
Rosalie Tracey
Mickey Davidson
Fatisha

REPERTOIRE: "From the Soul" (Aretha Franklin, Shirley Rushing), "Moments Remembered" (Doug and Jean Carne, Thomas Pinnock), "Creature" (Herbie Hancock, Rushing), "Joy" (Edwin Hawkins Swingers/War, Noel Hall), "Tenement Rhythms" (Bob Marley and the Wailers/Traditional, Pinnock), "Asakari" (Quincy Jones, Rushing), "Homo-Sapiens: Two Halves" (Weather Report/Alice Coltrane, (Pinnock), "Consummation' (Gladys Knight/Nina Simone, Hall), "Feline Feelings" (Aretha Franklin, Hall)

CONSTRUCTION COMPANY DANCE STUDIO
Wednesday, December 31, 1975.

BARBARA GARDNER
FOR NEW YEAR'S EVE

"Chapter 1: The New Dance" from "The Troublesome Fables of Achmed Flee"; Choreographed and danced by Barbara Gardner; Lights, Jenny Ball; Stage Manager, Linnea Pearson; Videotape, Joel Gold; Technical Assistants, Ted Cosbey, Richie Michaels, Rudy Lodichand, Pat Robinson

Lorraine Senna Photo

Shirley Rushing, Thomas Pinnock, Noel Hall in "Joy"

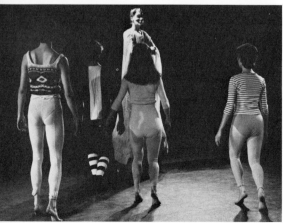

AMERICAN THEATRE LABORATORY
January 2, 3, 4, 1976

CLEO QUITMAN
DANCE EXPEDIENCE

Artistic Director-Choreographer-Costume Designer, Cleo Quitman; Production Manager-Lighting Designer, Gary Harris; Company Manager, Chuck Hodge; Assistants to Miss Quitman, Diane Hunt, Kathy Jennings

COMPANY
Cleo Quitman

Karen DiBianco	Joseph Cohen
Gina Fisher	David Gleaton
Diane Hunt	Chuck Hodge
Ida	Charles Neal

PROGRAM: "Inception" (Hubert Laws), "Quest" (Missa Bantu), "Angela Etcetera" (Mandrill/Deodato/Edgar Winter Group)

AMERICAN THEATRE LABORATORY
January 8–11, 1976

KATHERINE LITZ DANCE COMPANY

Artistic Director-Choreographer, Katherine Litz; Lighting Design, John Knudsen, Tina Charney; Costumes, B. J. Cooke, Patrique Magary, Adolphine Rott, Bill Maloney

COMPANY
Katherine Litz

Janis Ansley	Jeannie Hutchins
Jennifer Donohue (Guest Artist)	Scott Caywood
Grethe Holby	Bill Maloney

PROGRAM: "Score" (Dick Raaijmakers, "Baroque Suite" (Telemann/Couperin), "They All Came Home Save One Because She Never Left" (Al Carmines), and *PREMIERE* of "The Lure" (Schoenberg/Prideaux)

Katherine Litz Dance Company in "The Lure"
Above: Cleo Quitman Dance Expedience in
"Angela Etcetera"   *(Ron Reagan Photos)*

PEARL LANG & DANCE COMPANY
in
"The Possessed"

Based on the play "The Dybbuk" by S. Ansky; Choreography, Pearl Lang; Music and Sound Score, Meyer Kupferman, Joel Spiegelman; Lighting, Ken Billington; Set, Stuart Wurtzel; Projections, Virginia Hochberg; Costumes, A. Christina Giannini; General Manager, William Gatewood; Press, Tom Kerrigan; Stage Managers, Craig Miller, Judith Binus

COMPANY

Richard Arbach, Jerome Sarnat, Frank Colardo, Douglas Nielsen, Oded Kafri, Andrew Krichels, Larry Stevens, Philip Grosser, Christine Dakin, Susan McLain, Alice Coughlin, Jacqulyn Buglisi, Deborah Zalkind, Debra Arch, Wendy McDade

GUEST ARTISTS: William Carter, Paul Sanasardo

JOSE CORONADO & DANCERS

Artistic Director-Choreographer, Jose Coronado; Lighting Design, Tina Charney; Stage Manager, Robert Pierce

COMPANY

Betsyann Baron, Nancy Citeno, Kevin Clark, Ilona Copen, Cindi Green, Ralph Hewitt, Jocelyn Lorenz, Terry McClone, Ricardo Mercado, Micah, Nancy Mikota, John Obson, Victor Vargas, Whitney Weimer

PROGRAM

"Three Dimensional Pieces" (D. Erb), "From The Seer" (C. Ives), "Mujeres" (J. G. Handel), and *PREMIERES* of "Danza Mexicana #1: The Postcard" (J. P. Moncayo), "Danza Mexicana #2: Corrido" (S. Revueltas) in homage to Jose Limon, "Danses Sacree et Profane" (C. A. Debussy)

Kenn Duncan Photo

Pearl Lang and Dance Company in "The Possessed"
(Ron Reagan Photo)

Jose Coronado and Dancers in "Three Dimensional Pieces"

Wendy Osserman, Meredith Johnson in "Still Me"

WENDY OSSERMAN DANCE COMPANY

Artistic Director-Choreographer, Wendy Osserman; Stage Manager, Dennis Florio; Technical Assistants, Elaine Ashburn, Barnet Silver; Sound, Sheila Sobel; Press, Shelley Hainer; Lighting Vince Laloma

COMPANY

Joan Adams, Joyce Adams, Richard Burke, Marni Chambers, Shelley Hainer, Marty Herling, Wanda Pruska, Barnet Silver, Wendy Osserman

PROGRAM

"Cycles" (Balinese Gamelan), "Just Dance" (Chick Corea/Gary Burton, Shelley Hainer), "Still Me" (Walter Carlos, Osserman), "Elsh & Newy" (Bartok, Shelley Hainer), "Duet for Joyce and Joan" (Emerson/Lake/Palmer, Osserman), "Wanda's Solo" (Collage, Wanda Pruska), "Dream Animal Dream" Wendy Osserman)

HENRY STREET PLAYHOUSE
Friday & Saturday, January 23–24, 1976
Henry Street Settlement and Dance Visions Inc. present:

SOUNDS IN MOTION

Artistic Director-Choreographer, Dianne McIntyre; Administrative Director, Damon Wright; Technical Director, Sandra Ross; Costumes, Gwendolyn Nelson-Fleming, Kenneth McPherson, Linda Williams; Press, Howard Atlee; Manager, Lonnetta Gaines

COMPANY

Ronald Brown, Mickey Davidson, William Donald, Lonnetta Gaines, Linda Griffin, Bernadine Jennings, Kenneth McPherson, Dianne McIntyre, James Shorts

PROGRAM

"The Lost Sun" (Gene Casey, Dianne McIntyre), Piano Peace (work in progress)" (Mary Lou Williams, McIntyre), "Smoke and Clouds" (Shirley & Lee/Huey Smith/The Jacks/Akunyun, McIntyre), "Excerpts from Shadows" (Music and Choreography, Dianne McIntyre, Cecil Taylor), "Melting Song" (McIntyre), "Memories" (Eubie Blake, McIntyre)

FELT FORUM
January 27, 28, 29, 1976
Hurok Concerts presents:

MAZOWSZE POLISH SONG AND DANCE COMPANY

Founder, Tadeusz Sygietynski; Director and Artistic Director, Mira Ziminska-Sygietynska; Choreographer and Ballet Director, Witold Zapala; Conductors, Jan Grabia, Stanislaw Wysocki; Press, Sheila Porter, Robert Weiss

PROGRAM

Chodzony "Kolem Kolem," Oberek from Opoczno, Dances from Szamotuly, Songs and Dances of the Shepherds of Jurgow in Podhale, Dances from Kolbiel, Songs from Bilgoraj, Dances from Siepadz, Dances from Zielona Gora, Kazuby Dances, Comic Dances from Krakow, Krakowiak, Polonaise, Mazurka, Mountaineers' Dances, Dances from Zywiec, Kukuleczka, Kosciuszko Polonaise, The Lowicz Maiden, Mazurka and Oberek, Grand Finale

AMATO OPERA THEATRE
January 18 & 19, 1976

THE ALONSO CASTRO DANCE COMPANY

Director-Choreographer, Alosno Castro; Lighting, Joey Martin; Costumes, Bill Ortzar; Masks, Olga Ley; Company Manager, Ina Kahn

COMPANY

Alonso Castro, Shirley Hardie, Roberto Ghigliotty, Clifton Jones, Helen Breasted, Shirley Milgrom, Judith Giannada, W. Beveridge, Marty Feldman, Billy Toth, Cedilia Hewlett, Charles Karp, Jeanette Hardie, Phyllis Brilly

PROGRAM

"Vignettes of Carmina Burana" (Orff, Castro), "Threshold" (Bazelon, Castro), "The Inquisitors" (Bach/Block/Britten, Castro)

Ina Kahn Photo

ST. PETER'S CHURCH
January 22–25, 1976

OBERLIN DANCE COLLECTIVE

Eric Barsness — Mercy Sidbury
Margot Crosman — Doug Skinner
Carol Douglas — Brenda Way
Kimi Okada — Doug Winter
Pam Quinn — Bill Chetel

PROGRAM: "Format V" (Randy Coleman, Brenda Way), "You Again" (Carol Douglas), "Hide, Hide the Cow's Outside" (Doug Skinner), "Hit or Miss" (Kimi Okada), "Format VI" (Randy Coleman, Brenda Way), "Half-Drawn" (Margot Crosman), "A Coup from the Blues" (Blind James Campbell, Pam Quinn)

Top Left: Alonso Castro Dance Company in "Threshold"
Below: Oberlin Dance Collective in "Format VI"

Mazowsze Polish Dance Company
Above: Sounds in Motion in "Smoke and Clouds"

ITHACA DANCEMAKERS

Artistic Directors-Choreographers, Saga Ambegaokar, Barbara Dickinson, Janice Kovar, Peggy Lawler; Composer, Linda Fisher; Production Manager, Rosemary Harms; Administration, Sorrel Fisher; Guest Choreographer, Stephen Goldbas

COMPANY

Saga Ambegaokar
Barbara Dickinson
Janice Kovar
Peggy Lawler
Karen Bell
Sam Costa
Alix Keast

PROGRAM: "Thanks for a Lift" (David Borden, Ambegaokar), "Ocean Bird" (Vaughan Williams, Kovar), "Eulogy for Kitty and Jake" (Stephen Goldbas), "You and I" (David Reuther, Dickinson), "Throes" (Saga Ambegaokar), "Ultimathule" (Linda Fisher/Kris Miller, Ambegaokar)

Top Left: Ithaca Dancemakers in "Ultimathule"
Left: Frank Ashley Dance Company in "The Game"
(Vince Orgera Photo)

FRANK ASHLEY DANCE COMPANY

Artistic Director-Choreographer, Frank Ashley; Executive Director, Bertram Beck; Associate Executive Director, Atkins Preston; Managing Director, Eileen Robbins; Technical Director, C. Richard Mills; Stage Managers, Robert Foose, Francine Dobranski; Director Arts for Living, Mark Tilley; Costumes, Frank Ashley, Susan Sudert

COMPANY

Frank Ashley

Carole Simpson	Bill Chaison
Strody Meekins	Sylvia Rincon
Rosalie Tracey	Bernard Riddick
Wendy McDade	Paula Odellas

PROGRAM: "Rock Ready Suite" (White/Franklin/Ross/Withers, Ashley), "The Game" (Gheorghe Zamfir, Ashley), "Vakako" (Herbie Hancock, Ashley), "Manipulation" (Max Roach/Herbie Hancock, Ashley), and *PREMIERE* of "Garvey" (Burundi/Blackbirds/Weather Report/John Coltrane/Burning Spear, Ashley)

SATORU SHIMAZAKI
DAVID MALAMUT

PROGRAM: "Report from Arms" (choreographed by Satoru Shimazaki, and performed by Mr. Shimazaki, Nicky Tessler, Debra Gay Maslanko; "Boaz" (Jack Moore, David Malamut) performed by David Malamut; "A Study for Nancy" choreographed by Satoru Shimazaki and performed by Nancy Hall; "Volley" (Zen Flute, David Malamut; Costumes, Manja Todorovic; Lighting, George Stevenson, Tom Kane) Performed by Valerie Pullman, David Malamut

David Malamut, Valerie Pullman in "Volley"
(Christine Drake Photo)

111

HARLEM PERFORMANCE CENTER
Sunday, February 1, 1976
Harlem Cultural Council (Geanie Faulkner, Executive Director; Emory Taylor, Producing Director) presents:

ELEO POMARE DANCE COMPANY

Artistic Director-Choreographer, Eleo Pomare; Managing Director, Michael E. Levy; General Manager, Virgil D. Akins; Stage Manager, Sandy Ross

Company

Jennifer Barry	Joe Johnson
Robin Becker	Strody Meekins
Bill Chaison	Rosalie Tracey
Dyane Harvey	Mina Yoo

PROGRAM: "Serendipity" (Handel), "Roots" (American Folk-/Billie Holiday/Nikki Giovanni), " 'N'Other Shade of Blue" (Traditional/R. Flack/J. Collins/L. Nyro)

Top Right: Dyane Harvey in "Roots"

LEXINGTON AVENUE YWCA
Wednesday, February 4, 1976

NAVIDA

and the Oriental Dance Group: Gretchen Brown, Linda Hollig, Lorraine Mungioli, Janet Fonder, Aranka Kolmos, Nitza Loyola, with Eddie the Sheik Kochak, Haki Obadia, Khaleel Hallal, and Guest Artist Joan Gainesley; Production conceived, choreographed and directed by Navida; Stage Assistants, Millie Trupin, Frank O'-Keefe

PROGRAM

MOODS OF THE ORIENTAL DANCE: Joy, Love between Man and Woman, Religious Fervor, Celebration

Right: Navida

AMERICAN THEATRE LABORATORY
February 6, 7, 8, 1976

DONALD BLUMENFELD
& VIC STORNANT

Choreography by Donald Blumenfeld, Vic Stornant; Lighting Design-Stage Manager, Jeffrey Eichenwald; Assistant Stage Manager, Joan Gedney

COMPANY

Kent Baker, Janis Brenner, Candice Christakos, Susan Creitz, Felice Dalgin, Patrice Evans, Jill Feinberg, Pamela Francis, Jody Oberfelder, Sasha Spielvogel

PROGRAM

"Inescape" (George Crumb, Donald Blumenfeld), "Little Murders" (Poulenc/Francaix, Vic Stornant), "Revels" (Jethro Tull, Blumenfeld), "Film Solo" (Tape Collage, Stornant), "Black Magic" (Collage, Blumenfeld), *PREMIERE* of "Sign" (Donald Blumenfeld)

"Sign"
(William Berg Photo)

CUNNINGHAM STUDIO
February 19, 20, 21, 1976

DANCES BY ROSALIND NEWMAN

COMPANY: Livia Blankman, Tom Borek, Naomi Dworkin, Kent Fischer, Micki Geller, Susan Goldstein, Valerie Hammer, Gretchen Henry, Jonathan Hollander, Kate Johnson, Robert Kahn, Clarice Marshall, Stormy Mullis, Rosalind Newman, Vittoria Uris, Renee Wadleigh, Debra Wanner, Alyssa Nan Hess (Harp)

PROGRAM

"Orange Pieces" (Faust), "Chapter II," "Chapter III" (Frog sounds), "Third Watch" (Latin Mass), *New York Premiere* of "Flakes" (Steve Drews) danced by Rosalind Newman

**Right: Livia Blankman, Robert Kahn,
Ken Fischer in "Third Watch"**

BEACON THEATRE
February 23, 24, 25, 1976
Kazuko Hillyer presents:

POLISH MIME BALLET THEATER

Director-Choreographer, Henryk Tomaszewski; Assistant Director, Jerzy Koztowski; Technical and Lighting Director, Kazimierz Doniec; Music, Sbigniew Karnecki; Stage Supervisor, Gustaw Herman; Costumes, Wladyslaw Wigura; Setting, Kazimierz Wisniak

COMPANY

Danuta Kisiel Drzewinska, Ewa Czekalska, Zbigniew Zukowski, Grazyna Bielawska, Urszula Hosiej, Julian Hasiej, Marek Oleksy, Zbigniew Papis, Zygmunt Rozlach, Anatol Krupa, Janusz Pieczuro, Jerzy Reterski, Jerzy Stepniak, Jerzy Koztowski, Czeslaw Bielski, Ryszard Staw, Elzbieta Orlow, Zygmunt Rozlach, Krzysztof Szwaja, Feliks Kudakiewicz, Wojciech Hankiewicz, Wojciech Misiuro, Krzysztof Szwaja, Andrzej Musiat

PROGRAM: "Menagerie of the Empress Phylissa," in eight scenes with prologue and apotheosis. Inspired by Frank Wedekind's "Die Kaiserin von Neu Funland."

Right: Polish Mime Ballet Theatre

WASHINGTON SQUARE METHODIST CHURCH
Thursday & Friday, February 26–27, 1976

MARIAN SARACH/BRYAN HAYES
and Dancers

Choreography, Marian Sarach, Bryan Hayes; Costumes, Charles Stanley; Lighting Design, Ted Cosby; Sound, Scott Daywood; Stage Manager, Bettina Brooks; Lighting Assistant, George Titus

PROGRAM

"Private Collection" (Collage, Sarach) danced by Amy Harlib, Bryan Hayes, Irene Meltzer, Marian Sarach, Allan Seward, Robin Silver

"Cuffs" (Mozart) and "Garbo Waltz" (John Field) choreographed and danced by Marian Sarach

"Purcell Suite" (Henry Purcell) choreographed and danced by Bryan Hayes, with Elena Alexander, Janet Gerson, Linnea Pearson, Karen Robbins, Steve Witt

Tom Brazil Photo

"Private Collection"

CONWAY-ANSORGE LOFT
Friday & Saturday, February 27–28, 1976

CAROL CONWAY DANCE COMPANY

Artistic Director, Carol Conway; Costumes, Raya, Genevieve Kapuler; Lighting Design, Avi Davis

COMPANY

Djuna Moran, Caren Acker, Patricia Bardi, Genevieve Kapuler, Joan Schwartz, Sandy Wuliger, Anne Sailer, Molissa Fenley, Carol Martin, Janet Lilly, Janet Brecht

PROGRAM

"Good Evening, Ladies and Gentlemen" (Poem by Dylan Thomas, Chris Stevens), "Light Departing" (Rosemary Gaffney, Djuna Moran), "Through the Maze" (Skip LaPlante, Patricia Bardi), "Photographed Painting" (Neopolitan Traditional, Genevieve Kapuler/Djuna Moran/Joan Schwartz), "The Journey of the Oblong Sphere and the Parallel Journey of the Green Ocelot past the Lost 127th Latitude Who Collided Past You, Exploded into Space and Became You" (Kesahven, Sandy Wuliger), "Rebecca's Song" (Linda Thomas, Molissa Fenley), "Slow Fall" (Skip LaPlante, Carol Martin)

Top Right: Carol Conway in "Together Passing"
(Ron Reagan Photo)

THE ENERGY CENTER
February 27–28, March 5–6, 1976
The Energy Center presents:

TWO COMPANIES

MWC COMPANY: Sheila Sobel (Director-Choreographer), Eileen Claire, Carol-Lynne Rose, Marlene Novitsky, Cybele Waters, performing "Moving Road Song, Parts I & II"

WENDY OSSERMAN DANCE COMPANY: Wendy Osserman (Director-Choreographer), Richard Burke, Shelly Hainer, Maggie Higgs, Margo Bassity, performing "Dream Animal Dream," "Still Me" (Walter Carlos, Osserman), "Elsh & Newy" (Bartok, Shelly Hainer), "Heavy Light" (Michael Smolanoff, Osserman)

Left: Carol-Lynne Rose, Marlene Novitsky, Sheila Sobel in "Folkwalk"

AMERICAN THEATRE LABORATORY
February 27, 28, 29, 1976

HARRY

Director-Choreographer, Senta Driver; Lighting Design, Robin Kronstadt; Stage Manager, Tina Charney

Marianne Bachmann
Senta Driver
Andrea Stark

PROGRAM: "Two Dances from Dead Storage" (John Fahey/Tom Johnson), "Two Steps Outside" (Lukas Foss, Vera Blaine), "Board Fade Except" (Thomas Skelton), "Since You Asked" (Senta Driver), "Memorandum" (Driver), "Another Section from Gallery" (Fahey), "In Which a Position Is Taken, and Some Dance" (Gilbert & Sullivan)

Johan Elbers Photo

Harry in "In Which a Position Is Taken and Some Dance"

MARYMOUNT MANHATTAN THEATRE
February 27, 28, 29, 1976

MARIANO PARRA SPANISH DANCE COMPANY

Artistic Director, Mariano Parra; Lighting Designer, Mark Goodman; Company Manager, Ira Rubin

COMPANY

Mariano Parro
Jerane Michel

with Ines Parra, Mariana Parra, Liliana Lomas, Marcia Martinez, Lillian Ramirez, Domingo Alvarado (singer), Daniel Waite (pianist), Carlos Lomas, Guillermo Rios (guitarists)

PROGRAM

"Panaderos de la Flamenca" (Traditional), "Baile Para Dos" (Enrique Granados), "Las Mujeres de Cadiz" (Traditional), "Soleares" (Traditional), "Goyescas" (Granados), "Jota Valenciana" (Traditional), "Romanza Gitana" (Traditional), "Zapateado" (Sarasate), "La Cana" (Traditional), "Leyenda" (Albeniz), "Tablao Flamenco" (Traditional)

Mariano Parra Spanish Dance Company
(Ron Reagan Photo)

AMERICAN THEATRE LABORATORY
March 3–8, 1976
Dance Theater Workshop presents:

ZE'EVA COHEN

Solo Dance Repertory
Production Manager-Lighting Design, Edward I. Byers; Stage Manager, Tina Charney; Production Assistant, Kate Elliott

PROGRAM

"Three Landscapes" (Alan Hovhaness/John Cage/Ali Akbar Kahn) choreographed and performed by Ze'eva Cohen, "Listen" (George Crumb, Ze'eva Cohen) performed by guest artist Reuben James, Christman Edinger, "Mothers of Israel" (Margalit Oved, Oved) performed by Ze'eva Cohen

Left: Ze'eva Cohen in "Mothers of Israel"
(Ron Reagan Photo)

CONSTRUCTION COMPANY DANCE STUDIO
Friday & Saturday, March 5 & 6, 1976

GELMAN/PALIDOFSKY DANCE THEATRE

Artistic Directors, Linda Gelman, Meade Palidofsky; Lighting, Dave Gilbert; Sound, David Rothenberg; Business Manager, Paul Zuckerman

COMPANY

Linda Gelman
Meade Palidofsky
Meg Gilbert
Martha Hirschman

PROGRAM: "3 Dialogues for 2 Voices and 2 Bodies" (Palidofsky, Gelman/Hirschman), "Cat's Cradle" (Palidofsky/Karen Gelman, Gelman/Sarah Martens), "Lady on a Cliff" (Meade Palidofsky), "Your Feets Too Big" (Fats Waller, Gelman), "Untitled Solo" (James Taylor, Martha Hirschman), "Eoan: Figures of Dawn" (Palidofsky, Gelman/Palidofsky)

Paul Zuckerman Photo

Linda Gelman in "Your Feets Too Big"

AMERICAN THEATRE LABORATORY
March 11 - 14, 1976
Dance Theater Workshop presents:

ART BERGER/DORIS GINSBERG

PROGRAM: "Direction: Sunward" (Peruvian Folk, Ginsberg; Lighting, Tina Charney) performed by Doris Ginsberg; "Her Dream" (Steven Edmond Samuels, Doris Ginsberg; Narrator, Stephanie Gallas) danced by Mickie Geller and Valerie Pullman; "From Corner Windows" choreographed and danced by Art Berger; "Air for Five" (Claude Bolling, Ginsberg; Costumes, Manja Todorovic) danced by Mary-Pat Carey, Mickie Geller, Andrea Levine, Valerie Pullman, Kathy Robens; "Meadow" (Roger Kellaway, Art Berger) performed by Art Berger and Doris Ginsberg

Ron Reagan Photo

LILA ACHESON WALLACE AUDITORIUM
Sunday, March 14, 1976
Japan Society presents

AYAKO UCHIYAMA

in Japanese Classical Dances: "The Seven Gods of Good Fortune" (Kouta), "The Iris-Print Kimona" (Nagauta), "The Castle Maiden" (Tokiwazu), "The Soap Bubble Man" (Kiyomoto)

Mike Jakub Photo

CONSTRUCTION COMPANY DANCE STUDIO
March 18 - 21, 1976

BARBARA BAKER

performing "Oceanside"; Choreography, Barbara Baker; Costumes and Set Designer, Lohr Wilson; Lighting Design, Ted Cosbey; Sound, Rose Jordan; Stage Manager, Linnea Pearson

AMERICAN THEATRE LABORATORY
March 18 -21, 1976
Dance Theater Workshop presents:

JIM & LORRY MAY

PROGRAM: "Short Lecture and Demonstration on the Evolution of Rag-Time as Presented by Jelly Roll Morton" choreographed by Anna Sokolow; "March On" (Charles Ives, Ray Harrison), "Traveling Pair" (Billy Joel, Irene Feigenheimer), "Magrirte, Magritte" (Liszt/Ravel/Satie, Anna Sokolow), "Headquarters" (Collage, Art Bauman)

Stage Manager: Edward Effron
Pianist: Patricia DeVore

Lois Greenfield Photo

MARYMOUNT MANHATTAN THEATRE
Saturday & Sunday, March 20 - 21, 1976
Domani Productions presents:

FRED BENJAMIN DANCE COMPANY

Artistic Director-Choreographer, Fred Benjamin; Production Manager, Karen DeFrancis; Lighting Design, Don Coleman; Ballet Mistress, Thelma Hill; Wardrobe Master, Bruce Hawkins; Press, Howard Atlee, Clarence Allsopp

COMPANY

Fred Benjamin	Karen Burke
Marilyn Banks	Juanita Taylor
Milton Bowser	Brenda Braxton
Alfred Gallman	Donald Griffith
Ron McKay	Mark Rubin

PROGRAM: "Mountain High" (Ashfor/Simpson, Benjamin), "Ceremony" (African, Benjamin), "Dealing with the Facts and Pain" (Contemporary, Benjamin), "Parallel Lines" (Hubert Laws/-War, Benjamin), and *WORLD PREMIERE* of "Travels, Just Outside the House" (Yusef Lateef/Carlos Santana/Alice Coltrane, Fred Benjamin; Costumes, Fred Benjamin, Olon Godare)

Top: Doris Ginsberg in "Direction: Sunward"
Below: Fred Benjamin Dance Company in
"Mountain High" *(Ron Reagan Photos)*

Jim and Lorry May in "Traveling Pair"
Above: Ayako Uchiyama

WORKS BY AMY GREENFIELD

PROGRAM: "Dirt" danced by Amy Greenfield, E. Carl Brown, Don Young; "Transport" dance by Lee Vogt, Amy Greenfield; "Element" danced by Amy Greenfield; "Dialogue for Camera and Dancer" danced by Amy Greenfield; "Fragments: Mat/Glass" danced by Ben Dolphin; "Dervish" danced by Amy Greenfield; "Beach" danced by Amy Greenfield and Ben Dolphin

HUNTER COLLEGE PLAYHOUSE
Wednesday, March 24, 1976
Hunter College presents:

PEOPLE/DOROTHY VISLOCKY DANCE THEATRE

Director-Choreographer, Dorothy Vislocky; Lighting Designer-Stage Manager, Mark Litvin; Technical Assistant, Stefan Cohen; Costumes, Frank Garcia, Betty Williams

COMPANY

Shannon Connell	Frances Park
Margaret Hoeffel	Gail Rucker
Janna Jensen	Andrea Snyder
Frances Lucerna	Ilana Snyder
Barbara Mahler	

Guest Artists: Jana Feinman, Glorianne Jackson

PROGRAM: "Santosa (Peace) 1974" (Pachebel/McDowell), "People Games" (Improvisation), "Silent Images" (Subotnik/Riegger), "Flash Is Trash???" (Lareef/Cobham)

Nat Tileston Photo

Left: "Silent Images"
Top: Amy Greenfield in "Transport"
(Samuel Robbins Photo)

CONSTRUCTION COMPANY DANCE STUDIO
March 26, 27, 28, 1976

ERIC TRULES & JACKIE RADIS
from MoMing

PROGRAM: "Dance Reading" (Poem by Li Shang-Yin), "More Song and Dance by the Radish," "A Softly Automated Jigsaw Puzzle," "Improvisations," "BTR Blues, or An Accumulation of Things with Some Piano," "Cornflicks" (Erwin Helfer, Susan Kimmelman/Eric Trules), "A Conversation Piece" (Read by Eileen Shukofsky), "Girl Machine" (Kenword Elmslie), "Stein/Giorno", "April Seventh" (William Faulkner)

CHOREOGROUND THEATRE
Saturday & Sunday, March 27 -28, 1976

BRUCE KING DANCE COMPANY

Director-Choreographer, Bruce King; Lighting Design, John Dodd; Stage Manager, Michael Forcade; Management, Frances Schram

COMPANY
Bruce King
Dale Townsend
Dawn Da Costa
Rick Gomes

PROGRAM: "Ghosts" (Anton Webern), "Bamboo" (Lou Harrison), "Swarm" (Antonio Soler), "Vigil" (Charles Ives, "Omens and Departures" (Edgar Varese), "Leaves" (William Penn), "General Booth Enters into Heaven" (Charles Ives)

Jack Mitchell Photo

Dawn DaCosta, Bruce King, Dale Townsend in
"General Booth Enters into Heaven"
Above: Eric Trules, Jackie Radis *(Tom Behrens Photo)* **117**

KAUFMANN CONCERT HALL
March 30 -April 5, 1976
The Jose Limon Dance Foundation in association with the 92nd Street
YM-YWHA presents:

JOSE LIMON DANCE COMPANY

Artistic Director, Ruth Currier; Assistant Artistic Director, Carla
Maxwell; Lighting Design, Eugene Lowery; Production Manager,
John Toland; Costume Supervisor, Allen Munch; Wardrobe Master,
Herbert Binzer; Press, Tom Kerrigan; Management, HI Enterprises

COMPANY

Mark Ammerman, Ginga Carmany, Bill Cratty, Robyn Cutler, Ken
Ganado, Christopher Gillis, William Hansen, Gary Masters, Fred
Mathews, Carla Maxwell, Jennifer Scanlon, Holly Schiffer, Tonia
Shimin, Louis Solino, Risa Steinberg, Nina Watt

REPERTOIRE

"The Unsung" (Jose Limon), "Air for the G String" (Bach, Doris
Humphrey), "Two Ecstatic Themes" (N. Medtner/G. F. Malipiero,
recorded by Vivian Fine; Doris Humphrey, reconstructed by Ernes-
tine Stodelle), "The Shakers" (Traditional, Doris Humphrey, recon-
structed by Ruth Currier), *World Premier* of "Storm Warning"
(Scriabin, Ruth Currier), "Dances for Isadora" (Chopin, Limon),
"Concerto Grosso" (Vivaldi, Limon), *World Premiere* of "Solaris"
(Richard Cameron, Fred Mathews), "La Malinche" (Limon), "The
Exiles" (Schoenberg, Limon), "Night Spell" (Rainer, Humphrey)

Martha Swope Photos

Right: Gary Masters, Carla Maxwell in "The Exiles"
Tonia Shimin, Jennifer Scanlon in "Air for the G String"
Top Right: Louis Solino (C) in "Storm Warning"

Louis Solino, Risa Steinberg,
Mark Ammerman in "La Malinche"

Risa Steinberg, Gary Masters, Robyn Cutler in
"Concerto Grosso in D Minor"

Tuesday, March 30, 1976
The Performing Arts Program of the Asia Society in association with
Carnegie Hall Corporation and Department of Cultural Affairs of the City
of New York presents:

SITARA

in
KATHAK

WARD-NASSE GALLERY
April 3, 10, 17, May 1, 8, 1976

LAURA FOREMAN DANCE THEATRE

Director, Laura Foreman; Musical Director, John Watts; Sound,
Hank O'Neal; Stage Managers, Laurel Dann, Martha Ellen; Technical Assistants, Bernie Babinson, Susan Ferleger, Jean Lichty; Videotapes, Dennis Diamond, Andy Mann; Program Coordinator, Harry
Nasse; Company Manager, Martha Ellen

PROGRAM

PREMIERE of "Program" (Collage/John Watts, Laura Foreman),
performed by Roxanne Bartush, David Malamut, Lucie Signa,
Satoru Shimazaki, Jean Lichty, Cheryl Thacker, Zelda Suplee,
Marcia McBroom, Dalia Shapiro

Lois Greenfield Photo

Top Right: Susan Whelan, Satoru Shimazaki,
David Malamut, Carol Volanth in "city of angels"
Right: Shirley Rushing in "Rhythm Ritual"
(Oleaga Photo)

BARBIZON PLAZA THEATRE
Friday & Saturday, April 9 - 10, 1976

ROD RODGERS DANCE COMPANY

Artistic Director-Choreographer, Rod Rodgers; Executive Direc-
tor, Leon Denmark; Press, Joanne Robinson; Lighting, George
Vaughn Lowther; Costume Mistress, Rhema Pinnock; Assistant to
Choreographer, Thomas Pinnock

COMPANY

Shirley Rushing, Tamara Guillebeaux, Leslie Innis, Thomas Pinnock, Jeanne Moss, Rael Lamb, Noel Hall, Elaine Anderson, Bill
Chaison

PROGRAM

"Tangents" (Cowell/Harrison, Rodgers), "Need No Help" (Valerie
Simpson, Rodgers) "Intervals" (Gwendolyn Watson, Rodgers),
"Freedom! Freedom" (Coleridge-Taylor Perkinson, Rodgers), "Vi-
sions . . . of new blackness" (Coleridge-Taylor Perkinson, Rodgers),
"Rhythm Ritual" (Ron Rodgers, Rodgers)

SYNOD HOUSE
April 20 - May 9, 1976
The Synod House at the Cathedral of St. John the Divine presents:

KEI TAKEI'S MOVING EARTH

Artistic Director-Choreographer, Kei Takei; Technical Director-
Lighting Design, Vincent Lalomia; Costumes-Dialogue, Kei Takei;
Stage Manager, Thomas Drewke; Production Manager, Maldwyn
Pate; Production Assistant, Don Moore; Sets, Maxine Klein

COMPANY

Amy Berkman, Avi Davies, Richmond Johnstone, Regine Kunzle,
John de Marco, Elsi Miranda, Don Moore, John Parton, Maldwyn
Pate, Joseph Ritter, Lloyd Ritter, Joan Schwartz, Kei Takei, Laurie
Uprichard, Howard Vichinsky, John Vinton

PROGRAM: "Light" in nine parts.

Kei Takei's Moving Earth in "Light part 9"
(Don Manza Photo)

ENVIRON
Thursday & Friday, April 22 - 23, 1976

WASHINGTON SQUARE REPERTORY DANCE COMPANY

Director, Laura Brittain; Lighting Design, Robert W. Rosentel; Sound, Robert Sallier; Managerial Assistant, Vikki Pizzuta; Technical Assistants, Darryl Brittain, Lydia Curtis, Mary Sandy

COMPANY

Nancy Bain, Laura Brittain, Leon Felder, Anne Fogelsanger, Karen Giombetti, Amy Kaplan, Rochelle Levine, Mara Lewis, Elaine Perlmutter, Naomi Schaeffer, Leslie Seaman, Barbara Sherman, Roberta Wein, Jill Wender, and Guest Artist Richard Cabezas

PROGRAM

"Joints" (Stockhausen, Martha Rzasa), "Loss (My Dance for Leslie)" (Robert Sallier, Tom Wetmore), "On a Scarlatti Sonata" (Lucas Foss, Michelle Berne), "Disengage" (Villa Lobos, Laura Brittain), "Comforts" (Lynn/Haggard Williams, Laura Brittain; *Premiere*), "Recyle (work in progress)" (Hammer De Johnette, Michelle Berne)

Leon Felder in "Portraits"
(Elaine Perlmutter Photo)

Jan Wodynski Dance Company in "Royal Flush"
(Chuck Saaf Photo)

AMERICAN THEATRE LABORATORY
April 22 - 25, 1976
Dance Theater Workshop presents:

JAN WODYNSKI DANCE COMPANY

Direction, Choreography, Costumes, Jan Wodynski; Technical Director, Mike Wodynski; Technicans, Jim Hunter, Jodi Strano

COMPANY

Valerie Bergman
Joanne Edelmann
Ron Paul
Madeleine Perrone
Jan Wodynski
Mike Wodynski

PROGRAM: "Akshun," "Freekwensi" (Mike Wodynski), "Outing" (Ralph Towner), "Yeast" (Keith Jarrett) *PREMIERE* of "The Royal Flush" (Mike Wodynski Tape)

WESTBETH STUDIO
Friday & Saturday, April 23 - 24, 1976
Dance Theater Workshop presents:

PEOPLE/DOROTHY VISLOCKY DANCE THEATRE

Director-Choreographer, Dorothy Vislocky; Lighting Design, Andrew Tron; Costume Designer, Frank Garcia; Stage Manager, Michael Richardson

COMPANY

Jana Feinman   Barbara Mahler
Janna Jensen   Gail Rucker
Frances Lucerna   Andrea Snyder
     Ilana Snyder

PROGRAM: "Centering" (Scarlatti/Handel), "Streets: Karma I" (Tape), "Silent Images" (Subotnik/Riegger), "Walking Perceptions" (Reilly)

Nat Tileston Photo

Ilana Snyder, Frances Lucerna, Gail Rucker, Janna Jenson in "Waking Perceptions"

LARRY RICHARDSON & DANCE COMPANY

Artistic Director-Choreographer, Larry Richardson; Administrative Director, J. Antony Siciliano; Administrative Assistant, Myrtle Lada; Costumes, DeBenedetti; Masks, Salvatore Guida, Kap Soon Park; Lighting, Raymond Dooley; Pianist, Mimi Stern-Wolfe

COMPANY

Larry Richardson

Wendy Stein	Dennis Kocjan
Sandra Small	Cheryl Hartley
Cameron Burke	Seth Walsh
Karen Donelson	Karen Lashinsky
Nanette Rainville	Kristie Zinberg

REPERTOIRE

'Fusion" (Aaron Copland, Richardson), "Erebus" (Tzvi Avni, Richardson), "Rounds" (David Diamond, Richardson), "Kin" (Bach/Buxtehude/Schutz/Xenakis, Richardson, *New York Premiere* of "The Chameleons" (Rosenthal, Richardson), and *World Premiere* of "The Heart's Rialto" (Debussy/Bertoncini, Richardson)

Irving Freilich Photo

Larry Richardson and Dance Company in "The Heart's Rialto"

NIMBUS

Choreography by Erin Martin, Jack Moore, Linda Tarnay; Stage Manager, Elizabeth Emery; Lighting Design, John P. Dodd; Sound, Stephen Goldberg; Management, Philip Moser, Management Projects

PROGRAM

"Mirror" (Tape Collage, Erin Martin) performed by Erin Martin, Moss Cohen; "Residue-Variant #6" (Nancarrow, Jack Moore) performed by Linda Tarnay; "Love Song for Jason Mayhew" (J. J. Cale, Jack Moore) performed by Bill Bass, David Malamut

PREMIERES: "Cross-Fade" (Stephen Goldberg, Erin Martin) performed by Georgiana Holmes, Erin Martin; "November" (Mahler) choreographed and danced by Linda Tarnay; "Four Netsukes" (Evelyn de Boeck, Jack Moore) performed by Erin Martin, David Malamut

Nathaniel Tileston Photos

**Left: Erin Martin, Georgiana Holmes in "Crossfade"
Above: David Malamut, Bill Bass in "Love Song for Jason Mayhew"**

Thomas Holt

PROGRAM

THOMAS HOLT DANCE ENSEMBLE: Lucinda Gehrke, Thomas Holt, JoAnne Kuhn, David McComb, Ann Moser, performing "Arienata" (Vivaldi, Holt), "Duet for Summer" (Lee Holdridge, Holt)

GEORGE STEVENSON DANCE COMPANY: Reginald Browning, Thomas Holt, Diane Rosenthal, George Stevenson, William Slicker, Cynthia Yee, Sandra Rios, performing "Relections" (Joplin, Cynthia Yee), "Rodeo Hoe Down Duet" (Copland, Stevenson/Holt), "Eveloutions" (Bandings, Stevenson), "Moods" (Roberta Flack, Diane Rosenthal), "Gospel Suite" (Arranged, Stevenson)

LILA ACHESON WALLACE AUDITORIUM
Thursday, May 6, 1976
The Performing Arts Program of the Japan Society presents:

EIKO & KOMA
in
WHITE DANCE

Left: Eiko and Koma

THE BIG APPLE DANCE THEATRE
May 7 - 9, 1976

BIG APPLE DANCE THEATRE

Artistic Director-Choreographer, Kay Wylie; Lighting Designer, Cora Woogen; Technical Director, Deborah Barchat

COMPANY

Kay Wylie
Maggie Bohrer
Terria Joseph
Buffy Price
Christy Wilson
Cora Woogen

PROGRAM: "Glimpse" (Stanley Cowell, Kay Wylie), "Thoughts" choreographed and danced by Buffy Price, "Inconsistencies of an Egg Cream" (Leo Kottke, Claire Henry), "Clown" (Tape Montage, Claire Henry), "Let's Make a Woman" (PeeWee Hunt/Tchaikovsky/Bessie Smith/Stevie Wonder, Kay Wylie)

Glenn S. Treeson Photo

CHOREOGROUND
May 7, 8, 9, 14, 15, 16, 21, 22, 23, 28, 29, 30, 1976
(16 performances)

THEATRE DANCE COLLECTION

Rodney Griffin
Cynthia Riffle
Lynn Simonson
Lynne Taylor
Jaclynn Villamil

REPERTOIRE: "Rialto" (Gershwin, Griffin), "Diary" (Judith Lander, Taylor), "Spy" (Lander, Taylor), "New Work" (Debussy, Villamil), "Ends. . . . and odds" (Griffin)

Left Center: Theatre Dance Collection
(Romeo Mizzaro Photo)

MARYMOUNT MANHATTAN THEATRE
Tuesday & Wednesday, May 18 - 19, 1976

NEW WORK, NEW JERSEY

Director-Choreographer, Kathryn Bernson; Music Director, Robert Bonfiglio; Lighting Design, Nancy Golladay

COMPANY
Kathryn Bernson

Beth Cachat	Malinda Nelson
Kimi Cunningham	Leslie Rotman
Amy Gale	Susan Sklaroff
Stormy Mullis	Elizabeth Streb

PROGRAM: "Leslie's Dilemma," "Step Back," "Walking and Talking," "Emergent Turtle,' "My Folk Dance," Ragpickers"

The Pieces Company in "Mourning Sounds"

EXPERIMENTAL INTERMEDIA FOUNDATION
May 20, 21, 22, 1976
The Experimental Intermedia Foundation presents:

NANCY TOPF & JON GIBSON

Dances conceived and performed by Nancy Topf; Music, Slide Projections, Video Tape by Jon Gibson Technical Assistants, Kate Parker, Al Rossi, George Ashley

PROGRAM

THE GREAT OUTDOORS: "Gathering," "Melody III," "JM," "Song 3," "Three Trees"

Right: Nancy Topf, Jon Gibson in "Gathering"
(Babette Mangolte Photo)

KAUFMANN CONCERT HALL
May 23, 25, 26, 27, 1976

STINGS

Created and Directed by Margaret Beals and Lee Nagrin; Based on "Ariel," the final poems of Sylvia Plath; Choreography, Margaret Beals; Stage Manager, Richard Tauber; Scenery, Jim Meares; Costumes, Sally Ann Parsons; Lighting, Edward M. Greenberg; Sound, Antony Giovanetti

COMPANY

Margaret Beals
Booke Myers
Lee Nagrin

Suzanne Opton Photo

**Right: Lee Nagrin, Margaret Beals,
Brooke Myers (on floor) in "Stings"**

WASHINGTON SQUARE METHODIST CHURCH
Saturday & Sunday, May 24–25, 1976

THREE OF A FASHION

an evening of dance theatre by Candice Christakos, Bill Kirkpatrick, Gael Stepanek; Lighting Design, Chris Cunningham; Technical Assistant, Kevin Jones; Stage Manager, John Sillings; Sound Technician, Karen Levin

COMPANY

Candice Christakos, Bill Kirkpatrick, Gael Stepanek, with William Berg, Deborah Glaser, Kendall Klingbell, Brent Mason, Sandra Seymour, Janis Brenner, Richard Thorne, Eva Vasquez, Patricia Renawine, Andrea Borak, Pam Budner

PROGRAM

"Upon a Time Once" (Bach/Beethoven/Mancini, Gael Stepanek), "Castle Building" (Candice Christakos), "Fit to Be Tied" (Collage, Bill Kirkpatrick), and *PREMIERES* of "Shifted Gears" (Sound, Bill Kirkpatrick), "3 A.M. (Sound, Candice Christakos), "Untitled Voyage" (Rossini/Satie, Gael Stepanek)

LIBRARY & MUSEUM OF PERFORMING ARTS
May 24, 25, 26, 1976

THE PIECES COMPANY

John B. Giletto
Althea Leslie-Hilsendager
Kathy Pira
Mary D. Swoboda

in an evening of choreodram, staged by Joel Friedman; Technical Coordinators, Jerry Grabey, Bruce Charlick, Richard Jacobs, Deine Rowan

PROGRAM: "Mourning Sounds" (Brian Ross), "Letter from Ruth" (Ruth Froma Sijes), "Death as a Spectator Sport" (Joel Friedman)

Bill Kirkpatrick, Gael Stepanek in "Voyage sans Title"
(Ron Reagan Photo)

MARYMOUNT MANHATTAN THEATRE
May 26–29, 1976
Marymount Manhattan College presents:

RUDY PEREZ DANCE THEATRE

Artistic Director-Choreographer, Rudy Perez; Productio Manager-Lighting Design, Kenneth F. Merkel; Technical Directo Terrence Byrne; Press, Helen Lowe; Production Assistants, Jon An dreadakis, John Dodd, Peter Reitz, Steve Witt; Company Manage Sandra Fowlkes

COMPANY

Tom Brown	Jeffrey Urba
Leslie Koval	Candace Gilles-Brow
Karen Masaki	Irene Kasso
Rudy Perez	Thomas Wilkinso

PROGRAM: "Colorado Ramble" (George Reinholt, Rudy Perez "New Annual" (Collage, Perez), and *PREMIERES* of "System (Arranged, Rudy Perez), and "Update" (Noah Creshevsky, Rud Perez)

Johan Elbers Photo

**Top Left: Leslie Koval, Karen Masaki,
Tom Brown, Jeffrey Urban in "Update"**

TEARS
May 27–30, June 3–6, 1976

CLIFF KEUTER DANCE COMPANY

Artistic Director-Choreographer, Cliff Keuter; Costume and Set Designer, Walter Nobbe; Lighting Designer, Edward Effron; Musical Director, John Herbert McDowell; Managing Director, Alan Kifferstein; Administrator, Kaylynn Sullivan; Stage Manager, Jim Irwin

COMPANY
Cliff Keuter

Elina Mooney	Ellen Jacob
Karla Wolfangle	Ernest Pagnano
Ellen Kogan	Michael Tipton
Jean Finkelstein	John Dayger

REPERTOIRE

"Field" (Mahler, Cliff Keuter), "Sunday Papers" (McDowell, Keuter), "Visit" (Hellerman, Keuter), "The Murder of George Keuter" (Cliff Keuter, Keuter), and *PREMIERE* of "Tetrad" (Stravinsky, Keuter)

Ron Reagan Photo

**Right Center: John Dayger, Michael Tipton,
Elina Mooney in "Sunday Papers"**

AMERICAN THEATRE LABORATORY
May 28, 29, 30, 1976

PAUL WILSON'S
THEATREDANCE ASYLUM

Artistic Director-Choreographer, Paul Wilson; Associate Direc tor, Francis Witkowski; General Manager, Dennis Haines; Produc tion Manager, Jim Hunter; Lighting, Paul Dorphley; Stag Manager, Doris Fountain

COMPANY

Barry Barychko	Penelope Van
Joanne Edelmann	Scott Vol
Whit Carman	Paul Wilso
Rebecca Kelly	Francis Witkows
Joe Schwarz	Joan Witkows

PROGRAM: "Tossed the first law is survival ..." (Lou Gras i/Oliver Nelson, Paul Wilson), "Traditions" (Lehman Enge Charles Weidman), and *PREMIERES* of "Charles" (Chopi Rebecca Kelly; dedicated to Charles Weidman), "I-Cycles" (Ur bamba, Paul Wilson), "Late Nite TV Talk" (Conception, Directio Paul Wilson, Francis Witkowski; Music by Mozart)

Theatredance Asylum in "I-Cycles"
(Peter Hales Photo)

ANNUAL SUMMER DANCE FESTIVALS OF 1975

AMERICAN DANCE FESTIVAL
New London, Connecticut
June 26–August 2, 1975
Twenty-eighth Year

Director, Charles Reinhart; Dean, Martha Myers; Press, Meg Gordean, Becky Flora; Coordinator, Celia Halstead; Assistant to Director, Lisa Booth; Administrative Assistants, Heidi Crosier, Ron Robins; Project Director, Sheldon Soffer; Theatre Manager-Technical Director, Fred Grimsey; Assistant Technical Directors, Benjamin Howe, Chris Greene; Sound, Jon Ross; Lighting, Edward I. Byers, Tina Charney.

Thursday, June 26, 1975

ZE'EVA COHEN dancing "Three Landscapes" (Hovhaness/Cage/Kahn, Cohen), "32 Variations in C Minor" (Beethoven, Waring), "Escape" (Hopkins, Sokolow)

RAYMOND JOHNSON dancing "Fieldgoal" (Tape Collage, Perez), "Scherzo" (Chopin, Waring), "Three Faces" (Count Basie/Scott Joplin/Steve Reich, Johnson)

Friday & Saturday, June 27–28, 1975

DANCE THEATRE OF HARLEM (Arthur Mitchell, Karel Shook, Directors) with Lydia Abarca, Gayle McKinney, Susan Lovelle, Sheila Rohan, Karen Brown, Elena Carter, Laura Lovelle, Virginia Johnson, Laura Brown, Brenda Garrett, Melva Murray-White, Karen Wright, Yvonne Hall, Denise Nix, Walter Raines, Ronald Perry, Samuel Smalls, Homer Bryant, Roman Brooks, William Scott, Paul Russell, Joseph Wyatt, Allen Sampson, Mel Tomlinson dancing "Every Now and Then" (Jones, Scott), "Allegro Brillante" (Tchaikovsky, Balanchine), "Le Corsaire" (Drigo, Shook), "Dougla" (Holder, Holder).

Wednesday, July 2, 1975

ELIZABETH KEEN DANCE COMPANY: Elizabeth Keen, Michael Aiken, Hannah Kahn, Dalienne Majors, Jeannie Hutchins, Michael Rivera, Ted Striggles dancing "Line Drawing" (Faure, Keen), "Poison Variations" (Watson/Press, Keen), "Parentheses" (Keen), "A Polite Entertainment for Ladies and Gentlemen" (Foster, Keen)

Thursday, July 3, 1975

BHASKAR with Cindy Maddux dancing "Nantanam Adinar," "Thala Nirtham," "Naga Nirtham," "Surya Nirtham"

PAULINE KONER DANCE COMPANY: Deborah Pratt, Sam Tampoya, Tamara Grose, Martha Curtis, Michael Freed, George White, Karen Shields dancing *premiere* of "Solitary Songs" (Luciano Berio, Koner)

Friday, July 4, 1975

ALVIN AILEY JUNIOR COMPANY (Artistic Director, Sylvia Waters; Administrative Director, Wade Williams): Marla Bingham, Alistair Butler, Nancy Colahan, Merle E. Holloman, Daniela Malusardi, German Maracara, Lonne Moretton, Delila Moseley, Clayton Palmer, Martial Roumain, Jacqueline Smith-Lee, John Young dancing "Night Creature" (Ellington, Ailey), "Icarus" (Matsushita, Hoving), "Echoes in Blue" (Ellington, Myers), "Revelations" (Spirituals, Ailey)

Right: Bhaskar
Top: Ze'eva Cohen

Alvin Ailey Junior Company in "Revelations"

Raymond Johnson Dance Company
(M. B. Hunnewell Photo)

125

AMERICAN DANCE FESTIVAL

Saturday, July 5, 1975

ALVIN AILEY JUNIOR COMPANY dancing "40" (Ellington, Solomons), "Dance for Six" (Vivaldi, Trisler), "Untitled New Work" (Ellington, Alvin McDuffie), "Revelations" (Spirituals, Ailey)

Friday & Saturday, July 11–12, 1975

TWYLA THARP DANCES AND DANCERS: Twyla Tharp, Rose Marie Wright, Kenneth Rinker, Tom Rawe, Jennifer Way, Nanna Nilson dancing "Sue's Leg" (Waller, Tharp), "The First Fifty" (Tharp), "Bach Duet" (Bach, Tharp), *American Premiere* of "Ocean's Motion" (Chuck Berry, Twyla Tharp)

Monday, July 14, 1975

IOLANI LUAHINE with Hoakalei Kamauu in dances of Hawaii

Thursday, July 17, 1975

CHUCK DAVIS DANCE COMPANY CHAMBER GROUP (Artistic Director-Choreographer, Chuck Davis): Lynne Allen, Carol Awolowo, Tara Bernard, Marilyn Banks, Onika Bgemon, Milton Bowser, Brenda Braxton, Victor Braxton, Sandra Burton, Jackie Coban, Chuck Davis, Ayele Douglas, Linda Evans, William Fleet, Jr., Theresa Freeman, Normadien Gibson, Ben Jones, Jennifer Jones, Francine Quick, Larry Saunders, Charles Wynn dancing "Experiment with Death" Robin Kenyatta/Nina Simone, Davis), "Loving You" (Jesse Scott, Davis), "Today" (Scott, Davis), "Personal Statement," "Peace and Love" (Sweet Inspirations, Davis), "Dyembe and Chant" (Traditional, Onika Bgemon), "Kalunji-Yi" (Traditional, Davis), "Moly Yamee" (Traditional, Davis), "Konkoba" (Traditional, Davis), "Ritual"

Friday & Saturday, July 18–19, 1975

TRISHA BROWN AND COMPANY: Elizabeth Garren, Judith Ragir, Mona Sulzman, Trisha Brown dancing "Spiral," "Structured Pieces," "Floor of the Forest and Other Miracles," "Locus," "Theme and Variations," *Premiere* of "Chronology"

Friday & Saturday, July 25–26, 1975

VIOLETTE VERDY and HELGI TOMASSON dancing "Raymonda pas de Deux" (Glazounov, Balanchine), "Tchaikovsky pas de Deux" (Tchaikovsky, Balanchine)

NANCY MEEHAN DANCE COMPANY: Carol Conway, Risa Friedman, Emery Hermans, Craig Hoke, Amy Horowitz, Trude Link, Jeffrey Maer, Nancy Meehan, Anthony Pepiciello, Ellen Marshall Reifler, Mary Spalding dancing "Split Rock" (Jon Deak, Nancy Meehan), "Bones Cascades Scapes" (Eleanor Hovda, Meehan), "Grapes and Stones" (Deak, Meehan)

Friday & Saturday August 1–2, 1975

KATHRYN POSIN DANCE COMPANY: Bill Gornel, Kathryn Posin, Holly Reeve, Ricky Schussel, Susan Thomasson, Lance Westergard, Marsha White dancing "Waves" (Laurie Spiegel, Kathryn Posin), "Bach Pieces" (Bach, Posin)

PILOBOLUS DANCE THEATRE: Robert Morgan Barnett, Alison Chase, Moses Pendleton, Michael Tracy, Martha Clarke, Jonathan Wolken dancing "Monkshood's Farewell" (Company), and *Premiere* of "Untitles" (Bob Dennis, Company)

Right: Pilobolus Dance Theatre Above: Trisha Brown and Company in "Locus" Top: Tom Rawe, Twyla Tharp, Rose Marie Wright, Kenneth Rinker in "Sue's Leg"

Nancy Meehan in "Bones Cascades Scapes"
(Dave Sagarin Photo)

Kathryn Posin Dance Company in "Waves"
(Joel Gordon Photo)

DANCE FESTIVAL/THE MALL
New York, N.Y.
May 30–June 29, 1975

Director, Louise Roberts; Administrative Assistant, Joan Chanin;
ecial Assistant to Director, Karen DeFrancis; Production Man-
ement, Technical Assistance Group; Lighting, Jon Knudsen;
age Manager, Rosemary Cunningham; Technical Staff, Gordon
nk, Tony Marques, Robin Tannenbaum; Press, Howard Atlee,
arence Allsopp

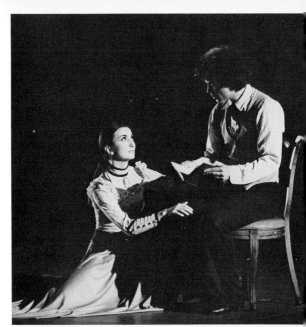

TY UNIVERSITY GRADUATE CENTER MALL
May 30, 31, June 1, 1975
HEATRE DANCE COLLECTION: Rodney Griffin, Don Lopez,
nthia Riffle, Audrey Ross, Justin Ross, Susan Sfreddo, Lynn Si-
nson, Lynne Taylor, Jaclynn Villamil, Miriam Welch, dancing
inetics" (Vivaldi, Lynne Taylor), "Mandragora" (Charles Tol-
er, Lynn Simonson/Rodney Griffin), "Double Solitude" (Britten,
ylor), "The Fools Almanac" (Rossini, Griffin), "Puppets" (Jeffrey
resky, Griffin), "Odd Man Out" (Steve Cagan, Taylor), "Fly with
e" (Jay Hirsch, Taylor), "Fordansak" (Debussy, Jaclynn Vil-
mil), "Epilog" (Cagan, Taylor), "Journey I" (Ravel, David Ander-
n), "Misalliance" (Ibert, Griffin)
June 6, 7, 8, 1975
IANNE McINTYRE SOUNDS IN MOTION: Ahmed Abdullah,
abafumi Akunyun, Phillip Bond, Victor Braxton, William Donald,
nnetta Gaines, Linda Griffin, Bernadine Jennings, Dianne McIn-
re, Clayton Strange, dancing "Free Voices," "Smoke and Clouds"
hirley & Lee Huey Smith, Dianne McIntyre), "Up North 1881"
ouisiana State Prison Singers/Rev. Gary Davis/Alabama Sacred
arp Singers/Fred McDowell, McIntyre), "Memories" (Eubie
ake, McIntyre), "Sounds from Inside," "Union" (Babafumi Aku-
un/Gwendolyn Nelson/ Ahmed Abdullah/Steven Solder, McIn-
re)
June 13, 14, 15, 1975

EW CHOREOGRAPHERS CONCERT '75: "The Lake" (Tradi-
nal Balinese, Patrice Regnier) danced by Carolann Cortese, Merci
nton, Elizabeth Fisher, Andrea Morris, Valencia Ondes; "The
gitive" (Fukushima, Luis Layag) danced by Luis Layag; "The
rd" (Vivaldi, Patricia Hruby) dance by Patricia Hruby; "Et Cet-
a" (Madeleine Denko) danced by Janice Cronin, Susan Matthews,
evon Wall; "Thirst" (Weather Report, Sandra Burton) danced by
renda Braxton, Monifa Olajorin, Francine Quick; "Out of the Cra-
e Endlessly Rocking" (Block, Katherine Liepe) danced by Kather-
e Liepe; "Closet Dancing" choreographed and danced by Stuart
nith; "Depart" (Correlli, Susan Dibble) danced by Alan Good,
zanne Brookhoff, Susan Emery, Donald Scheumann, Phillip
rosser, Jerome Sarnat, Diane Chavin, Gwyneth Jones, Gravia
ella Terza, Lisa Levart, Meralee Guhl
June 17–22, 1975
RED BENJAMIN DANCE COMPANY: Terrin Miles, Karen
urke, Marilyn Banks, Milton Bowser, Sharon Brooks, Donald
riffith, Henny Kamerman, Clayton Palmer, Tina Steinway, Juanita
yler, dancing "Parallel Lines" (Hubert Laws/War, Fred Benja-
in), "Double Solitude" (Britten, Lynne Taylor), "Dealing with the
acts and the Pain" (Contemporary, Benjamin), "Ember" (Isaac
ayes, Winston DeWitt Hemsley), "Vein Melter" (Herbie Han-
ck/Chico Hamilton/Isaac Hayes, Benjamin), "Personal Testi-
ony" (Ashford & Simpson, Benjamin), "Concupiscence" (Herbie
ancock, Benjamin), "New York Mambo" (Johnny Colon, Andy
orres), "Prey" (Alphonze Mouzon/War, Benjamin), "Our Thing"
saac Hayes, Benjamin), "Mountain High" (Ashford & Simpson,
enjamin), "902 Albany Street" (Contemporary, Benjamin), "From
e Mountain of the Moon" (Weather Report/Herbie Hancock-
Earth, Wind & Fire, Benjamin)
Sunday, June 29, 1975
LVIN AILEY REPERTORY WORKSHOP: Marla Bingham,
listair Butler, Nancy Colahan, Merle Holloman, Daniela Malu-
rdi, German Maracara, Lonne Moretton, Delila Moseley, Clayton
almer, Martial Roumain, Jacqueline Smith-Lee, John Young,
ncing "Night Creatures" (Ellington Ailey), "40" (Ellington, Gus
olomons, Jr.), "Echoes in Blue" (Ellington, Milton Myers), "Reve-
tions" (Spirituals, Ailey)

p Right: Lynne Taylor, Don Lopez in "Double Solitude"
(Theatre Dance Collection)
Below: Sounds in Motion in "Union"

Fred Benjamin Dance Company in "Facts and Pain"

127

JACOB'S PILLOW DANCE FESTIVAL
Lee, Massachusetts
July 1–August 23, 1975
Forty-third Season

Founder, Ted Shawn (1891–1972); Director, Norman Walker; Comptroller, Grace Badorek; Promotional Director, Donald Westwood; Technical Director, David M. Chapman
July 1–5, 1975

THEATRE DANCE COLLECTION: Cynthia Riffle, Miriam Welch, Audrey Ross, Jaclynn Villamil, Don Lopez, Rodney Griffin, Justin Ross, Christopher Stocker, Lynn Simonson, Lynne Taylor, dancing "Kinetics" (Vivaldi, Lynne Taylor), "Double Solitude" (Britten, Taylor), "Misalliance" (Ibert, Rodney Griffin)

CHIANG CHING with CHIH-MING LU dancing "Techniques and Dances" (Chinary Ung, Chiang Ching), "Journey" (Chiang Ching), "On the Steppes" (Ching)

LINDA DiBONA and CHRIS JENSEN dancing "Ballade" (Faure, Norman Walker), "Tchaikovsky Pas de Deux" (Tchaikovsky, Balanchine)
July 8–12, 1975

JOAN MILLER and the CHAMBER ARTS/DANCE PLAYERS: Lee Connor, Anita Littleman, Joan Miller, Seth Walsh, Frank Ashley, Lorn MacDougal performing "Thoroughfare" (Mayall/Watson, Joan Miller), "Pass Fe White" (Joan Miller)

LYNDA YOURTH and FRANK ANDERSEN dancing "William Tell Pas de Deux" (Rossini, Brenaa after Bournonville), "Flower Festival of Genzano Pas de Deux" (Paulli/Helsted/Gade, Hans Brenaa after Bournonville)

EMILY FRANKEL with David Anderson, Stephen Casko, John David Cullum performing the *World Premiere* of "Medea" (Alban Berg, Norman Walker; Costumes, Ben Benson)
July 15–19, 1975

MURRAY LOUIS DANCE COMPANY: Murray Louis, Michael Ballard, Richard Haisma, Helen Kent, Anne McLeod, Robert Small, Marcia Wardell, performing "Porcelain Dialogues" (Tchaikovsky, Louis), "Personnae" (Free Life Communication, Louis), "Hoopla" (Traditional, Louis)
July 22–26, 1975

CLIFF KEUTER DANCE COMPANY: Cliff Keuter, Michael Tipton, Joan Finkelstein, Ellen Jacob, Ellen Kogan, Karla Wolfangle, John Dayger, Ernest Pagnano, dancing "Musette di Taverni" (Couperin, Keuter), *World Premiere* of "Field" (Mahler, Keuter), "Amazing Grace" (Collage, Keuter), "Plaisirs d'Amour" (Keuter, Keuter)

NALA NAJAN dancing "Jhaptal," "Devarunama," "Idhubagya," "Homage to Vivaldi" (Vivaldi, Najan)

**Right: Joan Miller Above: Chiang Ching,
Chih-Ming Lu, Emily Frankel**

**Nala Najan Top Right: Theatre Dance Collection
in "Kinetics"**

Chris Jensen, Linda Di Bona
(Bil Leidersdorf Photo)

128

JACOB'S PILLOW DANCE FESTIVAL

July 29–August 2, 1975

MARIA ALBA SPANISH DANCE COMPANY: Maria Alba, Roberto Cartagena, Ana Maria Cristina, Melinda Montero, Jorge Navarro, Carlota Santana, Roberto Lorca (Guest Artist), Adonis Puerta (Guitarist), Luis Vargas (Vocalist), performing "Dansas Fantasticas" (Turina, Alba/Lorca), "Malaquena," "Jota Navarra" (Larregla, Cartagena), "Tarantos," "Martinete" (Roberto Cartagena), "Guajira" (Roberto Lorca), "Farruca," "Suite Colombiana" (Popular, Cartagena), "Baile para Dos" (Rios, Alba), "Noche en Seville" (Popular, Maria Rosa Merced)

August 5–9, 1975

BOSTON BALLET COMPANY: Tony Catanzaro, Anamarie Sarazin, Laura Young, Augustus Van Heerden, Kathryn Anderson, Stephanie Moy, Deidre Myles, Ilene Strickler, Mark Johnson, David Drummond, James Capp, Daryl Robinson, Ron Cunningham, Larry Robertson, Ellen O'Reilly, Leslie Woodies, dancing "Holberg Suite" (Grieg, Ron Cunningham), "Tarantella" (Gottschalk, Balanchine), "Allegro Brillante" (Tchaikovsky, Balanchine), "The Road of the Phoebe Snow" (Ellington/Strayhorn, Talley Beatty)

August 12–16, 1975

DANCERS: Dennis Wayne, Bonnie Mathis, Martine van Hamel, Elaine Kudo, Buddy Balough, Janet Popelski, Kenneth Hughes, performing "The Still Point" (Debussy, Bolander), "Lazarus" (Fiser, Walker), "The Murder of George Keuter" (Ratter, Keuter), "Solo from Solitaire" (Arnold, MacMillan)

MARGARET BEALS with Gwendolyn Watson performing "The Desperate Heart" (Segall, Bettis), "Wild Swans in Epitaph" (Millay, Beals), "Improvisations for Cellist and Dancer" (Watson, Beals), "Love Is a. . . ." (Beals)

August 19–23, 1975

LAWRENCE RHODES and ALBA CALZADA dancing "After Eden" (Hoiby, Butler), "Pas de Deux Glazounov" (Glazounov, Rodham)

5 by 2 DANCE COMPANY: Jane Kosminsky, Bruce Becker, with guest artists Carolyn Adams and Daniel (Williams) Grossman, performing "Duet" (Haydn, Taylor), World Premieres of "Suite Richard" (Traditional, Bruce Becker), and "Celestial Circus" (George Crumb, Norman Walker)

JACOB'S PILLOW DANCERS: Janis Brenner, Deborah Donaldson, Jennifer Donaldson, Nancy Gottlieb, Olgalyn Jolly, Barbara Kidd, Regina Larkin, Nancy Lushington, B. J. Manilla, Mary Ann Neu, Brenda Steady, Michael Cichetti, Paul Fiorino, Morris Freed, Oliver Freed, David Lukcso, Brian Marble, Wesley Robinson, dancing "Gloria" (Poulenc, Walker)

Right: Dennis Wayne in "Lazarus"
(Thomas Victor Photo)
Above: Jacob's Pillow Dancers in "Gloria"
(John Van Lund Photo)

Bruce Becker, Jane Kosminsky
Top Right: Maria Alba

Alba Calzada, Lawrence Rhodes
(Richard L. Bitner Photo)

129

NEW YORK DANCE FESTIVAL
Delacorte Theater, Central Park
New York, N.Y.
August 28–September 7, 1975

Producer, Joseph Papp; Executive Producer, Adam A. Pinsker; Associate Producer, Bernard Gersten; Production Supervisor, Jason Steven Cohen; Press, Merle Debuskey, Susan L. Schulman; Lighting, Thomas Skelton, Shirley Prendergast, Louise Guthman; Assistant to Executive Producer, Mathew Maine; Stage Manager, Louis Rackoff; Technical Coordinator, David Manwaring

PROGRAMS
Thursday & Friday, August 28–29, 1975

ERICK HAWKINS DANCE COMPANY: Cathy Ward, Robert Yohn, Nada Reagan, Natalie Richman, Kristin Peterson, Cori Terry, Erick Hawkins dancing "Greek Dreams with Flute" (Debussy/Ohana/Varese/Hovhaness/Matsudaira/Jolivet, Hawkins)

ELIOT FELD BALLET: Christine Sarry, Helen Douglas, Naomi Sorkin, Richard Fein, John Sowinski, George Montalbano, dancing "Intermezzo" (Brahms, Feld)

KATHRYN POSIN DANCE COMPANY: Sharon Filone, Bill Gornel, Kathryn Posin, Ricky Schussel, Susan Thomasson, Lance Westergard, Marsha White, dancing the *NY Premiere* of "Waves" (Laurie Spiegel, Posin)

ANNABELLE GAMSON performing "Dances by Isadora Duncan": "Water Study," "Five Waltzes," "Dance of the Furies," and "Etude"

CHUCK DAVIS DANCE COMPANY: Chuck Davis, Victor Braxton, Charles Wynn, Milton Bowser, Larry Sanders, William Fleet, Earl Mack, dancing "N'Tora Dance" (Traditional Watusi, Davis)

Right: Kathryn Posin, Lance Westergard
(Joel Gordon Photo)

Annabelle Gamson Top Right: Eliot Feld Ballet
(Martha Swope Photo)

Chuck Davis

130

NEW YORK DANCE FESTIVAL

Saturday & Sunday, August 30–31, 1975

TINA RAMIREZ' BALLET HISPANICO OF NEW YORK: Rachel Ticotin, Alicia Roque, Asha Coorlawala, Coco Pelaez, Valerie Contreras, Jose Suarez, Marcial Gonzalez, Roy Rodriguez, Antonio Iglesias, Sandra Rivera, Lorenzo Maldonado, dancing "Echoes of Spain" (Albeniz/Temptations/Mandrill, Louis Johnson), and "La Boda de Luis Alonso" (Gimenez, Paco Fernandez)

JEFF DUNCAN DANCE REPERTORY COMPANY: Jeff Duncan, Anne Sahl, Valerie Pullman, Timothy Haynes dancing "Winesburg Portraits" (American Traditional, Duncan)

CINCINNATI BALLET COMPANY: Wayne Maurer, Colleen Giesting, Michael Bradshaw, David Blackburn, Michael Rozow, Alyce Taylor, dancing "Face of Violence" (Lester Horton/Carmon DeLeone, James Truitte/Carmen de Lavallade after Lester Horton)

MOVEMENT PROJECTS' DIALOG (Michael Czajkowski) choreographed and danced by Art Bauman

LOUIS JOHNSON DANCE THEATER: Michelle Murry, Meahie, Kiki, Phoebie Redmond, Amii, Charles Augins, Clyde Barrett, David Cameron, Bernard Gibson, Robert Pittman, dancing "When Malindy Sings" (Narrator, Skipper Driscolle; Johnson)

PATRICIA McBRIDE and JEAN-PIERRE BONNEFOUS dancing "Le Corsaire Pas de Deux" (Drigo, Petipa)

Tuesday & Wednesday, September 2–3, 1975

MARYLAND BALLET: Misti McKee, Debra Van Cure, Yuri Chatal, Camille Izard, Norma Pera, Bojan Spassof, dancing "Designs with Strings" (Tchaikovsky, John Taras)

MAY O'DONNELL CONCERT DANCE COMPANY: Sheila Zadra, Dale Andree, Hazel Kandall, Sheila Nixon, Alice Gill, Marsha Franklin, Donna Tchapraste, dancing "Suspension" (Ray Green, O'Donnell)

SOPHIE MASLOW DANCE COMPANY: Jessica Chao, Ana Marie Forsythe, Cheryl Hartley, Jane Hedal, Nedra Marlin-Harris, Anthony Balcena, Joe Goode, Andy Miller, dancing "Folksay" (American Folk, Maslow)

MURRAY LOUIS DANCE COMPANY: Michael Ballard, Richard Haisma, Helen Kent, Anne McLeod, Robert Small, Marcia Wardell, dancing "Proximities" (Brahms, Louis)

SAN FRANCISCO BALLET: Tina Santos and Gary Wahl dancing the New York Premiere of "Pas de Deux from Shinju" (Paul Chihara, Michael Smuin)

LUIGI'S JAZZ DANCE COMPANY: Barry D'Angelo, Andy Handler, Marla Serlin, Paula Hirschberg, Ronnie De Marco, Nichole Vachon, Guillermo Gonzales, Jeff Phillips, Nina Williams, dancing "Jazz with Luigi" (Nyro/McFarland/Schifrin/Mandrill, Luigi)

Right: Valerie Pullman, Jeff Duncan in "Winesburg Portraits"
(V. Sladon Photo)

Top: Ballet Hispanico of New York
(Carleton Sarver Photo)

Murray Louis Dance Company in "Proximities"

Cincinnati Ballet in "Face of Violence"

NEW YORK DANCE FESTIVAL
Thursday & Friday, September 4–5, 1975

MATTEO with THE ETHNOAMERICAN DANCE THEATER: Socorro Santiago, Homer Garza, Terry Yorysh, Carlyn Deats, Deborah Novotny, Shanti Garcia, Bonnie Campos, Judith Landon, Sandra Fernandez, Barbara Arcelay Reynolds, Ingrid Ross, John Kirshy, Robert Chiarelli, dancing "Hansa Sarovaram" (Tchaikovsky, Matteo after La Meri)

CHARLES MOORE dancing "Sacred Forest Dance" (Traditional Mande Tribe)

BOB BOWYER and JO-ANN BRUGGEMANN dancing "Menutto" (Mozart, Bowyer), and "Rock 'n' Roll" (Elton John, Bowyer)

THE DANSCOMPANY: Clif de Raita, Cindy Bernier, Jacqulyn Buglisi, Milton Myers, Nancy Long, Lonnie Moretton, Laurie Kaplan, Miguel Antonio, dancing "Four Temperaments" (Hindemith, Joyce Trisler)

CHIANG CHING with Lu Chih-Ming performing "Journey," "Yang Kuan," "Three Folksongs" (Chou Wen-Chung, Chiang Ching)

REBECCA WRIGHT and KEVIN McKENZIE dancing "Pas de Deux from Cinderella" (Prokofiev, Ben Stevenson)

LES BALLETS TROCKADERO DE MONTE CARLO: Jack d'Aniels, Alexis Ivanovitch Lermontov, Vera Namethatuneva, Roland Deaulin, Tamara Karp, Natasha Veceslova, Zenia Xenophobia, Veronica-Malaise du Mer, Mlada Mladova, Olga Tchikabounskaya, Verenika-Malaise du Mer, Zamarina Zamarkova, Eugenia Repelskii, performing Act II of "Swan Lake" (Tchaikovsky, Karpova after Petipa)

Saturday & Sunday, September 6–7, 1975

BUZZ MILLER and ETHEL MARTIN dancing "Secret Agent" (Raymond Scott, Jack Cole)

LAURA FOREMAN DANCE THEATRE: Roxanne Bartush, Suzette Pompei, David Malamut, Lynn McNutt, Lucy Signa, Satoru Shimazaki, Carol Volanth, Susan Whelan, performing "city of angels" (John Watts, Foreman)

SOUNDS IN MOTION: Lonnetta Gaines, Linda Griffin, William Donald, Dianne McIntyre, Bernadine Jennings, Dorian Williams, Phillip Bond, Kenneth McPherson, dancing "Memories" (Eubie Blake, Dianne McIntyre)

PAUL RUSSELL and LYDIA ABARCA dancing "Pas de Deux from Romeo and Juliet" (Prokofiev, Gabriella Taub-Darvash)

MARIA BENITEZ' ESTAMPA FLAMENCO: Maria Benitez, Carlos Sanchez (guitar), El Pelete (singer) performing "Asturias" (Albeniz, Benitez), "Alegrias" (Traditional, Benitez)

2ND CENTURY DANCE THEATRE: Rodney Pridgen, David Gibson, George Giraldo, Joseph Pugliese, Clare Culhane, Anita Ehrler, Linda Haberman, Nancy Stewart, performing the *World Premiere* of "The Villain" (Crown Heights Affair, Ronn Forella)

Paul Russell, Lydia Abarca in "Romeo and Juliet"
(Martha Swope Photo)

Top: Chiang Ching, Chih-Ming Lu (R) Sounds in Motion in "Memories"

Above: Tamara Karpova *(John L. Murphy Photo)*

THE YARD
Chilmark, Massachusetts
July 12–August 29, 1975

Director, Patricia N. Woolner; Assistant Director, Jack Moore; Administrator, Robert Van Cleave; Consultant, Mildred Dunnock

Saturday, July 12, 1975

"Tribute to Isadora Duncan" (Chopin, reconstructed by Sincha Hong) performed by Valerie Bergman, Judith Feldman, Sincha Hong, Lisa Kraus, Claire Millardi, Lisa Nalven, Madeleine Perrone, Jan Wodynski, Patricia Yenawine

"Dandelion Garden" (Tomita, Jack Moore) danced by Bill Bass, Bill Holcomb, Sincha Hong, Bill Kirkpatrick, Lisa Kraus, David Malamut, Lisa Nalven, Madeleine Perrone

Thursday & Friday, July 24, 25, 1975

"Palette Cycle" (George Crumb/Caroline Worthington) performed by Valerie Bergman, Judith Feldman, Bill Holcomb, Sincha Hong, Bill Kirkpatrick, Patricia Yenawine, David Malamut, Erin Martin

Thursday & Friday, July 31, August 1, 1975

"Yardwork #1" (Collage, Claire Mallardi) performed by Valerie Bergman, Madeleine Perrone, Judy Feldman, Bill Bass, David Malamut; "Five by Two" (Sin Cha Hong) performed by Lisa Kraus, Bill Holcomb; "Dry Run" (Evelyn DeBoeck, Jack Moore) performed by Sin Cha Hong, Lisa Kraus, Erin Martin, Bill Bass, David Malamut; "Retainer" (Robert DeVoe) choreographed and performed by Bill Kirkpatrick; "Finale" (Keith Jarrett, Jan Wodynski) performed by Valerie Bergman, Judy Feldman, Lisa Nalven, Madeleine Perrone, Patricia Yenawine, Bill Bass, Bill Holcomb, Bill Kirkpatrick, David Malamut

Monday, August 18, 1975

"Yeast" (Keith Jarrett, Jan Wodynski) with Bill Bass, Valerie Bergman, Judy Feldman, Bill Holcomb, David Malamut, Patricia Yenawine; "Refractory" (Alice Cohen, Jan Wodynski) with Malvina Golden, Lisa Kraus, Francine Piggott, Holly Schiffer, Debbie Teller

Sunday, August 24, 1975

"Here Is Now" (Herbie Mann/Usef Lateef/Herbie Hancock, Patricia N. Woolner) performed by Daryl Knight, Carol Magee, Judy Kranz, Margaret Knight, Margaret Koski, Linda Glyman, Bill Holcomb, Linda Tarnay

Thursday & Friday, August 28–29, 1975

"Legacy–Noun/Feminine" (Schutz/Hindemith/Shostakovich/Alcantara/Stravinsky, Erin Martin) with Valerie Bergman, Alice Cohen, Francine Piggott, Holly Schiffer, Linda Tarnay; "Solo" choreographed and performed by David Malamut; "You Can't Eat It All" choreographed and performed by Lisa Kraus, David Malamut; "Rubber Shoes" (The Beatles/Vivaldi/Bach, Valerie Bergman) with Bill Bass, David Malamut, Francine Piggott, Holly Schiffer, Patricia Yenawine; "Jack and Jill" (Haydn, Linda Tarney) danced by Lisa Kraus, Bill Bass

**Top Right: Francis Piggot, Holly Schiffer,
Linda Tarnay in "Legacy—Noun/Feminine"**
(M. Zide Photo)

Linda Tarnay in "Here Is Now"

Bill Bass, Erin Martin in "Dry Run"

133

REGIONAL AND PROFESSIONAL DANCE COMPANIES
(Failure to meet deadline necessitated several omissions)

ALBERTA CONTEMPORARY DANCE THEATRE
Edmonton, Alberta, Canada

Artistic Directors, Jacqueline Ogg, Charlene Tarver; Managing Director, Ronald Holgerson; Technical Director, Colin Reese; Costume Mistress, Wendy Albrecht; Lighting, Colin Reese; Guest Choreographers, Iris Garland, Wallace Seibert, Sherrie Waggener, Bonnie Giese, Ronald Holgerson; Guest Designers, John Madill, Sean Wager, Pat Galbraith

COMPANY

Bonnie Giese, Littie Schroen, Maureen Herman, Sherrie Waggener, Robert Fleming, Ronald Holgerson, Oscar Riley, and apprentices Dan Damman, David Wensel, Janie Achtemichuk

REPERTOIRE

"Circles of Silence" (Malcolm Forsyth, Jacqueline Ogg), "Pendulum of the Mind" (Ravi Shankar, Charlene Tarver), and *PREMIERES* of "Untitled" (silent, Bonnie Giese), "The Weavers" (Paul Horn, Sherrie Waggener), "Verdict: Death by Famine" (Michael Oldfield, Ronald Holgerson), " 'Twas Mercy Brought Her?" (Charles Ives/African traditional, Ogg), "Snowflakes Are Dancing" (Debussy, Ogg), "Dans Cette Etable" (traditional French, Ogg), "23 Skiddoo" ('20's medley, Iris Garland), "Spiral Vortex" (Oliver Messiaen, Ogg), "From the Major Arcana" (John Mills-Cockell, Ogg), "Islands of Infinity" (Paul Horn, Charlene Tarver), "Moods II" (medly of jazz, Wallace Seibert), "There's Nothing to Say" (silent, Waggener)

Glenn Tooke Photo

ALICE TEIRSTEIN DANCE COMPANY
New Rochelle, N.Y.

Artistic Director-Choreographer, Alice Teirstein; Music, Earle Brown; Poetry, Miriam Solan

COMPANY

Art Bridgman	Ken Pierce
Anita Feldman	Marta Renzi
Kathy Kramer	Kathy Robens
Craig Sloane	

REPERTOIRE: "Nexus"

Lois Greenfield Photo

Alberta Contemporary Dance Theatre's "Vortex"

ANN ARBOR CIVIC BALLET
Ann Arbor, Michigan

Director, Sylvia Hamer; Co-Directors, Mary Jane Williams, Pamela Rutledge; Sets, Alan Peterson; Costumes, Esther Bissell; Wardrobe, Frances Cooper; Stage Manager, Jay King; Conductor, Edward Szabo; Guest Choreographers, Dom Orejudos, Alice Hinterman

COMPANY

PRINCIPALS AND SOLOISTS: Kathie Birchmieir, Sherry Fisher, Karen Aseltine, Patty Parkis, Caroline Billings, Zerrin Crippen, Jeff Miller, Steve Janick, Lee Ann Shankland, Marci Margeson, Kathryn Adams, Elaine Abbrecht, Sarah Crane, Carol Kiskitalo, Leslie Marich, Rebecca Nichols, Jan Nyquist, Melanie Siebert, Sue Ripple, TeDee Theofil, Barbara McGraw, Gwen Werner, Jennifer Wilkinson, Teresa Casey, Deborah Cooper, Lisa Pignanelli, Suzanne White, Tena Casey

GUEST ARTISTS: Dom Orejudos, Peggy Powell, Beth Fitts

REPERTOIRE

"Les Sylphides," "Eight to Eternity," "Orison," "Rodeo," and *Premieres* of "The Tin Soldier," "Babes in Toyland"

Ann Arbor Civic Ballet
(Van Dyck Dobos Photo)

134

THE ATLANTA BALLET
Atlanta, Georgia

Founder-Consultant, Dorothy Alexander; Artistic Director, Robert Barnett; Associate Directors, Merrilee Smith, Joanne Lee, Tom Pazik; Choreographers, Robert Barnett, Tom Pazik, Conrad Ludlow, Stanley Zompakos, Todd Bolender, Norbert Vesak, Ginger Prince Hall, Saeko Ichinohe; Conductor, John Head; Lighting, Charles Fischl; Executive Assistant, Linda C. Fischl; Costumes, Tom Pazik; Stage Managers, Lee Betts, Jeff Key; Press, Kathy Monahan; General Manager, Charles Fischl

COMPANY

PRINCIPALS: Rose Barile, Merry Clark, Amy Danis, Kathry McBerth, Joanne McKinney, Ellen Richards, Ben Hazard, Ronald Jones, Tom Pazik, Patrick Stines

CORPS: Lor Black, Nancy Boggs, Kristi Brininger, Becky Bryan, Victoria Cabrera, Martha Clarke, Nanette Clem, Lisa Davidson, Mary Linn Durbin, Joan Dvorscak, Caroline Fenlon, Lorenne Fey, Debby Goldberg, Fran Gould, Mary Gould, Julie Gresham, Sarah Harrell, Kandy Hodges, Belinda Holt, Celeste Jabczenski, Michele Laboureur, Brenda Monroe, Caron Osborn, Linda Pretz, Elise Rawson, Helene Richon, Lisa Riggs, Margaret Saunders, Caroline Spears, Elaine Wadsworth, Leslie Weiner, Gil Boggs, Patrick Brown, James Lee

GUEST ARTIST: Burton Taylor

REPERTOIRE

"Giselle Peasant pas de Deux" (Adam, Blair), "Gift to Be Simple" (Traditional, Vesak), "Lifeline '73" (Husa, Hall), "Minkus Pas de Trois" (Minkus, Balanchine), "Don Quixote Pas de Deux" (Minkus, Traditional), "Heloise and Abelard" (Suk, Ratcliff), "Cry without a Sound" (Brel/Hollander, Pazik), "Nutcracker Grand Pas de Deux" (Tchaikovsky, Balanchine), "The Good Morrow" (Mahler, Vesak), "Glinkadances" (Glinka, Barnett), "Great Scot" (Joplin, Pazik), "Still Point" (Debussy, Bolender), "Peasant Dancers" (Adam, Barnett), "Black Swan" (Tchaikovsky, Cranko), "Pas de Quatre" (Pugni, Dolin), "Nutcracker" (Tchaikovsky, Balanchine), "Giselle" (Adam, Blair), "Serenade" (Tchaikovsky, Balanchine)

PREMIERES: "Peter and the Wolf" (Prokofiev, Pazik), "Lumenesque" (Saint-Saens, Barnett), "Rococo" (Mozart, Zompakos), "L'Histoire de Soldat" (Stravinsky, Ludlow), "Circles" (Berio, Ichinohe)

**Right: Ben Hazard, Rose Barile in "Great Scott";
Kathryn McBeth, Ronald Jones in "Don Quixote"
Above: Tom Pazik, Amy Danis in "The Good Morrow"
Top: "Gift to Be Simple"**

Atlantic Dance Company in "Peter and the Wolf"

ATLANTIC DANCE COMPANY
New Smyrna Beach, Florida

Artistic Director, Jean Tepsic; Associate Directors, Mary W. Hall, Marjorie C. Tepsic; Technical Director, Jacqueline Gorman; Press, Ellen Page

COMPANY

PRINCIPALS: Elizabeth Elmquist, Jean Tepsic

CORPS: Dianne Downing, Deborah Moss, Aleta Rush, Kathy Blais, Katherine Pieters, Lynn Lauretta, Earl Dryden, John Pieters, Dan Casale

GUEST ARTISTS: Sari Newell, Richard Pulley, Rusti Brandman, Cheryl Wright, David Ross

REPERTOIRE

"Peter and the Wolf" (Prokofiev, Tepsic), "Renaissance Dances" (Traditional, Tepsic), "Courant" (Haydn, Tepsic), "4 X 6" (K. C. and the Sunshine Band, Tepsic)

Augusta Ballet

AUSTIN BALLET THEATRE

Austin, Texas

Artistic Director, Stanley Hall; Director, Judy Thompson; Costumes, Marguerite Wright, Mary Alice Ziegler, Liz Cameron; Lights, Peter McKinnon; Sound, Lee Thompson; Stage Manager, Mark Loeffler; Programs, Kate Berquist; Press, Michie Ward, Betty Adams

COMPANY

Brantley Bright, Terri Lynn Wright, Judy Thompson, Shelly Schleier, Lisa Frantz, Lisa Smith, Mary Claire Ziegler, Gina Adams, Bonnie Bratton, Nora Byrd, Susan Grubbs, Adriana Guajardo, Arletta Howard, Lea Johnson, Eve Larson, Lynda Lindsay, Lucy Nagle, Norma Shim, Rosemary Thomas, Lucia Uhl, Michie Ward, Steve Brule, Victor Culver, Byron Johnson, Ken Owen, George Stallings, Roberto Adams, Doug Becker, Brian Bullard, Russell Easley, Clint Fisher, James Haile, William Haile, Clark Johnston, Dave Larson

REPERTOIRE

"Rosenkavalier Waltz" (Strauss, Hall), "Rites of Joseph Byrd" (Byrd, Hall), "Tchaikovsky Suite" (Tchaikovsky, Hall), "Le Corsaire Pas de Deux" (Drigo, Traditional), "Concerto" (Tchaikovsky, Hall), "Le Combat" (Khatchaturian, Hall), "Tregonell" (Goldsmith, Hall), "Centennial Rags" (Hall), "Larks Tongue in Aspic" (King Crimson, Hall), "Aurora's Wedding" (Tchaikovsky, Hall), "Flickers" (Hall)

PREMIERES: "Graduation Ball" (Strauss, Stanley Hall), "Don Quixote Pas de Deux" (Minkies-Lanchbery, Traditional), "Vepres Siciliennes" (Verdi, Hall), "Snowflakes Are Dancing" (Debussy, Hall)

Carolyn Hubner in Austin Civic Ballet's "The Nutcracker"
also Right Center *(Bill Records Photo)*

AUGUSTA BALLET COMPANY

Augusta, Georgia

Artistic Director, Ron Colton; Assistant to Director, Zanne Beaufort; Production Manager, Jim Thomas; Wardrobe, Dot Bowers; Press, Suzanne Beaufort; President, Jane Cross

COMPANY

PRINCIPALS: Zanne Beaufort, Cammy Fisher, Catherine Harvir, Melinda Jordan, Renee Williams

CORPS: Kelly Bowers, Lil Easterlin, Jenny Elkins, Terri Levy, Jul Rece, Ann Sussman, Bet Willingham, Linda Woodward

GUEST ARTISTS: Patsy Adair, Ronald Jones, Tom Pazik

REPERTOIRE

"Nutcracker" (Tchaikovsky, Barnett after Balanchine), "Design" (Varese, Colton), "Love Song" (Suk, Noble), "Symphony 13" (Haydn, Noble), "Symphony in D" (Mozart, Zompakos), "Dans L Bois" (Ibert, Zompakos), "Mystere" (Albinoni, Noble), "Trio" (Mozart, Zompakos), "Peter and the Wolf" (Prokofiev, Colton), "Reflections with Voice" (Stockhausen, Colton), "The Rookery" (Zank Husa, Hall), "Brandenburg Movement" (Bach, Zompakos), "Minkus Pas de Trois" (Minkus, Balanchine), "Poems" (Ravel, Colton), "Classical Gas" (Williams, Colton), "Pictures at an Exhibition" (Prokofiev, Carlson), "Pageant" (Moore, Colton)

PREMIERES: "Bagatelles" (Tcheripnin, Zompakos), "Broadway Dream" (Hart, Adair), "Heads and Tails" (Alpert, Adair)

Lee Downing Photo

AUSTIN CIVIC BALLET

Austin, Texas

Directors, Eugene Slavin, Alexandra Nadal; Conductors, Kelly Hale; Sets, Marjorie Kuehne, Hugo Kuehne; Costumes, Alice McKenna, Betty Milstead; Lighting, Eugene Slavin; Stage Manager, Kay Hankinson; Press, Bill Parsons

COMPANY

Christine Aiello, Betsy Blitch, Isabel Clark, Suzanne Diercks, Michelle Dugi, Rona Ebert, Carol Elskes, Laura Gannon, Kathy Golden, Carolyn Hubner, Lisa Joiner, Charisse Kennison, Kimberly LaGrone, Catherine Leon, Joyce Lowe, Shelley Meadows, Debbie Milstead, Teresa Nation, Hilary Yarrington, Steve Barton, Kirk Broaddus, Chip Dameron, Scott Meynig, Gregory Easley, Tom Harrison, Marc Hughes, David Sanders, Tim Spragens, David Strother, Curt Wright

GUEST ARTISTS: Violette Verdy, Edward Villella

REPERTOIRE

"La Fille Mal Gardee" (Hertel, Igor Youskevitch), "Swan Lake, Act II" (Tchaikovsky, Slavin), "Raymonda, Act III" (Glaounov, Slavin), "Nutcracker" (Tchaikovsky, Slavin), "Helios" (Nielson, Slavin), "Bolero" (Ravel, Slavin), "Cherkeska" (Khachaturian, Slavin), "Scherzo Italiano" (Gottschalk, Slavin), *PREMIERE* of "Minkus Variations" (Minkus, Eugene Slavin)

BALLET PACIFICA

Laguna Beach, California

Founder-Artistic Director, Lila Zali; Artistic Adviser, Michel Panaieff; General Director, Douglas Reeve; Press, Sally Reeve; Ballet Mistress, Kathy Jo Kahn; Technical Director, Carl W. Callaway; Wardrobe Mistress, Myrth Malaby; Coordinator, Elizabeth W. Townsend; Choreographers, Kathy Jo Kahn, Carrie Kneubuhl, David Lichine, Victor Moreno, Michel Panaieff, Benjamin Sperber, Lila Zali; Sets, Tania Barton; Costumes, Tania Barton, Lila Zali; Lighting, Zachary Malaby, David Challis, Todd Elvins, Darci Linke, Mike Modiano

COMPANY

PRINCIPALS: Louis Carver, Roger Faubel, Louise Frazer, Kathy Jo Kahn, Carrie Kneubuhl, Molly Lynch, Paul Maure, Victor Moreno, David Panaieff, Lisa Robertson, Kristi Stephens, Cynthia Tosh

SOLOISTS: Randy Barnett, Charles Colgan, Jennifer Engle, Billie Pulliam, Sandra Rasmussen, Belinda Smith, Glenn Smith, Elizabeth Snyder, David Tygard

CORPS: Julie Bradley, Allison Bryant, Dee Dee Bychak, Terri Bychak, Andrea Daywalt, Heidi Edgren, Eve Henderson, Kathy Hunter, John Land, Kelly Meadows, Roma Meyer, Cynthia Miller, Lori Miller, Christine Rasmussen, Phyllis Schneider, Lisa Stolzy, Nancy Sutton, Tricia Toliver, Arabella Wibberley

REPERTOIRE

"Be-Bop Beach" (Shank, Sperber), "Black Swan Pas de Deux" (Tchaikovsky, after Ivanov), "Carmina Burana" (Orff, Zali), "Carnival of the Animals" (Saint-Saens, Kahn), "La Danse et la Musique" (Chopin, Panaieff), "Moldavian Dances" (Traditional, Moreno), "Peter and the Wolf" (Prokofiev, Zali), "Snow White and the Seven Dwarfs" (Compiled, Kneubuhl), "Space Race" (Preston, Kneubuhl), "Swan Lake Act II" (Tchaikovsky, after Ivanov), "Nutcracker" (Tchaikovsky, Zali), "The Seasons" (Glazounov, Panaieff), "Two Plus Three" (Bach, Zali), "Variations on a Theme by Haydn" (Brahms, Zali)

PREMIERES: "Coppelia" (Delibes, Panaieff), "Danse Classique" (Glinka, Panaieff), "Encounter Near Venus" (Wibberly-Russell, Zali), "Le Corsaire Pas de Deux" (Drigo, after Petipa), "Paquita" (Minkus, Moreno)

Ballet Repertory Company's
"Hanson Piano Concerto"

BALLET DES JEUNES

Merchantville, N.J.

Artistic Director-Choreographer, Ursula Melita; Choreographers, Ruth Skaller, Carmencita Lopez, Andrea Handler; Stage Director, George Landers; Costumes, Sherry Bazell; Pianist, Irene Andrews; Press, Lynn Vlaskamp, Jeanne O'Hara

COMPANY

Cindy Alberts, Myra Bazell, Ann Marie Bright, Kathleen Bright, Esther Cohen, Claudia Collings, Maria DeRosa, Amelia DeRosa, Lisa DiGiacomo, Joy Edelman, Andrea Elsner, Kim Forlini, Carolyn Franzen, Kathy Fuzer, Amanda Gamel, Terry Howell, Marina Iossifides, Sally Jackson, Sarah Jones, Sheila Jones, Shelly Gregory, Caroline Krakower, Diane Landers, Debbie Lang, Ginny Magee, Linda Marchione, Kathy Miller, Marylin Morris, Connie O'Hara, Debbi O'Hara, Gina Papatto, Linda Pfrommer, Jackie Reisman, Amy Orloff, Lisa Robbins, Holly Ruckdeschel, Carol Rubin, Debbie Saldana, Karen Schussler, Maryann Sinnott, Donna Tambussi, Marianne Trombetta, Renee Vekkos, Douglas Vlaskamp, Christine Vlaskamp, Evelyn Wang, Lisa Weinstein, Amy Wilen, Michele Wood, Anita Zypilli

REPERTOIRE

"Sorcerer's Apprentice" (Dukas), "Snow Queen" (Mayer), "Three Cornered Hat" (DeFalla), "Hoe Down" (Coplan), "Search for Spring" (Shostakovich), "Suite of Spanish Dances" (Folk), "Slavonic Dances" (Dvorak), "The Beauty of Dance and the Joy of Dance" (Chopin), "Serenade" (Mozart), "Hello World" (Mayer), "Exhibition of Degas Paintings" (Chopin), "Romanian Rhapsody" (Enesco), *PREMIERE* of "Glimpses of Art, 1776–1976" (Ronald Brown, Ursula Melita)

Dorothy Jackson Photo

Top Left: Sally Jackson

Ballet Pacifica in "Paquita"
(Rick Lang Photo)

BALLET REPERTORY COMPANY

New York, N.Y.

Director-Choreographer, Richard Englund; Company Manager, Robert Yesselman; Assistant to Director, Robin Woodward; Ballet Mistress, Joysanne Sidimus; Rehearsal Coach, Gage Bush; Stage Manager, Rosemary Cunningham; Lighting, Michael Piotrowski, Tony Tucci; Wardrobe Supervisors, Harriet Wallerstein, Natalie Garfinkle; Accompanist-Musical Consultant, Daniel Waite; Guest Teacher, Jeremy Blanton

COMPANY

David Cuevas, Rebecca Drenick, Ellen English, Peter Fonseca, Cynthia Gast, Lynn Huck, Jeffrey Jones, Lisa Lockwood, Linda Marx, Richard Prewitt, Cindy Reid, Anthony Sheldon, Carole Valleskey

REPERTOIRE

"Icarus" (Matsushita, Hoving), "Bournonville Divertissement" (Helsted/Gade/Paulli, Bournonville), "Spring Waters" (Rachmaninoff, Messerer), "Crazy Quilt" (Copland, Englund), "Le Corsaire Pas de Deux" (Drigo, Petipa),

PREMIERES: "Hanson Piano Concerto" (Hanson, Haigen), "Aeolian Passage" (Rachmaninoff, Englund), "Haiku Images" (Hovhaness, Englund)

Susan Cook Photos

BALLET ROYAL
Winter Park, Florida

Artistic Director-Choreographer, Edith Royal; Business Manager, Bill Royal; Designer, Phyllis Watson; Assistant Director, Carol Willson; Associate Director, Jack Everidge

COMPANY

Dawn Barker, William Bartlett, Cathy Behnke, Jane Bilven, Sharal Brown, Kim Bruce, Cindy Bryant, Elaine Chambers, Benita Cherry, Angel Casteleiro, Keith Coburn, Walty Davies, Susie Ellis, Neill Foshee, Tracy Goodson, Robin Grant, Caryl Howe, Pamela Jenkins, Carol Ann Karas, Jan Koshar, Teegie Lehmann, LuAnn Leonard, Lisa Lynn Lewenthal, Susie Lyle, Mickey Mance, Cindi Maxwell, Heidi Nelson, Luis Perez, Anita Phillips, Deanna Pitman, Brian Price, Lynne Rader, Cindy Ratcliffe Lisa Siegfried, Shelly Segrest, Dena Snider, Rhonda Sward, Jeanne Thiele, Jan Walker, Sharon Will, Trisha Will, Debbie Young

GUEST ARTISTS: Carol Willson, Michael Hall

REPERTOIRE

"Nutcracker" (Tchaikovsky, Edith Royal), "Swan Lake Act II" (Tchaikovsky, Thomas Armour), "That's How It Was 200 Years Ago" (Sherman Edwards, Carol Willson), "Variations from Day to Day" (Brahms, Norman Walker), "Stop Look and Listen" (Kraftwerk, Carol Willson), "The Village" (Egnos, Ron Daniels)

PREMIERES: "That's How It Was," "Stop Look and Listen," "The Village"

William Grover Photo

Top Right: Ballet Royal's "Song of the Wind"

Ballet Tacoma's "Roanoke River 1865"

BALLET TACOMA
Tacoma, Washington

Director-Choreographer, Jan Collum; Costume Designer, Judy Loiland; Decor, Paul Van Griffen; Press, Lois Hampson

COMPANY

Jolene Chaney, Cassandra Crowley, Immaculada Dodd, Deidre Gimlett, Valli Hale, Leslie Hull, Robyn Jones, Janet Kinsman, Lorna Newton, Maren Palmquist, Debbie Ramsey, Patty Shippy, Debbie Griffin, Lynn Jacobson, Monica Tarpenning, David Hitchcock, Hunter Hale, Michael Crouch, Russ Millar, Ed Staver, Charles Talamantes, Jim Williams

REPERTOIRE

"Le Lac Quiet" (Debussy, Collum), "Roanoke River 1865" (Buffy Sainte-Marie/Traditional, Charles Bennett), "Gracchus" (Stravinsky, Hunter Hale), "Cycle" (Lubos Fiser, Nelle Fisher) PREMIERES: "Magnificat" (Vivaldi, Jan Collum), "Almost Red, White and Blue" (Arif Mardin, Michael Kane), "Bailes de Fiesta" (DeFalla, Collum)

BALLET WESTERN RESERVE
Youngstown, Ohio

Director, Michael Falotico; Choreographers, Michael Falotico, Marilyn Jones, Edward Myers, Michael Mears; Conductors, Franz Bibo, C. Watson; Sets, Paul Kimpel, Robert Elden, Richard Gullickson, Galen Elser; Costumes, Robert Elden, Georgann Sherwood, Marilyn Jones, Bruce Mac, Roberta Johnson, Nancy Scott, Priscilla Taylor; Lighting, Kenneth Lowther; Stage Manager, Galen Elser; Press, Friedman and Associates; Business Manager, Catherine McPhee; Executive Producers, Harriet S. Dabney, Youngstown Ballet Guild

COMPANY

PRINCIPALS: Amy Taylor, Robin Miller, Robert Tupper, Michael Mears, James Russell Vogler

SOLOISTS: Nancy Tiberio, Lenore Pershing, Lisa Devine, Beth Rollinson, Suzanne Swan, Cathy Amendolara, Edward Patuto

CORPS: Laura Lou Anderson, Lisa Bannon, Elizabeth Dory, Marisa Manolukas, Gina Gangale, Holly Weibel

GUEST ARTISTS: Diana Byer, Edward Henkle, Leigh Ann Hudacek, Rachel List, Jose Mateo, Michael Tipton

REPERTOIRE

"End of the Morning" (Contemporary, Jones), "Rustic Variations" (Adam Falotico), "G & S for 8 + 2" (Sullivan, Falotico), "Giselle Act II" (Adam, Myers), "Nutcracker" (Tchaikovsky, Falotico), "Les Rendez-Vous" (Glazounov, Falotico), "Faschings Terzert" (Beethoven, Falotico), "Mindscape" (Contemporary, Jones), "Scott Joplin Gaieties" (Joplin, Falotico), "The Witching" (Moffatt, Falotico), "Grand Faux Pas de Deux" (Arr. Lanchbery, Falotico), "Peter and the Wolf" (Prokofiev, Falotico)

PREMIERES: "Romeo and Juliet Balcony Scene" (Prokofiev, Falotico), "Side Show" (Abramson, Falotico), "Masque" (Sessions, Falotico), "Navarra" (Minkus, Falotico), "Emily" (Dello Joio, Falotico), "TKO" (Mears)

Ballet Western Reserve's "Emily"

BALLET WEST

Salt Lake City, Utah

Artistic Director, Willam Christensen; Ballet Mistress, Sondra Sugai; Conductor, Ardean Watts; Musical Director, Ronald Mead Horton; Stage Manager, David K. Barber; Associate Production Manager-Lighting Designer, Greg Geilmann; Executive Vice President-General Manager, Robert V. Brickell; Company Manager, Steven H. Horton; Administrative Assistant-Company Manager, John V. Rettie; Press, Susan Gilbert

COMPANY

PRINCIPALS: Bruce Caldwell, Suzanne Erlon, Charles Fuller, Philip Fuller, John Hiatt, Victoria Morgan, Michael Onstad, Catherine Scott, Cynthia Young

SOLOISTS: Connie Burton, Vivien Cockburn, Christopher Fair, Frank Hay, Francine Kessler, Sharee Lane, Richard Lohr, Leonore Maez, Elizabeth Nesi, Clark Reid, Tenley Taylor, Michele White, Cheryl Yeager, Derryl Yeager

CORPS: Corey Farris, Linda Gudmundson, Tauna Hunter, Catherine Buzard, Kim Colosimo. Lynn Connolly, Diane Jenkins, Lesley Radoff, James Beaumont, Keith Kimmel, Karen Kuhn, Carole Ann Ramme, Nancy Clarke, Mark Lanham, Pamela Lehan, Leslie Lindstrom, Ann Morgan, Elizabeth Selz

REPERTOIRE

"Carmina Burana" (Carl Orff, John Butler), "The Nutcracker" (Tchaikovsky, William Christensen), "Serenade" (Tchaikovsky, George Balanchine), "Cinderella" (Prokofiev, William Christensen) PREMIERES: "Knoxville: Summer of 1915" (Samuel Barber, Bruce Caldwell), "Grand Pas de Deux from Don Quixote" (Nabokov, Bruce Marks after Petipa), "Don Juan" (Richard Strauss, Bruce Marks)

Vinnie Fish Photos

Right: "Serenade" Above: Vivien Cockburn, Michael Onstad in "The Nutcracker" Top: Catherine Scott in "Carmina Burana"

Michael Onstad, Suzanne Erlon in "Don Juan"

Elizabeth Nesi, Bruce Caldwell in "Carmina Burana"

BARTA BALLET
Rochester, N.Y.

Director-Choreographer, Karoly Barta; Costumes, Marcella Corvino; Lighting-Stage Manager, Ed Goetz

COMPANY

Tricia Allen, Mandy Bennett, Sharon Benny, Lisa Bouley, Wendy Brimstein, Heide Brunner, Kelly Cass, Chasey Clifford, Leslie Clirford, Tracy Coniglio, Debbie Deck, Ann Gaffney, Bonnie Garcia, Kathy Maher, Ann Mario, Tricia May, Beth Nackley, Karen O'-Keefe, Laura Oliver, Joanne Radomski, Carol Ralston, Linda Ralston, Lori Scarfarotti, Susan Scoville, Annette Van Slyke, Becky Soggs, Marty Soggs, Emily Taylor, Lynn Vance, Maia Wechsler, Amy Wilkin, Rose Marie Wurzer, Carl Askew, Leonard Askew, Marvin Askew, Peter Frame, Russell McKinnon, Karl Singletary

GUEST ARTISTS: Sara Leland, Susan Pilarre, Robert Weiss

Costas Photo

Susan Pilarre, Robert Weiss in "The Nutcracker"

BELLA LEWITZKY DANCE COMPANY
Los Angeles, California

Artistic Director-Choreographer, Bella Lewitzky; Costume-Lighting Designer, Darlene Neel; Art Director, Cliff Nelson; Production Managers, Harry Donovan, Joseph Ayres, Keith Gonzales; Wardrobe Mistress, Patricia Cook; Electronic Engineer, Scott Duncan; Guest Scenic Designer, Newell Taylor Reynolds

COMPANY

Christopher Burnside, David Caley, Wanda Evans, Sean Greene, Robert Hughes, Loretta Livingston, Cynthia Penn, Iris Pell, Nora Reynolds, Serena Richardson, Kurt Weinheimer, Joy Hubbert

REPERTOIRE

"Bella and Brindle" (Reginald Smith-Brindle, Lewitzky), "Ceremony for Three" (Cara Bradbury Marcus, Lewitzky), "Five" (Max Lifchitz, Lewitzky), "Orrenda" (Marcus, Lewitzky), "Pietas" (Marcus, Lewitzky), "Spaces Between" (Marcus, Lewitzky), "Game Plan" (Lewitzky), "Kinaesonata" (Ginastera, Lewitzky), "On the Brink of Time" (Subotnick, Lewitzky), *PREMIERE* of "V.C.O. (Voltage Controlled Oscillator)" (Cara Bradbury Marcus, Bella Lewitzky)

Left Center: "Spaces Between"

BURLINGTON BALLET COMPANY
Rancocas, N.J.

Artistic Director-Choreographer, Joan K. Stebe; Business Manager-Lighting-Stage Manager, Linda McConnell; Costumes, Joan Orfe; Press, Arline Inman, Peggy Moran; Consultant, Jeffrey K. Lemke

COMPANY

PRINCIPALS: Linda McMenamin, Dawn Tocci, Julie Stebe, Susan Frantz, Mark Galante, Tom Cordenzio, Debbie Dutton, Kathleen Nelboeck, Richard Walker, Yvonne Cook, Steve Huber

CORPS: Tricia Smith, Laurie Yengo, Marci Shannon, Kathleen Stebe, Donna Davies, Margurite Shumate, Linda McConnell

GUEST ARTIST: Paul Klocke

REPERTOIRE

"Ballade" (Chopin), "Waltz Bouquet" (Chopin), "Parthenon" (Greek Music), "Nocturne" (Chopin), "Little Women" (Charles Ives), "Kinetic Anemone" (Gwendolyn Watson), "Homespun Gathering" (Traditional), "Love's Dream" (Liszt), and *PREMIERES* of "Concerto" (Tchaikovsky), "Burlington Mosaic" (Debussy), "Vignette" (Selected). All choreography by Joan K. Stebe

Linda McConnell Photo

Burlington Ballet's "Little Women"

BOSTON BALLET

Boston, Massachusetts

Artistic Director, E. Virginia Williams; Conductor, Michel Sasson; Ballet Master, Lorenzo Monreal; Regiseusse, Ellen O'Reilly; Lighting, Thomas Skelton; Stage Manager, Aloysius Petruccelli; General Manager, Michael B. Judson; Administrative Director, Richard J. King; Press, Rosemary Polito, Brenn Stilley; Executive Director, Ruth G. Harrington; Ballet Mistress, Sydney Leonard; Wardrobe, Penelope Gardner

COMPANY

Elaine Bauer, Anamarie Sarazin, Laura Young, David Brown, James Capp, Tony Catanzaro, Ron Cunningham, James Dunne, Woytek Lowski, David Drummond, Mark Johnson, Augustus Van Heerden. Durine Alinova, Kathryn Anderson, Carinne Binda, Emmanuelle Davis, Kaethe Devlin, Robin Lyon, Patrick McDonald, Debra Mili, Stephanie Moy, Deirdre Myles, Clyde Nantais, Larry Robertson, Darryl Robinson, Pamela Royal, Judith Shoaff, Kitty Warren, Rachel Whitman, Alexandra Williams, Annabel Winston, Leslie Woodies

REPERTOIRE

"Les Sylphides" (Chopin, Michel Fokine), "Melodie" (Tchaikovsky, Frank Ohman), "Les Corsaire Pas de Deux" (Drigo, after Petipa), *WORLD PREMIERES* of "Carmina Burana" (Carl Orff, Lorenzo Monreal), "Hansel and Gretel" (Englebert Humperdinck, Ron Cunningham)

Right: "Les Sylphides" Top: "Hansel and Gretel"
(Ron Reagan Photos)

Laura Young, Tony Catanzaro

"Road of the Phoebe Snow" Above: "Melodie"

Douglas Hevenor, Marlene Jones and
California Ballet Company in "The Nutcracker"

Charleston Ballet's "Concerto in F"

Charleston Ballet Company

CALIFORNIA BALLET COMPANY
San Diego, California

Artistic Director-Choreographer, Maxine Mahon; General Direc
tor, Robert G. Mahon; Administrative Assistants, Geraldine E
Rogers, Gregory B. Smith; Conductor, David Hubler; Ballet Mis
tress, Linda Click; Technical Director-Lighting Design, Dea
Krause; Wardrobe, Flora Jennings, Ruth Small; Artistic Advisers
Charles Bennett, John Hart, David Ward-Steinman; Press, Rober
Mahon, Greg Smith; General Production Chairman, Richard Rum
ney

COMPANY

PRINCIPALS AND SOLOISTS: Marlene Jones, Douglas Hevenor
Robin Briceno, James Francis, Jeri Jones, Eugenia Keefer, Uch
Sugiyama

CORPS: Frank Doyle, Patrick Nollett, Linda Click, Cheryl Her
rington, Kevin Linker, Greg Smith, Susan Kroll, Michael Melcher
Tom Ashworth, Adriel Frumin, Nikki Adamo, Kathy Auten, Lorr
Grindle, Pamela Long, Laura Bail, Arturo Fernandez

REPERTOIRE

"Adagio" (Albinoni, Bennett), "Aurora's Pas de Deux" (Tchai
kovsky, after Petipa), "Bicycling Belle" (Poulenc, Deakin), "Black
Swan Pas de Deux" and "Blue Bird Pas de Deux" (Tchaikovsky
Petipa), "Cerements" (Miller, Turner), "Configuration on a Cloud"
(Brahms, Mahon), "Coppelia" (Delibes, Mahon), "Corsaire Pas d
Deux" (Drigo, Mazillier), "Courtrigues" (Britten, Turner), "Do
Quixote Pas de Deux" (Minkus, Petipa), "Fran Pas de Trois" (Doni
zetti, Mahon), "Harlequin and Columbine" (Drigo, Volinine), "In
terlude" (Copland, Weikel), "Jazz Rock" (Various, Sugiyama), "Le
Sylphides" (Chopin, Fokine), "Love, the Painter" (Mozart, Turner)
"Man, the Animal" (Various, Sorrell/Hansen/Hevenor), "Nut
cracker" (Tchaikovsky, Mahon), "Peasant Pas de Deux" (Adam
Perrot), "Pyramids" (Hindemuth, Turner), "Raymonda Variations"
(Glazounov, Mahon), "The Seasons" (Glazounov, Mahon), "Spin
ning Wild Rainbows" (Franklin, Turner)

THE CHARLESTON BALLET
Charleston, West Virginia

Director-Choreographer, Andre Van Damm; Stage Director
Strauss Wolfe; Lighting Designer, William Lutman; President, Dr
Arnold C. Burke; Costumes and Sets, Maggy Van Damme, A
Benoni
SOLOISTS: Jennifer Britton, Kim Pauley, Kathleen Rhodes, Ju
lianne Kemp, Nor Brunschwyler

REPERTOIRE

All Premieres: "Classica" (Francois Joseph Fetis, Andre Va
Damme), "Pavane pour une Infante Defunte" (Ravel, Van Damme)
"The Red Death" (Francois Joseph Gossec, Van Damme), "Rhap
sody in Blue" (George Gershwin, Van Damme), "Concerto in F"
(Gershwin, Van Damme)

CHARLESTON BALLET COMPANY
Charleston, S.C.

Directors, Don Cantwell, Robert Ivey; Sets and Costumes, Rober
Ivey, Don Cantwell, Ray Goodbred, Gail Shoudy, Toni Hall, Mrs
G. W. Chavous, James N. Sellers, Jr.

COMPANY

Ann Osborne, Geormine Stanyard, Debbie Horton, Lee Brunner
Gina Farrar, Kris Pierce, Camilla Tezza, Ann Bacot Igoe, Evelyr
Johnson, Lisa Moseley, Debbie Wolf, Vanessa Perot, Patricia
Strang, Louise Hall, Justin Geilfuss, Anita Lane, Mary McKeever
Christine Cantwell, Chris Harrelson, Merran Funderburg

REPERTOIRE

"The Emperor's New Clothes" (Nicode/Tchaikovsky, Don Cant
well), "Capriol Suite" (Warlock, Cantwell), "Cry Witch" (Thomp
son, Robert Ivey), and PREMIERES of "A Ceremony of Carols"
(Benjamin Britten, Robert Ivey), "A Choice of Darkness" (Gar
MacFarland, Lee Brunner), "The Lesson" (Russel Wragg, Ivey)
"Summernight Waltz" (Stephen Sondheim, Ivey), "In Exile" (Ben
jamin Britten, Ivey), "Picnic at Charlestowne" (Dimitri Shos
takovich, Don Cantwell), "Capriccio" (Franz von Suppe, Cantwell)
"Street Games" (Shostakovich, Ivey)

Bill Buggel Photo

CINCINNATI BALLET COMPANY
Cincinnati, Ohio

Executive Artistic Director, David McLain; Assistant Artistic Director, David Blackburn; Music Director, Carmon DeLeone; Designer-Production Coordinator, Jay Depenbrock; General Manager, R. Dean Amos; Company Manager, Patricia C. Losey; Press, C. Jeannine Kagan

COMPANY

Charlotte Belchere, Paula Davis, Diane Edwards, Collene Giesting, Renee Hallman, Janice James, Karen Karibo, Patricia Kelly, Carol Krajacic, Sheila McAulay, Patricia Rozow, Alyce Taylor, Katherine Turner, Pam Willingham, Lynn Ferszt, Peggy Howard, Marcia Sells, Katherine Thompson, John Ashton, Ian Barrett, David Blackburn, Michael Bradshaw, Michael McClelland, John Nelson, Michael Rozow, James Exum, Patrick Hinson, Eric Johnston, Woodward Louden

REPERTOIRE

"Aubade" (Poulenc, Sabline), "The Beloved" (Hamilton, Truitt/-Horton), "Concerto" (Poulenc, McLain), "Concerto Barocco" (Bach, Balanchine), "Divertissement Classique" (Burgmuller, Jasinski), "Face of Violence (Horton/DeLeone, Horton/Truitte/-DeLavallade), "Firebird" (Stravinsky, Jasinski/Larkin), "Frevo" (DeLeone, Truitte/Horton), "Guernica" (DeLeone, Truitte), "Guitar Concerto" (Castelnuovo-Todesco, McLain), "Night Soliloquies" (Barlow/Rogers/Hanson, McLain), "Nutcracker" (Tchaikovsky, Franklin), "Pas de Quatre" (Ougni, Dolin/Markova), "Serenade" (Tchaikovsky, Balanchine), "Tribute to Jose Clemente Orozco" (Klaus, Truitte/Horton), "Winter's Traces" (Verdi, McLain)

PREMIERES: "Le Combat" (DeBanfield, Dollar), "Dear Friends and Gentle Hearts" (Foster/DeLeone/Proto, Saddler), "Pas de Dix" (Glazounov, Franklin), "With Timbrel and Dance Praise His Name" (Arr. DeLeone, Truitte)

Sandy Underwood Photo

Right: "Dear Friends and Gentle Hearts"
Top: "Le Combat"

Leigh Ann Hudacek,
Ian Horvath in Cleveland Ballet's "Ballet No. 2"

CLEVELAND BALLET
Cleveland, Ohio

Artistic Director, Ian Horvath; Associate Director, Dennis Nahat; General Manager, Gerald Ketelaar; Company Manager, Helen Horvath; Choreographers, Dennis Nahat, Ian Horvath, Charles Nicoll; Ballet Master, Charles Nicoll; Ballet Mistress, Pamela Pribisco; Costumes, Ginger Shane; Press, Nancy McArthur; Technical Director, John Rolland; Lighting, Richard Coumbs

COMPANY

Barbara Boyle, Mary Beth Cabana, Margaret Carlson, Anita Converse, Susan Diana, James Fatta, Michael Gleason, Joseph Glowik, Alice Holloway, Ian Horvath, Leigh Ann Hudacek, Geoffrey Kimbrough, Gallia Kuharsky, Dennis Nahat, Patrick Nalty, Ted Oetting, Lisa Powell, Pamela Pribisco, Regan Quick, Thomas Schmitz, Veronica Soliz, Lisa Villarini, David Wolfe

GUEST ARTIST: Cynthia Gregory

REPERTOIRE

"Laura's Women" (Nyro, Horvath), "Budwings" (Ravel, Horvath), "A Sparkin'" (Thomson, Nicoll), "Ballet No. 2" (Tchaikovsky, Nahat)

PREMIERES: "Grand Pas de Dix" (Glazounov, Nahat), "US" (Berlin/Dorsey/Guthrie/Norton/Winter, Nahat/Horvath), "Things Our Fathers Loved" (Ives, Nahat)

Louis Peres Photos

COLORADO CONCERT BALLET
Denver, Colorado

Executive-Artistic Directors, Lillian Covillo, Freidann Parker; Guest Choreographers, George Zoritch, Wilfred Schuman, Richard Denny; Producer, Henry E. Lowenstein; Technical Supervisor, Timothy L. Kelly; Designer, Bruce Jackson, Jr.; Stage Manager, Cory Wamser; Costumes, Nancy Yeager, Penelope Stames; Ballet Mistress, Laura Walker; Coordinator, Erica Nicholson

COMPANY

PRINCIPALS AND SOLOISTS: Laura Walker, Nancy Shadwell, Dede Nieto, Susie Spencer

CORPS: Carolyn Ash, Wendi Beckwitt, Cynthia Elsey, Mary Dee Fischer, Sharon Gettel, Terri Gunnison, Maggie Hunt, Julie Kane, Carol Lepthian, Christine Martelon, Julie Lorenzo, Theresa McLellan, Paulette Niehoff, Desbah Organick, Carol Pirotte, Joyce Schuyler

GUEST ARTISTS: Burton Taylor, Starr Danias, Keith Kimmel

REPERTOIRE

"Giselle" (Adam, Michel Katcharoff after Perrot), "Straw Hats in the Park" (Poulenc, Richard Denny), and *PREMIERES* of "Trio" (Beethoven, Covillo), "American Innovators" (Covillo/Parker), "Jewel Ballet" (Covillo/Parker), "Under Western Skies" (Grofe, Zoritch), "Swan of Quonela" (Sibelius, Covillo), "Nutcracker" (Tchaikovsky, Covillo/Parker/Wilfred Schuman), "What's A Foot?" (Parker)

COBB MARIETTA BALLET
Marietta, Georgia

Artistic Director-Choreographer, Iris Hensley

COMPANY
(names not submitted)

REPERTOIRE

"Coppelia" (Delibes, Leon Folkine), "Graduation Ball" (Strauss, Vivian Phillips), "The Seven Last Words of Christ!" (Theodore DuBois, Iris Hensley)

(No photo submitted)

Left: "The Seven Last Words of Christ"

Susie Spencer	Laura Walker

Colorado Concert Ballet

THE DALLAS BALLET
Dallas, Texas

Artistic Directors, George Skibine, Marjorie Tallchief; General Manager, Mary Heller Sasser; Administrator, Moira Whitney; Choreographer, George Skibine; Guest Choreographers, Stuart Hodes, J. David Kirby; Conductors, Louis Lane, Michael Semenitzky; Costume Mistress, Ella Rose Hill; Sets, Peter J. Hall; Lighting, David Gibson; Sound, B. W. Griffith, Jr.; Stage Manager, Patricia Hyde; Press, Sarah Birge

COMPANY

Mark Borchelt, Kevin Brown, Angela Sloan Hagedorn, Kirt Anthony Hathaway, Cyndi Jones, Allan L. Kinzie, David Costellanos, Lisa F. Owen, Marcella Shannon, Michael Beall Southwell, David Stein, Deanne Tomlinson Browning, Karen Travis, Cameron Basden

GUEST ARTISTS: Edward Villella, Anna Aragno, Teena McConnell, Robert Maiorano, Judith Jamison

REPERTOIRE

"Annabel Lee" (Schiffman, Skibine), "Cantante Profana" (Bartok, Skibine), "Nutcracker Suite" (Tchaikovsky, Skibine after Petipa), "Sketches" (Rossini, Molbajoli), "Idylle" (Serrette, Skibine), "Design for Strings" (Tchaikovsky, Taras), "The Abyss" (Richter, Hodes), "Gaite Parisienne" (Offenback, Skibine), "Tempo Vivo" (Jolinet, Skibine), "La Peri" (Coralli, Skibine), "Suite de Danses" (Coupuin, Skibine), "Aubade" (Poulenc, Skibine), "Combat" (DeBanfield, Dollar), "Firebird" (Stravinsky, Skibine), "Bolero" (Ravel, Skibine after Nijinska), "Daphnis and Chloe" (Ravel, Skibine)

PREMIERES: "Tarantella Americana" (Gottschalk, Skibine), "American Salute" (Gould/Gershwin, Kirby), "A Shape of Light" (Foote, Hodes)

King Douglas Photo

Dallas Ballet

Concert Dance Company

CONCERT DANCE COMPANY
Natick, Massachusetts

Artistic Director, Barbara Kauff; Coordinator, Barbara Goldfinger; Lighting, Beverly Emmons Gombosi; Stage Managers, John Gates, Ann Botkin; Choreographers, Bill Evans, Deborah Wolf; Press, Kathryn Daniels

COMPANY

Ann Asnes, Shirley Benjamin, Peggy Brightman, Kathryn Daniels, Patrick Hayden, Faith Pettit, Keith Taylor, Roger Tolle, Robb Wallin, Deborah Wolf

GUEST ARTIST: Bill Evans, Gregg Lizenbery

REPERTOIRE

"For Betty" (Vivaldi, Bill Evans), "Pilobolus" (Appleton, Wolken/Pendleton), "Five Songs in August" (Sussman, Evans), "Day on Earth" (Copeland, Doris Humphrey), "I Wan Somebody, Yes I Do" (Rotter, Cliff Keuter), "Randance" (Elton John, Gus Solomons, Jr.), "Making and Doing" (Coryell, Richard Bull), "Cartouche" (Purcell, Phoebe Neville), "Headquarters" (Collage, Art Bauman)

PREMIERES: "Hard Times" (Deseret String Band, Bill Evans), "Lapses" (Collage, Deborah Wolf)

Donald Curran Photo

DALLAS METROPOLITAN BALLET
Dallas, Texas

Artistic Directors, Ann Etgen, Bill Atkinson; Executive Director, Pat Baker; Company Manager, Wayne Pitts; Technical Director, Jeannine Stegin; Costumes, Elrose Sullivan; Press, Kay Ellis; Guest Choreographers, Jo Emery, Dennis Poole

COMPANY

Suzette Mariaux, Wayne Pitts, Christy Dunham, King Douglas, Richard Condon, Trudi Perrin, Mitzi Smith, Michael Stammer, Tracy Forsyth, Brad Moranz, Sheikwa Nowlin, Karen Stevens, Suzanne Wagner, Jerry Kelley, Mary Hall, Kathy Chamberlain, Rusty Simmons, Billy Stephens, Byron Reynolds, Mary Kay Douglas

GUEST ARTISTS: Galina and Valery Panov, Anamarie Sarazin, David Drummond, Debra Mili, Darrell Barnett

REPERTOIRE

"Sonata" (Lesemann, Emery), "Rainbow Symphony" (Britten, Poole), "Rags" (Joplin), "Graduation Ball" (Strauss, Carow after Lichine), "Christina's World" (Collage, Vesak), "Gym Dandy" (Prokofiev), "Country Garden" (Grainger), "La Valse" (Ravel, Wilde), "Innamorati" (Wolf, Ferrari), and *PREMIERES* of "Suite for Fun" (Shostakovich), "Dance Baroque" (Tchaikovsky)

Right Center: Dallas Metropolitan Ballet's "Suite for Fun"

DANCE GUILD OF VIRGINIA
Virginia Beach, Virginia

Producer, Nancy A. McClees; Director, Vija M. Cunningham; Choreographers, Major Burchfield, Vija M. Cunningham, Judith Hatcher, Heidi Robitshek, Colin Worth; Stage Manager, Beth Hudson; Costumes, Gail Sedel; Sound, Ursula Jones; Press, Marilyn Jacobson; Narrator, Sunday Abbott

COMPANY

Debby Benvin, Major Burchfield, Heidi Robitshek, Theresa Coleman, Vija Cunningham, Judith Hatcher, Ann John, Charles Lipka, Kathy McDonald, Maggi Schmidt, Gail Sedel, Jeannie West

REPERTOIRE

"Seagull" (Santana/Britten, Burchfield), "Don Quixote" (Minkus, Mischa Morawski), "Impressions of Degas" (Chopin, Cunningham), "Mysterious Mountain" (Hovhaness, Cunningham), "Haiku Suite" (Miller/Dorough/Lohoefer, Cunningham), "H & R" (Hans Van Manen, Heidi Robitshek), "Ragtime Dance" (Joplin, Robitshek), "Composition X" (Erb, Cunningham), "Danse" (Stravinsky, Cunningham), "Hoe Down" (Copeland, Burchfield), "Abstractions" (Sauter & Finnegan, Cunningham), "The Elephant's Child" (Stravinsky/Varese/Lehman, Cunningham)

PREMIERES: "Symphonic Variations" (Frank, Colin Worth), "Courtly Dances" (Traditional, Major Burchfield, Judith Hatcher), "The Night before Christmas" (Glazounov/Cowell/Vivaldi/Folk/Rice, Vija Cunningham), "Peter Rabbit" (Kobalevsky/White/Ravel/Prokofiev, Cunningham)

Dance Guild of Virginia's "Abstractions"

THE DANCING MACHINE
Boston, Massachusetts

Director, Becky Arnold; Choreographers, Becky Arnold, Linda Rabhan, Gene Murray

COMPANY

Kathleen Caton
Jackie Ledgister
Richard Moses
Joanne Patriacia
Linda Rabhan
Dorsey Yearley

REPERTOIRE: "Sisters, Mothers, Warriors" (John Jay, Becky Arnold), "Duet" (Charles Mingus, Arnold), "Dancing Machine" (Jackson Five, Arnold), and *PREMIERES* of "Opening with the Crusaders" (Jazz Crusaders, Arnold), "From out of the Bible" (Gary McFarland, Linda Rabhan), "Lively Up Yourself" (Bob Marley, Arnold), "Satin Doll" (Duke Ellington, Gene Murray), "Tuxedo Junction" (Glenn Miller, Arnold), "Bamoja Transit" (Modern Jazz Quartet, Arnold)

Top Right: Kathleen Caton, Jackie Ledgister, Kerry Kennett, Richard Moses, Dorsey Yearly in "Dancing with the Crusaders"

Dayton Ballet Company's "Lincoln Portrait"
(Walt Kleine Photo)

DELAWARE REGIONAL BALLET
Dover, Delaware

Artistic Director-Artist in Residence, Cherie Noble; President, Marion Tracy; Choreographer, Bill Comer; Ballet Mistress, Beth Anne Riggi; Lighting, Judith Haynes, Kent Productions; Costumes, Pam Comer, Betty Mathews, Marianne Smith; Stage Managers, Bob Noble, Sharyn Williamson; Business Manager, Les Fels; Press, Ellie Boone; Guest Choreographer, Robert Ivey

COMPANY

Denise Bickling, Renee Breault, Mary Lu Bruner, Robin Burkett, Bill Comer, Lisa Cutchin, Elizabeth Fels, Susan Foster, Laurie LeBlanc, Carol Mathews, Susie Mathews, Raymond McKee, Karen Proudford, Ginny Portz, Beth Anne Riggi, Mike Shortell, Diana Snare, Tony Sterago, Arlene Villaroel, Donna Wilkinson

GUEST ARTISTS: Bob Belichick, Judith Bettinger, Curt Decker, Adam Miller

REPERTOIRE

"Free to Dream" (Shirley, Comer), "Interpretations on Edd Kalehoff" (Kalehoff, Mineo), "Nutcracker" (Tchaikovsky, Noble), and *PREMIERES* of "Adam's Eves" (Poulenc, Ivey), "Clover and Sal" (Joplin, Comer/Noble), "One Divided" (VillaLobos, Noble), "Pulse" (Collage, Comer), "Release" (Poulenc, Riggi), "To Life, Liberty and Love" (Mozart, Noble)

DAYTON BALLET COMPANY
Dayton, Ohio

Artistic Director, Josephine Schwarz; Associate Directors, Jon Rodriguez, Bess Saylor; Choreographers, Josephine Schwarz, Jon Rodriguez, Bess Saylor; Wardrobe Mistress, Barbara Trick; Set and Lighting Designer-Stage Manager, John Rensel; Pianist, Thomas Barret; Business Manager, Jack A. DeVelbiss

COMPANY

Beth Berdes, Cynthia Bowden, Summer Cast, Gregory Clough, Elena Comendador, Jimmy Daniel, Judy Denman, Ebony Barkley, DeAnn Duteil, Amy Eifert, Charles Hoffman, Ron Hollenkamp, Mary Louise Hubler, Daniel Jamison, Stewart Jarrett, Keith Kline, Susan Koenigsberg, Peter Means, Theresa Muth, Jeff Nelson, Meggin Rose, Earl Roosa, Camille Ross, Beth Saidel, Terri Schmidt, Jodi Smith, Diane Stapp, Elizabeth Tierney, Ann Vandevander, Karen Welch, Alison Willis

REPERTOIRE

"Celebrations" (Vivaldi, Yuriko), "Concertino" (Pergolesi, Koner), "Dance Overture" (Creston, Schwarz), "Die Linie" (Keats, Saylor), "Flower Festival" (Helsted, Bournonville), "Grand Pas Espagnol" (Vivaldi, Rodriguez), "Periphrastic" (Denisov, Saylor), "The Wheat Maiden" (Delibes), "Seaborne" (Britten, Saylor), "Concerto Barocco" (Bach, Balanchine), "Dulce et Decorum Est" (Penderecki, Rodriguez), "Homage to Georg Friderich" (Handel, Rodriguez), "Pas de Quatre" (Pugni, Stapp), "there are no roses in my garden" (Saylor, Rodriguez), "Trimorphous" (Bach, Rodriguez), "Anya's Journey" (Shostakovich, Saylor), "Cinderella" (Prokofiev, Rodriguez), "I Watch Myself Grow Up" (Wasson, Schwarz), "Amahl and the Night Visitors" (Menotti, Schwarz), "Tarantella" (Gottschalk, Balanchine), "Fliessende Tanschrifte" (Hindemith, Saylor), "Sleeping Beauty Pas de Trois" (Tchaikovsky, Rodriguez), "Nutcracker Act II" (Tchaikovsky, Rodriguez), "Ophelia" (Stravinsky, Saylor), "Willoughby" (Prokofiev, Sebastian), "Crucifixion" (Hindemith/Shostakovich, Saylor), "Ruth" (Jacobi, Saylor), "Pas de Quatre - Encore '75" (Santana, Ross/Duell/Gribler/Saylor), "Papillons" (Schumann, Schwarz), "Dialogues" (Poulenc, Rodriguez), "Chopin's Revenge" (Chopin, Clough), "Schubertiad" (Schubert, Rodriguez), "Movin' On" (Johnny Winter, Saylor), "At Half Past Six in the Afternoon" (Schuman, Rodriguez), "Lincoln's Portrait" (Copland, Saylor), "Billy the Kid" (Copland, Loring), "Trio" (Ibert, Rodham), "To Albinoni" (Albinoni, Saylor)

Members of Delaware Regional Ballet's "Clover and Sal"

DELTA FESTIVAL BALLET
New Orleans, Louisiana

Artistic Directors, Joseph Giacobbe, Maria J. Giacobbe; President, Mrs. Earl V. Magri, Jr.; Stage Manager, Karen Greenberg; Costumes, Marcos Paredes, Frank Bennett; Lighting, Karen Greenberg, Chenault Spence; Pianist, Julia Adams; Press, Rosalie Baker; Guest Choreographers, Fiorella Keane, Dom Orejudos, Richard Munro, Christina Munro, Rochelle Zide

COMPANY

Alden Adams, Holly Adams, Magda Canales, Lisa Everett, Kelly Fortier, Nancy Herren, Bonnie McCormack, Denise Pons, Laurie Volny, Sue Ellen Stewart, Tammie Magri, Melanie Montalto, Gwen Delle Giacobbe, Denise Oustalet, Barbara Waguespack, Gretchen Newburger, Mary Ann Louviere, Maureen Simeral, David Wedemeyer, Michael Brown, Ozzie Laporte, Tom Quintini, Rick Kelly, Cutting Jahncke, Ronnie Fine, Michael Taormina

GUEST ARTISTS: Martin Van Hamel, Clark Tippet, Richard Schafer, Rochelle Zide, Edward Villella, Kay Mazzo, Violette Verdy

REPERTOIRE

"Sleeping Beauty" (Tchaikovsky, Fiorella Keane), "Songs of a Wayfarer" (Mahler, Dom Orejudos) "Jigs 'n' Reels" (Malcolm Arnold, Richard Englund), "Saddles and Sashes" (Copland, Joseph Giacobbe), "Variations from Day to Day" (Brahms, Norman Walker), "Capriccio" (Mendelssohn, Englund), "Les Sylphides" (Chopin, Giacobbe after Fokine), "Second Thoughts" (Albinoni, Giacobbe)

(No photos submitted)

Top Right: Delta Festival Ballet's "Les Sylphides"
(David Sandberg Photo)

DISCOVERY DANCE GROUP
Houston, Texas

Director-Choreographer, Camille Long Hill; Choreographers, Lynn Reynolds, Pam Stockman, Martha Bratton Owens; Stage Manager, Jerry Springhorn

COMPANY

Valentine Boving, Kathleen Buck, Linda Castillon, Jay Fullinwider, Gary Hardy, Kathleen Parker, Pam Stockman, and Paul Clements, Bonnie McMillian, Martha Owens, Jeff Smith, Lisa Trussel, Sara Whitaker

REPERTOIRE

"Sounds of Silence" (Don Sebesky, Camille Hill), "Etude" (Mauriat, Hill), "Jazz Bit" (Drums, Hill), and *PREMIERES* of "Rhapsody" (Debussy, Hill), "I of Me" (Mingus, Hill), "Jungle Plum" (K. Barron, Hill), "Inhibitions" (Mingus, Hill), "Being Beginning" (P. Horn, Lynn Reynolds), "Unholy Trinity" (J. Lord, Pam Stockman)

Horace F. Oleson Photo

**Right Center: Valentine Boving,
Jay Fullinwider in "Rhapsody"**

ELMIRA-CORNING BALLET
Elmira, N.Y.

Founder-Artistic Director-Choreographer, Madame Halina; Conductors, Theodore Hollebrach, Fritz Wallenburg, David Einfeld; Technical Director, Floyd Lutomski; Stage Manager, Lauren Trescott; Lighting, Jack Westervelt; Costumes, Donna Jump

COMPANY

Stephanie Schmid, Dorothy Lindsay, Elizabeth Howell, Carla Chamberlain, Mary Ellen Hagy, Margaret Thompson, Darlene Errett, Betsy Buch, Mark Smith, Wanalyn Aronson, Jeanine Clare, Wendy Tuller, Gaye-Lin Horton, Lindsay O'Connor, Margaret Kornu, Debbie Carroll, Lorreine Gile, Karen Minch, Sally Updyke, Cathy Curran, Kirsten Winsor, Luke Smith, Joan Russen, Jackie Meckes

REPERTOIRE

"Cirque" (Shostakovitch, Halina), "Stars and Stripes" (Sousa, Halina), "Cakewalk" (Gottschalk, Falotico), "Nutcracker" (Tchaikovsky, Halina), and *PREMIERES* of "Witching" (Bernstein, Falotico), "American Gaieties" (Joplin, Falotico)

Elmira-Corning Ballet's "Witching"

EMPIRE STATE BALLET THEATRE
Buffalo, N.Y.

Artistic Director-Choreographer, Barbara Striegel; Executive Director, Thomas Banasiak; Scenery and Lighting, Joseph Aveilhe

COMPANY

Jean Bacon, Michelle Becker, Vicki Bogacki, Marianne Carpenter, Carol Clendenning, Ruth Ann Jaworski, Susan Lafferty, Lisa Mast, Moira Murphy, Marion Phelan, Carolyn Pulk, Maryanne Scully, Tara Valone

Joseph Aveilhe, Randy Banasiak, Thomas Banasiak, Harry Ferris, John Osborn

APPRENTICES: Jacquelyn Aveilhe, R. J. Busch II, Margaret Heather, Maureen Kelly, Dianne Marra, Maria Messina, Melissa Phelan, Susan Scully

REPERTOIRE

"Sleeping Beauty" (Tchaikovsky, Barbara Striegel), "Nutcracker" (Tchaikovsky, Striegel), "Coppelia" (Delibes, Striegel), "Petrouchka" (Stravinsky, Striegel), "Firebird" (Stravinsky, Striegel), "Concerto" (Tchaikovsky, Striegel), "Pas de Quatre" (Pugni, Perrot/Striegel), "Gluck Ballet Suite" (Gluck, Striegel)

Thomas Banasiak Photo

**Top Right: Thomas Banasiak,
Michelle Becker in "Sleeping Beauty"**

**Douglas Hevenor, Donna Silva, Frank Bays,
Rita Agnese, Flemming Halby in "Assorted Rags"**

GEORGIA DANCE THEATRE COMPANY
Augusta, Georgia

Artistic Director-Choreographer, Frankie Levy; Ballet Mistress, Bebe Graham; Assistant to Director, Ann-Toni Estroff; Costumes and Sets, Randa Yvel, Ann-Toni Estroff, Keith Cowling, Claude Astin; Lighting, Frankie Levy, Ann-Toni Estroff; Sound, Bernard Chambers

COMPANY

Bebe Graham, Dede Shiver, Tina Hagler, Lynn Harp, Ann Marie Schweers, Martha Teets, Andrea Lum, Kim Hale, Laura Hensley, Charlene Linder, Kim Kortick, Joy Shapiro

GUEST ARTISTS: Violette Verdy, Edward Villella, Allegra Kent, Bonnie Mathis, Dennis Wayne, Frank Ohman, Nolan T'Sani, Linda Yourth, Polly Shelton, Susan Hendl

REPERTOIRE

"The Little Match Girl," "Holy, Hopping, Hallelujah" (Geld-/Udell, Giordano), "Chopin Today" (Chopin, Levy), "Garden Dances" (Chopin, Levy), "Danzas Espanol" (Moszkowski, Levy), "Grand Esprit" (Bach, Levy), "Pas de Quatre" (Pugni, Levy), "et mors" (Saint-Saens, Levy), "Summer Song" (Mozart, Levy)

Ann-Toni Estroff Photo

FIRST CHAMBER DANCE COMPANY
Seattle, Washington

Artistic Director-Choreographer, Charles Bennett; Executive Administrator-Music Director, Harriet Cavalli; Costumes, Alan Madsen; Technical Director, Richard Weil; Stage Manager, Frank Simons; Choreographers, Charles Bennett, Raymond Bussey, Teodoro Morca

COMPANY

Rita Agnese
Frank Bays
Sara de Luis
Flemming Halby
Douglas Hevenor
Alexis Hoff
Donna Silva

REPERTOIRE: "Recollection of an Age" (Boieldieu, Bennett), "Leyenda" (Albeniz, Morca), "Contrasts" (Ramsey Lewis, Jay Norman), "The Moor's Pavane" (Purcell, Jose Limon), "La Chasse" (Massenet/Anonymous, Lotte Gosler), "By Candlelight" (Buffy Ste-Marie, Bennett), "Spring Waters" (Rachmaninoff, Asaf Messerer), "Under Green Leaves" (Telemann, Bennett), "Les Sylphides" (Chopin, Fokine/Bennett), "Nutcracker Grand Pas de Deux" (Tchaikovsky, Petipa), "Flower Festival Pas de Deux" (Helsted, Bournonville), "Nagare" (Japanese Traditional, Bennett), "Pas de Quatre" (Pugni, Dolin), "Albinoni Adagio" (Albinoni, Bennett)

Carol Beach Photo

**Tina Hagler, Ann Marie Schweers, Andrea Lum
of Georgia Dance Theatre Company**

GLORIA NEWMAN DANCE THEATER

Orange, California

Artistic Director-Choreographer, Gloria Newman; General Manager, Charles M. Schoenberg; Company Manager, Lenita Kellstrand; Stage Manager, Tom Grond; Technical Director, Stan Lanich; Costumes, Carol Warner, Charles Berliner, Charles Tomlinson, Remy Charlip; Lighting, Tom Grond, Ken Olcott, Jennifer Tipton, Beverly Emmons

COMPANY

JoElla Lewis	Sandra Puerta
Lynn Rempalski	Arthur Mikaelian
Barbara Dobkin	Dennis Holderman
Wanda Lee Evans	Alvin Mayes
Gladys Kares	Larry Ham

Guest Artists: Carol Warner, Clay Taliaferro

REPERTOIRE

"Encounters" (Leopold Weiss, Gloria Newman), "Mulligan Stew" (Gerry Mulligan, Newman), "Tromperie" (Paul Bowles, Newman), "Parentheses" (Elizabeth Keen), "Magazine" (Newman), "Rushes" (Keen), "Of Winds and Time" (Lou Harrison, Newman), "Rooms" (Kenyon Hopkins, Anna Sokolow), "Games" (Traditional, Donald McKayle)

Gloria Newman Dance Theater in "Magazine"

HAMPTON ROADS CIVIC BALLET

Hampton, Virginia

Directors, Edgerton B. Evans, Muriel Shelley Evans; Choreographers, Edgerton B. Evans, Muriel Shelley Evans, Lisa Shaw; Sets, Mary Beaven, Duff Kliewer, Jr.; Lighting, Tim Van Noy, David Messick; Stage Managers, C. O. Seaman, Stephanie Messick; Auditions, Joanne Crum

COMPANY

SOLOISTS: Michelle Cawthorn, Cathy Welsh, Michele Lequeux, Darcy Evans, Lisa Shaw, Susan McAllister, Ron Braswell, Leigh Catlett, Jr.

SENIOR COMPANY: Teresa Adams, Lauri Aunan, Kari Buttles, Michelle Cawthorn, Joanne Crum, Darcy Evans, Kathy Johnson, Michele Lequeux, Mary Leath, Susan McAllister, Karen Peters, Lisa Shaw, Carolyn Wilson, Cathy Welsh, Ron Braswell, Leigh Catlett, Jr.

APPRENTICE COMPANY: Kathryn Blevins, Sidney Sale, Jane White, Joanna Wallberg, Margaret Zehmer, Connie Alvis, Leslie Driver, Mary Guy, Bella Karr, Kim Kulp, Jill Spielberger, Anne Stafford

GUEST ARTISTS: Leo Schmidt, Bronwyn Thomas, Manuel Gomez

REPERTOIRE

"Nutcracker" (Tchaikovsky, Petipa/Ivanov), "City Mouse, Country Mouse" (Beethoven, M. Evans), "Travail et Jou" (Chopin, Lisa Shaw/E. Evans), "The Moldau" (Smetna, M. Evans), "Rosenkavalier Waltzes" (Strauss, M. Evans), "Pavanne" (Ravel, E. Evans), "Old World Dances" (Traditional)

Carl Brown Photo

GUS GIORDANO
JAZZ DANCE COMPANY

Evanston, Illinois

Director-Choreographer, Gus Giordano; Dance Coordinator, Lea Darwin; Manager, Libby Beyer

COMPANY

Gus Giordano	Clarence Teeters
Julie Walder	Jeff Mildenstein
Erik Geier	Pattie Obey
Charlene Clark	Kim Darwin

REPERTOIRE: "The Matriarch" (Ingle, Giordano), "Solstice" (Subnotick, Bill Evans), "Judy" (Judy Garland, Giordano), "Glitzville, U.S.A." (Songs of the 1950's, Debbie Hallak), "Fluctuation" (Bernstein, Jim Kolb), "The Rehearsal" (Stevens, Giordano), "Solar Wind" (Pointer Sisters, Ernest Morgan), "Bach to Bach to Honegger" (Bach/Honegger, Giordano/Walder), "Tribute" (Hayes, Giordano), "On the Town" (Bernstein, Giordano/Walder), "Ragtime to Rock" (American music from the 1920's to now, Company), "New York Export: Opus Jazz" (Prince, Giordano), "Holy Hoppin' Hallelujah" (Gold/Udell, Giordano)

Left Center: Gus Giordano's Jazz Dance Company

**Lisa Shaw, Leigh Catlett of
Hampton Roads Civic Ballet**

HARTFORD BALLET

Hartford, Connecticut

Artistic Director, Michael Uthoff; Managing Director, Ellsworth Davis; Press, Sue Conner; Company Manager, Michael Simson; Assistant to Director, Lisa Bradley; Music Adviser, Peter Woodard; Stage Manager, Jerry Kelch; Technical Director, Mark Anson; Costumer, Mary Wolfson; Wardrobe Mistress, Beulah Cole; Sets, James Steere, Morton Fishman, Anni Albers, Carl Michell

COMPANY

Lisa Bradley, Jack Anderson, Kevin Aydelotte, Noble Barker, Robert Buntzen, Jeff Giese, Thomas Giroir, Judith Gosnell, Karen Kelly, Clover Mathis, Debra McLaughlin, Joan Merrill, John Perpener, Martha Purl, Sandra Ray, Roland Roux, John Simone, Jeanne Tears, Michael Uthoff, Joan Watts

REPERTOIRE

"Brahms Variations" (Brahms, Uthoff), "Cantata" (Ginastera, Uthoff), "Come, Come Travel with Dreams" (Scriabin, Anna Sokolow), "Concerto Grosso" (Vivaldi, Uthoff), "Danza a Quattro" (Donizetti, Uthoff), "Duo" (Clark, Uthoff), "Dusk" (Satie, Uthoff), "F. Jasmine's Quiet Space" (Wakeman, Katherine Gallagher), "La Malinche" (Lloyd, Jose Limon), "Leggieros" (Beethoven, Lotte Goslar), "Marosszek Dances" (Kodaly, Uthoff), "The Nutcracker" (Tchaikovsky, Enid Lynn/Uthoff), "Meatwaves" (Miller, Enid Lynn), "Pastorale" (Handel, Uthoff), "Quartet in D Minor" (Schubert, Lois Bewley), "White" (Traditional Japanese, Jennifer Muller), "Windsong" (Elgar, Uthoff)

PREMIERES: "Antumalal (Corral of the Sun)" (Ginastera, Uthoff), "Arcady" (Debussy, Stuart Sebastian), "Aves Mirabiles" (Foss, Uthoff), "Little Improvisations" (Schumann, Antony Tudor), "Primavera" (Rossini, Uthoff), "Three for the Mountain" (Zummo, Katherine Gallagher)

Right: "Leggieros" (also top) Below: Jack Anderson, Clover Mathis in "Antumalal (Corral of the Sun)", Lisa Bradley in "Aves Mirabiles"

"Concerto Grosso" Above: Judith Gosnell, John Simone in "Antumalal (Corral of the Sun)"

HARTFORD BALLET CHAMBER ENSEMBLE

Hartford, Connecticut

Artistic Directors, Michael Uthoff, Enid Lynn; Managing Director, Ellsworth Davis; Press, Sue Conner; Company Manager, Michael Simson; Production Manager, Ron Brissette; Costumer, Mary Wolfson

COMPANY

Allyson Barker, Kristen Corman, David Corwen, Deborah Evens, Elizabeth Fisk, Nicolas Humphrey, Robert Kowalski, Christel Meyer, Page Perry, June Ellen Rosenfeld, Susan Ross, Brad Roth, Jeffrey Schweizer, Sharon Stivers

REPERTOIRE

"Concerto Grosso" (Vivaldi, Michael Uthoff), "Dusk" (Satie, Uthoff), "F. Jasmine's Quiet Space" (Wakeman, Gallagher), "Marosszek Dances" (Kodaly, Uthoff), "Meatwaves" (Miller, Enid Lynn), "Nutcracker Divertissements" (Tchaikovsky, Lynn/Uthoff), "Peter and the Wolf" (Prokofiev, Uthoff), "Primavera" (Rossini, Uthoff), "Something Happened" (Laws, John Perpener), "Variations for Tape and Choreography" (Tal, Lynn), and *PREMIERE* of "An American Portrait" (Compiled, Enid Lynn)

HOUSTON BALLET
Houston, Texas

Artistic Director, Ben Stevenson; Acting Artistic Director-Choreographer, James Clouser; Ballet Masters, Hiller Huhn, Nicholas Polajenko; Ballet Mistress, Anne Polajenko; Conductors, Hugo Fiorato, Charles Rosekrans; Lighting, Jennifer Tipton; Company Manager, Jane V. Hayes; Stage Managers, Patrick Ballard, William Banks; Costumer, Brauna Ben-Shane; Wardrobe, Marion Eggers, Ray Delle Robbins; Production Assistant, V. A. Cirpulis; General Director, Henry Holth; Press, Lorraine Gress

COMPANY

PRINCIPALS: Leo Ahonen, Soili Arvola, Barbara Pontecorvo, Matti Tikkanen, Andrea Vodehnal

SOLOISTS: Brian Andrew, Whit Haworth, Mary Margaret Holt, Nancy Onizuka, Robert Raimondo, Denise Smokoski, Bruce Steivel

CORPS: Gloria Brisbin, Sharon Caplan, Gloria de Santo, Jean Doornbos, Rodwic Fukino, Jeff Giese, Cynthia Graham, Jory Hancock, Richard Hazelton, Michael Job, Kathy Kepler, Melissa Lowe, Julie Racca, James Sutton, Kathleen Vander Velde, Michele White

GUEST ARTISTS: Edward Villella, Jean-Pierre Bonnefous, Patricia McBride

REPERTOIRE

"Allen's Landing" (Tull, James Clouser), "Black Swan Pas de Deux" (Tchaikovsky, Petipa), "Caprichos" (Bartok, Herbert Ross), "Carmina Burana" (Orff, Clouser), "Concerto Barocco" (Bach, Balanchine), "Con Spirito" (Smetana, Clouser), "Constantia" (Chopin, Dollar), "Coppelia" (Delibes, Sergeyev after Saint-Leon, staged by Frederick Franklin), "Danse Brillante" (Glinka, Franklin), "Designs with Strings" (Tchaikovsky, John Taras), "Gershwin Songbook" (Gershwin, Clouser), "Homage" (Gounod, Franklin), "Le Combat" (deBanfield, Dollar), "Le Corsaire Pas de Deux" (Drigo, Petipa), "Napoli Act III" (Helsted/Gade/Paulli, Bournonville), "The Nutcracker" (Tchaikovsky, Franklin), "Paquita" (Minkus, Petipa), "Pas de Dix" (Glazounov, Balanchine), "Pas de Quatre" (Pugni, Anton Dolin), "Prodigal Son" (Prokofiev, Balanchine), "Suspension" (Ray Green, May O'Donnell), "Swan Lake Act II" (Tchaikovsky, Petipa), "Pas de Deux" (Tchaikovsky, Balanchine), "Three Preludes" (Rachmaninoff, Ben Stevenson), "Three Trios" (Bartok, Clouser), "Through a Glass Lightly" (Collage, Clouser), "Waltz and Variations" (Glazounov, Balanchine), "Water Music" (Handel, Taras)

PREMIERES: "Moonscape" (Michael Horvit, Jan Stockman Simonds), "Charley Rutlage, A Cowboy Dreams of Heaven" (Ives, Clouser), "A Rose for Matti" (Leroy Anderson, Clouser), "Rag Time" (Scott Joplin, Ruthanna Boris)

Michael von Helms Photos

**Right: Whit Haworth in "Moonscape", Leo Ahonen,
Soili Arvola in "Nutcracker"
Above: Melissa Lowe, Whit Haworth
in "Three Preludes" Top: Jory Hancock,
Denise Smokoski in "Caliban"**
(Walt Frerck Photos)

**Claudia Chapline, Reiko, Harold Schwarm in
"The Telephone Book"**

I.D.E.A. COMPANY
Santa Monica, California

Artistic Director-Choreographer-Designer, Claudia Chapline; Composer-Lighting Designer, Leonard Ellis; Video Director, Lyn DelliQuadri; Stage Manager, Robert Grauch; Business Manager, Michelle Lefcoe

COMPANY

Claudia Chapline, Lyn DelliQuadri, Leonard Ellis, Robert Graunch, Harold Schwarm, Iris Tansman, Lisa Walford, and apprentices Judith Hill, Holly Rosenwald, Gillian Warren

REPERTOIRE

ALL PREMIERES: "Builders, Jumpers, Sounder" (Collaborative), "Cycles" (Leonard Ellis, Claudia Chapline), "The Telephone Book" (Ellis, Chapline), "Crossection" (David McCall, Iris Tansman), "Flash Point Four" (Ellis, Chapline), "Bicentribute Parable" (Lisa Walford), "Ash Can Blues" (Ellis), "Chair Events" (Lyn DelliQuadri), "Mud Dance" (Collaborative), "Riding Down the Seven Stars" (McCall, DelliQuadri), "Chondra" (Gregory Watson/Billy Greene, Chapline/Tansman)

Lyn Smith Photo

151

JACOBS LADDER DANCE COMPANY
New York, N.Y.

Artistic Director-Choreographer, Judith Jacobs

COMPANY

Lynn Frielinghaus
Timothy Knowles
Judith Jacobs
Terre Rossman
Carol Slate

PREMIERE: "Yankee Doodling" (Taped Collage, Judith Jacobs)

Top Left: Judith Jacobs

KANSAS CITY BALLET
Kansas City, Missouri

Artistic Director, Tatiana Dokoudovska; Choreographers, George Skibine, Dennis Landsman, Shirley Weaver, Zachary Solov; Conductor, James Paul; Designer, Frank Szasz; Ballet Mistress, Vicki Allen Reid; Business Manager, Barbara R. Scanlon; Technical Director-Stage Manager, Carlton Carroll; Lighting Designer, Ron Coles

COMPANY

Dolly Allard, Sandra Balot, Toinette Biggins, Kelli Buckles, Benecia Carmack, Stephen Eads, Cathy Eberhart, Carol Feiock, Patricia Frizzell, Flora Hall, Michele Hamlett, Maryhelen Hanson, Melissa Kelly, Linda Lyon, Wendy Macafee, Ernest Mavis, Lisa Merrill, Jean Q. Niedt, Richard Orton, Dawn Parrish, Laura Ply, Peggy Ply, Anita Porte, Lois Scanlon, Debrah Shore, John Charles Smith, Mary Lynn Soli, William Stannard, Lisa Swanson, Curtis Sykes, Deborah Ummel, Nita Watson, Carl Welander, John Wells

GUEST ARTISTS: Violette Verdy, Richard Dryden, Kay Mazzo, Peter Martins

REPERTOIRE

"The Nutcracker" (Tchaikovsky, Dokoudovska after Ivanov), "Rhapsody in Blue" (Gershwin, Solov/Vicki Allen Reid), "Les Sylphides" (Chopin, Dokoudovska after Fokine), "Iridice" (Ravel, Carlos Carvajal/Reid)

PREMIERES: "Symphonic Metamorphosis" (Paul Hindemith, George Skibine), "Abendsterne Walzer" (Joseph Lanner, Shirley Weaver), "Aftermath" (Alan Hovhaness, Dennis Landsman), "Bicentennial Jubilee" (G. Chadwick/Benjamin Franklin/Benjamin Carr/W. Steffe, Zachary Solov)

David Scanlon Photo

**Curtis Sykes, Peggy Ply, Flora Hall,
Michele Hamlett in Kansas City Ballet's "Iridice"**

KUNI DANCE THEATRE COMPANY
Los Angeles, California

Artistic Director-Choreographer, Masami Kuni; Choreographers, Linda Wojcik, Paul Edwards, Miriam Tait; Electronic Music, Ken Heller, Masami Kuni; Lighting, Larry Wiemer, Fred Sutton, Jerry McColgan; Costumes, Henrietta Soloff, Becky Wiemer, Saburo Ohba; Stage Managers, Fred Sutton, Paul Edwards

COMPANY

Linda Wojcik, Stephanie Romeo, Miriam Tait, Becky Wiemer, Tomiyo Nagahashi, Valerie Sied, Henrietta Soloff, Jeanette Triomphe, Paul Edwards, Joyce Shrode, Aki Ishimi, Chris Yamaga, Janey McCoy, Lois Greyston

GUEST ARTISTS: Judy Jarvis, Kazuo Kamizawa, Sachi Ogasawara

REPERTOIRE

"Room," "Song of Chain," "The Sea," "Circle without Circumference," and *PREMIERE* of "Terra Incognito" (Masami Kuni/Ken Heller, Kuni)

Kuni Dance Theatre Company in "Virgo"

LES GRANDS BALLETS CANADIENS

Montreal, Canada

Founder-Director, Ludmilla Chiriaeff; Artistic Director-Choreographer, Brian Macdonald; Musical Director-Conductor, Vladimir Jelinek; Resident Choreographer, Fernand Nault; Ballet Mistress, Linda Stearns; Ballet Master, Brydon Paige; Repetiteur and Production Assistant, Daniel Jackson; Lighting, Nicholas Cernovitch; General Manager, Colin McIntyre; Press, John Burgess, Gilles Morel; Production Coordinator, Evelyne DuBois; Technical Director, Tex Pinsonneault; Stage Manager, Maxine Glorsky; Director of Wardrobe, Nicole Martinet; Wardrobe Master, Richard Bergeron; Sound, Jean Benoit

COMPANY

Annette av Paul, Maniya Barredo, James Bates, Alexandre Belin, Christiane Berardelli, Lucien Bordeianu, Richard Bouchard, Cathy Buchanan, Patti Caplette, Sylvie Chevalier, Robert Dicello, Jerilyn Doucette, Leslie-May Downs, Heather Farquharson, Jean-Guy Gerome, David Graniero, Manon Hotte, Barbara Jacobs, Ondine Kozlov, David LaHay, Maurice LeMay, Candace Loubert, Michele Morin, Mannie Rowe, Dwight Shelton, Jacques St.-Cyr, John Stanzel, Robert Steele, Christopher Tabor, Susan Toumine, Sonia Vartanian, Shauna Wagner, Vincent Warren, Wendy Wright

REPERTOIRE

"Quatre Temperaments" (Hindemith, Balanchine), "Villon" (Starer, Butler), "Tam Ti Delam" (Vigneault, Macdonald), "Serenade" (Tchaikovsky, Balanchine), "Romeo and Juliet" (Freedman, Macdonald), "Firebird" (Stravinsky, Bejart), "Jeu de Cartes" (Stravinsky, Macdonald), "La Loterie" (Stravinsky, Macdonald), "Au-dela du Temps" (Stravinsky, Macdonald), "Variations Diabelli" (Beethoven, Macdonald), "Variations pour une Voix Tenebreuse" (Somers, Paige), "Variations pour une Souvenance" (Mortifee, Rabin), "Variations Polissones" (Confrey, Macdonald), "Casse Noisette" (Tchaikovsky, Nault), "Concerto Barocco" (Bach, Balanchine), "Liberte Temperee" (Mercure, Nault), "Lignes et Points" (Mercure, Paige/Macdonald), "Cantate pour une Joie" (Mercure, Macdonald), "Artere" (Mercure, Chiriaeff), "Marathon" (Macdonald)

Top: (L) Vincent Warren, Sonia Vartanian in "Concerto Barocco" (R) Vincent Warren, Helene Heineman in "La Loterie" Right Center: Annette av Paul, Alexandre Belin in "The Shining People of Leonard Cohen"

Sonia Vartanian, David LaHay, Mannie Rowe, Maniya Barredo in "Lignes et Points"

**Johnna Kirkland, John Clifford and
Los Angeles Ballet's "Pas de Dix"**
(Ted Petit Photo)

LOS ANGELES BALLET
Los Angeles, California

Artistic Director-Choreographer, John Clifford; Executive Director, Betty Empey; Business Manager, Newman E. Wait III; Ballet Mistress, Irina Kosmovska; Music Director, Clyde Allen; Technical Director-Lighting, Zuben Ornelas; Costumes, Ardeth; Scenic Designer, Philip Gilliam

COMPANY

Nancy Davis, Colette Jeschke, Johnna Kirkland, Polly Shelton, John Clifford, Charles Flemmer, Ken Mraz, Reid Olson

April Anderson, Martha Ashley, Ellen Bauer, Tom Blair, Suzann Chapin, Jenny Crain, Richard Fritz, Jeri Gaile, Jarnette Jones, James Lane, Jana Malloy, Juliana Mathewson, Mark McLaughlin, Kolleen McQuillen, Risa Oganesoff, Charlton O'Neal, David Rodriguez, Evette Voss, Lesli Wiesner, Eyzah Zoe

REPERTOIRE

(All premieres, and all choreographed by John Clifford) "Stravinsky Piano Concerto" (Stravinsky), "Dvorak Serenade" (Dvorak), "Harlequinade Pas de Deux" (Drigo), "Firebird" (Stravinsky), "Prokofiev Violin Concerto" (Prokofiev), "Rachmaninoff Suite" (Rachmaninoff), "Serenade in A" (Stravinsky), "Sonata" (Debussy), "Zolotoye Concerto" (Shostakovich), "Le Quattro Stagioni" (Verdi), "Annenberg Variations" (Bach), "Concerto Grosso" (Vivaldi), "Terpsichore Dances" (Praetorius)

LOUIS TUPLER DANCE COMPANY
Washington, D.C.

Artistic Director-Choreographer, Louis Tupler; Assistant Director, Terry Parresol; Technical Director, Michael Buck; Stage Manager, Janice Connors

COMPANY

Terry Parresol	Pamela Lasswell
Beth Shumway	Peter Nathan
Diane Johnson	Camille Smith
Allyn Enderlin	Lynne Strader

REPERTOIRE

"Classical Suite" (Vivaldi), "Bach Suite" (Bach), "New Intensities" (Winter), "Crescence" (Hovhaness), "Reed" (Tupler), "Here's the Show" (Tupler), "Cubed" (R. Gerhard, Terry Parresol), "Chug Chug Chuga Baby" (P. Schaeffer, Parresol), and *PREMIERES* of "Spheres of Time" (Choreography, Diane Johnson), "Twilight and Dawn" (Oregon, Pamela Lasswell). All choreography by Louis Tupler except where noted.

Right: Louis Tupler's "Crescence"

LOYOLA UNIVERSITY BALLET
New Orleans, Louisiana

Director, Lelia Haller; Artistic Director, Rene J. Toups; Choreographers, Lelia Haller, Rene J. Toups; Stage Manager, Bill Murphy

COMPANY

PRINCIPALS: Rene J. Toups, Joel Stassi Laciura

SOLOISTS: Dianne Preston Eustis, Louann King, Michael Willis Tassain, Mary Meade Murphy, Lynn Berry

CORPS: Mary Davidsaver, Joan Wolf, Mary Emma Pierson, Kay Rotert, Mary Ann Bragg, Andrea Canale, Bunny Kelly, Lisa Miller, Bonnie Barnes, Dianne Cresson, Celeste Ford, Martha Ghio, Maureen Marshall, Julie Tinsley, Ark Nelson, Harry Juarez, Richard Edwards, Mark Scully, Paul Watkins, Larry Armstrong, Forrest Snelling, Bob Jeanfreau, Pam Casey, Ann Plamondon, Debbie Puthoff, Vikki Rasmussen-Taxdal, Susan Smola, Cindie Schaefer, Natasha Arceneaux, Joan Buttram, Mary Roberts

REPERTOIRE

"Le Sacre du Printemps" (Stravinsky, Haller), "Snegourochka" (Traditional, Haller), and *PREMIERES* of "Le Baiser de la Fee" (Stravinsky, Haller), "Lt. Kije" (Prokofiev, Haller), "An American in Paris" (Gershwin, Haller), "Largo from the New World Symphony" (Dvorak, Toups)

Rene J. Toups, Joel Stassi Laciura in "Le Baiser de la Fee"
(Russ Cresson Photo)

MACON BALLET GUILD
Macon, Georgia

Artistic Director, Gladys Lasky; President, Binks Solomon Hart; Stage Manager, T. M. Northington; Music, Bill Allen; Press, Elizabeth Drinnon; Lighting, E. C. McMillan

COMPANY

Judy Friedel, Cathy Willis Sheffield, Lauren Drinnon, Mary O'-Shaughnessey, Mary Frances Weber, Melissa Garrette, Edith Newton, Karen Hinson, Ellen McKelvey, Cheryl Andrews, Mary Virginia Kay, Fabia Rogers, Lucy Holliday Elliott, Mary Holliday

GUEST ARTISTS: Dulce Anaya, Ronald Jones, Marion Schlosburg

REPERTOIRE

"The Nutcracker" (Tchaikovsky, Gladys Lasky after Ivanov), and *PREMIERES* of "Rhapsody in Blue" (Gershwin, Mary Frances Weber), "Fanfare for the Common Man" (Aaron Copland, Susan Buckman)

Photo by Robert

Top Left: Melissa Garrette, Edith Newton, Mary Virginia Kay of Macon Ballet Guild

MARIN CIVIC BALLET
San Rafael, California

Director, Leona Norman; Associate Director, Grace Doty; Association President, Jean Knox; Technical Director, Robert Finley; Wardrobe Mistress, Nancy Gallenson; Press, Phyllis Thelen

COMPANY

Colleen Caudill, Rita Cunningham, Rosemary Cunningham, Kathleen Gould, Rachel Hay, Mindy Jonas, Marianne Knox, Allison Leidel, Anne Little, Lesa Martin, Margo Motter, Moira O'Sullivan, Christina Rolling, Lynn Rothman, Michelle Sabella, Michelle Shibate, Nell Stewart, Leslie Vanderville, Susan Weisenberg, and Guest Artists Richard Cook, Peter Hempel, Ed White

REPERTOIRE

"Nutcracker" (Tchaikovsky, Norman), "Golden Moments of Ballet" (Guckenheimer Sour Kraut Band, Norman), "Paquita" (Minkus, Howard), "Les Pas de Quatre" (Pugni, Dolin), "Les Sylphides" (Chopin, Fokine), "Harp Concerto" (Boieldeux, Sutowski), "Brahms Waltzes" (Brahms, Weidman), "The Gift to Be Simple" (Vesak), "Graduation Ball" (Strauss, Lichine), "Gymnopedies" (Satie, Guidi), "Brandenburg Concerto #3" (Brandenburg, Wilde), "Sage of Silver Creek" (Copland, Gladstein), "Peasant Pas de Deux" "Vinasa" (Wilde), "Don Quixote Pas de Deux," "Romeo and Juliet Pas de Deux" (Howard), "Afternoon of a Faun" (Wilde)

Right Center: Allison Leidel, Richard Cook of Marin Civic Ballet in "Afternoon of a Faun"

MATTI LASCOE
DANCE THEATRE COMPANY
Huntington Beach, California

Artistic Director-Choreographer, Matti Lascoe; Executive Director, Jerry Lascoe; Directors, Anita Metz Grossman, Sonya Newberg, Phyllis Wapner; Sets, James Bertholf; Lighting, Thomas Ruzika; Stage Manager, Tom Grond; Sound, John Williams; Press, Bette Barr

COMPANY

Lynn Coghill	Sandy Asay
Arie Fleischer	Lou Dewey
Stephen Gray	Marilyn McCarthy
Diane Baughman	Byron Marks

REPERTOIRE

"Quasi" (Pachelbel, Lascoe), "Ellipsis" (none, Lascoe), "fiveforoctoberfive" (Milhaud, Lascoe), "Little Green Box on Modale" (R. Lewis), and *PREMIERES* of "The Great American Marble" (Keith Jarrett), "130-22-3528" (Subotnick, Lascoe)

Lyn Smith Photo

Sandy Asay, Arie Fleischer, Marilyn McCarthy, Lynn Coghill

METROPOLITAN BALLET COMPANY OF MARYLAND

Bethesda, Maryland

Director-Choreographer, Charles Dickson; Assistant Director-Choreographer, Alan Woodard; Sets, Richard C. Hankins; Lighting, Guy Le Valley; Costumes, Claudia Mangan, Katherine Larson; Wardrobe Mistress, Gladys Fuller

COMPANY

PRINCIPALS: Cathy Caplin, Michael Kessler

SOLISTS AND CORPS: Gayle Abbott, Elizabeth Chastka, Roanne Duncan, Cindy Faulkenberry, Connie Oxford, Cynthia Haley, David Lee, Jody Menick, Georgina Slavoff, Valerie Striar, Nancy Szabo

GUEST ARTISTS: Merle Park, Sylvester Campbell, Katie Murphy

REPERTOIRE

"Snow Maiden" (Tchaikovsky, Dickson/Woodard), "Sylvia" (Delibes, Dickson/Woodward), "Britten Variations" (Britten, Woodard), "Waltzes" (Tchaikovsky, Dickson), "Ballet Romantique" (Helsted, Woodard), "Sestetto" (Marcello, Dickson), "The Death of Actaeon" (Poulenc, Dickson), and *PREMIERE* of "Balletese" (Glazounov, Dickson)

Metropolitan Ballet Company's "Balletese"

METROPOLITAN BALLET OF ST. LOUIS

St. Louis, Missouri

Artistic Director-Choreographer, Nathalie LeVine; Associate Director, Gary Hubler; President of the Board, Richard Halbert; Lighting, Jim Renner; Stage Manager, Bernie Corn; Costumes, Judy Halbert, Wendy Eckart, Nathalie LeVine

COMPANY

Lisa Armantrout, Patti Barry, Marianne Bellinger, Paul Cavin, Dina Duckworth, Elizabeth Eckart, Janet Ferguson, Kim Gavin, Anna Marie Harris, Leslie Herrin, Patricia Kelsten, Karen Kemp, Melinda Koblick, Gus Licare, Valerie Ratts, Laura Reynolds, Mary Lou Sinnott, Kathleen Sutton, Marvin Sunnenschein

Ellen Barry, Jane Barry, Cindy Butler, Halli Cohn, Ellen Cook, Rosemary Cook, Lisa Dellinger, Anita DeMarco, Amy Eckart, Scott Eckart, Richard Fischer, Elizabeth Guller, Laura Halbert, Denise Harris, Beth Katz, Nikki LeVine, Ted LeVine, Angela Liao, Kelly McGinnis, Susan Rowe, Laurie Stream, Karen Van Meter, Kathleen Webber

REPERTOIRE

"Trilogy on Love, Marriage, and Children from 'The Prophet'" (Arif Mardin, Sherry Londe), "Mississippi River Portraits" (Traditional, Gregg Mayer/Bob Fehrmann), "Salute" (John Phillip Sousa, Gary Hubler), "Games" (Morton Gould, Jill Engel Tulchinsky/Bobbi Niman), "Black Swan Pas de Deux" (Tchaikovsky, Larry Long), "Bluebird Pas de Deux" (Tchaikovsky, Nathalie LeVine), "Consumer's Guide" (TV Commercials, Sherry Londe)

Left Center: Lisa Armantrout,
Gary Hubler, Karen Kemp in "Back to Bach"
(Michael Eastman Photo)

MIAMI BALLET COMPANY

Miami, Florida

Artistic Director-Choreographer, Thomas Armour; Co-Directors, Robert Pike, Martha Mahr, Renee Zintgraff; Conductor, Akira Endo; Costumes, Renee Zintgraff, Robert Pike, Peter Farmer, Francois Cloutier; Sets, Demetrio Menendez, Peter Farmer, Francois Cloutier, Robin Ironside, Christopher Ironside; Lighting; Richard Mix; Stage Manager, Demetrio Menendez

COMPANY

Barbara Abbott, Sydney Bredenberg, Susie Caswell, Cathy Contillo, Rio Cordy, Diana Dismuke, Paula Donelan, Ann England, Helen Frost, Rebecca Granda, Lynne Lardizabal, Maritza Moreno, Adlaida Munez, Kate Prahl, Tracy Poulter, Lenore Redmond, Sheleva Schill, Julie Smith, Karen Smith, Grace Suarez, Marcia Sussman, Nancy Undt, Cathy Wilson, Phyllis Vasquez, Susan Willig, Wendy Wine, Dennis Arroyo, Roy Dunan, Steven Undt, Richard Schill

GUEST ARTISTS: Karena Brock, Natalia Makarova, Frederic Franklin, Ted Kivitt, Ivan Nagy, Gregory Begley, John Davis, Mark Diamond, Richard Rock, Jorge Samaniego

REPERTOIRE

"La Sylphide" (Lovenskjold, Bournonville), "Raymonda" (Glazounov, Petipa), "Prince Igor" (Borodine, Fokine), "Le Corsaire Pas de Deux" (Adam, Perrot), and *PREMIERES* of "Straussiana" (Johann Strauss, Thomas Armour), "Americana 1876" (Don Gillis, Robert Pike)

Miami Ballet's "Raymonda"

MID-HUDSON BALLET COMPANY
Poughkeepsie, N.Y.

Artistic Directors, Estelle & Alfonso; President, Joseph V. Towers; Sets, Lloyd Waldon, Ruth Waldon; Costumes, Olive Pearson; Company Manager, Shirley Sedore; Stage Manager, Robert McCord; Ballet Mistress, Karen Cassetta; Press, Betty L. Eisele.

COMPANY

Karen Cassetta, Mary Anne Fiorillo, Kathy Meggison, Sharon Moore, Jan Silkworth, Betty Jean Theysohn, Tracey Vita, Mary Chris Wall, Taryn Noel Weinlein

REPERTOIRE

(All choreography by Estelle & Alfonso)
"Let Freedom Ring" (Public Domain), "The American Bride" (Gilbert & Sullivan), "The Big Country" (J. Moross), "Origins in Geometric Progressions" (Peter Sinfield), "Little Drummer Boy" (H. Simeon/H. V. Onorati/K. Davis), "Etudes"

Top Right: Mid-Hudson Ballet Company

MISSISSIPPI COAST BALLET
Gulfport, Mississippi

Director-Choreographer, Delia Weddington Stewart; Conductor, James Shannon; Stage and Business Manager, Bennie Stewart; Press, Jerry Kinser

COMPANY

Delia Weddington Stewart, Hazle White, Merrily Bertucci Carter, Julie Stewart, Christina Backstrom, Molly Pisarich Johnson, Barbara Gayle Titler, Jill Wilson, Cheryl Dawson, Mark Hamilton, Ellen Booth

Rebecca Fountain, Tammy Fulton, Beth Shanks, Patsy Williams, Donna Necaise, Lisa McCardle, Michele Thigpin

GUEST ARTIST: Bruce Wells

REPERTOIRE

"Romanza" (Wallingford Riegger, Hazle White), "Canon in D Major" (J. Pachelbel, Bruce Wells), "Moon Child" (Erik Satie, Hazle White), "Mahalia's Spirituals" (Mahalia Jackson, Merrily Carter/-Delia Stewart), "Onegin Waltz" (Tchaikovsky, Delia Stewart), "Air" (Bach, Cheryl Dawson), "Meditations" (Dowland/Bull/-Gluck, Merrily Carter/Delia Stewart), "In the Wind" (Maurice Ravel, Bruce Wells), and *PREMIERES* of "Spirituals" (Morton Gould, Merrily Carter/Delia Stewart/Hazle White), "I Know My Love" (American Folk Songs, Bruce Wells)

MINNESOTA DANCE THEATRE
Minneapolis, Minnesota

Artistic Director-Choreographer, Lyce Houlton; Balletmater, Daniel Job; General Manager, Jim Kerr; Production Manager, John Linnerson; Press, Kathleen Perkins; Costumiere, Gail Bakkom; Designers, Judith Cooper, Jack Barkla, Robert Ellsworth; Lighting, Lance Olson, Robert Hutchings, Ed Kuharski, Jon Baker; Guest Choreographer, John Butler.

COMPANY

Jon Benson, Cynthia Carlson, Cathy Fox, Cheryl Gomes, Marianne Greven, Michael Hackett, Peter Hauschild, Sandra Machala, Glen Martin, Pamela Pilkenton, Andrew Rist, Nicole Sowinski, Andrew Thompson, Susan Thompson, David Voss, Geol Weirs

Tina Forsberg, Neil Greenberg, Elizabeth Harrison, Stephanie Karr, Katherine Kranda, Alan Land, Karen Larsen, Toni Pierce, Robin Stiehm, Lea Thompson, Mark Townes, Donald Young

REPERTOIRE

"Circles" (Igor Stravinsky, Loyce Houlton), "Requiem" (Stravinsky, Houlton), "Seedless Stonemoons" (George Crumb, Houlton), "Slaughter on Tenth Avenue" (Richard Rodgers, Houlton), "293.6" (Anton von Webern, Houlton), "Yellow Variations" (Vivaldi, Houlton)

PREMIERES: "Knoxville: Summer of 1915" (Samuel Barber, Houlton), "Threnodies" (Tadeusz Baird, Daniel Job), "The God Is Lonely" (Hans Werner Henze, John Butler), "Kaleidoscope, View of American Dance" (Compiled, Houlton), "Carmina Burana" (Carl Orff, Houlton)

Left Center: Andrew Thompson,
Marianne Greven in "Knoxville: Summer of 1915"

Mississippi Coast Ballet

NANCY SPANIER DANCE THEATRE
Boulder, Colorado

Artistic Director-Choreographer, Nancy Spanier; Technical Director-Lighting Designer, Debora L. Stoll; Manager, Thomas Hast

COMPANY

Nancy Spanier
Paul Oertel
Emily Wadhams
Jane Franklin
Douglas Jessop

REPERTOIRE: "Class Camelias" (Pink Floyd, Spanier), "Time Wounds All Heals" (Collage/Stephen Elliott, Spanier), "Witness" (Kraftwerk, Wadhams), "Swine Luck" (Collage, Spanier/Oertel)

PREMIERES: "Foreplay" (Improvisation, Wadhams), "Peak to Peak" (Pachabel/Temptations, Spanier/Oertel), "Third Facings" (Vivaldi, Jessop), "Chronicles" (Collage/Stephen Elliott, Oertel), "Labyrinth 1, 2, 3" (Chavez, Franklin), "Earthreach" (Selleck, Wadhams), "Witness" (Kraftwerk, Wadhams), "Abundance" (Bach, Spanier)

Top Left: Nancy Spanier Dance Theatre

NEW JERSEY DANCE THEATRE GUILD
Edison, N.J.

Artistic Director-Choreographer, Alfredo Corvino; Ballet Mistress, Andra Corvino; Ballet Chairman, Patricia McCusker; Business Director, Helen Bechtold; Administration and Production Consultant, Yvette Cohen; President, Gertrude Weinberg; Costumes, Gail Rae, Marcella Corvino; Sets, Norman Cohen; Stage Managers, Verne Fowler, Jackie Lynn; Choreographer, Andra Corvino

COMPANY

Judy Bolanowski, Nancy Butchko, Eileen Byrne, Ruth Capaldo, Cecily Douglas, Kathy Gatto, Melanie Geigel, Diane Gressing, Dawn Lore, Karen Lowande, Michelle Massa, Claire Miller, Mary Ruth Nollstadt, Margaret Rock, Patricia Scarangello, Janice Sorrentino, Maryellen Stickles, Mary Stoltenberg, Debbie Strauss, Leslie Strauss, Lisa Torcicollo

GUEST ARTISTS: Christine Sarry, John Sowinski, Gregory Cary, Joseph Fernandez, Edilio Ferraro, Mercie Hinton, Jack Scalici, Jay Seaman, Victor Vargas

REPERTOIRE

"The Nutcracker" (P. I. Tchaikovsky, Corvino after Ivanov)

Right Center: "Dance of the Snowflakes"

NEW REFLECTIONS DANCE THEATRE
Charlotte, N.C.

Artistic Directors, Mary Ann Mee, Gerda Zimmermann; Costume Designers, Robert Croghan, Terri Watson

COMPANY

Roy Cooper, Noel Goodman, Rebecca Hutchins, Jean Johnson, Mary Ann Mee, Elizabeth Petty, Kista R. Tucker, Pamela Sofras, Stacy R. Williams, Rosemary M. Wyman, Gerda Zimmerman, and apprentices Hardin Minor, Jim Rivers

REPERTOIRE

"Merry Clydeneddie" (Charles Ives, Kista R. Tucker), "June 1936" (Poem by James Agee, Tucker) "Soctober Song" (Copland, Tucker), "Kinnapump" (Sound, Cathy Kaemmerlen), "Ogam" (Toru, Mary Ann Mee), "Jam" (Bette Midler/Helen Reddy, Noel Goodman), "Do It" (Arranged/Stones, Raymond Johnson), "Lot's Wife" (Thomas Turner, Gerda Zimmermann), "Luna Park" (Perrey-Kingsley, Zimmermann), "Apokatastase" (Maurice Ravel, Zimmermann), "Strahlungen" (Chavez, Zimmermann), "Silhouettes" (Russell/Cowell/Perry-Kingsley/Turner, Zimmermann), "Jeux Variation on a Theme" (Beethoven, Zimmermann), "Phases and Faces" (Friedrich Leinert, Zimmermann), "Sidewalk Interlude" (Edgar Varese, Zimmermann), "Contrasts" (Rich O'Donnell, Zimmermann)

PREMIERES: "Charlotte Ruby" (Harold Winokuer, Kista R. Turner), "Arachne" (Thomas Turner, Gerda Zimmermann) "Untitled" (Pamela Sofras), "Brahms Waltz" (Johannes Brahms, Charles Weidman)

Members of New Reflections Dance Theatre

Caroll Sue Dodd, Glenn White in
Norfolk Civic Ballet's "Raymonda Variations"

NORTH CAROLINA DANCE THEATRE
Winston-Salem, N.C.

Director, Robert Lindgren; General Manager, Rod J. Rubbo; Press, Louise A. Bahnson; Lighting, Gary Barnes; Stage Manager, Larry Starr; Technical Director, Skip Sherman; Wardrobe Mistress, Marita Marsili

DANCERS

Jan Adams, Margaret Anders, Michael Auer, Terri Cox, Charles Devlin, Tamara Grose, Larry Harper, Carey Homme, Janine James, Liz Kuethe, Mike Michael, Susan Rowe, Gwen Spear, Katie Starr, Rodney Wynfield

REPERTOIRE

"A Time of Windbells" (Tape Collage, Norbert Vesak), "Bach Brandenburg Three" (Bach, Charles Czarny), "Fugitive Visions" (Serge Prokofiev, Job Sanders), "The Grey Goose of Silence" (Ann Morrifee, Vesak), "Myth" (Igor Stravinsky, Alvin Ailey), "Nocturnal Sun" (Michael Colina, Richard Kuch), "Raymonda" (Alexander Glazounov, Balanchine/Danilova)

PREMIERES: "Changes" (Honegger, Carlos Carvajal), "Reflections" (Johannes Brahms, Sanders), "Virginia Sampler" (Leo Smit, Valerie Bettis)

NORFOLK CIVIC BALLET
Norfolk, Virginia

Artistic Director-Choreographer, Gene Hammett; Assistant Director, Teresa Martinez; Choreographers, Randy Strawderman, Glenn White; Costumes, Angelina Martinez, Peggy Jones; Ballet Mistress, Patricia Sorrell

COMPANY

PRINCIPALS: Lisa Headley, Caroll Sue Dodd, Deborah Dougherty, Sandra Flader, Jane Meredith

SOLOISTS: Alexis Brown, Stacie Caddell, Kim Fielding, Melissa Hoffer, Mark Holland Croston, Rick Karsten, John Medlin, Gregory E. Pope, Tom Luna, Lee Thompson, Steve Pasco, Charles Gies, Michael Webster

CORPS: Paula Bass, Sandra Barth, Lori Buckley, Lisa Buckley, Maria Ten Braak, Mary Baker, Leona Dodd, Loretta Dodd, Denise Hernandez, Marina Maroto, Ana Maria Martinez, Kathleen Mullen, Kim Olinger, Lynne Owen, Sherri Foshee, Beth Richardson, Donna Sheppard, Patti Sawyer, Catherine Anne Smith, Ginny Thumm, Ami Tsao, Joan Tsao, Terri Tompkins, Debbie Vastano, Virginia Vaughan, Jan Zartman, Michael Barriskill, John Senter

GUESTS: Richard Prewitt, David Cuevas, Ralph Hewitt, Clark Tippet, Steve Revelino

REPERTOIRE

"Raymonda Variations" (Glazounov, Balanchine/Danilova), "Cinderella" (Offenbach, Hammett), "Spring Waters" (Rachmaninoff, Messerer), "Rhapsody in Blue" (Gershwin, Strawderman)

PREMIERES: "Cinderella" (Offenbach, Hammett), "Grande Tarantella" (Gottschalk, Hammett), "These Three" (Debussy, Hammett), "Slaughter on 10th Avenue" (Rodgers, Strawderman), "Salute for Susan" (Sousa, White)

North Carolina Dance Theatre's "Virginia Sampler"

NORTH CAROLINA PROGRESSIVE DANCE TROUPE
Chapel Hill, N.C.

Artistic Director, Jamie Sims; Managing Director, Glen Tig; Technical Director, Christopher Stamey; Choreographer, Jamie Sims; Music Consultant, Steve Riley; Designers, Gregory Vines, Glen Tig, Jamie Sims

COMPANY

Karin Bradford
Jim Clark
Glen Tig
Gregory Vines
Olivia Wu
Jane Wyche

REPERTOIRE: All premieres: "Cocktails" (Spoken, Jamie Sims), "A Day at the Vet's" (Portsmouth Sinfonia/Light Classics/WYVD Radio Station, Jamie Sims), "Les Saltimbanques" (Silence/Sousa, Sims), "Giblets" (Ulmer-Koger/Company, Sims)

North Carolina Progressive Dance Troupe in
"Les Saltimbanques"

NUTMEG BALLET COMPANY
Torrington, Connecticut

Artistic Director-Choreographer, Sharon E. Dante; President, Arthur LePage; Press, James Hodson; Technical Director, Arthur LePage; Wardrobe Mistress, Claire LePage; Musical Adviser, Neil Pagano

COMPANY

Denise LePage	Charlene Jacobs
Donna Neri	Darlene Jacobs
Deborah Tyczenski	Jeanne Diorio
Julie Danaher	Cheryl Hart
Donna Bonasera	Christina Andreoli

James Trimble

GUEST ARTISTS: Denise Warner, Janet Shibata, David Coll, Denis Marshall

REPERTOIRE

"Coppelia Variations" (Delibes, Saint-Leon), "Le Corsaire" (Drigo, Petipa), "Holberg Suite" (Grieg, Dante), "On Our Way Back" (Complied, Dante), "White Swan Pas de Deux" (Tchaikovsky, Petipa/Ivanov), "La Petite Danseuse" (Mozart, Dante), "Pas Classique Pas de Deux" (Auber, Petipa), "Romeo and Juliet Pas de Deux" (Prokofiev, Lavrovsky), "Untitled" (Compiled, Dante)

Nutmeg Ballet Company

OHIO STATE UNIVERSITY DANCE COMPANY
Columbus, Ohio

Director-Choreographer, Vera Blaine; Company Assistant, Miguel Diaz; Lighting, Louise Guthman; Costumes, Victoria Angel, Angela Nicolosi; Press, Charles McCloud, Marguerite Fishman, Marilyn Jones; Choreographer-in-Residence, Nina Wiener

COMPANY

Mary Ambrose, Betty Bruen, Timothy Buckley, Miguel Diaz, Marguerite Fishman, Denise Gabriel, Karen Gober, Marilyn Jones, Alison Katz, Lynda Knapp, Alison Pearl, Claire Porter, Anthony Rabara, Nancy Scotford, Robert Sonnenschein, Randy Thomas, Marcia Trees, Linn Walker

REPERTOIRE

ALL PREMIERES: "Inside-Out" (Collage, Linda Knapp), "Apparitions" (Johann Joachim Quanz, Rosalind Pierson), "Tracks" (Collage/Tom MacDonald, Vera Blaine), "Dance with Chairs" (Collage and Choreography, Alison Pearl), "A Friend Is Better Than a Dollar" (Traditional, Nina Wiener), "Dan's Run Penny Supper" (Traditional country western, Dan Wagoner)

Ohio State University Dance Company
(Harry R. Blaine Photo)

OLYMPIA BALLET
Olympia, Washington

Artistic Director-Choreographer, Virginia Woods; Music Director, Ken Olendorf; Stage Manager, Chuck Foster; Art Director, Ray Gilliland; President, Carole Shoop

COMPANY

Debbi Haverlock, Debi Campbell, Dan Hentzmann, Nancy Isely, Kathy Minnitti, Susan Foster, Mary Ann Murphy, Kendra Olendorff, Krystal Shoop, Gail Tveden, Fred Knittle, Vicki Ross, Frankie Nelson, Michiko Yamane, Kathy Coniff, Eric Foster

REPERTOIRE

"The Nutcracker" (Tchaikovsky, Woods), "Frankie and Johnny" (Gershwin, Woods), "Entrance to Hades" (Hindemith, Woods), "Bicentennial of Dance" (Traditional, Woods)

PREMIERES: "The Night before Christmas" (Traditional, Woods), "We Believe in Music" (Popular, Woods)

Virginia Woods of Olympia Ballet

PACIFIC BALLET
San Francisco, California

Artistic Directors, Sue Loyd, Henry Berg, John Pasqualetti; Choreographer, John Pasqualetti; Administrator, Mary Ann Seymour; President of the Board, Francesca Howe; Stage Manager, John O'-Neil

COMPANY

Susan Alleluia	John Loschmann
Zola Dishong	Carolyn Meyerhoffer
Deborah Frates	Peter Reed
Allen Gebhardt	Jeffrey Sherwood
Nancy Henderson	Gay Wallstrom
Fred Johnston	Kahz Zmuda

REPERTOIRE

All premieres, and all choreographed by John Pasqualetti except where noted) "Rhapsody in Blue" (Leonard Bernstein), "Six Wives of Henry VIII" (Rick Wakeman), "Symphony for a Man Alone" (Pierre Henry/Pierre Schaeffer), "Voice of the Whale" (George Crumb), "Symphony of Psalms" (Stravinsky), "Namaska" (Maurice Ravel, Sue Loyd), "Bagatelles" (Beethoven, Henry Berg), "Intermezzo" (Brahms, Berg), "Makrokosmos III" (Crumb, Berg), "Aurora" (Ralph Towner, Allen Gebhardt), "Basha Bella" (Berberian, Nancy Henderson), "Murder in the Cathedral" (Gustav Holst, Gebhardt), "Sonata" (Aaron Copland, Ann Butler), "Pas de Deux" (Tchaikovsky, David Lopes), "Walk to Paradise Garden" (Delius, John Loschmann), "Fifth Position" (Prokofiev, Butler)

Nancy Henderson, John Loschmann,
Henry Berg of Pacific Ballet in "Daphne of the Dunes"
(Arne Folkedal Photo)

PENINSULA BALLET THEATRE
San Mateo, California

Director-Choreographer, Anne Bena; Sets, Hu Pope, Lila Vultee; Costumes, Jeanette Owlett, Alice Weiner; Lighting, David Arrow; Stage Manager, Edward Bena; Press, Annette Cowan

COMPANY

PRINCIPALS AND SOLOISTS: Rosine Bena, Sam Weber, and Ulf Esser, Jeanne Harman, Linda Triplett, Don Harriss

CORPS: Tina Amarillo, Loretta Bartlett, Amy Butler, Leslie Gaumer, Helen Kjolby, Kymberly Kish, Kristin Laak, Bonnie Manzon, Cathleen McCarthy, Liz McCarthy, Karstyn McCoy, Jennifer Myers, Diana Riola, Anne Rosenberg, Gigi Stephansen, Marge Walsh, Beth Weiner

REPERTOIRE

"The Nutcracker" (Tchaikovsky, Anne Bena), "Paradoz" (Kylian, Kylian), "Roundabout" (Malcolm Arnold, Martin Buckner), "Carnival Tu Tu" (Darius Milhaud, Dick Ford), "Entre Cinq" (Faure, Antony Valdor), and *PREMIERE* of "Swan Lake" (Tchaikovsky, Sallie Wilson)

Left Center: Peninsula Ballet Theatre's "Swan Lake"

PREMIERE DANCE ARTS COMPANY
Denver, Colorado

Artistic Director, Gwen Bowen; Choreographers, Gwen Bowen, Holly Cope, Linda Jacoby, Carrie Taylor, Crystal Chapman, David Miller, Mark Schneider, John Landovsky, Dean Crane; Conductor, Gordon Parks; Production Manager, Dixie Turnquist; Stage Managers, Matt Reid, Rique Bowland, Hal Herr; Sets, Gwen Bowen, Rod Miller; Costume Mistress, Norma Chapman; Lighting, Kathleen Caldwell, Rod Miller; Props, Kathryn Gunderson; Press, Don Taylor, Dixie Turnquist

COMPANY

SOLOISTS: Holly Cope, Dixie Turnquist, Evan Jaffe, Carrie Taylor, Tim Stewart

CORPS: Crystal Chapman, Jayne Cacciatore, Suzanne Cacciatore, Vicky Fields, Gina Gray, Linda Jacoby, Rise Kelly, Nikki Killian, Irene Kropwiansky, Carol March, Colette Porter, Joyce Rider, Beth Shafer, Valerie Thornberg, DeAnne Warden, Anne West, Alexandra Geronikos

REPERTOIRE

(Choreography by Gwen Bowen unless otherwise noted) "The Web" (Barber), "Moldovian Suite" (Traditional, John Landovsky), "Deux et Trois" (Adam), "Beethoven" (Beethoven), "Palaszt" (Brahms), "Invitation to the Dance" (Weber), "Prince Igor" (Borodin), "Reflections" (Selected), "Hansel and Gretel" (Humperdinck), "Pastel Symphony" (Tchaikovsky, Carrie Taylor, Crystal Chapman), "Peacocks 'Round the Glass, Alas!" (Tchaikovsky, Holly Cope), "Valse" (Strauss, Linda Jacoby), "Night on Bald Mountain" (Moussorgsky/Shubert, Crystal Chapman), "Pas Classique Hongrois" (Glazounov, David Miller), "Ghost Town" (Selected), "Anthology on Sousa" (Sousa)

Vicky Fields, Beth Shafer and
Premiere Dance Arts Company in "Ghost Town"

RIO GRANDE VALLEY CIVIC BALLET
McAllen, Texas

Artistic Director-Choreographer, Doria Avila; Administrative Director, Alfred J. Gallagher; Company Manager, Jeanne Ross; Conductor, Vasilios Priakos; Ballet Mistress, Colette Ross; Sets, Peter Wolf Associates; Costumes, Michelle Ross, Barbara Woodall, Jeanne Ross, Doria Avila; Lighting-Stage Manager, Maurine Rockhill; Sound, Alfred J. Gallagher, Donnie Ross; Props, Severa Zambrano; Press, Aurora Pena, Nelda Gonzalez

COMPANY

PRINCIPALS: Bonnie Bazar, Carlos Cantu, Rosemary Cavazos, Colette Ross

SOLOISTS: Linda Acevedo, Willie Shives, Sheryl Uhlaender, Douglas Woodall

CORPS: Lisa Acevedo, Dianne Anderson, Lori Anderson, Terri Anderson, Diedre Arechiga, Melissa Barrera, Mike Cattaruzza, Tina de los Santos, Linda Eanes, Michelle Fesler, Linda Garza, Cindy Gonzalez, Cynthia Gonzalez, Jackie Graham, Laura Guerra, Michael Guerra, Debra Handy, Lezlie Hollister, Linda Jaime, Dede Johnson, Jackie Lynn, Steven Lyssy, Kim Maddux, Venezia Mancilla, Donna Patrick, Wendy Patrick, Maritza Pena, Jaime Perez, Patty Putz, Polly Putz, Gabriel Reyes, Linda Rosales, Olaya Solis, Tracy Tarvin, Mark Wilder, Ann Williams

GUEST ARTISTS: Judith Aaen, Anthony Sellers, Olga Plushinskaya, David Kent

REPERTOIRE

"The Nutcracker" (Tchaikovsky, Bill Martin-Viscount/Doria Avila), "Fiesta de Huapango" (Moncayo, Avila), "Feria en Espana" (Massenet, Avila), "Fiesta Mexicana!" (Traditional, Avila), "Dance of the Liberation of the American People" (Tchaikovsky, Olga Plushinskaya)

PREMIERES: "America Hurrah!" (Sousa, Doria Avila; Pas de Deux, Aaen/Sellers), "Caracole" (Lecocq, Avila), "Green Mansions" (Villa Lobos, Avila), "Miss Mariachi" (Traditional, Avila), "Variations on America" (Ives, Avila)

RAM ISLAND DANCE COMPANY
Portland, Maine

Founder-Director, Millicent Marks; Artistic Director, Bryn Mehl; Manager, Frank Wicks; Lighting, Ed Effron

COMPANY

Jan Peterson
Jan Schwartz
Sandy Lovell
John Carrara
Bob Dhondt
Brynar Mehl
Harriet Lutz

REPERTOIRE: ". . . And Autumn Past," "Spacecraft," "Quatette," "Wheel of Time" (Wagner)

Top Left: Brynar Mehl

Rio Grande Valley Civic Ballet's "Caracole"
(Bill Records Photo)

RONDO DANCE THEATRE
Bedford, N.Y.

Director-Choreographer, Elizabeth Rockwell; Lighting Desig Myra Koutzen; Stage Manager, Michael Smart; Manager, Cla Miller

COMPANY

Carol Hess
Kate Johnson
Hannah Kahn
Dennis Kocjan
Edward Zawacki

Susan Osbe
Tony Sm
Catherine Sulliv
Evan Willia

REPERTOIRE: "Line Drawing" (Faure, Keen), "The Executio (Purcell, Rockwell), "Creatures All" (Elizabethan, Newton/Roc well/company), "Spill/Quell" (Evans/Hall, Kahn), "Rin (Haydn, Genter), "Sunday Go to Meeting" (Glenn, Myers), "Ran dance" (Elton John, Solomons), "Holy Moses" (John/Traupin, M ers), "Afro Duo" (Iron Butterfly, Holmes), "Tout de Suite" (Dav Folin), "Triptych" (Villa-Lobos, Rockwell), "Duo" (Coplan Rockwell), "Scorpio" (Coffey, Griffith), "Genesis" (Collage, Roc well), "Take Five" (Desmond, Rockwell), "Poison Variation (Watson/Press, Keen), "Palomas" (Oliveros, Alum)

PREMIERES: "Debussy Dance" (Debussy, Hannah Kahn), "Bla Angels" (George Crum, Kazuko Hirabayashi)

Susan Osberg, Edward Zawacki, Catherine Sullivan in Rondo Dance Theater's "Debussy Dance"

SAN FRANCISCO BALLET
San Francisco, California

Artistic Directors, Lew Christensen, Michael Smuin; President-General Manager, Richard E. Leblond, Jr.; Company Manager, Philip Semark; Press, Penelope McTaggart; Production Managers, Parker Young, Roger Heffner; Choreographers, Lew Christensen, Michael Smuin, Robert Gladstein, John McFall, Tomm Ruud; Music Director, Denis Decoteau; Assistant Conductor, Jean-Louis Leroux; Costumes, Robert O'Hearn, Robert Fletcher, Seppo Nurmina, Jose Varona, Marcos Paredes, Paul Cadmus, Tony Duquette, Russell Hartley, Rouben Ter-Arutunian, Cal Anderson, Tony Walton, Willa Kim, Williams Pitkin, Ariel, Victoria Gyorfi; Sets, Robert Fletcher, Ming Cho Lee, Paul Cadmus, Seppo Nurmima, Tony Walton, Tony Duquette, Russell Hartley, Rouben Ter-Aruntunian, William Pitkin, Ariel, Willa Kim; Lighting, Jennifer Tipton, Gilbert Hemsley, Sara Linnie Slocum, Parker Young; Wardrobe, Patricia Bibbins, Read Gilmore; Regisseurs, Richard Cammack, Virginia Johnson; Ballet Master, Robert Gladstein

COMPANY

Damara Bennett, Sherron Black, Madeleine Bouchard, Maureen Broderick, Val Caniparoli, Gardner Carlson, Laurie Cowden, Allyson Deane, Nancy Dickson, Michael Dwyer, Betsy Erickson, Attila Ficzere, Michael Graham, Victoria Gyorfi, Stephanie Jones, Susan Magno, Keith Martin, John McFall, Lynda Meyer, Cynthia Meyers, Anton Ness, Gina Ness, Anita Paciotti, Roberta Pfeil, Laurie Ritter, Tomm Ruud, Rina Santos, Jim Sohm, Michael Thomas, Elizabeth Tienken, Paula Tracy, Vane Vest, Gary Wahl, Diana Weber, Jerome Weiss, Deborah Zdobinski

GUEST ARTISTS: Valery Panov, Galina Panov, Fernando Bujones, Paolo Bortoluzzi, Ted Kivitt, Carmen de Lavallade, Marge Champion, Suzanne Farrell, Peter Martins

REPERTOIRE

"Airs de Ballet" (Gretry, Christensen), "Cinderella" (Prokofeiv, Christensen/Smuin), "Con Amore" (Rossini, Christensen), "Danses Concertantes" (Stravinsky, Christensen), "Don Juan" (Rodrigo, Christensen), "Don Quixote Pas de Deux" (Minkus, Petipa), Eternal Idol (Chopin, Smuin), "Fantasma" (Prokofiev, Christensen), "Four Temperaments" (Hindemith, Balanchine), "Harp Concerto" (Reinecke, Smuin), "Mobile" (Khachaturian, Ruud), "N.R.A." (Jepson, Gladstein), "Nutcracker" (Tchaikovsky, Christensen), "Pulcinella Variations" (Stravinsky, Smuin), "Serenade" (Tchaikovsky, Balanchine), "Shinju" (Chihara, Smuin), "Symphony in C" (Bizet, Balanchine), "Tealia" (Holst, McFall), "Variations de Ballet" (Glazounov, Christensen/Balanchine)

PREMIERES: "Agon" (Stravinsky, Balanchine), "Les Chansons de Bilitis" (Debussy, de Lavallade), "Garden of Love's Sleep" (Khachaturian, McFall), "Heart of the Mountains" (Kozhlayev, Panov), "Opus I" (Webern, Cranko), "Romeo and Juliet" (Prokofiev, Smuin), "Songs of Mahler" (Mahler, Smuin), "Souvenirs" (Barber, Bolender), "Stravinsky Pas de Deux" (Stravinsky, Christensen)

Right: Gina Ness, Vane Vest in "Airs de Ballet"
Top: Betsy Erickson, Gary Wahl in
"Garden of Love's Sleep"
(Arne Folkedal Photo)

John McFall in "Cinderella"

Attila Ficzere, Madeleine Bouchard in "Eternal Idol"

Cary Tidyman in Sacramento Ballet's "Coppelia"

ST. LOUIS CIVIC BALLET

St. Louis, Missouri

Artistic Director-Choreographer, Stanley Herbertt; Associate Directors, LaVerne Meyering, Betty McRoberts; Choreographers, Ross Winter, Betty McRoberts, LaVerne Meyering; Conductor, Gary Zimmerman; Designers, Stanley Herbertt, Ross Winter, Betty McRoberts, Marion Wehmueller; Lighting, Stanley Herbertt, Ross Winter, Cheryl Brown; Stage Manager, Cheryl Brown; Press, Barbara Corday; Repetiteur, Kyle Wehmueller; President, James Burt; Prop Manager, Marge Salem

COMPANY

Jim Akman, Monica Albers, Laurie Bartram, Ginny Burt, Amy Corday, Karen Cracchiola, Linda Grimme, Stephanie Hamilton, Mary Heidbreder, Stephanie Kretow, Tiffany Maierhoffer, Kathleen Massot, Tony Parise, Kim Reitz, Michelle Sapienza, Lisa Schallert, Patti Smith, Kyle Wehmueller

GUEST ARTISTS: Laura Young, Tony Catanzaro

REPERTOIRE

"The Nutcracker" (Tchaikovsky, Stanley Herbertt), "Oneself Unreal" (Contemporary, Herbertt), "Gentlemen, Be Seated" (Traditional, Herbertt), and *PREMIERES* of "The History of Dance in America" (Compiled, Herbertt/Betty McRoberts), "In a Glass Darkly" (Chopin, Herbertt), "Opus" (Tchaikovsky, Herbertt), "High Jinx" (Contemporary, Herbertt), "Symphonie" (Bach, Herbertt)

William Webber Photo

**Members of San Jose Dance Theatre's
"Golden Moments of Ballet (Circa 1920)"**

SACRAMENTO BALLET

Sacramento, California

Artistic Director-Choreographer, Barbara Crockett; Associate Directors, Cary Tidyman, McGarry Caven; General Manager, Albert Gallo; Stage Manager-Lighting Designer, Bruce Kelley; Costume Coordinator, Marjorie Bader

COMPANY

Danielle Anderson, Mary Anderson, Sarah Arnold, Didi Boyer, Cheryl Chalmers, Debora Dildine, Jody Downes, Teresa Dryden, Margie Francis, Shelley Gilchrist, Julie Leneave, Barbara Nyland, Ron Ortman, Erin Saberi, Ron Shepherd, Kim Sherwood, Jill Stewart, David Takacs, Elizabeth Thompson

GUEST ARTISTS: Starr Danias, Robert Weiss, Allyson Deane, Michael Dwyer, Michael Onstad, Ron Thiele, Leslie Crockett

REPERTOIRE

"Coppelia" (Delibes, Alicia Alonso/Barbara Crockett), "The Nutcracker" (Tchaikovsky, Crockett/Lew Christensen), and *PREMIERES* of "The Wonder Phenomena" (Stevie Wonder, McGarry Caven), "Mobile" (Aaron Khatchaturian, Tomm Ruud), "Imaginary Dialogue" (John McLaughlin, Caven), "La Favorita" (Donizetti, Crockett)

St. Louis Civic Ballet's "Oneself Unreal"
(Art Vasterling Photo)

SAN JOSE DANCE THEATRE

San Jose, California

Directors-Choreographers, Paul Curtis, Shawn Stuart; Conductor, Lewis Keizer; Sets, Stephen C. Wathen, Shawn Stuart; Costumes, Shawn Stuart; Lighting, James R. Earle, Jr.; Production Coordinator, Patricia Poe; President-General Manager, Raymond Poe

COMPANY

PRINCIPALS: Nancie Berridge, Gloria Vauges Mohr, Leila Parello, Shawn Stuart

CORPS: Karen Anderson, Joan Brobst, Mary Callahan, Sally Clish, Denise Croft, Barbara Dando, Letitia DeVillar, Cheryl Elliot, Kim Gardner, Kae Guy, Diana Hayes, Charlene Horvath, Jennifer Johnson, Jacqueline Kamber, Kathleen Kane, Marti Kennedy, Sonja Krusic, Becky Meyers, Sharon Nagle, Sandy Noda, Robert Norton, Kelcey Poe, Sally Ross, Erin Silva, Melanie Spencer, Howard Timoney, Lynn Wingrove, Valinda White, Jamie Zimmerman

GUEST ARTISTS: Ted Kivitt, Karena Brock, John Tucker

REPERTOIRE

"Nutcracker" (Tchaikovsky, Paul Curtis/Shawn Stuart), "Peter and the Wolf" (Prokofiev, Shawn Stuart), "Golden Moments of Ballet" (Guckenheimer Sauerkraut Band, Leona Norman; "Danzas de las Pulgas" (Traditional, Stuart), "Pink Panther" (Mancini, Stuart), "Lilac Fairy Variations" (Tchaikovsky, Stuart), "Don Quixote Variations" (Minkus, Stuart), "I've Got Rhythm" (Gershwin, Stuart)

PREMIERES: "The Sting" (Scott Joplin, Nancie Berridge), "Kuan Yin" (Bach, Stuart), "Sin Gar Adja" (Traditional, Patrick Crommett), "Tarantella" (Rossini, Stuart)

Jenny Anderson
Marilyn Brda
Ruth Emerson
Patricia Hruby
Deborah Riley
Deborah Lowen

REPERTOIRE: "Suite People" (Barry Brosch, Anderson), "Portrait" (Bach, Anderson), "Waltz" (Ted Kalom, Anderson), "SFZ" (Tiger Benford/Jerry Fiddler/Stuart Smith, Brda), "Event" (Brda), "What Time Is This" (William Barnes, Brda), "Canon as Game" (Philip Carlsen, Emerson), "Septet" (Ben Johnston, Emerson), "Jasper" (Barry Brosch, Emerson), "Lean 2" (Cherry Wolfarth, Emerson), "Ripstop" (Patrick Beckman, Emerson), "Birds" (Vivaldi/birdsongs, Hruby), "Match" (Delibes, Hruby), "Daystar" (Eastern Music, Riley), "One More than Three" (Arthur Stidfole, Riley), "Progression" (William Barnes, Riley), "Blue Moon" (Bosch, Riley), "Just Back from Ted Mack" (Don Redman, Lowen)

Top Left: Somedancers in "Suite People"

SOUTHERN REPERTORY DANCE THEATER
Carbondale, Illinois

Artistic Director-Choreographer, Lonny Joseph Gordon; Coordinator, Holly Catchings; Music Director, Bill Evans; Wardrobe Mistress, Jean Kistler

COMPANY
Steven Budas
Robert Hollister
Devi Piper
Andrew Skalko
Elizabeth Thompson
Rosalind Zeisler

GUEST ARTISTS: Gale Ormiston, Nana Shineflug, Mildred Dickinson, Don Redlich

REPERTOIRE: "Phrases for Louise," "Tangoes Inmortales" (Libertad Lamarque, Gordon), "When Things Come Quick and Clear," "Victor Borge's Piano Bench," "Paper Women" (Bette Midler, Gordon), "Christina's View" (Elizabeth Allyn Thompson)

PREMIERES: "Tune My Heart to Sing Thy Grace" (Folk Hymn, Holly Catchings), "Memories of My Childhood" (Kenny Takaoka, Nana Shineflug), "Fourteen Summers on Padre Island" (Bill Evans, Gordon), "Night of the Rich/Night of the Poor" (Elizabeth Allyn Thompson), "Early American Social Dance Suite" (Traditional, Mildred Dickinson)

Right Center: Lonny Joseph Gordon in "Phrases for Louise"

SOUTHERN THEATRE BALLET COMPANY
Jacksonville, Florida

Founder-Artistic Director-Choreographer, Marta Jackson; Guest Choreographers, Gayle Parmelee, Magda G. de Aunon; Technical Director-Lighting Design, Virginia Fox; Sound, Ernest Boada; Costumes, Mary Lovelace; Ballet Mistresses, Pam Davis, Virginia Pelegrin, Lori Childers; Press, Leonardo Favela

COMPANY

Nancy Bock, Sharon Booth, Lori Childers, Pam Davis, Staci Deane, Susan Donziger, Pam Farber, Joy Farris, Becky Hardin, Sara Howell, Pamela Huelster, Gentry Linville, Caroline Lovelace, Melody Susanne McCombs, Traci Owens, Virginia Pelegrin, Mary Saltmarsh, Connie Simmons, Dane Smith, Neyda Castells, Annie Coroalles, Neri Llorente, Gigi Morales, Marta Lopez, Sharon Lasky, Lisa Ossi, Ceci Mari Perez, Lourdes Palomino, Barbara Spraggins, Susu Saltmarsh, Theresa Thweatt, Stacia Stine, Shirley Thomas, Elaine Underwood, Karen Wood, Randy Wood

GUEST ARTISTS: Judith Odell, Donald Van Vleet

REPERTOIRE

(All choreography by Marta Jackson except where noted) "All Rights Reserved (even on the moon)" (Satie, Parmelee), "Arabescos" (Flotow), "Aurora's Wedding" (Tchaikovsky), "Ballet School" (Strauss), "Carmina Burana" (Orff, Ratcliff), "Con Bravura!" (Kay), "El Amor Brujo" (DeFalla), "Esprit" (Britten, Parmelee), "Grand Pas de Quatre" (Pugni), "Highlights" (Drigo), "Isle of Loneliness" (Wagner), "Nutcracker" (Tchaikovsky), "Paquita" (Minkus), "Quadrille" (Strauss), "Reflections" (Debussy), "Rochene" (Glazounov), "Swan Lake Act II" (Tchaikovsky), "Solitude" (Ravel), "Visions" (Debussy), and *PREMIERES* of "The River" (Smetana, Jackson), "Concerto" (Bach, de Aunon after Alberto Alonso)

Belton S. Wall Photo

Southern Theatre Ballet Company

STANZE PETERSON DANCE THEATRE

San Francisco, California

Artistic Direction, Choreography and Costume Design by Stanze Peterson; Technical Direction, Lighting Design, Kevin Myrick; Stage Manager, Jody Mahoney

COMPANY

Stanze Peterson
Janet Ross
Jose Corrales
Virginia Kester

Frances Parham
Mimi Platner-Mills
Don McKing
Esther Platner

REPERTOIRE

"The Sameness Wheel" (Jones/Maldron/Nyro), "I Won't Pass By Here Again" (Jagger/Green/West/Yarbrough), "Cortege" (John Lewis), "Ships" (Olly Wilson)

PREMIERES: "Untitled Solo" (Rodrigo, Maclovia), "Lament for Things to Come" (Fontella Bass), "Ears of Stone" (Anton Webern), "Sugar Man" (Kris Kristofferson, Janet Ross), "Legend" (Elton John/Steven A. Chambers/Oregon/Traditional)

Stanze Peterson in "Cortege"
(David Brooks Photo)

TANCE AND COMPANY

San Francisco, California

Artistic Director, Tance Johnson; Musical Director, Jon Sims; Lighting Design, Carl Sitton; Stage Manager, Patty Ann Farrell; Costumes, Thea Goulis, Narda

COMPANY

Evelyn Ante, Claire Dixon, Teresa de la Cruz, Narda Gillespie, Yvonne Prucha, Maria Goulis, Ercilia Santos, Yvonne Murray, Estella Sisnernos, John Riley, Gilbert Chun, Rosa Wang, Dennis Parlato, Brion Charles, Gerry Luckham

GUEST ARTISTS: Virgil Pearson-Smith, Katherine Warner, Bruce Bain, Jerome Frazer

REPERTOIRE

"Canticle" (Chopin, Tance Johnson), "Aleatoric Thing" (Orff, Johnson), "Encounter" (Benson, Johnson), "The Chase" (rock, Evelyn Ante), "Deja Vu" (Russell, Narda Gillespie), "Trisagion" (Webern, Johnson), "Lovescape" (Brahms, Virgil Pearson-Smith), "Mayuzumi: (Mayuzumi, company)

PREMIERES: "Magnetic Rag" (Scott Joplin, the company), "Ethnic Suite" (Stravinsky, Tance Johnson)

THEATRE FLAMENCO

San Francisco, California

Artistic Director-Choreographer, Adela Clara; Choreographers, Dini Roman, Miguel Santos; Designers, Cal Anderson (sets), Keith Gonzales (lighting); Technical Director, Clive Shephard

COMPANY

PRINCIPALS: Adela Clara, Miguel Santos, SOLOISTS: Ernesto Harnandez, Cruz Luna, Dini Roman, Paula Caro, Damita Prado, CORPS: Mimi Bartolome, Regine Boetius, Leslie Correll, Constancia Lorca, Patricia Roiacono, Julia Thomas, Miguel Vasquez, Teo Greso (guitarist), Jorge Marin (singer), Larry Canaga (piano)

GUEST ARTISTS: William Earl, Diane Moss

REPERTOIRE

"La Vida Breve" (de Falla, Eugenia), "Cordoba" (Albeniz, Eugenia), "Alegrias de Cadiz" (Traditional, Santos), "Balada de la Placeta," "Zapateado" (Traditional, Triana), "Triana" (Albeniz, Vega), "Romance Gitano" (Traditional, Clara), "Viva la Jota" (Traditional, Santos), "El Barberillo de Lavapies" (Barbieri, Eugenia), "Seguiriyas" (Traditional, Roman), "Gitanerias" (Lecuona, Clara), "Jarabe Tapatio" (Traditional), "La Bamba" (Traditional, Santos), "Malambo" (Traditional), "Juerga Flamenca" (Traditional, Clara), "Siva-Mora-Americana-Damballa" (Various, Clara), "La Soltera" (de Falla, Roman)

PREMIERES: "Misa Flamenca" (Traditional, Santos), "Orgia" (Turina, Alba), "Columbian Suite" (Traditional, Cartagena)

Left Center: Yvonne Murray,
Rosa Wang, Dennis Parlato in "Wespero"
(Pete Peters Photo)

Theatre Flamenco of San Francisco
(Mort Fryman Photo)

THELMA OLAKER YOUTH CIVIC BALLET COMPANY
Hopewell, Virginia

Artistic Director, Christin Parks; Ballet Mistress, Karmon Oliver; Technical Director, Ben Keys; Costume and Set Design, Barbara Hebert; Wardrobe Mistress, Hattie McMillan; Lights and Sound, Steve King

REPERTOIRE

"King's River Legends," "Susanna Bolling Story" (Gluck, Christin Parks/Karmon Oliver), "Evelyn Byrd Story" (Mendelssohn, Parks/Oliver), "Windowpanes of Brandon" (MacDowell/Gottschalk, Parks/Oliver), "The Puppets" (Gilbert & Sullivan, Parks), "Bees. . . . the Spirit of the Hive" (Ravel, Parks)

Top Right: Susan Smallwood

TULSA CIVIC BALLET
Tulsa, Oklahoma

Artistic Directors-Choreographers, Roman Jasinski, Moscelyne Larkin; Conductor, Thomas Lewis; Sets, Albert Martin, Jerry Harrison, Katherine Phelps, Ross Young; Costumes, Moscelyne Larkin, Mrs. L. E. Maines; Lighting, Avrome Schuman, Roman Jasinski; Technical Director, M. M. Donnelly; Manager, Charles Ellis

COMPANY

PRINCIPALS: Gail Gregory, Donna Grisez, Edward Tuell

SOLOISTS: Timothy Fox, Jerri Kumery, Kimberley Bell

CORPS: Cynthia Ball, Dorothy Bridwell, Lisa Collins, Lynn Collins, Peyton Foster, Kimmy Jin, Tracy Lockwood, Lisa Mahuron, Carolyn Paddock, Emily Palik, Kimberly Smiley, Hope Theodoras, Annette Wean, Amy Bechtel, Lisa Bethell, Mary Beth Bigbie, Kimberly Dooley, Julie Harris, Joni Myers, Lucy Tuttle, Emily Worrall

APPRENTICES: Deidre Cartmill, Diane Cougler, Melissa Goodman, Nancy Hoopert, Gloria Jo Kumery, Debra McReynolds, Susan Mobley, Lisa Myers, Lisa Poppenhouse, Diane Schooley, Tracie Treece, LaDawn Vinson, Amy Whitney

GUEST ARTISTS: Patricia McBride, Helgi Tomasson, Kay Mazzo, Richard Hoskinson, Kaleria Fedicheva, Dennis Marshall, Charles Ellis, Bob Barnes, Georgia Snoke

REPERTOIRE

"The Nutcracker" (Tchaikovsky, Larkin/Jasinski after Ivanov), "Les Sylphides" (Chopin, Larkin after Fokine), "Stars and Stripes Pas de Deux" (Sousa/Kay, Balanchine), "Concerto" (Mendelssohn, Jasinski), "Mozartiana" (Mozart, Jasinski), "The Dying Swan" (Saint-Saens, Fokine), "Le Corsaire Pas de Deux" (Drigo, Adam), "Rossini Pas de Deux" (Rossini, Tchernicheva/Fedicheva)

PREMIERES: "Bach for a Hep Margrave" (Bach, Jasinski), "Grande Tarantelle" (Gottschalk, Jasinski), "Classical Symphony" (Prokofiev, Jasinski)

R. J. Kumery Photo

TOLEDO BALLET
Toledo, Ohio

Artistic Director-Choreographer, Marie Vogt; President, Carl Hibscher; Conductor-Music Director, Serge Fournier; Customieres, Roz Gonia, Evelyn Davis; Sets, Bill Smith; Lighting, Sue Blaser Bearringer; Production Chairman, Evelyn Brandman

COMPANY

Kerry Culleru, Nagiva Mikhail, Jean Peterson, Judith Nasater, Alison Booth, Kathy Carter, Susan Carter, Amanda Davis, Pam Gordon, Sarah Mott, Kim Parquette, Laura Wade, Renate Wolgast, Craig Barrow, Hillary Sujkowski, Steve Donahue

REPERTOIRE

"Stars and Stripes" (Sousa/Kay), "Symphony for Fun" (Gillis), "Water Music" (Handel), "Saltarello" (Mendelssohn), "Nutcracker" (Tchaikovsky), "American Dance Suite" (Smith), "Les Patineurs" (Meyerbeer), "Graduation Ball" (Strauss, Lichine/Kriza)

Left Center: Alison Booth, Steve Donahue, Kim Parquette, Hillary Sujkowski

Tulsa Civic Ballet's "Classical Symphony"

Rich Burrows, Kay Clark in "Earth"
(Doug Bernstein Photo)

VALENTINA OUMANSKY DRAMATIC DANCE EMSEMBLE

Hollywood, California

Valentina Oumansky

Marilyn Carter	Robin Levin
Keith Clifton	Dellamaria Marino
Janet Dolan	Oscar Nieto
Beth Gage	Tarumi Takagi

(All choreography by Ms. Oumansky)
REPERTOIRE: "A Bow Is a Bow Is a Bow" (Bach/Purcel), "Adoration" (Hovhaness), "Afro-American Jazz Legend" (Compilation), "Cortez, the Conqueror" (Ginastera), "Conversations in Silence and Sound" (Klauss), "El Popol Vuh" (Waldo), "Facade" (Sitwell/Walton), "Ghazals" (Hovhaness), "God in a Box" (Berio), "Homage to the Southwest Indian" (Stein), "In the Hills" (Hovhaness), "Rin Tin Tin Superstar" (Hovhaness), "With Apologies to Aesop" (Stein), "The Horse" "Zen Zen", and *PREMIERE* of "Poe-Pourri" (Herman Stein, Valentina Oumansky; Lighting, Tom Rodgers)

UTAH REPERTORY DANCE THEATRE

Salt Lake City, Utah

Production Manager-Lighting Design, M. Kay Barrell; Company Manager, Sherryn C. Barrell; General Manager, Bruce A. Beers; Design/Costumer, Marina Harris; Stage Manager, Gary Justesen; Production Assistant, Deward Wilson

COMPANY

Ellen Bromberg, Michael Bruce, Rich Burrows, Kay Clark, Martin Kravitz, John Malashock, Ruth Jean Post, Ron Rubey, Thom Scalise, Linda C. Smith, Karen Steele, Lynne Wimmer

GUEST ARTISTS: Bill Evans, Donald McKayle, Lar Lubovich, Jennifer Scanlon, Bruce Marks

REPERTOIRE

"Between Me and Other People There Is Always a Table and a Few Empty Chairs" (Burt Alcantara, Jennifer Muller), "Earth" (Roberto Gerhardt, Paul Sanasardo), "Fatal Birds" (Alberto Ginastera, Sanasardo), "For Betty" (Vivaldi, Bill Evans) "Lyric Suite" (Alban Berg, Anna Sokolow), "Nocturne" (Moondog, Donald McKayle), "Spotlight" (John Cage, Ruth Jean Post), "Synapse" (Songs of the Humpbacked Whale, Karen Steele), "The Brood" (Pierre Henry, Richard Kuch)

PREMIERES: "Games" (Donald McKayle), "Getting Off" (Ellen Bromberg), "My Brother's Keeper" (Hal Cannon/Chris Montague, Lynne Wimmer), "Session" (Lar Lubovich)

Valentina Oumansky in "Zen Zen"
(Garo Photo)

VIRGINIA BEACH CIVIC BALLET

Virginia Beach, Virginia

Artistic Director-Choreographer, Colin Worth; Producer-Executive Director, Nancy A. McClees; Ballet Mistress, Sylvia Worth; Stage Manager, Beth Hudson; Costumes, John Jones, Dona McCloud, Edith Caldwell, Joyce Gaus, Phyllis Hale, Ursula Jones, Elizabeth Marquette, Neil Templeton, Sylvia Worth; Sound, Ursula Jones; Props, Mary Louise Hepner; Technical Crew, Bruce Calkins, Judith Hatcher, Gary John, John Jones, Theresa Pagano; Press, Marilyn Jacobson; Sets, Stan Fedyzen

COMPANY

PRINCIPALS: Debby Benvin, Major Burchfield, Charles Lipka, Heidi Robitshek

CORPS: Audrey Bender, Sarah Bender, Kenya Benitez, Lolly Brenn, Catherine Caldwell, Dawn Dodson, Frank Gruber, Nancy Lew Guarnieri, Julianna Holm, Lisa Hunt, Elizabeth Hurd, Deborah Jakubec, Ann John, Joe Johnson, Monique McCloud, Kathy McDonald, Irene Meert, Andrea Michalos, Deborah Nadell, Deborah Nonni, Leslie Redden, Medina Stiff, Ann Tate, Ann Watkins, Dottie Watkins, Jeanne West, Lauren Wiesner, Valerie Wilson, Colin Worth, Sylvia Worth, Ridgely Balderson, John Conrad, Barry Frankenfield

REPERTOIRE

"Snow Scene from "The Nutcracker" (Tchaikovsky, Colin Worth), "Coppelia" (Delibes, Colin Worth after Saint-Leon)

Virginia Beach Civic Ballet's "Chopin Suite"
(Ursula Jones Photo)

Janet Smith, Scott Hollifield in Virginia Beach
Community Ballet's "Voice from the River"

VIRGINIA BEACH COMMUNITY BALLET COMPANY
Virginia Beach, Virginia

Artistic Director-Choreographer, Virginia Biggs; Ballet Mistresses, Betty Jean Walker, Janet Smith; Sets and Designs, Mike Bell; Wardrobe, Kim Crosby

COMPANY

PRINCIPALS: Janet Smith, Jody Norris, Melinda Sullivan, Dana Snead, Shelia Francis, Terri Earley, Tiffany Biggs, Lisa Biggs, John Vanauken, Scott Hollifield

CORPS: Kaven Addison, Maria Griffith, Kim Griffith

REPERTOIRE

"Dance Romantique" (Schumann, Walker), "Reflection" (Satie, Walker), "The Enchanted Ogre" (Shostakovich, Smith), "Voice from the River" (Ravel, Walker), "Pas de Deux" (Minkus, Biggs), "Expectation" (Quincy Jones, Smith), "Now I Have Everything" (Ferrante and Teicher, Biggs)

David L. St. Clair Photo

WASHINGTON DANCE THEATRE
Washington, D.C.

Artistic Director-Choreographer, Erika Thimey; Stage and Lighting Directors, Guy LeValley, Bill De Mull; Conductors, William J. Akers, Karl Halvorson; Costumes, Dagmar Wilson, Hertha Woltersdorf; Masks and Sets, David Komuro, E. Raye LeValley

COMPANY

Sharon Bodul, Margaret Chinn, Miriam Cramer, Ellie Grayson, Lorraine Johnson, Stephen Johnson, E. Raye LeValley, Carol O'-Toole, Diana Parson, Kevin Tolson

REPERTOIRE

"Playthings of the Wind" (Gassman/Sala), "Folk Cantana, Santa Maria de Iquique" (Luis Advis), "Noisy Hello" (Butler), "Galoob and Galick" (Kazoo/Improvisations), "First Totem Pole" (Lohoefer), and *PREMIERE* of "Rejoice in the Lamb" (Britten)

Howard Millard Photo

Right Center: E. Raye LeValley, Stephen Johnson, Julie Houghton, Diana Parson, Sharon Bodul in "Rejoice in the Lamb"

WESTCHESTER BALLET COMPANY
Ossining, N.Y.

Artistic Director-Choreographer, Iris Merrick; Conductor, Stephen Simon; Designers, Janet Crapanzano, Jacqueline Stoner

COMPANY

PRINCIPALS: Vivian Crapanzano, Lenore Meinel, Micaela Ceballos, Heather Behling, Patricia Morrissy, Tom Grant, Richard Roistacker, Gregory Ismailov

CORPS: Elizabeth Wedge, Nancy Wellman, Laurie Beckett, Sue Kenney, Nell Compo, Inga Sterner, Jill Robie, Michele Brucellaria, Phyliss Crowder, Carolyn Ellis, Nancy Fry, Karin Berzins, Pamela Packard, Nanci Turner, Wendy Garber, Laurie Offenberg, Charles Compo, Tim Rowell, Gareth Houghman, William Wedge, Ken Pierce, Richard Moore

GUEST ARTISTS: Cathryn Rhodes, Dennis Marshall, Gregory Mitchell

REPERTOIRE

"Romeo and Juliet" (Tchaikovsky), "Cinderella" (Prokofiev), "Holiday" (Anderson), "Le Retour" (Kabelevsky), "Sleeping Beauty" (Tchaikovsky), "Caprice" (Shostakovich), "Emperor Valse" (Strauss), "Peter and the Wolf" (Prokofiev), "Nutcracker" (Tchaikovsky), "East of the Sun" (Grieg), "Seasons" (Chausson), "The Tailor and the Doll" (Rossini/Britten), "Come What May" (Riisager), "Star Maiden" (McDowell), "Swan Lake Act II" (Tchaikovsky), "Dream Toy Shop" (Rossini), "Summer Day" (Prokofiev), "Secret River" (Leyden), "Suite of Shubert Dances of Isadora Duncan directed by Julia Levien" (Shubert), "Tarkus" (Emeraon/Lake and Palmer, Edward Roll)

Curt R. Meinel Photo

Lenore Meinel, Richard Roistacher in
Westchester Ballet Company's "Nutcracker"

Alvin Ailey

Lucette Aldous

Joseph Albano

Maria Alba

Dick Andros

BIOGRAPHIES OF DANCERS AND CHOREOGRAPHERS

ABARCA, LYDIA. Born Jan. 8, 1951 in NYC. Studied at Fordham U., Harkness House. Debut 1968 with Dance Theatre of Harlem.

ADAIR, TOM. Born in Venus, Tex. Joined American Ballet Theatre in 1963, elevated to soloist in 1966.

ADAMS, CAROLYN. Born in N.Y.C. Aug. 16, 1943. Graduate Sarah Lawrence Col. Studied with Schonberg, Karin Waehner, Henry Danton, Wishmary Hunt, Don Farnworth. Member of Paul Taylor Co. since 1965. Director of Harlem Dance Studio.

ADAMS, DIANA. Born in Stanton, Va. Studied with Edward Caton, Agnes de Mille. Made professional debut in 1943 in "Oklahoma!" Joined Ballet Theatre in 1944. N.Y.C. Ballet 1950. Now ballet mistress-teacher at School of American Ballet. N.Y.C.

AHONEN, LEO. Born June 19, 1939 in Helsinki, Finland. Studied at Kirov Theatre. Scandinavian School of Ballet. Joined company and rose to principal. Appeared with Bolshoi Ballet. Joined National Ballet of Holland as dancer and ballet master; Royal Winnipeg Ballet 1966; San Francisco Ballet 1968. Since 1972 principal and teacher with Houston Ballet.

AIELLO, SALVATORE. Born Feb. 26, 1944 in N.Y. Attended Boston Cons. Studied with Danielian, Stanley Williams. Rosella Hightower, Professional debut with Joffrey Co. in 1964, subsequently with Donald McKayle, Pearl Lang, Patricia Wilde, Alvin Ailey, Harkness Ballet, and in Bdwy musicals. Joined Royal Winnipeg Ballet 1971. Promoted to principal 1972.

AILEY, ALVIN. Born Jan. 5, 1931 in Rogers, Tex. Attended UCLA. Studied with Lester Horton, Hanya Holm, Martha Graham, Anna Sokolow, Karel Shook, and Charles Wiedman. Debut 1950 with Lester Horton Dance Theatre, and became choreographer for company in 1953. Formed own company in 1958 and has toured U.S. and abroad. Now N.Y. City Center based.

AITKEN, GORDON. Born in Scotland in 1928. Joined Saddler's Wells Ballet in 1954. Soloist with Royal Ballet.

ALBA, MARIA. Born in China of Spanish-Irish parentage. Began studies in Russian School of Ballet, Peking. Moved to Spain, studied with Regla-Ortega, and La Quica. After professional debut in teens, became one of world's foremost Spanish dancers at 21. Toured with Iglesias Co., and Ballet Espagnol. With Ramon de los Reyes, formed company in 1964 that has toured U.S., S. America and Europe.

ALBANO, JOSEPH. Born Dec. 29, 1939 in New London, Conn. Studied with Vilzak, Legat, Bartholin, Hightower, Danielian, Graham, Weidman, and Limon. Performed with Charles Wiedman Co., Ballet Russe, Martha Graham, Joos-Leeder, N.Y.C. Ballet. Founder-artistic director-choreographer of Hartford Ballet Co., Established Albano Ballet 1971. First dancer to serve as Commissioner for Conn. Commission for the Arts.

ALBRECHT, ANGELE. Born Dec. 12, 1942 in Frieburg, Ger. Studied at Royal Ballet, and with Lula von Sachnowsky, Tatjanti Granzeva, Rosella Hightower. Debut 1960 with Ntl. Theater Mannheim; Hamburg Staatsoper 1961–7; Ballet of 20th Century from 1967.

ALDOUS, LUCETTE. Born Sept. 26, 1938 in Auckland, N.Z. Studied at Royal Ballet School. Joined Rambert, London's Festival Ballet (1963), Royal Ballet (1966), Australian Ballet (1971).

ALENIKOFF, FRANCES. Born in N.Y.C.; graduate Bklyn Col. Studied with Graham, Limon, Horton, Anthony, Sanasardo, Humphrey, Sokolow, Barashkova, Dunham, Fort, Flores. Debut 1957. Since 1959 toured with own company, and as soloist. Has choreographed Bdwy musicals.

ALEXANDER, ROD. Born Jan. 23, 1922 in Colo. Studied with Cole, Holm, Maracci, Riabouchinska, Horton, Castle. Debut with Jack Cole Dancers, then in Bdwy musicals before forming own company and becoming choreographer for Bdwy and TV.

ALLEN, JESSICA. Born Apr. 24, 1946 in Bryn Mawr, Pa. Graduate UCol., NYU. Debut 1970 with Jean Erdman Dance Theatre. Also appeared with Gus Solomons, Matt Maddox.

ALLENBY, JEAN. Born Apr. 29, 1946 in Bulawayo, Rhodesia and began training there. Debut 1966 with Cape Ballet. Joined Stuttgart in 1971 and promoted to principal.

ALONSO, ALICIA. Born Alicia Martinez, Dec. 21 in Havana; married Fernando Alonso. Studied with Federova, and Volkova, and at School of American Ballet. Made debut in musicals. Soloist with Ballet Caravan 1939–40. Ballet Theatre 1941. In 1948 formed own company in Havana. One of world's greatest ballerinas.

ALUM, MANUEL. Born in Puerto Rico in 1944. Studied with Neville Black, Sybil Shearer, Martha Graham, Mia Slavenska. Joined Paul Sanasardo Company in 1962, and is its assistant artistic director. Has appeared with The First Chamber Dance Quartet, and American Dance Theatre Co. Also teaches and choreographs, and formed own company 1972.

ALVAREZ, ANITA. Born in Tyrone, Pa. in 1920. Studied with Marth Graham, and appeared with her company 1936–41. Since 1941 has appeared in Bdwy musicals.

AMOCIO, AMEDEO. Born in 1942 in Milan, Italy. Studied at LaScala, and joined company, rising to soloist. Has created many ballets and choreographed musicals and films.

AMMANN, DIETER. Born Feb. 5, 1942 in Passau, Ger. Attended Essen Folkway School. Joined Stuttgart Ballet in 1965.

ANAYA, DULCE. Born in Cuba; studied with Alonso, at School of Am. Ballet; joined Ballet Theatre at 15, Ballet de Cuba where she became soloist. In 1957 was prima ballerina of Stuttgart Opera before joining Munich State Opera Ballet for 5 years, Hamburg Opera for 3. Returned to U.S. and joined Michael Maule's Dance Variations, Ballet Concerto. Founder-Director of Jacksonville (Fla.) Ballet Theatre since 1970.

ANDERSON, CAROLYN. Born Apr. 28, 1946 in Salt Lake City. Graduate Univ. Utah. Studied with William Christensen, Patricia Wilde, Peryoslavic, Cayton, Weisburger, Danilova, Vladimiroff. Principal dancer with Ballet West before joining Pa. Ballet as soloist.

ANDERSON, REID. Born Apr. 1, 1949 in New Westminster, BC, Can. Studied with Dolores Kirkwood, and Royal Ballet School. Appeared in musicals before joining London's Royal Opera Ballet 1967, Stuttgart Ballet 1969.

ANDERSSON, GERD. Born in Stockholm June 11, 1932. Pupil of Royal Swedish Ballet, and Lilian Karina. Joined company in 1948; became ballerina in 1958.

ANDROS, DICK. Born in Oklahoma City, March 4, 1926. Trained with San Francisco Ballet, American Theatre Wing, Ballet Arts, Met Ballet, Ballet Theatre, Ballet Russe. Has appeared with San Francisco Ballet, Irene Hawthorne, Marian Lawrence, John Beggs, Eve Gentry, Greenwich Ballet, Lehigh Valley Ballet, and Dance Originals. Now choreographs and operates own school in Brooklyn.

ANTONIO. Born Antonio Ruiz Soler Nov. 4, 1922 in Seville, Spain. Studied with Realito, Pericet, and Otero. Made professional debut at 7. Became internationally famous with cousin Rosario as "The Kids From Seville." Formed separate companies in 1950's, his becoming Ballets de Madrid. Made N.Y. debut in 1955 and has returned periodically.

ANTONIO, JUAN. Born May 4, 1945 in Mexico City. Studied with Xavier Francis. Am. Ballet Center, Ballet Theatre School. Made debut 1963 in Mexico with Bellas Artes, N.Y. debut 1964 with Ballet Folklorico, subsequently danced with Glen Tetley, Louis Falco, Pearl Lang, Gloria Contreras, and Jose Limon. Now associate director of Falco Co.

ANTUNEZ, OSKAR. Born Apr. 17, 1949 in Juarez, Mex. Studied with Ingeborg Heuser, and at Harkness School. Made debut with Les Grands Ballets Canadiens in 1968. Joined Harkness Ballet in 1968.

Bene Arnold

Gerald Arpino

Soili Arvola

Frank Augustyn

Shawneequa
Baker-Scott

APINEE, IRENE. Born in Riga, Latvia where she began training at 11. Moved to Canada; founded school in Halifax. Became leading dancer with National Ballet of Canada, and in 1956 became member of Les Ballets Chiriaeff, now Les Grands Ballets Canadiens. Soloist with Ballet Theatre in 1959. Rejoined Les Grands Ballets in 1965.

APONTE, CHRISTOPHER. Born May 4, 1950 in NYC. Studied at Harkness House, and made debut in 1970 with the Harkness company. Joined Alvin Ailey 1975.

ARMIN, JEANNE. Born in Milwaukee. Aug. 4, 1943. Studied with Ann Barzel, Stone and Camryn, Ballet Russe, and in Paris with Mme. Nora. Made debut with Chicago Opera Ballet in 1958, joined Ballet Russe (1959) American Ballet Theatre (1965). Has appeared on Bdwy.

ARMOUR, THOMAS. Born Mar. 7, 1909 in Tarpon Springs, Fla. Studied with Ines Noel Armour. Preobrajenska, Egorova. Debut with Ida Rubenstein, followed by Nijinska's company, Ballet Russe, Ballet Russe de Monte Carlo. Founder-Artistic Director Miami Ballet.

ARNOLD, BENE. Born in 1935 in Big Springs, Tex. Graduate UUtah. Trained with Willam, Harold, and Lew Christensen at San Francisco Ballet. Joined company in 1950, becoming soloist in 1952, Ballet Mistress 1960–63. Joined Ballet West as Ballet Mistress 1963.

AROVA, SONIA. Born June 20, 1927 in Sofia. Bulgaria. Studied with Preobrajenska; debut 1942 with International Ballet, subsequently appearing with Ballet Rambert, Met Opera Ballet, Petit's Ballet, Tokyo-Kamaski Ballet, Ballet Theatre, Ruth Page Ballet Co., Norwegian State Opera Ballet. Co-Director San Diego Ballet from 1971.

ARPINO, GERALD. Born on Staten Island, N.Y. Studied with Mary Ann Wells. May O'Donnell, Gertrude Shurr, and at School of American Ballet. Made debut on Bdwy in "Annie Get Your Gun." Toured with Nana Gollner, Paul Petroff Ballet Russe; became leading male dancer with Joffrey Ballet, and NYC Opera. Currently choreographer and assistant director of Joffrey Ballet and co-director of American Ballet Center.

ARTHUR, CHARTHEL. Born in Los Angeles. Oct. 8, 1946. Studied with Eva Lorraine, and at American Ballet Center. Became member of Joffrey Ballet in 1965.

ARVE, RICHARD. Born in Clemson, S.C. Studied with Graham, Cunningham, Joffrey, Hayden; soloist with Ruth Page Ballet, Chicago Opera Ballet, Flower Hujer, Phyllis Sabold, Erica Tamar, Maggie Kast. Now teaches, and director of Richard Arve Dance Trio.

ARVOLA, SOILI. Born in Finland; began ballet studies at 8; joined Finnish Ballet at 18; San Francisco Ballet 1968–72; Houston Ballet 1972–. Also choreographs and appears with Ballet Spectacular.

ASAKAWA, HITOMI. Born Oct. 13, 1938 in Kochi, Japan. Studied and made professional debut in Nishino Ballet 1957. Joined Ballet of 20th Century 1967.

ASAKAWA, TAKAKO. Born in Tokyo, Japan, Feb. 23, 1938. Studied in Japan and with Martha Graham. Has appeared with Graham Co., and with Alvin Ailey, Donald McKayle, and Pearl Lang, and in revival of "The King and I." Now permanent member of Graham company.

ASENSIO, MANOLA. Born May 7, 1946 in Lausanne, Switz. Studied at LaScala in Milan. Danced with Grand Theatre de Geneve (1963–4), Het Nationale Ballet (1964–6), NYC Ballet (1966–8), Harkness Ballet 1969–.

ASHLEY, FRANK. Born Apr. 10, 1941 in Kingston, Jamaica. Studied with Ivy Baxter, Eddy Thomas, Neville Black, Martha Graham. Has appeared with National Dance Theatre of Jamacia, Helen McGehee, Pearl Lang, Marth Graham, Yuriko, Eleo Pomare. Also choreographs.

ASHTON, FREDERICK. Born in Guayaquil, Ecuador, Sept. 17, 1906. Studied with Massine and Marie Rambert. Joined Ida Rubinstein Co. in Paris in 1927, but soon left to join Rambert's Ballet Club for which he choreographed many works, and danced. Charles Cochran engaged him to choreograph for his cabarets. In 1933 was invited to create works for the newly formed Vic Wells Co. and in 1935 joined as dancer and choreographer. Moved with company to Covent Garden, and continued creating some of world's great ballets. Was knighted in 1962; first man so honored for services to ballet. After serving as associate director of Royal Ballet, became its director with the retirement of Dame Ninette de Valois in 1963. Retired in 1970.

ASTAIRE, FRED. Born Frederick Austerlitz in Omaha, Neb. May 10, 1899. Began studying at 5; was in vaudeville with sister Adele at 7; Bdwy debut in 1916 in "Over The Top." Appeared in many musicals and films.

ATWELL, RICK. Born July 29, 1949 in St. Louis, Mo. Studied with Dokoudovsky, Mattox, Krassovska, and Wilde. Joined Harkness Ballet in 1967 after appearing in several musicals.

AUGUSTYN, FRANK. Born Jan. 27, 1953 in Hamilton, Ont., Can. Studied at Ballet School of Canada. Joined Natl. Ballet of Canada in 1970, rising to principal in 1972.

av PAUL, ANNETTE. (Wiedersheim-Paul). Born Feb. 11, 1944 in Stockholm. Studied at Royal Ballet School, and made debut with Royal Opera House Ballet. Appeared with Royal Winnipeg Ballet before joining Harkness Ballet in 1966.

AYAKO. (See Uchiyama. Ayako)

BABILEE, JEAN. Born Jean Gutman Feb. 2, 1923 in Paris. Studied at School of Paris Opera. In 1945 became premier danseur in Les Ballets des Champs-Elysees. Toured with own company. Guest artist with ABT.

BAGNOLD, LISBETH. Born Oct. 10, 1947 in Bronxville, N.Y. UCLA graduate. Studied with Gloria Newman, Limon, Nikolais, Murray Louis. Joined Nikolais Dance Theatre in 1971.

BAILIN, GLADYS. Born in N.Y.C. Feb. 11, 1930. Graduate Hunter Col. Studied with Nikolais and joined his company in 1955. Has also appeared with Murray Louis and Don Redlich.

BAKER-SCOTT, SHAWNEEQUA. Born in Bronx; attended Hunter Col., CCNY. Studied with Holm, Humphrey-Wiedman, NDG, Ailey, Beatty, Holder, Clarke, Graham. Debut 1952 with Donald McKayle, subsequently with Destine, New Dance Group, Ailey, Marchant, Dancers Theatre Co., Eleo Pomare.

BALANCHINE, GEORGE. Born Georges Malitonovitch Balanchivadze in St. Petersburg, Russia Jan. 9, 1904. Studied Imperial School of Ballet. Debut 1915 in "Sleeping Beauty." Began choreographing while still in school. Left Russia in 1924 to tour with own company. Became associated with Diaghilev in Paris where he choreographed more than 10 works. Thence to Copenhagen as Ballet Master of Royal Dutch Ballet, then joined newly formed Russes de Monte Carlo. Formed Les Ballets in 1933 and toured Europe. Invited to establish school in N.Y., and in 1934 opened School of American Ballet, followed by American Ballet Co. Choreographed for Met (1935–8). Bdwy musicals, and for such companies as Original Ballet Russe, Sadler's Wells Theatre Ballet, Ballet Russe de Monte Carlo, Ballet Theatre, and Ballet Society. Formed NYC Ballet which premiered in 1948, and won international acclaim under his direction and with his brilliant choreography.

BALLARD, MICHAEL. Born July 17, 1942 in Denver, Colo. Studied with Nikolais and Louis at Henry Street Playhouse, and made professional debut with Alwin Nikolais Co. in 1966. Joined Murray Louis Co. in 1968.

BALOUGH, BUDDY. Born in 1953 in Seattle, Wash. where he began studying at 9. Trained at ABT School, and in 1970 joined Am. Ballet Theatre, rising to soloist in 1973. Also joined Ballet of Contemporary Art in 1973, for which he choreographs.

BANKS, GERALD. Born Feb. 4 in NYC. Attended CCNY, American Ballet Center. Joined Dance Theatre of Harlem 1969.

BARANOVA, IRINA. Born in Petrograd, Russia in 1919. Studied with Olga Preobrajenska. Soloist with Opera; Ballet Russe 1932–40; ballerina with Ballet Theatre 1941–2. More recently has been appearing in plays and musicals, and teaching at Royal Academy.

BARI, TANIA. formerly Bartha Treure). Born July 5, 1936 in Rotterdam. Studied with Netty Van Der Valk, Nora Kiss, Asaf Messerer. Joined Bejart's Ballet in 1955; principal from 1959.

BARKER, JOHN. Born in Oak Park, Ill., Nov. 20, 1929. Studied at Chicago U., and with Bentley Stone, Walter Camryn, Margaret Craske, Antony Tudor, Pierre Vladimiroff, Anatole Oboukoff, Valentina Perevaslavic, and Maria Nevelska. Made professional debut with Page-Stone Camryn Co. in 1951. Has appeared with Chicago Opera Ballet, Juilliard Dance Theatre, and Jose Limon Co.

BARNARD, SCOTT. Born Oct. 17, 1945 in Indianapolis, Ind. Graduate Butler U. Studied with Perry Bronson, Robert Joffrey, Gerald Arpino, Richard Englund, Hector Zaraspy. Debut 1963 with St. Louis Opera. Joined Joffrey Ballet in 1968.

BARNES, NERISSA. Born Feb. 2, 1952 in Columbus, Ga. Attended UIll. Debut 1969 with Julian Swain Inner City Dance Co. Joined Alvin Ailey company in 1972.

BARNETT, DARRELL. Born Sept. 24, 1949 in Miami, Okla. Attended Okla U. Studied with Mary Price, Ethel Winter, Betty Jones, Martha Graham. Debut in 1970 with Ethel Winter, subsequently with Yuriko, Mary Anthony, Pearl Lang, Erick Hawkins, Richard Gain, Kazuko Hirabayashi. Joined Harkness Ballet in 1971. Made soloist 1973.

BARNETT, ROBERT. Born May 6, 1925 in Okanogan, Wash. Studied with Nijinska, Egoroba, Preobrajinska, and at School of American Ballet. Made debut with Original Ballet Russe; joined NYC Ballet in 1950; Atlanta Ballet in 1958, and its director from 1963. Choreographs, and operates own school.

BARREDO, MANIYA. Born Nov. 19, 1952 in Manila, PI. Attended St. Paul Col., American Ballet Center. Debut 1965 with Philippine Hariraya Dance Co. Joined Joffrey Ballet 1972.

BARTA, KAROLY. Born Aug. 5, 1936 in Bekescsaba, Hungary. Debut there at 11 with folk ensemble. Studied at Hungarian State Ballet Inst.; performed with Budapest opera and ballet. First choreographic work at 15. Joined Hungarian National Folk Ensemble before emigrating to U.S. in 1957. Attended Met Opera Ballet, and Stone-Camryn School. Joined Chicago Opera Ballet, and continued to choreograph for various groups. Co-founder of Hungarian Ballets Bihari, Barta Ballet Co., was teacher-director for Birmingham Civic Ballet, and now operates his own school in Washington, D.C.

BARYSHNIKOV, MIKHAIL. Born Jan. 27, 1948 in Riga, Latvia. Began training at Latvian Opera Ballet School. Moved to Kirov school and joined company at 18 as soloist. Was guest artist with Bolshoi Ballet in Toronto, Can., when he defected in 1974. Has appeared with ABT, Australian Ballet, Hamburg and Paris Opera Ballets.

BATES, JAMES. Born Feb. 8, 1949 in Dallas, Tex. Studied with Moreno, Nault, Danilova, Fallis, and Harkarvy. Joined Les Grands Ballets Canadiens in 1968.

BAUMAN, ART. Born in Washington, D.C. Studied at Juilliard, Met, and Martha Graham schools. Has danced with Lucas Hoving, Paul Sanasardo, Charles Weidman. Has choreographed numerous works and teaches. Is asst. director of DTW.

BAYS, FRANK. Born June 6, 1943 in Bristol, Va. Attended King Col. Studied with Perry Brunson, and at Am. Ballet Center. Debut with American Festival Ballet 1964; joined Joffrey Ballet 1965; First Chamber Dance Co. 1972.

BEALS, MARGARET. Born Mar. 5, 1943 in Boston. Studied with Mattox, Graham, Sanasardo, Slavenska. Has appeared in musicals, and with Valerie Bettis, Jean Erdman, Pearl Lang, Jose Limon, and Paul Sanasardo. Also choreographs, and performs in concert.

BEATTY, TALLEY. Made professional debut in Bdwy musicals. Joined Ballet Society in 1947. Has more recently toured, given solo performances, formed own company for which he choreographs, and teaches.

BECKER, BRUCE. Born May 28, 1944 in NYC. Graduate Utah State U. Studied at O'Donnell-Shurr, Graham, and Don Farnworth studios. Debut 1961 with Norman Walker, subsequently on Bdwy, with Tamiris-Nagrin, Limon, O'Donnell; joined Batsheva in 1969.

BECKLEY, CHRISTINE. Born Mar. 16, 1939 in Stanmore, Eng. Studied at Royal Ballet School, joined company and advanced to solo artist.

BEJART, MAURICE. Born Jan. 1, 1927 in Marseilles, France. Studied at Opera Ballet School, and with Leo Staats. Danced with Opera Ballet until 1945; Ballets de Roland Petit (1947–49); International Ballet (1949–50); Royal Swedish Ballet (1951–2). In 1954 organized Les Ballets de l'Etoile and debuted as choreographer. Company became Ballet Theatre de Maurice Bejart. In 1959 appointed director of Theatre Royale de la Monnaie, Brussels, and its name was changed to Ballet of the 20th Century.

BELHUMEUR, CHANTAL. Born Mar. 20, 1949 in Montreal, Can. Studied with Graham, Les Grands Ballets Canadiens and became member 1965; joined Eleo Pomare in 1971.

BELIN, ALEXANDRE. Born Apr. 3, 1948 in Mulhouse, France. Made debut in 1966 with Les Grands Ballets Canadiens.

BENJAMIN, FRED. Born Sept. 8, 1944 in Boston. Studied with Elma Lewis, ABT, Claude Thompson, Talley Beatty. Has danced in musicals, with Boston Ballet, and Talley Beatty Co. Also teaches and choreographs.

BENJAMIN, JOEL. Born Feb. 21, 1949 in NYC. Attended Juilliard, Columbia; studied with Alwin Nikolais, Martha Graham, and at American Ballet Center. Made debut in Paris in 1963. Formed own company in 1963. Director American Chamber Ballet.

BENNETT, CHARLES. Born Apr. 8, 1934 in Wheaton, Ill. Studied with Bentley Stone, made debut with Ruth Page's Ballet before joining American Ballet Theatre. Member of NYC Ballet before formation of First Chamber Dance Quartet, now First Chamber Dance Co.

BENTLEY, MURIEL. Born in NYC. Studied with Tomaroff, Tarasoff, Swoboda, Fokine, Ruth St. Denis, Dolin and at Met Opera School. Made debut with Ruth St. Denis in 1931. Has appeared with Jose Greco 1936–7, at Met 1938–9; joined Ballet Theatre in 1940. Has since danced with Jerome Robbins' Ballets: U.S.A.

BERG, BERND. Born Nov. 20, 1943 in East Prussia. Began training at 11 in Leipzig. Joined Stuttgart Ballet in 1964; became soloist in 1967.

BERG, HENRY. Born in Chicago, Apr. 4, 1938. Studied with DeRea, Morrelli, Lew Christensen. Made professional debut with Ballet Alicia Alonso in 1958, subsequently joining San Francisco Ballet (1962), and Joffrey Ballet (1967).

BERGSMA, DEANNE. Born Apr. 16, 1941 in South Africa. Studied with Royal Ballet and joined company in 1958. Became soloist in 1962, principal in 1967. Co-artistic director Pacific Ballet.

BERIOSOVA, SVETLANA. Born Sept. 24, 1932 in Lithuania. Came to U.S. in 1940; studied at Vilzak-Shollar School. Debut with Ottawa Ballet Co. in 1947. Appeared with Grand Ballet de Monte Carlo 1947. Appeared with Grand Ballet de Monte Carlo 1947; Met Opera 1948; Sadler's Wells 1950, and became ballerina in 1954 with Royal Ballet.

BERTRAM, VICTORIA. Born Feb. 26, 1946 in Toronto, Can. Studied at National Ballet School and joined National Ballet of Canada in 1963.

BESWICK, BOB. Born Nov. 11, 1945 in San Francisco. Studied with Cunningham, Sokolow, Waring, Louis, Bailin, Nikolais. Made debut in 1967 with Utah Repertory Dance Theatre, subsequently with Nikolais Co. Choreographer and teacher.

BETHEL, PEPSI. Born in Greensboro, NC. Attended Adelphi Col. Toured Africa and performed during 1969–70. Since 1971 has been artistic director-choreographer for Pepsi Bethel Authentic Jazz Dance Theatre.

BETTIS, VALERIE. Born in 1920 in Houston, Tex. Studied with Hanya Holm. Debut with Miss Holm's company in 1937, and as a choreographer in 1941. Subsequently appeared as dancer-choreographer for several Bdwy productions, and own company that toured U.S. and abroad. Teaches in own studio in NYC.

BEWLEY, LOIS. Born in Louisville, Ky. Studied with Lilias Courtney. Made debut with Ballet Russe de Monte Carlo; subsequently with ABT, Ballets U.S.A., NYC Ballet.

BHASKAR. Born Bhaskar Roy Chowdhury in Madras, India, Feb. 11, 1930. Studied with G. Ellappa. Made debut in Madras in 1950 as concert dancer with own company which he brought to NYC in 1956. As dancer and/or choreographer, has appeared on Bdwy, and internationally; teaches.

BIEVER, KATHRYN. Born May 9, 1942 in Bryn Mawr, Pa. Studied in Ballet Russe School, Pa. Ballet School. Made debut in 1964 with American Festival Ballet before joining Pennsylvania Ballet. Joined Les Grands Ballets Canadiens 1972.

BILES, RICHARD. Born in Salem, Ore. Attended Ill. Inst. of Tech., UWisc. Joined Dance Repertory Theater. With Nikolais Dance Theatre 1970–71. Formed own company with which he tours. Also teaches.

BIRCH, PATRICIA. Born in Englewood, N.J. Studied at School of Am. Ballet, Cunningham, and Graham schools. Made debut with Graham company. Has appeared in concert, on Bdwy, and with Donald Saddler, Valerie Bettis. Also choreographs.

BJORNSSON, FREDBJORN. Born in Copenhagen in 1926. Entered Royal Danish Ballet school 1935; graduated into company and became soloist in 1949; became one of great leading mimes and exponent of Bournonville style.

BLACKSTONE, JUDITH. Born May 10, 1947 in Iowa City, Iowa. Studied with Donya Feuer, Paul Sanasardo, Mia Slavenska, Karoly Zsedenyi. Debut with Sanasardo Co. in 1958.

BLAIR, DAVID. Born in Yorkshire, Eng. July 27, 1932. Trained at Royal Ballet School. Subsequently joined its company, rising to principal dancer in 1955. Honored by Queen Elizabeth with title Commander of the Order of the British Empire.

BLANKSHINE, ROBERT. Born Dec. 22, 1948 in Syracuse, N.Y. Studied at American School of Ballet. Professional debut in 1965 with Joffrey Ballet which he left in 1968. Joined Berlin Opera Ballet in 1970.

Frank Bays

Victoria Bertram

Roman Brooks

Karena Brock

Homer Bryant

BOARDMAN, DIANE. Born Jan. 17, 1949 in NYC. Bklyn. Col. graduate. Began training at 6, studying with Murray Louis, James Truitte, Wilson Morelli, and John Medicros. Has appeared with Murray Louis, Alwin Nikolais, Phyllis Lamhut companies. Also teaches and choreographs.

BOLENDER, TODD. Born in Canton, O. in 1919. Studied with Chester Hale, Vilzak, and at School of American Ballet. Soloist with Ballet Caravan in 1937, Littlefield Ballet in 1941; founder-director of American Concert Ballet in 1943; joined Ballet Theatre in 1944, Ballet Russe de Monte Carlo in 1945. First choreography in 1943. Became dancer-choreographer for Ballet Society, and has continued to choreograph for various companies; was director of Cologne and Frankfurt Opera Ballets.

BONNEFOUS, JEAN-PIERRE. Born Apr. 25, 1943 in Paris. Attended Paris Opera School of Dance. Made debut in 1964 with Opera Ballet and became premier danseur. Appeared with companies in Frankfort, Moscow, Milan, Berlin, Oslo, Toronto before joining NYC Ballet in 1970 as a principal.

BORIS, RUTHANNA. Born in 1918 in Brooklyn. Studied at Met Opera School, with Helene Veola, and Fokine. Member of American Ballet in 1935, Met soloist in 1936, and premiere danseuse 1939–43. Joined Ballet Russe de Monte Carlo in 1943. Has choreographed a number of works. Now teaches.

BORTOLUZZI, PAOLO. Born May 17, 1938 in Genoa, Italy. Debut 1958 with Italian Ballet. Joined Bejart Ballet in 1960, rising to principal dancer. Joined ABT in 1972 as principal.

BOUTILIER, JOY. Born in Chicago, Sept. 30, 1939. Graduate of U. Chicago. Studied at Henry St. Playhouse, and with Angelina Romett. Debut with Nikolais in 1964, subsequently with Mimi Garrard, Phyllis Lamhut, and Murray Louis. Has choreographed and appeared in own concerts.

BOWMAN, PATRICIA. Born in Washington, D.C. Studied with Fokine, Mordkin, Legat, Egorova, and Wallman. Ballerina at Roxy and Radio City Music Hall, with Mordkin Ballet in 1939, Ballet Theatre in 1940, and appeared with Chicago Opera, Fokine Ballet, and in musicals and operettas. Now teaches.

BRADLEY, LISA. Born in Elizabeth, N.J. in 1941. Studied at Newark Ballet Academy, American Ballet Center, and with Joyce Trisler. Appeared with Garden State Ballet before joining Joffrey Ballet in 1961. Invited to study classic roles with Ulanova. Joined First Chamber Dance Co. in 1969; Hartford Ballet 1972 where she also teaches. Returned to Joffrey 1976.

BRASSEL, ROBERT. Born Nov. 3, in Chicago. Attended Ind. U., American Ballet Center. Trained with Robert Joffrey, Hector Zaraspe, Lillian Morre. Joined Joffrey Ballet in 1965, ABT in 1968.

BRIANSKY, OLEG. Born in Brussels Nov. 9, 1929. Studied with Katchourovsky, Gsovsky, Volkova. Joined Les Ballets des Champs-Elysees; became lead dancer in 1946. Subsequently with Ballets de Paris, London Festival Ballet, Chicago Opera Ballet. Formed own company, and teaches.

BRIANT, ROGER. Born May 4, 1944 in Yonkers, N.Y. Studied at Joffrey Center, Martha Graham Studio, O'Donnell-Shurr Studio. Has appeared on Bdwy, and with Martha Graham, Glen Tetley, Donald McKayle, Norman Walker companies.

BROCK, KARENA. Born Sept. 21, 1942 in Los Angeles. Studied with Lanova, Lichine, Riabouchinska, DuBoulay, and Branitzska. Danced with Natl. Ballet of Netherlands before joining American Ballet Theatre in 1963. Became soloist in 1968, principal 1973. Has appeared in musicals and films.

BROOKS, ROMAN. Born July 5, 1950 in Millington, Tenn. Attended Harbor-Compton Jr. Col. Studied with Eugene Loring. Joined Dance Theatre of Harlem 1973.

BROWN, CAROLYN. Born in Fitchburg, Mass. in 1927. Graduate of Wheaton College. Studied with Marion Rice, Margaret Craske, Antony Tudor and Merce Cunningham. Professional debut with Cunningham in 1953 and appeared in almost entire repertoire of the company in roles she created. Left company in 1973 to choreograph.

BROWN, KAREN. Born Oct. 6, 1955 in Okmulgee, OK. Studied at American Ballet Center. Joined Dance Theatre of Harlem in 1973.

BROWN, KELLY. Born Sept. 24, 1928 in Jackson, Miss. Studied with Bentley Stone, Walter Camryn. Made professional debut with Chicago Civic Opera Ballet in 1946; soloist with Ballet Theatre (1949–1953). Has since appeared in films, musicals, and on TV.

BROWN, LAURA. Born Sept. 1, 1955 in San Francisco, Cal. Studied at Ballet Celeste, San Francisco Ballet. Joined Dance Theatre of Harlem 1972.

BROWN, SANDRA. Born Jan. 6, 1946 in Ft. Wayne, Ind. Studied with Tudor, Craske, Graham, Limon. Made Debut in Juilliard concert in 1967, subsequently dancing with DTW, James Clouser, James Waring, and Lucus Hoving.

BREUER, PETER. Born in Tegernsee, Ger. Joined Munich Opera Ballet in 1961, Dusseldorf Ballet in 1965 as soloist. Has appeared with many companies as guest artist, including ABT 1976.

BRUHN, ERIK. Born Oct. 3, 1928 in Copenhagen. Attended Academie of Royal Danish Theatre, and received training with Royal Danish Ballet with which he made his debut in 1947. Became its leading dancer, and has appeared on tour with the company, and as guest soloist with all leading companies throughout the world. For brief period was a principal dancer with American Ballet Theatre, and a permanent guest artist. Is considered one of world's greatest classical dancers. Appointed Director of Ballet of Royal Swedish Opera in 1967. Retired in 1972. Resident Producer National Ballet of Canada 1973. Resigned 1976.

BRYANT, HOMER. Born Mar. 29, 1951 in St. Thomas, VI. Attended Adelphi U. Debut 1970 with Manhattan Festival Ballet; Joined Dance Theatre of Harlem 1973.

BUCHTRUP, BJARNE. Born Aug. 11, 1942 in Copenhagen. Studied with Birger Bartholin. Leon Danielian. Appeared in musicals before joining West Berlin Ballet Co. in 1963. Danced with Manhattan Festival Ballet (1965–66) and joined American Ballet Theatre in 1967.

BUIRGE, SUSAN. Born in Minneapolis, June 19, 1940. Graduate of U. Minn. Studied at Juilliard, Henry St. Playhouse, Conn. College. Made professional debut with Nikolais Co. in 1964. Has also appeared with Murray Louis, Mimi Garrard, Bill Frank, Juilliard Dance Ensemble, and Jose Limon. Also choreographs, and teaches.

BUJONES, FERNANDO. Born Mar. 9, 1955 in Miami, Fla. Attended Cuban Ntl. Ballet School, School of American Ballet, Juilliard. Debut 1970 with Eglevsky Ballet, followed by Ballet Spectacular 1971–2, American Ballet Theatre 1972. Raised to soloist 1973.

BURKE, DERMOT. Born Jan. 8, 1948 in Dublin, Ire. Studied at Royal School of Dance. Appeared with Royal Concert Group before joining Joffrey Company in 1966, National Ballet 1972, Joffrey 1975.

BURR, MARILYN. Born Nov. 20, 1933 in New South Wales. Studied at Australian Ballet School; made debut with Ntl. Ballet Co. in 1948. Joined London Festival Ballet in 1953 as soloist; became ballerina in 1955. Joined Hamburg State Opera Co. in 1963. Has danced with Natl. Ballet of Wash.

BUSHLING, JILISE. Born in 1957 in Santa Monica, Ca. Studied at American Ballet Theatre School, Sch. of Am. Ballet. Made debut in 1972 with Joffrey II Co. Joined NYCB in 1974.

BUSSEY, RAYMOND. Born Mar. 8, 1946 in Pawtucket, R. I. Studied with Perry Brunson, Tupine, and at Joffrey School. Made professional debut with American Festival Ballet in 1962. Joined Joffrey Company in 1964.

BUSTILLO, ZELMA. Born in Cartagena, Columbia, but came to N.Y.C. at 6. Graduate HS Performing Arts. Appeared with Thalia Mara's Ballet Repertory, at Radio City Music Hall, with American Festival Ballet, Joffrey Ballet Co. (1965), National Ballet (1970).

BUTLER, JOHN. Born in Memphis, Tenn., Sept. 29, 1920. Studied with Martha Graham and at American School of Ballet. Made debut with Graham company in 1947. Appeared in Bdwy musicals before becoming choreographer. Formed own company with which he toured.

CALDWELL, BRUCE. Born Aug. 25, 1950 in Salt Lake City, U. Studied with Bene Arnold, Willam Christensen at UUtah. Joined Ballet West in 1967; became principal in 1973.

CALZADA, ALBA. Born Jan. 28, 1947 in Puerto Rico. UPR graduate. Studied in San Juan and made debut with San Juan Ballet in 1964. Was guest with Eglevsky and Miami Ballets before joining Pa. Ballet. in 1968. Now a principal.

CAMMACK, RICHARD L. Born Oct. 24, 1945 in Knoxville, Tenn. Graduate Butler U. Studied at Harkness House, American Ballet Theatre School. Joined ABT in 1969.

CAMPANERIA, MIGUEL. Born Feb. 5, 1951 in Havana, Cuba. Studied at Ntl. Ballet of Cuba, and made debut with company in 1968. Joined Harkness Ballet and became soloist in 1973.

CAMPBELL, SYLVESTER. Born in Oklahoma. Joined NY Negro Ballet 1956, and subsequently Het Netherlands Ballet 1960, Ballet of 20th Century, Royal Winnipeg Ballet 1972.

CAMRYN, WALTER. Born in Helena, Mont, in 1903. Studied with Bolm, Maximova, Swoboda, Novikoff, and Muriel Stuart. Appeared with Chicago Civic Opera Ballet. Page-Stone Ballet, and Federal Theatre as premier danseur and choreographer. Teacher at Stone-Camryn School, Chicago. Has choreographed more than 20 ballets.

CANDELARIA, SANSON. Born July 13, 1947 in Albuquerque, NMex. Joined Les Grands Ballets Canadiens 1965, Lisbon's Gulbenkian Ballet 1969, American Classical Ballet 1971, Boston Ballet 1972.

CARAS, STEPHEN. Born Oct. 25, 1950 in Englewood, N.J. Studied at American Ballet Center, School of American Ballet. Made debut in 1967 with Irene Fokine Co. Joined N.Y.C. Ballet in 1969.

CARLSON, CAROLYN. Born in Oakland, Calif., Mar. 7, 1943. Graduate of U. Utah. Studied at San Francisco Ballet School, and Henry St. Playhouse. Professional debut in 1965 with Nikolais Co. Has also appeared with Murray Louis, and in New Choreographers Concert.

CARROLL, ELISABETH. Born Jan. 19, 1937 in Paris. Studied with Sedova, Besobrasova. Made debut in 1952 with Monte Carol Opera Ballet; joined Ballet Theatre in 1954, Joffrey Ballet in 1962, and Harkness Ballet in 1964.

CARTER, RICHARD. Became principal male dancer of San Francisco Ballet in 1958. With wife, Nancy Johnson, performed in more than fifty countries around the world. Was director and premier danseur of the San Diego Ballet Co. for which he created 14 ballets. Now with San Francisco Ballet.

CARTER, WILLIAM. Born in 1936 in Durant, Okla. Studied with Coralane Duane, Carmalita Maracci. Joined American Ballet Theatre in 1957, N.Y.C. Ballet in 1959. Helped to organize and appeared since 1961 with First Chamber Dance Co. Joined Martha Graham Co. 1972, ABT 1972.

CARTIER, DIANA. Born July 23, 1939 in Philadelphia, Pa. Studied with Tudor, Doubrouska, Balanchine, Joffrey, Griffith, and Brunson, Debut 1960 with Met Opera Ballet, subsequently with John Butler, N.Y.C. Opera Ballet, Zachary Solov, and Joffrey Ballet since 1961.

CASEY, SUSAN. Born in April 1949 in Buffalo, N.Y. Studied at Ballet Russe, and Harkness Schools, and with Kravina, Danielian, Shollar, Vilzak, and Volkova. Joined American Ballet Theatre in 1965; became its youngest soloist in 1969.

CASTELLI, VICTOR. Born Oct. 9, 1952 in Montclair, N.J. Studied at Newark Ballet Acad., School of American Ballet. Appeared with Garden State Ballet, and Eglevsky Ballet before joining NYC Ballet in 1971.

CATANZARO, TONY. Born Nov. 10, 1946 in Bklyn. Studied with Norman Walker, Sanasardo, Danielian, Lillian Moore, Lang, Joffrey, Jaime Rogers. Debut 1968 in musicals, subsequently appearing with Norman Walker, Harkness Youth Ballet, N.J. Ballet, Boston Ballet; joined Joffrey in 1971. Returned to Boston Ballet 1973.

CATON, EDWARD. Born in St. Petersburg, Russia. Apr. 3, 1900 Studied at Melidova's Ballet School, Moscow, and made professional debut in 1914. Joined Max Terptzt Co. (1918), Ourkransky-Pavley Co. (1919), Pavlova (1924), Chicago Opera Ballet (1926), American Ballet (1934), Catherine Littlefield (1935), Mikhail Mordkin (1938), Ballet Theatre (1940), retired in 1942 to become teacher and choreographer.

CAVRELL, HOLLY. Born Sept. 2, 1955 in NYC. Attended Hunter Col., studied with Pearl Lang, Patsy Birch, Rod Rodgers, Alwin Nikolais, American Dance Center, Debut 1972 with Ballet Players; Joined Martha Graham Co. 1973.

CEBRON, JEAN. Born in Paris in 1938. Made debut in 1956 in London. Joined Joos Folkwangballet. Tours world in concert.

CESBRON, JACQUES. Born May 10, 1940 in Angers, France. Studied at Paris Opera Ballet School, and joined company in 1958. Member of Harkness Ballet before becoming soloist with Pennsylvania Ballet in 1966. Left in 1969.

CHAIB, ELIE. Born July 18, 1950 in Beirut, Lebanon. Began studies in Beirut in 1966. Made debut 1969 as soloist with Beirut Dance Ensemble. Came to U.S. in 1970; appeared in Joffrey's "Petrouchka," Chamber Dance Ensemble before joining Paul Taylor Co. 1973.

CHAMBERLIN, BETTY. Born Nov. 10, 1949 in Madison, Wisc. Studied with Armour, LaVerne, Nault, Skibine, and at ABT. Joined American Ballet Theatre in 1969.

CHAMPION, GOWER. Born in Geneva, Ill., June 22, 1920. After appearing in vaudeville, night clubs, and on Bdwy, made debut as choreographer for "Lend An Ear" in 1946. Is now in great demand as choreographer and director of musicals, and films.

CHAPLINE, CLAUDIA. Born May 23, 1930 in Oak Park, Ill. Graduate George Washington U. Studied with Davis, Weidman, Hoving, Humphrey, Horst, Nikolais, Deitz, Limon, Graham, Cassan, Maracci, Rousellat. Debut 1948 with Evelyn Davis Co.; subsequently with Doris Humphrey, Gloria Newman, Instant Theatre, and in 1973 formed IDEA Co. for which she directs and choreographs.

CHARLIP, REMY. Born Jan. 10, 1929 in Brooklyn, NY. Attended Cooper Union, Reed Col. Studied at New Dance Group, with Merce Cunningham, Jean Erdman. Appeared with Cunningham for 11 years. Now choreographs.

CHASE, DAVID. Born June 18, 1948 in Mill Valley, Cal. Graduate URochester. Studied with Walter Nicks, Karl Shook, Graham School, Joffrey School, Nadia Potts, Norbert Vesak. Debut 1971 with Norbert Vesak, subsequently with Walter Nicks Co., Kazuko Hirabayashi; joined Martha Graham Co. 1972.

CHASE, LUCIA. Born March 24, 1907 in Waterbury, Conn. Studied at Theatre Guild School, and with Mikhail Mordkin. Became member of his company and danced title role in "Giselle" in 1937. Was principal dancer with Ballet Theatre when it was founded in 1939. In 1945 became co-director with Oliver Smith of American Ballet Theatre. In recent years has appeared only with her company in "Fall River Legend." "Swan Lake," and "Las Hermanas."

CHAUVIRE, YVETTE. Born Apr. 22, 1917 in Paris. Studied at Paris Opera School. Appeared with Paris Opera Ballet, London Festival Ballet, Royal Ballet (1959). In 1963 appointed director of Paris Opera Ballet School.

CHING, CHIANG. Born Jan. 26, 1946 in Peking, China. Graduate Peking School of Dance. Producer-Director of Great Wall Dancers of San Francisco. Also teaches and choreographs.

CHIRIAEFF, LUDMILLA. Born in 1924 in Latvia. Began training at early age in Berlin with Alexandra Nicolaieva. Joined de Basil's Ballets Russe, was soloist with Berlin Opera Ballet, and prima ballerina at Lausanne Municipal Theatre. Opened own academy in Geneva and choreographed for Ballet des Arts, Geneva. Moved to Canada in 1952 and organized own company, ultimately leading to her being founder and artistic director of Les Grands Ballets Canadiens.

CHOUTEAU, YVONNE. Born in Ft. Worth, Tex. in 1929. Studied with Asher, Perkins, Vestoff, Belcher, Bolm, at Vilzak-Shollar School of American Ballet. Made debut as child in American Indian dance company at Chicago's 1933 Fair. Joined Ballet Russe de Monte Carlo in 1943. Now teaches, makes guest appearances, and is Co-Director of Okla. Civic Ballet.

CHRISTENSEN, HAROLD. Born Dec. 24 in Brigham City, Utah. Studied with Balanchine. Appeared with Met Opera Ballet (1934), Ballet Caravan, San Francisco Opera Ballet, San Francisco Ballet. Retired to teach and direct San Francisco Ballet School.

CHRISTENSEN, LEW. Born May 9, 1906 in Brigham City, Utah. Studied with uncle Lars Christensen at American School of Ballet. Performer and choreographer since 1934, on Bdwy, for Met Opera, Ballet Caravan, American Ballet Co., and N.Y.C. Ballet. In 1938, with brothers Harold and William, founded San Francisco Ballet; has been general director since 1951.

CHRISTENSEN, WILLAM. Born Aug. 27, 1902 in Brigham City, Utah. Studied with uncle Lars Christensen, Nescagno, Novikoff, and Fokine. Made debut with Small Ballet Quartet in 1927, subsequently becoming choreographer, ballet master, director and teacher. With brothers Harold and Lew, formed San Francisco Ballet which he directed until 1951 when he established School of Ballet at U. of Utah. Is director-choreographer for Utah Civic Ballet which he organized in 1952, now Ballet West.

CHRISTOPHER, ROBERT. (formerly Robert Hall). Born Mar. 22, 1942 in Marion, Md. Studied with Harry Asmus, Vincenzo Celli, Celo Quitman. Made debut in 1960 with National Ballet of Venezuela; subsequently with Stuttgart Ballet, ABT, Anne Wilson, Valerie Bettis, Sophie Maslow; soloist and ballet master for Garden State Ballet, and appears with Downtown Ballet.

CHRYST, GARY. Born in LaJolla, Calif. Studied with Walker, Hoving, Limon, Jaime Rogers, Nina Popova, ABC. Debute at 16 with Norman Walker, subsequently with McKayle, Washington Ballet, N.Y.C. Opera, before joining Joffrey Ballet in 1968.

CLARE, NATALIA. Born in Hollywood, Calif. Studied with Nijinska, Egorova; joined de Basil's Ballet Russe, then Markova-Dolin Co., Ballet Russe de Monte Carlo. In 1956, established school in North Hollywood, and founded Ballet Jeunesse for which she is artistic director and choreographer.

| Elisabeth Carroll | Tony Catanzaro | Diana Cartier | William Christensen | Donna Cowen |

CLARKE, THATCHER. Born Apr. 1, 1937 in Springfield, Ohio. Made professional debut with Met Opera Ballet in 1954, subsequently joined Ballet de Cuba, Ballet Russe de Monte Carlo, San Francisco Ballet, and American Ballet Theatre. Has appeared in several musicals.

CLAUSS, HEINZ. Born Feb. 17, 1935 in Stuttgart. Studied at Stuttgart Ballet School, and with Balanchine. Joined Stuttgart Ballet in 1967 after appearing with Zurich Opera Ballet, and in Hamburg.

CLEAR, IVY. Born in Camden, Maine, Mar. 11, 1948. Studied at Professional Children's School of Dance and School of American Ballet. Made professional debut in 1963 with N.Y.C. Ballet. Soloist with Joffrey Ballet from 1965 to 1969.

CLIFFORD, JOHN. Born June 12, 1947 in Hollywood. Studied at American School of Dance and School of American Ballet. Appeared with Ballet of Guatemala and Western Ballet before joining N.Y. City Ballet in 1966. Soloist since 1969. Has choreographed 7 works for the company, in addition to works for other companies. Left in 1974 to become artistic director-choreographer for Los Angeles Ballet.

CLOUSER, JAMES. Born in 1935 in Rochester, N.Y. Studied at Eastman School of Music, Ballet Theatre School. Joined ABT in 1957, Royal Winnipeg Ballet in 1958, rising to leading dancer in 1959, subsequently choreographed, composed and designed for it, and became ballet master and assistant director. Has appeared in concert, taught, and tours with wife Sonja Zarek. Ballet master for Houston Ballet.

COCKERILLE, LILI. Born in Washington, D.C. Studied at Fokine School. Wash. School of Ballet and School of American Ballet. Made professional debut with N.Y.C. Ballet in 1963, joined Harkness Ballet in 1964, Joffrey Co. in 1969.

COFFMAN, VERNON. Born Dec. 5, 1947 in Tucson, Ariz. Studied with Lew and Harold Christensen. Made professional debut with San Francisco Ballet in 1964. Joined Joffrey Ballet in 1966, and American Ballet Theatre in 1967.

COHAN, ROBERT. Born in N.Y.C. in 1925. Soloist with Martha Graham Co. Opened own school in Boston, joined faculty of Harvard's Drama Center, made solo tours here and abroad, taught in Israel and choreographed for Batsheva Co. Now director of London Contemporary Dance Theatre.

COHEN, ZE'EVA. Born Aug. 15, 1940 in Israel. Studied at Juilliard, and appeared with its Dance Ensemble. Joined Anna Sokolow Co. 1961, subsequently with Pearl Lang, and in solo concerts. Choreographs and teaches.

COLEMAN, LILLIAN. Born Nov. 21, 1949 in N.Y.C. Attended SUNY, Harkness School. Made debut with New Dance Group.

COLL, DAVID. Born Mar. 20, 1947 in Chelsea, Mass. Studied with Vilzak. Nerden, Van Muyden, Fallis, Christensen. Made debut in 1965 with San Francisco Ballet. Joined American Ballet Co. in 1969. ABT in 1970. Became soloist in 1972.

COLLIER, LESLEY. Born Mar. 13, 1947 in Kent, Eng. Studied at Royal Academy of Dancing, Royal Ballet School. Joined Royal Ballet in 1965.

COLLINS, JANET. Born in New Orleans in 1917. Studied with Carmalita Maracci, Bolm, Lester Horton, Slavenska and Craske. Appeared in solo concerts before becoming premiere danseuse of the Met Opera Ballet (1951–54). Now teaches.

COLTON, RICHARD. Born Oct. 4, 1951 in N.Y.C. Attended Hunter Col., ABT School, American Ballet Center. Debut 1966 with James Waring Co.; joined Joffrey Ballet 1972.

COMELIN, JEAN-PAUL. Born Sept. 10, 1936 in Vannes, France. Studied at Cons. of Music and Art; made debut with Paris Opera Ballet in 1957. Soloist for London Festival Ballet in 1961, principal in 1962. Joined National Ballet for 1967, Pa. Ballet in 1970; Left in 1972. Associate Director Sacramento Ballet. Director Milwaukee Ballet 1975.

CONDODINA, ALICE. Born in Phildelphia; graduate of Temple U. Studied with Tudor, Zaraspe, Danielian, and at Met Opera Ballet, Ballet Theatre, and American Ballet Schools. Danced with Ruth Currier, Lucas Hoving, Sophie Maslow, Jack Moore, and Jose Limon Companies. Director-choreographer for own company since 1967.

CONOVER, WARREN. Born Feb. 5, 1948 in Philadelphia, Pa. Studied with Peter Conlow, Harkness House. Debut 1966 with Pa. Ballet. Subsequently with Harkness Ballet, Eglevsky Ballet, Niagara Ballet, Richmond Ballet; joined ABT 1971, soloist 1973.

COREY, WINTHROP. Born in 1947 in Washington, D.C. Studied with Ntl. Ballet and appeared with company. Joined Royal Winnipeg Ballet in 1966; Ntl. Ballet of Canada 1972; principal 1973.

CORKLE, FRANCESCA. Born Aug. 2, 1952 in Seattle, Wash. Studied with Virginia Ryan, Perry Brunson, Robert Joffrey. Joined Joffrey Ballet in 1967.

CORKRE, COLLEEN. Born in Seattle, Wash. and began training at 4. Debut with Chicago Opera Ballet. Dancer and choreographer for several musicals. Formed own company that tours every season.

CORVINO, ALFREDO. Born in Montevideo, Uruguay, where he studied with Alberto Poujanne. Also studied with Margaret Craske, Antony Tudor. Was premier danseur, assistant ballet master, and choreographer for Municipal Theatre, Montevideo. Appeared with Jooss Ballet, Ballet Russe de Monte Carlo, Metropolitan Opera Ballet. Juilliard dance faculty since 1952.

COSI, LILIANA. Born in Milan, and entered LaScala School in 1950. Was exchange artist with Bolshoi; made debut as prima ballerina in 1965 in "Swan Lake" with Bolshoi. Named prima ballerina of LaScala in 1968, and Assoluta in 1970. Has appeared as guest artist with many companies.

COWEN, DONNA. Born May 2, 1949 in Birmingham, Ala. Studied with Gage Bush, Richard Englund, School of American Ballet, Joffrey. Made debut in 1968 with Huntington Dance Ensemble; joined Joffrey Ballet in 1969.

CRAGUN, RICHARD. Born in Sacramento, Cal. Studied in London's Royal Ballet School and in Denmark. Joined Stuttgart Ballet in 1962 and quickly emerged as principal.

CRANE, DEAN. Born Jan. 5, 1932 in Logan, Iowa. Made professional debut at 14 as aerialist with Pollock Circus. Studied with Nimura, Dokoudovsky, Tudor and Petroff. Became first dancer and choreographer with Ballet Arts Co. Has also appeared on Bdwy and in clubs. Teaches.

CRASKE, MARGARET. Born in England. Studied with Cecchetti. Appeared with Diaghilev Ballets Russe, de Valois group. Became Ballet Mistress for Ballet Theatre in 1946, subsequently joined Met Opera Ballet School staff and became its assistant director. Currently with Manhattan School of Dance.

CRAVEY, CLARA. Born July 1, 1950 in West Palm Beach, Fla. Trained at Harkness School, and made debut with company in 1968.

CRISTOFORI, JON. Born in Buzzard's Bay, Mass., and began training at 15. Became lead student dancer in National Ballet of Wash., and toured with it until joining Joffrey Ballet. Left in 1969.

CROLL, TINA. Born Aug. 27, 1943 in N.Y.C. Bennington Col. graduate. Studied with Cunningham, Fonaroff. Debut 1964 in Kaufmann Hall. Has danced and choreographed for DTW since 1965. Formed own company in 1970 for which she choreographs.

CROPLEY, EILEEN. Born Aug. 25, 1932 in London. Studied with Sigurd Leeder, Maria Fay, Martha Graham, Don Farnworth. Made debut in 1966 with Paul Taylor Co.

CUNNINGHAM, JAMES. Born Apr. 1, 1938 in Toronto, Can. Graduate UToronto, London Academy Dramatic Arts. Studied at Martha Graham School. Choreographed for and performed with own company from 1967.

CUNNINGHAM, MERCE. Born Apr. 16 in Centralia, Wash. Studied at American School of Ballet. Professional debut as soloist with Martha Graham in 1940; with company through 1945. Began choreographing in 1946; in 1952 formed own company that has toured extensively every year. Teaches in his N.Y.C. studio.

CUNNINGHAM, RON. Born in Chicago; graduate Roosevelt U. Studied with Robert Lunnon, Eric Braun, Wigman, Cunningham, Humphrey, Weidman. Debut 1965 with Allegro American Ballet. Subsequently with Lucas Hoving, Kazuko Hirabayashi, Daniel Nagrin, Lotte Goslar, Zena Bethune, Ballet Concepts, Boston Ballet 1972.

CURRIER, RUTH. Born in 1926 in Ashland, Ohio. Studied with Doris Humphrey and Elsa Kahl. Made debut in 1949 with American Dance Festival. Soloist with Jose Limon Co. 1949–63. Since 1956 has been director-choreographer for own company which has toured U.S. Also teaches. Director Jose Limon Co.

CUTLER, ROBYN. Born May 25, 1948 in Atlanta, Ga. Attended Juilliard. Made debut 1972 with Jose Limon Co.

DABNEY, STEPHANIE. Born July 11, 1958 in Philadelphia, PA. Studied at Youngstown Academy, Dance Theatre of Harlem whose company she joined in 1975.

d'AMBOISE, JACQUES. Born July 28, 1934 in Dedham, Mass. Joined N.Y.C. Ballet at 15 after 7 years at School of American Ballet; rapidly rose to premier danseur in 1953. Has appeared in films and on TV and choreographed.

DANA, JERILYN. Born in Portland, Me., where she began dancing at 6. Studied with Boston Ballet, and graduated into company. Became soloist in 1969.

DANIAS, STARR. Born Mar. 18, 1949 in N.Y.C. Studied at School of Am. Ballet. Debut 1968 with London Festival Ballet, subsequently joined Joffrey Ballet in 1970.

DANIELIAN, LEON. Born Oct. 31, 1920 in N.Y.C. Studied with Mordkin and Fokine. Debut with Mordkin Ballet in 1937. Appeared with Original Ballet Russe, Ballet Russe de Monte Carlo, Ballet Theatre, Ballet des Champs Elysees, and San Francisco Ballet. Was choreographer-director of Ballet de Monte Carlo. Now with American Ballet Theatre School.

DANIELS, DANNY. Born in 1924 in Albany, N.Y. Studied with Thomas Sternfield, Jack Potteiger, Vincenzo Celli, Elisabeth Anderson-Ivantzova, Anatole Vilzak. Appeared in musicals, as soloist with orchestras, and Agnes de Mille Dance Theatre before becoming choreographer for TV and Bdwy musicals.

DANILOVA, ALEXANDRA. Born Nov. 20, 1906 in Peterhof, Russia. Graduate of Imperial School of Ballet, and became member of company. Subsequently with Balanchine's company, Les Ballets Russes de Diaghilev, Ballet Russe de Monte Carlo (both de Basil's and Massine's). Made N.Y.C. debut in 1948 at Met with Massine's company. Has appeared with and choreographed for N.Y.C. Ballet. In 1954 formed and toured with own company, The Concert Dance Group; choreographer for Met 1961–62. Now teaches.

DANTE, SHARON. Born Jan. 8, 1945 in Torrington, Conn. Graduate UHartford. Studied with Graham, Limon, Weidman, ABT School. Appeared with Charles Weidman, Larry Richardson, Rudy Perez, Jose Limon. Founder-Director of Nutmeg Ballet.

D'ANTUONO, ELEANOR. Born in 1939 in Cambridge, Mass. Danced with Ballet Russe de Monte Carlo for 6 years before joining Joffrey Ballet in 1960. Became member of American Ballet Theatre in 1961; principal since 1963.

DAVIDSON, ANDREA. Born in 1955 in Montreal, Can. Studied at Ntl. Ballet School, and joined company in 1971; Promoted to soloist in 1972.

DAVIS, GARY. Born in Washington, D.C. Graduate UMd., UIll. Studied at National Academy of Dance. Debut 1954 with Charles Weidman, subsequently with Jeff Duncan, Tina Croll, NY Dance Collective, Mimi Garrard, Paul Taylor. Also choreographs.

DAVIS, MARTHA HILL. Born in East Palestine, O. Graduate Columbia, NYU. Debut with Martha Graham (1929–31). Director of Dance, Bennington (1934–42), NYU (1930–51), Juilliard since 1951. Founder Conn. Col. School of Dance and American Dance Festival.

DAVIS, ROBERT. Born March 13, 1934 in Durham, N.C. Studied at Wash. School of Ballet, and with Fokine, Franklin, and Joffrey. Debut in 1960 and has appeared as principal dancer with Washington Ballet, National Ballet of Canada, and Joffrey Ballet. Is also director and choreographer.

DEAN, LAURA. Born Dec. 3, 1945 on Staten Island, NY. Studied with Lucas Hoving, Muriel Stuart, Matt Mattox, Martha Graham, American Ballet Center, Mia Slavenska. Appeared with Paul Taylor, Paul Sanasardo. Formed own company in 1971.

DEANE, MICHAEL. Born Nov. 4, 1950 in NYC. Graduate UColo. Studied with Larry Boyette, Robert Christopher, Dan Wagoner, Joffrey School. Debut 1974 with Paul Taylor Co. Member Repertory Dance Theatre 1974–75.

DeANGELO, ANN MARIE. Born Oct. 1, 1952 in Pittston, Pa. Trained at San Francisco Ballet School and made debut with its company in 1970. Joined Joffrey 1972.

DE BOLT, JAMES. Born in Seattle, Wash. Studied with Marian and Illaria Ladre, and at U. Utah. Debut with Seattle's Aqua Theatre. Joined Joffrey Ballet in 1959, subsequently with N.Y.C. Opera Ballet, N.Y.C. Ballet 1961, Manhattan Festival Ballet 1965. Is also a costume designer and choreographer. Re-joined Joffrey Co. in 1968. Currently premier danseur of Oslo's Den Norske Opera.

DE GANGE, ANN. Born Sept. 22, 1952 in New London, Conn. Juilliard graduate. Studied with Corvino, Tudor, McGehee, Winters. Debut 1971 with Kazuko Hirabayashi, subsequently with Martha Graham Co. from 1972.

DE JONG, BETTIE. Born in Sumatra, and moved to Holland in 1947. Made debut with Netherlands Pantomime Co. Studied with Martha Graham and joined company; subsequently with Pearl Lang and Lucas Hoving. Joined Paul Taylor in 1962.

DELAMO, MARIO. Born during January 1946 in Havana, Cuba. Studied with May O'Donnell, Gertrude Shurr, Norman Walker. Debut 1966 with Norman Walker Co.; Glenn Tetley 1969; Alvin Ailey 1970; Martha Graham Co. 1972.

DELANGHE, GAY. Born Aug. 21, 1940 in Mt. Clemens, Mich. Studied at Severo School. Professional debut in 1960 and toured with "The Dancemakers." Choreographer, performer, and teacher since 1965. Joined Lucas Hoving Co. in 1967.

de LAPPE, GEMZE. Born Feb. 28, 1922 in Woodhaven, Va. Attended Hunter Coll. and Ballet Arts School. Studied with Duncan, Fokine, Nimura, Caton, and Nemtchinova. Has appeared with Ballet Theatre and Agnes de Mille Dance Theatre and in Bdwy productions.

de LAVALLADE, CARMEN. Born March 6, 1931 in Los Angeles. Attended LACC, and studied with Lester Horton. Professional debut with Horton Dance Theatre. Bdwy debut in 1954. Has appeared with John Butler, Met Opera, de Lavallade-Ailey, Donald McKayle, and Ballet Theatre.

DELZA, SOPHIA. Born in N.Y.C. Studied in China. Professional debut 1953 in program of Chinese dances. Has toured world in concert, and been choreographic consultant for Met Opera, LCRep. Theatre, and Bdwy musicals.

de MAYO, FRED DOUGLASS. Studied at Abbey Theatre, and with Fokine, Youskevitch, Pereyaslavec, and in Paris with Preabrajenska. Appeared with National Ballet, Met. Opera Ballet. Founder of Newburgh Ballet. Now Director of Dance at West Point, and teaches at New Paltz SUNY.

de MILLE, AGNES. Born in N.Y.C. in 1909. Graduate of UCLA. Studied with Kosloff, Rambert, Karsavina, Tudor, Sokolova, Caton, Craske, Stroganova, and Dolmetsch. Debut in 1928 in own dance compositions and toured with them in Europe. Became leading choreographer for Bdwy. Created first ballet "Black Ritual" for Ballet Theatre in 1940. In 1953 organized Agnes de Mille Dance Theatre which toured U.S. Has also choreographed for Ballet Russe de Monte Carlo, and Royal Winnipeg Ballet. In 1973 organized and choreographs for Heritage Dance Theatre.

DENARD, MICHAEL. Born Nov. 5, 1944 in Dresden, Germany. Studied in Toulouse and Paris. Has appeared with Berlin Opera, and Paris Opera Ballets, with Bejart, and joined ABT (1971) as principal.

DENVERS, ROBERT. Born Mar. 9, 1942 in Antwerp. Studied with Nora Kiss, Tania Grantzeva, Peretti; joined Bejart's Ballet in 1963; Ntl. Ballet of Canada.

De SOTO, EDWARD. Born Apr. 20, 1939 in The Bronx. Attended Juilliard, AADA, New Dance Group Studio. Danced with Gloria Contreras, Judith Willis, Sophie Maslow, Art Bauman, Valerie Bettis, before joining Limon Co. in 1966.

DESTINE, JEAN-LEON. Born in Haiti, March 26, 1928. Attended Howard U. Made professional debut at Jacob's Pillow in 1949. Formed own company and has toured U.S., Europe, and Japan. Also teaches.

DeVILLIERS, JOHN R. Born Apr. 22, 1951 in Sacramento, CA. Attended Chico State, UCal., American Ballet Center. Debut 1975 in "Nureyev and Friends."

DIAMOND, MATTHEW. Born Nov. 26, 1951 in N.Y.C. Attended CCNY. Debut 1967 with Matteo and the Indo-American Dance Co. Subsequently with Norman Walker, N.Y.C. Opera, Louis Falco, Jose Limon 1975.

DI BONA, LINDA. Born July 21, 1946 in Quincy, Mass. Studied at Boston Ballet School and made debut with company in 1965. Joined Harkness Ballet 1972.

DICKSON, CHARLES. Born June 30, 1921 in Bellwood, Pa. Studied with Fokine, Massine, Dolin, Tudor, Volkova, Preobrajenska, Egorova, Balanchine, Volkova, Markova, Loring, Nijinska. Debut 1938 with Ballet Russe de Monte Carlo; AmBalTh 1940–42; Alicia Alonso Ballet 1952–55; Borovansky Ballet of Australia 1955–58; ballet master London Festival Ballet 1958–61; artistic director-ballet master Ballet Municipal de Santiago 1963–76; from 1971 director Metropolitan Academy, and Metropolitan Ballet Co.

DISHONG, ZOLA. Born Aug. 4, 1945 in Albany, Cal. Studied with Lew Christensen, Anatole Vilzak, Michael Lland, Patricia Wilde. Debut 1962 with San Francisco Ballet, subsequently with ABT 1967.

DOBRIEVICH, LOUBA. Born Feb. 9, 1934 in Bajina Basta, Yugoslavia. Studied at Belgrade Academy of Dance. Debut 1954 with Opera Zagreb; subsequently with Paris Theatre Ballet 1958, Maurice Bejart Co. from 1959.

DOBRIEVICH, PIERRE. Born Dec. 27, 1931 in Veles, Yugoslavia. Studied at Etudes de Droit. Debut 1955 with Opera Zagreb; subsequently with Paris Theatre Ballet 1957, Ludmila Cherina 1958, Les Etoiles de Paris 1959, Maurice Bejart from 1960.

DOBSON, DEBORAH. Born June 23, 1950 in Sacramento, Ca. Studied at San Francisco Ballet Sch., Sch. of Am. Ballet. Debut 1968 with Andre Eglevsky Co., joined ABT in 1969; promoted to soloist in 1973; joined Stuttgart 1975.

Stephanie Dabney

Gary Davis

Starr Danias

Leon Danielian

Ellen Everett

DOKOUDOVSKY, VLADIMIR. Born in 1922 in Monte Carlo. Studied with Preobrajenska; made debut at 13; became soloist with Ballet Russe de Monte Carlo, Mordkin Ballet, Ballet Theatre. Premier danseur with Original Ballet Russe (1942–52). Has choreographed several ballets. Now teaches.

DOLIN, ANTON. Born Sydney Francis Patrick Chippendall Healey-Kay in Slinfold, Sussex, Eng. July 27, 1904. Studied with Astafieva, Nijinska. With Diaghileff Company 1921–9, principal dancer with Sadler's Wells 1931–5. Ballet Russe 1939, 1946–8. Founder, director, and dancer with Markova-Dolin Co. 1935–8, 1945, 1947–8. Danced, restaged, and choreographed for Ballet Theatre from inception to 1946. 1949 organized and danced with London Festival Ballet until 1961. Currently artistic adviser of Les Grands Ballets Canadiens.

DOLLAR, WILLIAM. Born Apr. 20, 1907 in East St. Louis, Mo. Studied with Fokine, Mordkin, Balanchine, Vladimiroff, and Volinine. Lead dancer with Philadelphia Opera, American Ballet 1936–7, Ballet Caravan 1936–8, Ballet Theatre 1940, American Ballet Caravan 1941, New Opera Co. 1942, Ballet International 1944, ballet master for American Concert Ballet 1943, Ballet Society 1946, Grand Ballet de Monte Carlo 1948, N.Y.C. Ballet. Has choreographed many works, and teaches.

DONN, JORGE. Born Feb. 28, 1947 in Buenos Aires. Attended School of Teatro de Colon. Appeared in musicals before joining Bejart Ballet in 1963, rising to leading male dancer.

DORADO, THIERRY. Born in 1950 in Paris, France. Studied with Nina Tikanova, Paris Opera School. Debut with Paris Opera Ballet; appeared with Nice Opera Ballet, Ballets de Roland Petit, Stuttgart (1969–70). Joined Ballet West as principal 1973.

DOUGLAS, HELEN. Studied with Maggie Black, Karoly Zsedenyi, Vincenzo Celli, Margaret Craske. Debut 1966 with Met Opera Ballet. Joined Joffrey 1966–68; ABT 1968–71, Eliot Feld 1973. Also lecturer.

DOUGLAS, SCOTT. Born June 16, 1927 in El Paso, Tex. Studied with Lester Horton and Ruth St. Denis. Appeared with San Francisco Ballet, Ballets U.S.A., John Butler, Ballet Theatre, Nederlands National Ballet, Glen Tetley Co. Ballet Master for ABT.

DOWELL, ANTHONY. Born in London Feb. 16, 1943. Studied with June Hampshire, entered Royal Ballet School at 10. Debut as hunter in "Swan Lake" at Covent Garden Opera House. Joined Sadler's Wells Opera Ballet, and Royal Ballet in 1961. Is now a principal.

DOYLE, DESMOND. Born June 16, 1932 in South Africa. Joined Royal Ballet in 1951. Became soloist in 1953; is now a principal and teacher.

DRAPER, PAUL. Born 1909 in Florence, Italy. Began studies at early age, and became tap soloist, elevating it to ballet-tap concert form. Made debut in 1932 in London. Continues to give solo performances, teaches, and is photographer.

DRIVER, SENTA. Born Sept. 5, 1942 in Greenwich, Conn. Graduate Bryn Mawr, Ohio State U. Studied with Maggie Black, Don Farnworth, and at O'Donnell-Shur Studio. Joined Paul Taylor Company in 1967, left in 1973 to choreograph and direct Harry.

DU BOULAY, CHRISTINE. Born in 1923 in Ealing, Eng. Trained in Sadler's Wells Ballet School. Soloist with International Ballet before joining Sadler's Wells. Settled in U.S. in 1950, and with husband, Richard Ellis, became founders and directors of Illinois Ballet Co.

DUBREUIL, ALAIN. Born in Monte Carlo, Mar. 4, 1944. Studied at mother's ballet school until awarded scholarship at Arts Educational School (1960). Joined London Festival Ballet in 1962 and became soloist in 1964.

DUDLEY, JANE. Dancer-choreographer. Born in N.Y.C. in 1912. Studied with Martha Graham, Hanya Holm, Louis Horst. Leading dancer with Graham Co. (1937–44). With Sophie Maslow and William Bales, formed concert Dance Trio. Retired in 1954 to teach.

DUELL, DANIEL. Born Aug. 17, 1952 in Rochester, NY. Attended Fordham U., School of American Ballet. Debut 1971 with Edward Villella Co., subsequently with Eglevsky Ballet, Dayton Ballet, Lincoln Center Repertory Dancers, NYCB 1974.

DUFFY, DIANE. Born in Philadelphia, Pa. Studied at Pa. Ballet Sch., Harkness House. Debut at 15 with Pennsylvania Ballet; joined Harkness, National, Eliot Feld Ballet (1973).

DUNCAN, JEFF. Born Feb. 4, 1930 in Cisco, Tex. Attended N. State Tex. U., studied with Holm, Nikolais, Limon, Cunningham, Schwetzoff, Tomkins, Joffrey. Assistant to Doris Humphrey and Anna Sokolow. Debut 1952 at Henry St. Playhouse. Has appeared with New Dance Group, Juilliard Dance Theatre, Anna Sokolow, Jeff Duncan Dance Co., and is founder-director of Dance Theatre Workshop. Has also appeared in Bdwy musicals.

DUNHAM, KATHERINE. Born June 22, 1912, in Chicago. Debut with Chicago Opera Co. in 1933. Bdwy debut 1940 in "Cabin In The Sky." Formed own company for which she choreographed; toured with it in 1943, and subsequently in 57 other countries. Founded Katherine Dunham School of Cultural Arts in N.Y.C. in 1943.

DUNNE, JAMES. Born in Waldwick, N.J. Studied with Irene Fokine, and at School of American Ballet, Harkness House. Joined Harkness Ballet for 4 years, then Joffrey Ballet.

EBBELAAR, HAN. Born Apr. 16, 1943 in Hoorn, Holland. Studied with Max Dooyes and Benjamin Harkarvy. Danced with Nederlans Dans Theater before joining American Ballet Theatre in 1968 as soloist; promoted to principal in 1969, Dutch Natl. Ballet (1970).

EBBIN, MICHAEL. Born June 5, 1945 in Bermuda. Studied at Patricia Gray's, National Ballet, American Ballet, American Ballet Center, and Harkness Schools. Has danced with Eleo Pomare, Cleo Quitman, Australian Dance Theatre, Anna Sokolow, Talley Beatty, and Rod Rodgers companies, and appeared on Bdwy. Joined Ailey company 1972.

EDWARDS, LESLIE. Born Aug. 7, 1916 in Teddington, Eng. Studied with Marie Rambert and at Sadler's Wells School. Debut 1933 with Vic-Wells Ballet, subsequently joined Ballet Rambert, Royal Ballet, Now teaches and makes guest appearances.

EGLEVSKY, ANDRE. Born in Moscow Dec. 21, 1917. Received training in France. At 19 joined Rene Blum's Ballet de Monte Carlo. Came to U.S. in 1937, and after appearing with all major companies, joined Ballet Theatre. In 1947 appeared with Grand Ballet du Marquis de Cuevas. In 1950 joined N.Y.C. Ballet and danced leading male roles until 1958, also created "Scotch Symphony" and other ballets for the company. In 1955, with his wife, prima ballerina Leda Anchutina, opened school in Massapequa, L.I., and in 1960 formed local classical ballet company which he directs.

EISENBERG, MARY JANE. Born Mar. 28, 1951 in Erie, Pa. Attended Hunter, New School. Studied at Graham, ABT, Harkness schools. Debut 1969 with Glen Tetley, subsequently with Keith Lee, Contemporary Dance Ensemble, Louis Falco.

ELLIS, RICHARD. Born 1918 in London. At 15 joined Vic-Wells Ballet which became Sadler's Wells Ballet. Important member of company until 1952. After touring U.S. with company in 1949–50, settled in Chicago. With wife, Christine Du Boulay, became founders and co-directors of Illinois Ballet Co.

ENCKELL, THOMAS. Born in Helsinki, Finland, Oct. 14, 1942. Studied with Margaret Craske. Professional debut with Met Opera Ballet in 1962. Joined Finnish Natl. Opera Ballet 1965. Manhattan Festival Ballet 1966.

ENGLUND, RICHARD. Born in Seattle, Wash. Attended Harvard, Juilliard. Studied with Tudor, Graham, Volkova. Appeared with Limon, Met Opera, Natl. Ballet of Canada, ABT, and in musicals. Currently teaches and choreographs.

ENTERS, ANGNA. Dancer, choreographer, and mime was born in 1907 in N.Y.C. Created own style of dance and pantomime that she has performed all over the world. Is also a writer and painter.

ERDMAN, JEAN. Born in Honolulu, Hawaii. Graduate of Sarah Lawrence College (1938). Studied at Bennington, American School of Ballet, Hisamatsu, Martha Graham, Pukui and Huapala Hawaiian Dance Schools. Professional debut 1938 with Martha Graham, and as a choreographer in 1942. Organized own company in 1950, and made annual tours through 1960. World tour 1963–5 with "The Coach With The Six Insides" which she conceived and staged. Head of NYU Dance Dept. for 5 yrs.

ERICKSON, BETSY. Born in Oakland, Cal. Attended Cal. State U., San Francisco Ballet School. Debut with San Francisco Ballet. Joined American Ballet Theatre 1967; returned to SF Ballet 1973.

ESTELLE & ALFONSO. Born in N.Y.: trained with Haakon, Mattox, Juarez, LaSylphe, Nettles, Chileno, Wills, Thomas. Toured widely as team. Currently operate school in Poughkeepsie, N.Y., and artistic directors for Mid-Hudson Regional Ballet.

ESTNER, ROBERT. Born in North Hollywood, Calif. Attended Los Angeles City Valley Jr. Col. Studied with Robert Rossalatt, Natalie Clare, Andre Tremaine, Carmalita Maracci, and at ABC. Appeared with Ballet Concerto, Pacific Ballet, Ballet La Jeunesse, before joining Joffrey Co.

EVANS, BILL. Born Apr. 11, 1946 in Lehi, Utah. Graduate Univ. Utah. Studied at Harkness House, American Dance Center, ABT School. Made debut in 1966 with Ruth Page Ballet. Joined Repertory Dance Theatre in 1967 as dancer and choreographer.

EVERETT, ELLEN. Born in Springfield, Ill. June 19, 1942. Studied in Chicago and School of American Ballet. Professional debut 1958 with Ruth Page's Chicago Opera Ballet. Soloist with American Ballet Theatre from 1967. Raised to principal 1973. Has also appeared on Bdwy.

FADEYECHEV, NICOLAI. Born in Moscow in 1933. Studied at Bolshoi School and joined company in 1952; became soloist in 1953, and subsequently premier danseur.

FAISON, GEORGE. Born Dec. 21, 1945 in Washington, D.C. Attended Howard U. Studied with Louis Johnson, Claude Thompson, Alvin Ailey, Dudley Williams, Elizabeth Hodes. Appeared on Bdwy and with Universal Dance Experience (1971).

FALCO, LOUIS. Born in N.Y.C.; studied with Limon, Weidman, Graham, and at American Ballet Theatre School. Danced, choreographed, and toured with Jose Limon, Co., as principal dancer for 10 years, choreographed for other groups, and own company which he formed in 1967.

FALLET, GENEVIEVE. Born Aug. 2, 1943 in Switzerland. Studied at Royal Ballet, and with Yuriko, Cunningham, Wagoner, DTW. Has danced with London and Paris companies, with Frances Alenikoff, and solo.

FALLIS, BARBARA. Born in 1924 in Denver, Colo. Moved to London in 1929. Studied at Mona Clague School. Vic-Wells and Vilzak-Shollar Schools. Debut 1938 in London. With Vic-Wells Ballet 1938–40; Ballet Theatre in 1941; Ballet Alicia Alonso (1948–52), N.Y.C. Ballet (1953–58). Now teaches.

FARBER, VIOLA. Born in Heidelberg. Ger., Feb. 25, 1931. Attended American U. and Black Mt. College. Studied with Katherine Litz, Merce Cunningham, Alfredo Corvino, and Margaret Craske. Debut 1952 with Merce Cunningham, subsequently with Paul Taylor, and Katherine Litz. More recently, choreographing, and guest artist with Merce Cunningham.

FARRELL, SUZANNE. Born Roberta Sue Ficker Aug. 16, 1945 in Cincinnati. Began ballet studies in Cincinnati, subsequently attending School of American Ballet. After 15 months joined N.Y.C. Ballet, and became a principal dancer in 1965. Joined National Ballet of Canada in 1970, Bejart (1970), returned to NYCB in 1975.

FAXON, RANDALL. Born Sept. 26, 1950 in Harrisburg. Pa. Studied with Elizabeth Rockwell. Martha Graham, Paul Sanasardo, Alfredo Corvin, and at Juilliard. Debut 1969 with Ethel Winter; joined Lucas Hoving in 1970.

FEDICHEVA, KALERIYA. Born in Leningrad in July 1937. Attended Kirov School; joined company in 1956; Resigned in 1974 and came to U.S. in 1975. Appeared with Terpsichore Co.

FEDOROVA, NINA. Born Apr. 24, 1958 in Philadelphia, Pa. Studied at Pa. Ballet School, Sch. of Am. Ballet. Made Debut with NYC Ballet in 1974.

FEIGENHEIMER, IRENE. Born June 16, 1946 in N.Y.C. Attended Hunter Col. Studied with Holm, Graham, Cunningham, ABC. Debut 1965 with Met Opera Ballet, subsequently danced with Merry-Go-Rounders, Ruth Currier, Anna Sokolow, Cliff Keuter, Don Redlich.

FEIN, RICHARD. Born in Los Angeles where he studied with Don Hewitt, Joey Harris, and performed with the Harris Co. Joined National Ballet of Canada 1972, Eliot Felt Ballet 1974.

FEIT, VALERIE. Born July 17, 1956 in Johannesburg, SAf. Studied at Harkness and ABT schools. Joined Eliot Feld company 1974, Alvin Ailey 1975.

FELD, ELIOT. Born 1943 in Brooklyn. Studied with Richard Thomas and at School of American Ballet. Appeared with N.Y.C. Ballet, and on Bdwy before joining American Ballet Theatre in 1963. Co-founder (1969), director, dancer, and choreographer for American Ballet Co. Rejoined ABT in 1971. Debuted Eliot Feld Ballet 1974.

FERNANDEZ, ROYES. Born July 15, 1929 in New Orleans. Studied with Lelia Hallers and Vincenzo Celli. Appeared with Ballet Russe, Markova-Dolin, Ballet Alicia Alonso, de Cuevas' Ballet, before joining Ballet Theatre. Premier danseur since 1957. Retired in 1973 to teach. Has appeared with several companies as guest artist.

FIBICH, FELIX. Born May 8, 1917 in Warsaw, Poland; attended

dance and theatre schools, and made professional debut there in 1936. Became dancer-choreographer in 1939. Formed own company that has toured widely with Israeli and Chassidic dancers. Also teaches.

FIFIELD, ELAINE. Born in Sydney, Aust. Studied at Sadler's Wells, RAD. Debut 1948 with Sadler's Wells Co., subsequently appeared with Royal Ballet, Australian Ballet.

FIGUEROA, ALFONSO. Born May 24, 1947 in N.Y.C. Graduate Boston Cons. Studied with Virginia Williams, Thomas-Fallis, Pearl Lang. Debut 1967 with Boston Ballet; subsequently Pearl Lang, American Ballet 1968, Alvin Ailey 1970, Boston Ballet 1971.

FILIPOV, ALEXANDER. Born Mar. 19, 1947 in Moscow. Studied at Leningrad Kirov School. Debut with Moiseyev Ballet, defected and appeared with Pa. Ballet, Eglevsky Ballet, ABT (1970), Pittsburgh Ballet 1971, San Francisco Ballet 1974.

FISHER, NELLE. Born Dec. 10, 1920 in Berkeley, Cal. Appeared with Martha Graham Co., in Bdwy musicals; choreographs and teaches.

FITZGERALD, HESTER. Born Oct. 1, 1939 in Cleveland, O. Trained with Nedjedin, Levinoff, and at Ballet Russe, American, and Ballet Theatre schools. Debut with Ballet Russe 1956; subsequently with N.Y.C. Ballet, ABT, and Harkness Ballet.

FLINDT, FLEMMING. Born Sept. 30, 1936 in Copenhagen. Entered Danish Royal Ballet School at 10; became member at 18. Invited by Harald Lander to appear in London; returned to Danish Ballet and became leading dancer before joining Paris Opera as danseur etoile, and choreographing. Ranks among world's greatest male dancers, and has achieved recognition as choreographer. Became director of Royal Danish Ballet in 1966.

FLINDT, VIVI. Born Feb. 22, 1943 in Copenhagen, Den. Studied at Royal Danish Ballet and joined company in 1965.

FONAROFF, NINA. Born in N.Y.C. in 1914. Studied with Martha Graham, at School of American Ballet. Danced with Graham (1937–46) before forming own company in 1945. Is now teacher-choreographer.

FONTEYN, MARGOT. Born May 18, 1919 in Surrey, Eng. Began training at 14 with Astafieva, and a few months later entered Sadler's Wells School. Solo debut with company in 1934 in "The Haunted Ballroom." In 1935, succeeded to ballerina roles of Markova. Unrivaled in roles of Aurora and Chloe. Made Dame of British Empire by Queen Elizabeth. Guest star of Royal Ballet, and considered Prima Ballerina Assoluta of the world.

FOREMAN, LAURA. Born in Los Angeles. U. Wisc. graduate. Danced with Tamiris-Nagrin, Marion Scott, Harriet Anne Gray, Ann Halprin. Director of Laura Foreman Dance Company; Founder/Director of Choreographers Theatre/ChoreoConcerts; director New School Dance Dept.

FOSSE, BOB. Born in Chicago June 23, 1927. Appeared in musicals and clubs before becoming outstanding choreographer for Bdwy, films, and TV.

FOSTER, RORY. Born Feb. 3, 1947 in Chicago, Ill. Attended Ill. Benedictine Col. Studied with Robert Lunnon, Doreen Tempest, Vincenzo Celli. Debut 1962 with Allegro American Ballet; joined American Ballet Theatre 1970.

FOWLER, TOM. Born Feb. 18, 1949 in Long Beach, Cal. Graduate U. Cin. Studied with David Howard, Claudia Corday, David McLean, Margaret Black, Richard Thomas, Harkness House. Debut 1971 with American Ballet Company. Joined Joffrey 1974.

FRACCI, CARLA. Born Aug. 20, 1936 in Milan, Italy. Began training at 8 at La Scala with Edda Martignoni, Vera Volkova, and Esmee Bulnes. Became prima ballerina of La Scala in 1958; joined London Festival Ballet as guest artist. Now permanent guest artist with American Ballet Theatre.

FRALEY, INGRID. Born Nov. 1, 1949 in Paris, France. Studied at San Francisco Ballet, and made debut with company in 1964. Subsequently with Kiel-Lubeck Opera Ballet, Fokine Ballet, Eglevsky Ballet, joined American Ballet Theatre 1969; Joffrey 1975.

FRANKEL, EMILY. Born in N.Y.C. Studied with Weidman, Holm, Graham, Craske, Tudor, and Daganova. Professional debut 1950. Founder, director, choreographer, and dancer with Dance Drama Co. since 1955. Has made 8 transcontinental tours, a State Dept. sponsored tour of Europe, and British Arts Council tour of England and Scotland.

FRANKLIN, FREDERIC. Born in Liverpool, Eng. in 1914. Studied with Legat, Kyasht, and Pruzina. Made debut as child dancer; went to London at 17; appeared in music halls, night clubs, and musicals before joining Markova-Dolin Co. 1935–7. Premier danseur with Ballet Russe de Monte Carlo from 1938; became its ballet master in 1944. Artistic adviser ABT (1961). Director National Ballet (1962–74); Artistic Director Pittsburg Ballet Theatre from 1974.

FRAZER, SUSAN. Born in NYC. Studied at Sch. of Am. Ballet, and with Jean Hamilton, Vladimir Dokoudovsky. Joined National Ballet 1968; promoted to soloist 1972. Joined ABT 1974.

FREDERICK, JULIA. Born in Boston. Studied and performed with Boston Ballet, Harkness Ballet, N.Y.C. Ballet. Also danced

Louis Falco

Valerie Feit

Flemming Flindt

Susan Frazer

Robert Gladstein

with Penn. Ballet, Garden State Ballet, and N.Y.C. Opera Co. Resident soloist with Hartford Ballet.

FREEDMAN, LAURIE. Born July 7, 1945 in N.Y.C. Graduate Bennington Col. Studied with Graham, Cunningham, Zena Rommett. Debut 1967 with Merry-Go-Rounders, subsequently with Batsheva Dance Co. (1968).

FREEMAN, FRANK. Born July 16, 1945 in Bangalore, India. Studied at Royal Ballet School. Joined company in 1963. Joined London Festival Ballet as soloist in 1971.

FUENTE, LUIS. Born in 1944 in Madrid where he began studies at early age. Joined Antonio's Ballets de Madrid in 1963; Joffrey Ballet 1964–1970. National Ballet (1970) as principal; London Festival Ballet 1972. Rejoined Joffrey 1976. Organized own company in Madrid.

FUERSTNER, FIONA. Born Apr. 24, 1936 in Rio de Janeiro. Attended San Francisco State College. Studied at San Francisco Ballet School (debut with company 1952). School of American Ballet, Ballet Rambert, Royal Ballet, Ballet Theatre schools. Has danced with Les Grands Ballets Canadiens, San Francisco, N.Y.C. Center, and Philadelphia Opera ballet companies. Principal dancer with Pennsylvania Ballet. Became Ballet Mistress in 1974.

GABLE, CHRISTOPHER. Born 1940 in London, began studies at Royal Ballet School. At 16 joined Sadler's Wells Opera Ballet, and next year Covent Garden Opera Ballet. In 1957 became member of Royal Ballet and at 19 advanced to soloist. Retired in 1967 to act.

GAIN, RICHARD. Born in Belleville, Ill. Jan. 24, 1939. Studied with Lalla Baumann, and Martha Graham. Professional debut with St. Louis Municipal Opera, followed by musicals. Became member of Graham Co. in 1961, also danced with Jazz Ballet Theatre, Lotte Goslar, Sophie Maslow, and Pearl Lang, and formed concert group "Triad" that performed in N.Y. and on tour. Joined Joffrey Co. in 1964; ABT in 1967. Teaches at N.C. School of Arts.

GARDNER, BARBARA. Born June 7, 1940 in Lynbrook, NY. Graduate Stanford U. Studied with Wigman, Sanasardo, Cunningham. Has appeared with Nikolais, Marion Scott, Phoebe Neville, Clina Mooney, and her own company. Also teaches.

GARRARD, MIMI. Born in Gastonia, N.C. Attended Sweet Briar College. Studied at Henry St. Playhouse, with Julia Barashkova, Angelina Romet. Has appeared with Alwin Nikolais and Murray Louis companies, and own company for which she choreographs.

GARRETT, BRENDA. Born Jan. 25, 1954 in Georgetown, Guiana. Studied at London's Royal Ballet School. Joined Dance Theatre of Harlem in 1973.

GARTH, MIDI. Born in N.Y.C. Studied with Francesca de Cotelet, Sybil Shearer, Louis Horst. Has choreographed and performed solo concerts in N.Y. and on tour. Also teaches.

GARY, M'LISS. Born Nov. 8, 1951 in Lisbon, Port, Graduate Natl. Ballet Academy. Studied with Oleg Tupine, Richard Thomas, Barbara Fallis. Debut 1969 with National Ballet, joined American Ballet Co. in 1971.

GAYLE, DAVID. Born July 10, 1942 in Yorkshire, Eng. Appeared in Covent Garden opera ballets before joining Royal Ballet. Left in 1970 to teach in Buffalo.

GENNARO, PETER. Born 1924 in Metairie, La. Studied at American Theatre Wing. Debut with Chicago San Carlo Opera 1948, and Bdwy bow same year. After several musicals and TV, choreographed "Seventh Heaven" in 1955. Is much in demand as dancer and choreographer on television.

GENTRY, EVE. Born Aug. 20, in Los Angeles. Used own name Henrietta Greenhood until 1945. Studied with Holm, Graham, Humphrey, Weidman, Tamiris, Barashkova, at Ballet Arts Studio, and American Ballet Center. Debut with Hanya Holm. Since 1949, director-choreographer-soloist with own company.

GERMAINE, DIANE. Born July 5, 1944 in N.Y.C. Studied with Martha Graham. May O'Donnell, Norman Walker, Paul Sanasardo. Debut with Sanasardo in 1963. Has appeared in concert with Norman Walker, and teaches.

GEVA, TAMARA. Born 1908 in St. Petersburg, Russia. Studied at Maryinsky Theatre. Joined Diaghilev. Came to U.S., signed by Ziegfeld, subsequently appeared in musicals and films and with American Ballet.

GIELGUD, MAINA. Born Jan. 14, 1945 in London. Studied with Karsavina, Idzikovski, Egorova, Gsovsky, Hightower. Debut 1961 with Petit Ballet, subsequently with Ballet De Marquis de Cuevas, Miskovitch, Grand Ballet Classique, joined Bejart Ballet in 1967.

GILMORE, RICHARD. Born in Franklin, PA. Attended Butler U. Studied at Harkness House. Joined Eliot Feld Ballet in 1973.

GILPIN, JOHN. Born in 1930 in Southsea, Eng. Was child actor; joined Ballet Rambert 1945, London's Festival ballet, becoming artistic director and principal dancer. Guest artist with ABT and Royal Ballet. Resigned as artistic director Festival Ballet but remains premier danseur.

GIORDANO, GUS. Born July 10, 1930 in St. Louis. Graduate U. Mo. Debut at Roxy N.Y.C., 1948, subsequently appeared in musicals on TV before becoming choreographer. Currently director of Giordano Dance Studio in Evanston, Ill., and his own company.

GLADSTEIN, ROBERT. Born Jan. 16, 1943 in Berkeley, Calif. Attended San Francisco State College, and studied at San Francisco Ballet School. Became member of San Francisco Ballet in 1960 and choreographed 13 ballets. Joined American Ballet Theatre in 1967, became soloist in 1969. Rejoined S.F. Ballet 1970.

GLASSMAN, WILLIAM. Born 1945 in Boston and began dance studies at 7. Scholarship to School of American Ballet. Studied with Alfredo Corvino and Margaret Craske. Appeared in musicals, with N.Y.C. Opera, and on TV, before joining American Ballet Theatre in 1963. Promoted to soloist 1965. Now with Niagara Frontier Ballet.

GLENN, LAURA. Born Aug. 25, 1945 in N.Y.C. Graduate Juilliard. Joined Limon Co. in 1964. Has also performed with Ruth Currier, Sophie Maslow, Valerie Bettis, and Contemporary Dance Sextet.

GLUCK, RENA. Born Jan. 14, 1933. Juilliard graduate. Studied with Graham, Tudor, Horst, Blanche Evans. Founding member of Batsheva Dance Co. in 1963. Also choreographs.

GLUSHAK, NANETTE. Born Dec. 31, 1951 in NYC. Studied at School of Am. Ballet. Made debut with American Ballet Theatre in 1967. Promoted to soloist 1973.

GODREAU, MIGUEL. Born Oct. 17, 1946 in Ponce, P.R. Studied at Joffrey Ballet Center, School of American Ballet, Ballet Russe, and with Martha Graham. Debut 1964 with First American Dance Co., subsequently with Ailey, McKayle, and Harkness Ballet. After appearing on Bdwy, organized and danced with own company in 1969. Returned to Ailey Co. in 1970. Left to appear in London. Now principal with Birgit Cullberg Co. in Sweden.

GODUNOV, ALEKSANDR. Born in 1950 on the island of Sakhalin, north of Japan. Began training in Riga, Latvia. Debut at 17 with Igor Moiseyev's Young Classical Ballet. Made debut with Bolshoi in 1970 as principal.

GOLLNER, NANA. Born 1920 in El Paso, Texas. Studied with Kosloff. Soloist with American Ballet 1935, de Basil's Ballet Russe 1935–6. Blum's Ballet Russe 1936–7. Ballet Theatre 1939–48. Only American to achieve rank of ballerina in foreign country.

GOODMAN, ERIKA. Born Oct. 9 in Philadelphia. Trained at School of American Ballet, and American Ballet Center. Debut with N.Y.C. Ballet 1965. Appeared with Pa. Ballet, and Boston Ballet before joining Joffrey Ballet in 1967.

GOPAL, RAM. Born Nov. 20. Hindu dancer, came to U.S. in 1938, and with own company has toured world as its soloist. Operates own school.

GORDON, LONNY JOSEPH. Born in Edinburg, Tex. Graduate of U.Tex and U.Wisc. Studied at Grand Kabuki Theatre in Tokyo, and with Koisaburo Nishikawa, Richo Nishikawa. Has given solo performances throughout Japan and U.S. Director Southern Repertory Dance Theatre.

GORDON, MARVIN. Born in N.Y.C. Graduate Queens Col. Studied with New Dance Group, Met Opera Ballet, Graham, Humphrey, and Weidman. Appeared on Bdwy and TV, in concert with Doris Humphrey, and Pearl Lang. Choreographed before becoming founder-director of Ballet Concerts, that has appeared in N.Y. and on tour throughout U.S.

GORDON, MEG ELIZABETH. Born May 6, 1953 in NYC. Attended New School, NYC Ballet. Joined Alvin Ailey Co. 1973.

GORRISSEN, JACQUES. Born Apr. 21, 1945 in Ghent, Bel. Studied at Ballet School Royal Flemish Opera. Debut 1962 with Ballet Royal Flemish Opera. Joined National Ballet of Canada in 1968.

GOSLAR, LOTTIE. Born in Dresden, Ger. Studied at Mary Wigman School. Toured Europe as dance mime before coming to U.S. in 1937. Formed own pantomime company for tours of U.S. and Europe. Also teaches.

GOVRIN, GLORIA. Born Sept. 10, 1942 in Newark, N.J. Studied at Tarassof School, American Ballet Academy, School of American Ballet. Joined N.Y.C. Ballet in 1957. Promoted to soloist at 19.

GOYA, CAROLA. Born in N.Y.C. Studied with Fokine, Otero, LaQuica, Maria Esparsa. Danced with Met Opera before solo debut as Spanish dancer in 1927. Appeared with Greco before partnership with Matteo in 1954.

GRAHAM, MARTHA. Born May 11, 1893 in Pittsburgh. Studied at Denishawn School of Dance; made debut with its company in 1919, and danced with them until 1923. First choreographed and appeared in N.Y.C. in a program of 18 original works in 1926, followed by annual concerts until 1938. A founder of Bennington (Vt.) Dance Festival where she staged several premieres of her works. Formed own company with which she has made numerous successful tours throughout world. Founded Martha Graham School of Contemporary Dance in 1927, and remains its director. Has created over 100 dances.

GRANT, ALEXANDER. Born Feb. 22, 1925 in Wellington. New Zealand. Entered Sadler's Wells School in 1946, and five months later joined company. Has created more major roles than any other male dancer with Royal Ballet. Appointed Director National Ballet of Canada in 1976.

GRAY, DIANE. Born May 29, 1944 in Painesville, Ohio. Attended Juilliard. Studied with Graham, Tudor, Youskevitch, Schwezoff, Melikova, Hinkson, Winter, McGehee, Ross. Debut 1964 with Martha Graham Co. Has also appeared with Helen McGehee, Yuriko, Pearl Lang, Sophie Maslow, Jeff Duncan.

GRECO, JOSE. Born Dec. 23, 1919 in Montorio-Nei-Frentani, Compobasso, Italy. Studied with Mme. Veola in N.Y.C. Argentinita and La Quica in Madrid. Debut as soloist 1935 with Salmaggi Opera Co. Partner with La Argentinita 1943–4. Pilar Lopez 1946–8, before organizing own company in 1949, with which he has become internationally famous.

GREENFIELD, AMY. Born July 8, 1940 in Boston. Studied with Graham, Cunningham, Fonaroff, Robert Cohan, American Ballet Center. Made debut in 1965. Has appeared in concert and with DTW.

GREGORY, CYNTHIA. Born July 8 in Los Angeles where she studied with Lorraine, Maracci, Panaieff, and Rossellat. Danced with Santa Monica Civic Ballet, L.A. Civic Light Opera in 1961 joined San Francisco Ballet, subsequently S.F. Opera Ballet, and American Ballet Theatre in 1965, became principal in 1968; Resigned in 1975.

GREY, BERYL. Born in Highgate, England, June 11, 1927. Began studies at Sadler's Wells Ballet School, and at 15 danced "Swan Lake" with its company. Left in 1957 but returned for guest appearances. Appointed in 1966 to head Arts Education School, London. Director London Festival Ballet, made Commander British Empire in 1973.

GRIFFITHS, LEIGH-ANN. Born Dec. 5, 1948 in Johannesburg, S.A. Studied at Royal Ballet School. Joined Stuttgart Ballet in 1968.

GRIGOROVICH, YURI. Born in Leningrad Jan. 2, 1927. Graduated from Leningrad Ballet School and became one of leading soloists with Kirov Co. In 1964 became choreographer for Moscow Bolshoi Ballet Co.

GROMAN, JANICE. Born in New Britain, Conn. Joined N.Y.C. Ballet at 16. Later with ABT, and First Chamber Dance Quartet.

GUERARD, LEO. Born Jan. 18, 1937 in Boston, Mass. Studied at School of American Ballet. Debut 1952 with ABT; subsequently with Grand Ballet de Cuevas 1957, Skandinavian Ballet 1960, Royal Winnipeg Ballet 1963, Western Theatre Ballet 1964, Intl. Ballet Caravan 1968, Boston Ballet 1968.

GUNN, NICHOLAS. Born Aug. 28, 1947 in Bklyn. Studied with Ellen Segal, Helen McGehee, June Lewis, Don Farnworth. Appeared with Stuart Hodes Co. Joined Paul Taylor Co. in 1969.

GUTELIUS, PHYLLIS. Born in Wilmington, Del. Studied with Schwetzoff, Tudor, Graham. Joined Graham Company in 1962. Has appeared on Bdwy. with Glen Tetley, Yuriko, Sophie Maslow, John Butler.

GUTHRIE, NORA. Born Jan. 2, 1950 in N.Y.C. Studied with Marjorie Mazia, Martha Graham, and at NYU. Debut 1970 with Jean Erdman Co.

GUZMAN, PASCHAL. Born in Arecibo, P.R. Attended Harkness, National Ballet, Graham, Dalcroze schools. Debut 1964 with National Ballet, subsequently with Baltimore Ballet, Washington Dance Repertory, Penn. Ballet, New America Ballet, Ballet Concerto, Downtown Ballet.

GYORFI, VICTORIA. Born in Wenatchee, Wash. Studied at San Francisco Ballet, and made debut with its company. Appeared with Munich Ballet, Bayerische Staats Oper, and returned to SF Ballet.

HAAKON, PAUL. Born in Denmark in 1914 Studied at Royal Danish Ballet School, with Fokine, Mordkin, and at School of American Ballet. Debut with Fokine in 1927. Danced and toured with Anna Pavlova. Became premier danseur with American Ballet in 1935. Appeared in musicals and nightclubs. In 1963 became ballet master and instructor of Jose Greco Co.

HACKNEY, PEGGY. Born Dec. 28, 1944 in Miami, Fla. Graduate Duke U., Sarah Lawrence Col. Has performed with Deborah Jowitt, Micki Goodman, Jose Limon Co., Tina Croll, and Jeff Duncan. Teaches extensively.

HAGGBOM, NILS-AKE. Born Apr. 20, 1942 in Stockholm, Swed. Studied at Royal Swedish Ballet, with Raymond Franccetti, Vera Volkova, Erik Bruhn, William Griffith, Stanley Williams, Royal Ballet. Joined Royal Opera Ballet in 1959, quickly rising to danseur noble. Guest artist with many companies.

HAISMA, RICHARD. Born Aug. 6, 1945 in Grand Rapids, Mich. Studied with Nancy Hauser and appeared with her company before joining Murray Louis Co. in 1973.

HALL, YVONNE. Born Mar. 30, 1956 in Jamaica, WI. Studied at Dance Theatre of Harlem and made debut with company in 1969.

HAMILTON, PETER. Born in Trenton, N.J. Sept. 12, 1915. Attended Rutgers. Danced in Broadway musicals before becoming choreographer and teacher.

HAMMONS, SUZANNE. Born Aug. 26, 1938 in Oklahoma City Attended San Francisco Ballet, American Ballet Center, and Harkness schools. Debut in 1958 with San Francisco Ballet; subsequently joined Harkness, and Joffrey Ballet companies.

HANITCHAK, LEONARD R., JR. Born July 24, 1944 in Oklahoma City. Studied with Ethel Butler, Graham, and Cunningham Has danced with DTW, and Rudy Perez Co.

HANKE, SUSANNE. Born in 1948 near Berlin. Studied with Anneliese Morike, Anne Woolliams, and at Royal Ballet School. Debut 1963 in Wuerttemberg State Theatre Ballet. Joined Stuttgart Ballet in 1966.

HARKAVY, BENJAMIN. Born in N.Y.C. in 1930. Studied with Chaffee, Caton, Preobrajenska, and at School of Am. Ballet. Made debut with Bklyn. Lyric Opera, for which he also choreographed Opened school in 1955 and formed concert group. Ballet master for Royal Winnepeg, and Nederlands Ballet. Artistic Director of Pa Ballet 1972.

HARKNESS, REBEKAH. Born in St. Louis, Mo. Promoted American dancers for several years before establishing Harkness Ballet in 1965, and Harkness Ballet School.

HARPER, LEE. Born Nov. 10, 1946 in Hickory, N.C. Juilliard graduate. Studied with Tudor, Limon, Koner, Lindgren, Cunningham, Alvin Ailey.

HARPER, MEG. Born Feb. 16, 1944 in Evanston, Ill. Graduate of U. Ill. Studied with Merce Cunningham and made professional debut with his company in 1968.

HARRIS, RANDAL. Born in Spokane, Wash. Attended Pacific Lutheran U. Studied with Joffrey, Edna McRae, Jonathan Watts ABC. Joined Joffrey Ballet in 1970.

HART, DIANA. Born Apr. 21, 1952 in Lansing, Mich. Attended Juilliard, and Martha Graham schools. Made debut 1973 with Graham Company. Has also appeared with Saeko Ichinohe Co.

HART, JOHN. Born in London in 1921. Studied with Judith Espinosa, and at Royal Acad. Joined Sadler's Wells in 1938, and rose to principal. Became ballet master in 1951, asst. director in 1962

HARUM, EIVIND. Born May 24, 1944 in Stavanger, Nor. Attended Utah State U. Debut 1959 with Stuart Hodes company, and subsequently with Helen Tamiris, Harkness Ballet, Alvin Ailey Co Martha Graham (1975). Has also appeared in several musicals.

HARVEY, DYANE. Born Nov. 16, 1951 in Schenectady, N.Y Studied with Marilyn Ramsey, Paul Sanasardo. Appeared with Schenectady Ballet, Dance Uptown, Miguel Godreau, Eleo Pomare Movements Black, Story Time Dance Theatre.

HARWOOD, VANESSA. Born June 14, 1947 in Cheltenham, Eng Studied with Betty Oliphant, Ntl. Ballet School, Rosella Hightower Debut 1965 with National Ballet of Canada; became principal in 1970.

HASH, CLAIRE RISA. Born May 18, 1946 in Norwich, Conn Studied at U. Colo. and NYU. Debut 1970 with Jean Erdman Co

HAUBERT, ALAINE. Born in N.Y.C. Attended U. Utah. Studied with Helen Averell, Raoul Pause, Kira Ivanovsky, Dorothy Dean Alan Howard, William Griffith. Debut with Monterey Peninsula Ballet, subsequently with Pacific Ballet, ABT, Joffrey Ballet.

HAUPERT, LYNN. Born Aug. 16, 1954 in Syracuse, NY. Studied with Paul Sanasardo, Dance Theatre of Harlem. Debut 1972 with Paul Sanasardo Dance Co.

HAWKINS, ERICK. Born in Trinidad, Colo. Studied at School of American Ballet. Appeared with American Ballet 1934–7, Ballet Caravan 1936–9, and with Martha Graham Company, before becoming choreographer, teacher, and director of his own company.

HAYDEE, MARCIA. Born April 18, 1940 in Rio de Janeiro. Studied at Royal Ballet School, London. Debut with Marquis de Cuevas Ballet. Joined Stuttgart Ballet in 1961, becoming its prima ballerina and in 1976 its artistic director.

cques Gorrissen   **Lotte Goslar**   **Nils-Aka Haggbom**   **Cynthia Gregory**   **Eivind Harum**

AYDEN, MELISSA. Born in Toronto, Can. April 25, 1923, where she received early training before becoming charter member f N.Y.C. Ballet in 1949. Has appeared with Natl. Ballet of Canada, allet Theatre, and Royal Ballet. In great demand as educator and cture-demonstrator. Has also appeared on Bdwy. Director "Ballet estival." Retired 1973 to teach.

AYMAN-CHAFFEY, SUSANA. Born Jan. 31, 1948 in Tenerden, England, Studied at Sadler's Wells School, and with Lepeinskaya, Graham, Cunningham. Made debut in 1968 with Merce unningham.

AYWARD, CHARLES SUMNER. Born May 2, 1949 in Providence, R.I. Attended Juilliard. Debut in 1968 with Jose Limon ompany.

EINEMAN, HELEN. Born Aug. 13, 1947 in Highland Park, Ill. ttended Hunter Col. Studied with Sybil Shearer, Mme. Swoboda. ebut 1963 with National Ballet; became soloist before leaving in 966. Ballet Russe 1967; Nederlands Dans Theater 1968-9; Harkess Ballet 1970.

ELPMANN, ROBERT. Born April 9, 1909 in Mt. Gambier, ustl. Attended King Alfred Col.; studied with Laurent Novikov. ebut in Austl. musicals; in 1933 joined Sadler's Wells (now Royal allet), and rose to soloist from 1933-50. Became choreographer, nd created ballet "Hamlet" in 1942. Recently has devoted time to cting, guest performances, and directing Australian Ballet. Made ommander of British Empire in 1964.

ERBERTT, STANLEY. Born in Chicago in 1919. Studied with udor, Caton, Ivantzova. Member of Polish Ballet, Littlefield, hicago and San Carlo Opera Ballets before joining Ballet Theatre 1943. Founder-Director of St. Louis Ballet. Also teaches and horeographs.

ERMANS, EMERY. Born June 25, 1931, in Seattle. Studied with aunda Carter, and at Henry St. Playhouse. Debut 1968 with Nikois Co. Has danced with Carolyn Carlson, Al Wunder, and in own orks.

ESS, LISA CAMILLE. Born in Amarillo, TX. Studied at School f American Ballet; joined NYC Ballet in 1975; appeared with "Nueyev and Friends."

IATT, JOHN. Born Oct. 5, 1939 in St. George, U. Studied at Utah, and became charter member and principal of Ballet West in 963.

IGHTOWER, ROSELLA. Born Jan. 30, 1920 in Ardmore, Okla. tudied at Perkins School. Appeared with Ballet Russe de Monte arlo 1938-41. Ballet Theatre 1941-5. Markova-Dolin 1946. Origial Ballet Russe 1946-7. Teaches in Cannes and makes guest appearnces.

ILL, CAROLE. Born Jan. 5, 1945 in Cambridge, Eng. Studied at oyal Ballet School and made debut with Royal Ballet Co. in 1962.

ILL, MARTHA. (see DAVIS, MARTHA HILL).

INKSON, MARY. Born in Philadelphia, March 16, 1930. Graduate of U. Wisc. Studied with Graham, Horst, Shook, June Taylor, chwezoff. Debut with Graham Co. in 1952. Also danced with John utler, N.Y.C. Opera, and N.Y.C. Ballet.

OCTOR, HARRIET. Born in Hoosick Falls, N.Y. Studied with arasov, Chalif, Dolin, Legat. Danced in vaudeville, theater, and ms before opening own school in Boston in 1941, where she aches.

ODES, STUART. Born in 1924. Studied with Graham, Lew hristensen, Ella Daganova, and at School of American Ballet. eading dancer with Graham (1947-58), appeared in Bdway musials, and as soloist in own works. Choreographer and instructor with arkness Ballet. Now teaches, and heads NYU Dance Dept.

OFF, ALEXIS. Born Aug. 31, 1947 in Chicago. Studied with elba Cordes, Betty Gour, Edna MacRae and at Stone-Camryn hool. Made debut with Chicago Lyric Opera Ballet in 1961. Joined arkness Ballet in 1965, becoming soloist in 1968.

OFF, STEVEN-JAN. Born June 24, 1943, in Hilversum, Holland. udied at Amsterdam Academie of Dance. Appeared in musicals fore joining American Ballet Theatre in 1966. Became soloist in '69. Joined Garden State Ballet 1970. Formed own "Film and ance Theatre" in 1971.

HOFFMAN, PHILLIP. Born in Rochester. N.Y. Attended Miami Dade Jr. Col. Studied with Thomas Armour, and at Harkness House, ABC. Joined Joffrey Ballet in 1969.

HOGAN, JUDITH. Born Mar. 14, 1940 in Lincoln. Neb. Studied with Martha Graham. Made debut with Bertram Ross in 1964. Danced with Glen Tetley before joining Graham Co. in 1967.

HOLDEN, RICHARD. Born Aug. 8 in Braintree, Mass. Graduate of London Inst. of Choreology. Appeared with George Chaffee Ballet, Met Opera, Ballets Minerva. Choreologist for Harkness Ballet, and director of Tucson Civic Ballet.

HOLDEN, STANLEY. Born in London, Jan. 27, 1928. Studied with Marjorie Davies Romford. Made professional debut in 1944 with Royal Ballet and remained until 1969. Now teaches, and makes guest appearances.

HOLDER, CHRISTIAN. Born in 1950 Trinidad. Studied in London, and with Martha Graham, Bella Malinka, ABC, Joined Joffrey Ballet.

HOLDER, GEOFFREY. Born in Port-of-Spain, Trinidad, Aug. 1, 1930. Attended Queens Royal College. With brother's dance company in Trinidad, later its director. With own company, made first U.S. appearance in 1953. Besides touring, and giving annual concerts with his group, has appeared on Bdwy, with Met opera, and John Butler Co., also choreographs and designs.

HOLM, HANYA. Born in 1898 in Worms-am-Rhine, Germany. Attended Hoch Conserv., Dalcroze Inst., Wigman School. U.S. debut with own company in 1936, followed by annual performances and transcontinental tours. Came to U.S. in 1931 to found N.Y. Wigman School of Dance which became her school in 1936. Has choreographed musicals and operas in U.S. and London.

HOLMES, GEORGIANA. Born Jan. 5, 1950 in Vermont. Studied with Pauline Koner, Duncan Noble, Job Sanders, Boston School of Ballet. Debut 1969 with Norman Walker; subsequently with Pearl Lang, Louis Falco, Paul Sanasardo, Manual Alum. Also teaches.

HONDA, CHARLOTTE. Born June 2, 1940 in San Jose, Calif. Graduate Ohio State U. Studied with Cunningham, Graham, Hoving, Limon, Sanasardo, Farnworth. Debut in 1967 with Larry Richardson; subsequently with Katherine Litz, ChoreoConcerts, and Laura Foreman.

HORNE, KATHRYN. Born in Ft. Worth, Tex., June 20, 1932. Studied with Margaret Craske, Antony Tudor. Debut 1948 with Ft. Worth Opera Ballet. Appeared with American Ballet Theatre as Catherine Horn (1951-56), a principal dancer Met Opera Ballet (1957-65), Manhattan Festival Ballet (1963-8), also ballet mistress and teacher for MFB.

HORVATH, IAN. Born in Cleveland, O., June 3, 1945. Studied with Danielian, Joffrey. Appeared in musicals, and on TV before joining ABT in 1967, soloist in 1969.

HOSKINS, PAUL. Born Sept. 5, 1952 in Collinsville, Ill. Attended Southern Ill. U. Studied with Katherine Dunham. Joined Alvin Ailey Co. 1972.

HOVING, LUCAS. Born in Groningen, Holland. Attended Dartington Hall, and Kurt Jooss School. Professional debut with Kurt Jooss Ballet in 1942. Has appeared with Graham, Limon, and his own company. Has also appeared in Bdwy musicals.

HOWARD, ALAN. Born in Chicago. Studied with Edna MacRae and in Europe. Joined Ballet Russe de Monte Carlo in 1949 and became premier danseur. Appeared with N.Y.C., and Met Opera Ballets before being appointed director of Academy of Ballet in San Francisco. Founded and is artistic director of Pacific Ballet.

HOWELL, JAMES. Born in Yakima, Wash. Attended U. Wash. Studied with Else Geissmar, Martha Graham, Doris Humphrey, Mary Wigman, Margaret Craske, Alfredo Corvino, Robert Joffrey. Original member of Joffrey Ballet.

HUANG, AL. Born in Shanghai, came to U.S. in 1955. Attended Oregon State U., Perry-Mansfield School, graduate UCLA and Bennington. Studied with Carmelita Maracci. Appeared with Lotte Goslar before forming own co., with which he tours when not teaching.

HUGHES, KENNETH. Born in Norfolk, Va. attended NC School of Arts, School of Am. Ballet. Debut 1969 with American Ballet; subsequently with Lar Lubovitch, American Classical Ballet, Les Grands Ballets Canadien, ABT 1972, Eliot Feld Ballet.

HUGHES, MICHAELA. Born Mar. 31, 1955 in Morristown, NJ. Made debut 1973 with Houston Ballet. Joined Eliot Feld Co. in 1974.

HUHN, HILLER. Born in New Orleans, LA. Danced with Royal Winnipeg Ballet; joined National Ballet (Washington, DC) as principal in 1971. Now ballet master of Houston Ballet.

HUJER, FLOWER. Born in Hollywood, Calif. Studied with Theodore Kosloff, Charles Weidman. Has toured in solo concerts and choreographs.

HUNTER, JENNY. Born Aug. 20, 1929 in Modesto, Calif. Studied with Merce Cunningham, Charles Weidman, Marjorie Sheridan. Debut 1951 with Halprin-Lathrop Co. With Dancers' Workshop Co. until 1958 when she left to found, direct, and choreograph for own company, Dance West.

HYND, RONALD. Born in London, April 22, 1931. Studied with Marie Rambert, Angela Ellis, Volkova Idzikowski, and Pereyaslavee. Professional debut 1949 with Ballet Rambert. Joined Royal Ballet in 1951, and graduated from corps to principal dancer.

INDRANI. Born in Madras, India. Studied with Pandanallur Chokkalingam Pillai, Sikkil Ramaswami Pillai, Devas Prasad Das, Narasimha. First dancer to present Orissi classic dance outside India. Tours extensively in solo and with company.

IRION, CYNTHIA. Born in Montclair, NJ. Studied at NJ School of Ballet, and joined NJ Ballet. Joined Eliot Feld Ballet in 1975.

ISAKSEN, LONE. Born Nov. 30, 1941 in Copenhagen where she studied with Edithe Feifere Frandson. Accepted in Royal Danish Ballet School at 13. In 1959 joined group organized by Elsa Marianne Von Rosen and Allan Fredericia, and shortly elevated to soloist. In 1961 studied at Joffrey's American Ballet Center, and appeared with his company. In 1965 joined Harkness Ballet, and became one of its principal dancers until 1970, when she joined Netherlands Natl. Ballet.

ISRAEL, GAIL. Born in Paterson, N.J. Studied with Alexandra Fedorova. Rose to soloist with Ballet Russe before joining American Ballet Theatre in 1962.

JACKSON, DENISE. Born in N.Y.C.: attended ABC. Danced with N.Y.C. Opera Ballet, joined Joffrey Ballet in 1969.

JAGO, MARY. Born in 1946 in Henfield, Eng. Trained at Royal Ballet School. Joined Covent Garden Opera Ballet in 1965; Natl. Ballet of Canada 1966; now a principal.

JAMES, JANICE. Born Feb. 14, 1942 in Salt Lake City, U. Studied with William and Lew Christensen; Joined NYC Ballet in 1963; joined Ballet West 1965, and is now a principal, and teacher.

JAMISON, JUDITH. Born in 1944 in Philadelphia. Studied at Judimar School, Phila. Dance Acad., Joan Kerr's School, Harkness School, and with Paul Sanasardo. Debut 1965 with ABT. Joined Ailey Co. in 1965, Harkness Ballet in 1966, and rejoined Ailey in 1967.

JAYNE, ERICA. Born Aug. 8, 1945 in Amersham, Eng. Studied at Royal Ballet School, RAD. Debut 1962 with Royal Opera Ballet. Currently principal with Les Grands Ballets Canadiens.

JEANMAIRE, RENEE ZIZI. Born Apr. 29, 1924 in Paris. Studied at L'Opera de Paris with Volinine, and with Boris Kniaserf. Debut with Ballet de Monte Carlo in 1944. Joined Ballet Russe de Colonel de Basil (1945–47), Petit's Ballets de Paris in 1948. Has appeard in musicals and films.

JENNER, ANN. Born March 8, 1944 in Ewell, Eng. Began studies at 10 with Royal Ballet School. Debut with Royal Ballet in 1962. Became soloist in 1966, principal in 1970.

JENSEN, CHRIS. Born Jan. 24, 1952 in Los Angeles, Cal. Studied with Albert Ruiz, Harriet DeRea, Carmelita Maracci, and at School of Am. Ballet. Debut 1970 with Ballet du Grand Theatre de Geneve; joined Harkness Ballet 1972.

JERELL, EDITH. Studied with Antony Tudor, Margaret Craske, Dokoudovsky, Brenna, Pereyaslavee, Joffrey, Popova, Gentry, Norman Walker, Nona Schurman, Nancy Lang. Lazowski, Dunham, and Nimura. Appeared with Met Opera Ballet as principal or solo dancer for 10 years. Is now teacher, concert and guest artist.

JHUNG, FINIS. Born May 28, 1937 in Honolulu where he began training. Gradute of U. Utah. Appeared on Bdwy before joining San Francisco Ballet in 1960. Advanced to soloist then joined Joffrey Ballet in 1962. Joined Harkness Ballet as soloist in 1964. Now teaches.

JILLANA. Born Oct 11, 1936 in Hackensack. N.J. After studying from childhood at School of American Ballet, joined N.Y.C. Ballet in teens rising rapidly to ballerina. With ABT (1957–8) returned to NYCB (1959). Retired in 1966. Is active in teaching and touring U.S. Artistic Adviser for San Diego Ballet.

JOFFREY, ROBERT. Born Dec. 24, 1930 in Seattle, Wash. Began studies with Mary Ann Wells, later attended School of American Ballet, and studied with May O'Donnell and Gertrude Shurr. Debut as soloist with Petit's Ballets de Paris. Appeared with O'Donnell company, and taught at HS Performing Arts and Ballet Theatre School before starting his own American Ballet Center in 1950. Formed first company in 1952 that was resident co. of N.Y. Opera, and made tours in his own works in the U.S. and abroad. Reorganized group appeared in 1965 and has been internationally acclaimed. Is now City Center Company.

JOHNSON, BOBBY. Born Oct. 26, 1946 in San Francisco. Studied at Harkness House and with Joffrey, Mattox, Jack Cole, Fokine. Has appeared on Bdwy and with Fred Benjamin Co.

JOHNSON, LOUIS. Born in Statesville, N.C. Studied with Doris Jones, Clara Haywood, and at School of American Ballet. Debut with N.Y.C. Ballet in 1952. Appeared in musicals before forming, choreographing for, and dancing with own group. Teaches, and on staff of Negro Ensemble Co.

JOHNSON, NANCY. Born in 1934 in San Francisco. Studied with Harold and Lew Christensen at San Francisco Ballet School, eventually becoming principal dancer of S.F. Ballet Co. With Richard Carter, toured world, appearing in fifty nations. Was prima ballerina with San Diego Ballet Co.

JOHNSON, PAMELA. Born in Chicago where she studied with Richard Ellis and Christine Du Boulay. Made debut with their Illinois Ballet Co. Joined Joffrey Ballet in 1966, American Ballet Theatre 1972.

JOHNSON, RAYMOND. Born Sept. 9, 1946 in N.Y.C. Graduate Queens Col. Studied with Alwin Nikolais, Murray Louis, Gladys Bailin, Phyllis Lamhut. Debut 1963 with Nikolais, joined Murray Louis in 1968; subsequently with Rod Rodgers, Joy Boutilier, Rudy Perez. Also teaches and choreographs.

JOHNSON, VIRGINIA. Born Jan. 25, 1950 in Washington, DC. Attended NYU, Washington School of Ballet. Debut 1965 with Washington Ballet; joined Capitol Ballet 1968: Dance Theatre of Harlem 1971.

JOHNSON, WILLIAM. Born Aug. 13, 1943 in Ashland, Kan. Attended San Francisco City Col., SF Ballet School. Debut 1961 with San Francisco Ballet; joined NYC Ballet 1970.

JONES, BETTY. Born in Meadville, Pa. Studied with Ted Shawn, Alicia Markova, La Meri, Doris Humphrey, and Jose Limon. Debut 1947 with Limon Co. and toured world with it. Has own lecture-performance, and teaches master classes throughout U.S. Has appeared in Bdwy musicals.

JONES, MARILYN. Born Feb. 17, 1940 in Newcastle, Australia. Studied with Tessa Maunder, Lorraine Norton, Royal Ballet School. Debut 1956 with Royal Ballet, subsequently with Borovansky Ballet, Marquis de Cuevas, London Festival, and Australian Ballets.

JONES, SUSAN. Born June 22, 1952 in York, Pa. Studied at Washington School of Ballet. Joined Joffrey company 1968, NYC Opera Ballet 1969, Am. Ballet Theatre 1971.

JORGENSEN, NELS. Born in New Jersey in 1938. Studied with Rose Lischner, and toured with her co. before beginning studies at School of American Ballet in 1953. Appeared in musicals and on TV before joining Joffrey Ballet as soloist in 1958. Artistic director Louisville Ballet.

JURKOWSKI, KRYSTYNA. Born June 15, 1954 in Nottingham, Eng. Appeared with Joffrey II, NJ Ballet, before joining City Center Joffrey Ballet in 1973.

KAGE, JONAS. Born in Stockholm, Swed. Began training at 9 in Royal Swedish Ballet School, and joined company in 1967. Joined ABT in 1971, rising to principal in 1973; Stuttgart 1975.

KAHN, ROBERT. Born May 31, 1954 in Detroit, Mich. Attended NYU. Made debut 1975 with Jose Limon Co., subsequently joined Paul Taylor Co.

KAHN, WILLA. Born May 4, 1947 in NYC. Attended Bklyn Col., CCNY. Studied with Paul Sanasardo, Mia Slavenska, Karoly Zsedbnyi. Debut 1959 with Paul Sanasardo Dance Co.

KAIN, KAREN. Born Mar. 28, 1951 in Hamilton, Ontario, Can. Trained at Ntl. Ballet School, and joined Ntl. Ballet of Canada in 1969; promoted to principal in 1971.

KARNILOVA, MARIA. Born in Hartford, Conn., Aug. 3, 1920. Studied with Mordkin, Fokine, Charisse, and Craske. First appeared with Met corps de ballet (1927–34). Became soloist with Ballet Theatre, and Met Opera Ballet. Recently in several Bdwy musicals.

KATAYEN, LELIA. Born in N.Y.C.: studied with Francesca de Cotelet, Sybil Shearer, Nanette Charisse, Joseph Pilates. In 1960 formed Katayen Dance Theatre Co, for which she is director-choreographer. Head of Southampton College Dance Dept.

KATO, MIYOKO. Born Sept. 26, 1943 in Hiroshima, Japan. Studied at Tachibana Ballet School. Made U.S. debut in 1965 with Met. Opera Ballet. Member of Harkness Ballet; joined Joffrey 1975.

KAYE, NORA. Born in N.Y.C. Jan. 17, 1920. Studied at Ballet School of Met Opera, and with Michel Fokine. Debut at 7 with Met's children's corps de ballet. Joined American Ballet Theatre as soloist in 1940 and N.Y.C. Ballet in 1950. Now assistant to her husband, choreographer Herbert Ross.

KEHLET, NIELS. Born in 1938 in Copenhagen where he began studies at 6, subsequently going to Royal Danish Ballet School. Teachers include Vera Volkova, Stanley Williams, Nora Kiss, Melissa Hayden. First solo at 16 in Royal Danish Ballet's "Sleeping Beauty." Made concert tour of Africa, and guest artist with Cuevas' Ballet, London Festival Ballet, and ABT (1971).

KEHR, DOLORES. Born May 11, 1935 in Boston. Studied with Fokine, Danielian, Doukodovsky, Vikzak. Made debut in 1952 with Ballet Russe; former ballerina with National Ballet. Now has school in Ft. Lauderdale, Fla., and is director of "Classiques," Denver Civic Ballet.

Janice James

Robert Joffrey

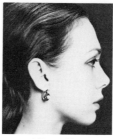
Allegra Kent

Michael Kidd

Gelsey Kirkland

KEIL, BIRGIT. Born Sept. 22, 1944 in Kowarschen, Sudetanland. Studied at Royal Ballet School. Made debut 1961 with Stuttgart Ballet.

KELLY, DESMOND. Born in 1945 in Bulawayo, Rhodesia. Studied at London's Royal Acad. Joined London Festival Ballet, becoming principal in 1963; subsequently with New Zealand Ballet, Zurich Opera Ballet, National Ballet 1968, Royal Ballet as principal in 1970.

KELLY, GENE. Born Aug. 23, 1912 in Pittsburgh. Graduate of U. Pittsburgh. Teacher and choreographer before appearing in Bdwy musicals and films. Currently choreographing and directing films.

KELLY, KAREN. Born Feb. 1, 1951 in Philadelphia. Trained at Thomas-Fallis School. Debut 1969 with American Ballet Co.

KENT, ALLEGRA. Born Aug. 11, 1938 in Los Angeles where she began her studies. At 13 went to School of American Ballet, and 2 years later joined N.Y.C. Ballet. Quickly rose to one of company's leading ballerinas.

KENT, HELEN. Born Dec. 30, 1949 in N.Y.C. U. Wisc. graduate. Studied with Waring, Cunningham, Nikolais. Made debut in 1971 with Murray Louis Co.

KENT, LINDA. Born Sept. 21, 1946 in Buffalo, N.Y. Juilliard graduate. Studied with Graham, Limon, Sokolow, Craske, Corvino, Tudor. Joined Alvin Ailey Co. in 1968, Paul Taylor Co. 1975.

KESSLER, DAGMAR. Born in 1946 in Merchantville. N.J. Studied with Thomas Cannon. Joined Penn. Ballet 1965, Hamburg State Opera 1966, London's Festival Ballet in 1967, Pittsburgh Ballet 1973.

KEUTER, CLIFF. Born in 1940 in Boise, Idaho. Studied with Welland Lathrop, Graham, Farnworth, Slavenska, Sanasardo. Debut in 1962 with Tamiris-Nagrin Co. Formed own company in 1969 for which he choreographs.

KIDD, MICHAEL. Born in N.Y.C. Aug. 12, 1919. Attended City College, and School of American Ballet. Studied with Blanche Evan, Ludmilla Scholler, Muriel Stewart, and Anatole Vitzak. Appeared as soloist with Ballet Caravan in 1938, and with Eugene Loring Co. Solo dancer with Ballet Theatre (1942–47), before becoming popular choreographer for musicals and films.

KIM, HAE-SHIK. Born Apr. 29, 1944 in Seoul, Korea. Graduate of Ewha U. Studied at Royal Ballet, London. Made debut in 1959 with Lim Sung Nam: subsequently with Zurich Opera Ballet (1967) and from 1969 with Les Grands Ballets Canadiens; promoted to soloist in 1970.

KIMBALL, CHRISTINA. Born Dec. 22, 1954 in Otsu, Japan. Debut 1972 with Alvin Ailey Co.

KINCH, MYRA. Born in Los Angeles. Graduate of U. of Calif. Solo and concert dancer, and choreographer of satirical ballets. Also teaches.

KING, BRUCE. Born in Oakland, Calif. Graduate of U. Calif. and NYU. Studied at Holm, Met Opera Ballet and Cunningham Schools. Debut 1950 with Henry St. Playhouse Dance Co. Toured with Merce Cunningham and is choreographer and teacher.

KIRBY, CHARLES. Born Apr. 28, 1926 in Little Rock, AR. Attended Little Rock U. Studied with Vera Nemtchinova, Hitchins, Nijinska, Agullo. Joined National Ballet of Canada in 1965 as soloist and character dancer.

KIRKLAND, GELSEY. Born in 1953 in Bethlehem, Pa. Studied at School of American Ballet. Joined N.Y.C. Ballet in 1968, promoted to soloist in 1969, principal in 1972. Joined ABT 1974.

KIRPICH, BILLIE. Born in N.Y.C., graduate of NYU. Studied with Graham, and at American School of Ballet. Debut 1942 with Pittsburgh Dance Co. Has appeared with New Dance Group, NYC Opera Ballet, on TV, and in musicals.

KITCHELL, IVA. Born in Junction City, Kan., March 31, 1912. Appeared with Chicago Opera Ballet before making solo debut as dance satirist in 1940. Has continued as concert artist and teacher.

KIVITT, TED. Born in Miami, Fla., Dec. 21, 1942. Studied with Alexander Gavriloff, Thomas Armour, Jo Anna Kneeland, and George Milenoff. Debut 1958 in night club revue. Appeared in Bdwy musicals before joining American Ballet Theatre in 1961. Elevated to soloist in 1964, principal dancer in 1967.

KLOS, VLADIMIR. Born July 1, 1946 in Prague. Studied at Konservatory Prag. Joined Stuttgart Ballet and quickly rose to principal.

KNAPP, MONICA. Born Jan. 23, 1946 in Germany. Made debut in 1963, and appeared with several companies before joining Stuttgart Ballet in 1971; promoted to principal.

KOESUN, RUTH ANN. Born May 15, 1928 in Chicago. Studied with Suoboda, Nijinksa, Tudor, and Stone-Camryn. Debut with Ballet Theatre in 1946, and became one of its principal dancers. Retired in 1968 but makes guest appearances.

KOLPAKOVA, IRINA. Born in 1933 in Leningrad. Studied with Kirov company and made debut at 18. Elevated to principal ballerina. Now prima ballerina for Leningrad Kirov Co.

KONDRATYEVA, MARINA. Born Feb. 1, 1933 in Kazan, Russia. Enrolled in Bolshoi School in 1943; graduated into company in 1953. One of company's principal ballerinas.

KONER, PAULINE. Born 1912 in NYC. Studied with Fokine, Michio Ito, Angel Cansino. Debut 1926 with Fokine Ballet. Debut as choreographer-solo dancer 1930. Formed own company (1949–1964). In addition to solo-performances, now teaches and choreographs.

KONING, LEON. Born July 5, 1947 in Zandvoort, Netherlands. Studied with Peter Leoneff, Benjamin Harkarvy, Richard Gibson, Hans Brenner. Debut 1967 with Netherlands Dance Theater.

KOSMINSKY, JANE. Born in Jersey City, N.J. in 1944. Attended Juilliard, CCNY. Debut 1960 with May O'Donnell. Joined Paul Taylor Co. in 1965. Has appeared with Helen Tamiris, Daniel Nagrin, and Norman Walker.

KRASSOVSKA, NATHALIE. Born June 3,1918 in Leningrad. Studied with Preobrajenska, Fokine, Massine, Balanchine, and Nijinska. Prima ballerina with Ballet Russe de Monte Carlo and London Festival Ballet. Currently teaches and dances with Dallas Civic Ballet, and appears with other companies as guest artist.

KRONSTAM, HENNING. Born in Copenhagen in 1934. Studied at Royal Danish Ballet School and joined company in 1952. Became premier danseur in 1956. Has appeared as guest artist with many companies.

KRUPSKA, DANIA. Born Aug. 13, 1923 in Fall River, Mass. Studied at Ethel Phillips, and Mordkin Ballet Schools. Began dancing at 6 in Europe as Dania Darling. On return to U.S., joined Catherine Littlefield Ballet. Became member of American Ballet Co. in 1938. More recently has been busy as choreographer.

KUCHERA, LINDA M. Born Jan. 28, 1952 in Monongahela, Pa. Studied at Wash. School of Ballet. Debut 1970 with NYC Opera Ballet; Joffrey II 1970, Ballet Brio 1972–3, ABT 1973.

KUNI, MASANI. Started career in Japan at 13. Gained international fame in solo recitals throughout Europe. Graduate of German Dance College, and studied with Mary Wigman and Max Terpis. Has taught and choreographed in Berlin, London, Copenhagen, Italy, Argentina, and Israel. Is currently director of Kuni Inst. of Creative Dance in Tokyo and Los Angeles.

LAERKESEN, ANNA. Born in 1942 in Copenhagen. Studied at Royal Danish Ballet School and joined company in 1959. Became soloist in 1961.

LaFONTSEE, DANE. Born Nov. 9, 1946 in Lansing, Mich. Studied at School of Am. Ballet. Debut in 1966 with National Ballet; joined Pa. Ballet in 1967, promoted to soloist in 1972.

LaFOSSE, EDMUND. Born in Beaumont, TX. Danced with National Ballet of Washington before joining Eliot Feld Ballet in 1974.

LAING, HUGH. Born in 1911 in Barbados, B.W.I. Studied in London with Craske and Rambert. Long career with Ballet Rambert, and Ballet Theatre, before joining N.Y.C. Ballet in 1950. Now a commercial photographer.

LA MERI. Born Russell Meriwether Hughes in Louisville, Ky., May 13, 1899. Professional debut in 1928. Annual tours throughout world until 1957. Established Ethnologic Dance Center and Theater in 1943, which she closed in 1956, and retired in 1960. Has written several books on dance, and teaches. Organized Festival of Ethnic Dance 1970.

LAMHUT, PHYLLIS. Born Nov. 14, 1933 in N.Y.C. where she began her studies in Henry St. Settlement Playhouse. Also studied with Cunningham, and at American Ballet Center. Debut in title role of Nikolais' "Alice in Wonderland." In 1957 gave concert of own works, and has appeared with Murray Louis. In addition to dancing, teaches and choreographs.

LAMONT, DENI. Born in 1932 in St. Louis, Mo. Appeared in musicals before joining Ballet Russe de Monte Carlo in 1951, Ballet Theatre 1953, N.Y.C. Ballet in 1954, now soloist.

LANDER, TONI. Born June 19, 1931 in Copenhagen, and studied there with Leif Ornberg, and in School of Royal Danish Ballet. Became member of its company at 17. In 1951, joined Paris Opera Ballet. Later joined London Festival Ballet, Ballet Theatre Francais. ABT in 1960 becoming principal ballerina. Rejoined Royal Danish 1971.

LANDON, JANE. Born Jan. 4, 1947 in Perth, Australia. Attended Royal Ballet School, London. Joined company in 1963 rising to principal dancer in 1969. Member of Stuttgart Ballet from 1970.

LANG, HAROLD. Born Dec. 21, 1920 in Daly City, Calif. Debut with S.F. Opera Co., subsequently dancing with Ballet Russe de Monte Carlo, and Ballet Theatre. More recently has appeared in musicals, and teaches.

LANG, PEARL. Born May 29, 1922 in Chicago. Attended U. of Chicago, and studied at Frances Allis, Martha Graham, American Ballet, Nenette Charisse, and Vicente Celli Schools. Debut with Ukrainian Folk Dance Co. in 1938, subsequently appearing with Ruth Page, Martha Graham companies before forming her own. Became active choreographer and teacher and has appeared on Bdwy.

LANNER, JORG. Born Mar. 15, 1939 in Berlin. Studied with Kurt Jooss, Nora Kiss, Menia Martinez. Debut 1958 in Ballet Babilee; joined Bejart in 1959.

LANOVÁ, MERRIEM. Born in California. Attended San Francisco State, and U. Cal. Studied with Nijinska, Lichine, Danilova, and at School of Am. Ballet, and Ballet Arts. Appeared with Ballet International, and Ballet Russe de Monte Carlo. Now operates own school, choreographs for and directs Ballet Celeste International.

LAPZESON, NOEMI. Born in Buenos Aires, Argentina, June 28, 1940. Studied at Juilliard, and with Corvino, Tudor, Limon, Nikolais, and Graham. Debut in Buenos Aires in 1955. Has appeared with Yuriko, Sophie Maslow, Helen McGehee, Bertram Ross, and Martha Graham. Has appeared in several musicals, and teaches.

LARSEN, GERD. Born in Oslo in 1921. Studied with Tudor. Debut with London Ballet, followed with Ballet Rambert, International Ballet, Sadler's Wells (now Royal) becoming soloist in 1954. Also teaches.

LASCOE, MATTI. Born Feb. 24, 1932. Graduate UCal. Trained with New Dance Group, Merce Cunningham, Herbert Ross. Premiered her own Dance Theatre Co. in 1972.

LATIMER, LENORE. Born July 10, 1935 in Washington, D.C. Graduate Juilliard. Joined Jose Limon Co. in 1959. Has appeared with Valerie Bettis, Anna Sokolow. Also teaches.

LAVROVSKY, MIKHAIL. Born Oct. 29, 1941. Studied at Bolshoi and graduated into company, rapidly rising to principal.

LAYTON, JOE. Born May 3, 1931 in N.Y.C. Studied with Joseph Levinoff. Bdwy debut in 1947. After many musicals, joined Ballet Ho de George Reich in Paris (1945–6). Returned to N.Y. and has become popular director and choreographer.

LECHNER, GUDRUN. Born Nov. 7, 1944 in Stuttgart, Ger. Studied at Stuttgart, and Royal Ballet School, London. Debut 1962 with Stuttgart Ballet; promoted to principal.

LEDIAKH, GENNADI. Born in 1928 in Russia. Entered Bolshoi School in 1946, and was graduated into company in 1949.

LEE, ELIZABETH. Born Jan. 14, 1946 in San Francisco. Studied with Harriet DeRea, Wilson Morelli, Richard Thomas. Debut 1964 with Pennsylvania Ballet. Joined American Ballet Theatre in 1967. American Ballet Co. 1969. Rejoined ABT in 1971; Eliot Feld Ballet 1974.

LEE, KEITH. Born Jan. 15, 1951 in the Bronx. Studied at Harkness, and Ballet Theatre Schools. Has danced with Norman Walker, Harkness Youth Co., and own company. Joined ABT in 1969; became soloist in 1971.

LEES, MICHELLE. Born Mar. 18, 1947 in Virginia. Studied at Wash. School of Ballet. Made debut 1964 with National Ballet.

LEIGH, VICTORIA. Born July 3, 1941, in Brockton, Mass. Studied with Georges Milenoff and at JoAnna-Imperial Studio. Debut 1958 with Palm Beach Ballet. Joined American Ballet Theatre in 1961, and became soloist in 1964.

LELAND, SARA. Born Aug. 2, 1941 in Melrose, Mass. Studied with E. Virginia Williams, Robert Joffrey, and at School of Am. Ballet. Debut with New England Civic Ballet, and subsequently with N.Y.C. Opera (1959), Joffrey Ballet (1960), N.Y.C. Ballet from 1960. Appointed principal in 1972.

LERITZ, LARRY. Born Sept. 26, 1955 in Alton, Ill. Trained with Harkness, Joffrey, and School of Am. Ballet. Debut 1974 with Harkness Ballet. With NY Dance Ensemble (1974–75), American Chamber Ballet 1975.

LERNER, JUDITH. Born in Philadelphia, Dec. 30, 1944. Attended Hunter College, American Ballet School, Ballet Theatre School, and studied with Nenette Charisse and Antony Tudor. Debut as soloist with Eglevsky Ballet in 1961, and joined American Ballet Theatre same year.

LESINS, MARCIS. Born Jan. 6, 1946 in Neustadt, WGer. Studied with Elisabeth Curland, Helen Uraus-Natschewa, Leonid Gonta.

Debut 1963 with Munich Opera Ballet; joined Stuttgart Ballet 1970; promoted to principal.

LEVANS, DANIEL. Born Oct. 7, 1953 in Ticonderoga, N.Y. Studied at HS Performing Arts, N.Y. School of Ballet. Debut in 1969 with American Ballet Co. Joined ABT in 1971, promoted to soloist in 1972, principal 1973. Joined NYCB 1974, U.S. Terpischore Co. 1975.

LEVINE, MICHELLE. Born Jan. 24, 1946 in Detroit, Mich. NYU graduate. Studied with Nenette Charisse, Gladys Bailin, Jean Erdman. Debut 1970 with Erdman Co.

LEWIS, DANIEL. Born July 12, 1944 in Bklyn. Juilliard graduate. Joined Limon Co. in 1963. Has appeared with Ruth Currier, Felix Fibich, Anna Sokolow companies.

LEWIS, JAMES J. Born July 30, 1946 in Denver, Colo. Graduate U. Mich. Studied with Sandra Severo. Debut 1969 with Boston Ballet. Joined American Ballet Co. in 1970.

LEWIS, MARILYN. Born June 15, 1947 in Winnipeg, Can. Attended United Col. Debut in 1966 with Royal Winnipeg Ballet; subsequently with Deutsche Operam Phein, and Wuppertal Opera in Germany, Netherlands Dans Theatre.

LIEPA, MARIS. Born July 27, 1930 in Riga, Latvia. Studied at Riga, and Bolshoi schools. Joined Bolshoi in 1961, quickly rising to principal.

LINDEN, ANYA. Born Jan. 3, 1933 in Manchester, Eng. Studied in U.S. with Theodore Koslov, entered Sadler's Wells School in 1947; joined company (now Royal) in 1951; ballerina in 1958. Now retired.

LINDGREN, ROBERT. Born in 1923 in Vancouver, Can. Studied with Vilzak, Swoboda, Preobrajenska. Joined Ballet Russe in 1942, N.Y.C. Ballet in 1957. Retired to teach.

LINN, BAMBI. Born in Brooklyn. April 26, 1926. Studied with Mikhail Mordkin, Helen Oakes, Hanya Holm, Agnes de Mille, and Helene Platava. Debut 1943 in "Oklahoma!" Subsequently danced with Ballet Theatre, Met Opera Ballet, Dance Jubilee Co., and American Ballet Co.

LISTER, MERLE. Born in Toronto, Can., where she began training and had own dance troupe. After moving to N.Y.C., organized dance company in 1964 with which she has appeared in N.Y. and on tour. Also teaches.

LITTLEMAN, ANITA. Born Jan. 4, 1952 in San Francisco, CA. Attended UHawaii, UWash. Trained with Jack Claus, Robert Joffrey. Joined Joffrey company in 1970. Has appeared with Donald McKayle, George Faison, Eleo Pomare, currently with Alvin Ailey.

LITZ, KATHERINE. Born in 1918 in Denver, Colo. Studied with Humphrey, Weidman, Horst, Platova, Thomas. Debut with Humphrey-Weidman Co. in 1936. Soloist with Agnes de Mille Co. (1940–42), and in Bdwy musicals. Debut as choreographer in 1948 in Ballet Ballads, followed by solo and group works. Also teaches.

LLAND, MICHAEL. Born in Bishopville, S.C. Graduate U.S. Car. Studied with Margaret Foster. Debut 1944 in "Song of Norway." Joined Teatro Municipal Rio de Janeiro (1945), ABT (1948) rising to principal in 1957, Ballet Master Houston Ballet (1968), ABT (1971).

LOKEY, BEN. Born Dec. 15, 1944 in Birmingham, Ala. Graduate U. Utah. Studied with Wm. Christensen, Caton, Peryoslavic, Weisberger, Morawski, Patricia Wilde. Made debut in 1966. Principal with Ballet West, and soloist with Pa. Ballet.

LOMBARDI, JOAN. Born Nov. 18, 1944 in Teaneck, N.J. Parsons graduate. Studied with Raoul Gelebert, Igor Schwezoff, Paul Sanasardo, Richard Thomas. Debut 1967 with Sanasardo Co. Has appeared with N.Y.C. Opera Ballet, and John Butler.

LOMMEL, DANIEL. Born March 26 in Paris. Studied with Joseph Lazzini, Nora Kiss. Made debut in 1966 with Grand Ballet Marquis de Cuevas. Joined Bejart Ballet in 1967 and is now a principal dancer.

LORING, EUGENE. Born in Milwaukee in 1914. Studied at School of American Ballet, and with Balanchine, Muriel Stuart, Anatole Vilzak, and Ludmilla Schollar. Debut 1934 in "Carnival." Subsequently with Met Opera Ballet, and Ballet Caravan, for whom he choreographed and starred in "Billy The Kid." Has become a leading choreographer for all media. Owns and operates American School of Dance in Hollywood.

LORRAYNE, VYVYAN. Born April 20, 1939 in Pretoria, South Africa. Entered Royal Ballet School in 1956 and company in 1957. Became principal in 1967.

LOUIS, MURRAY. Born Nov. 4, 1926 in N.Y.C. Graduate of NYU. Studied with Alwin Nikolais, and made debut in 1953. Has appeared annually in concerts and on tour with Nikolais, and own company, for which he also choreographs. Co-director of Chimera Foundation for Dance.

LOUTHER, WILLIAM. Born 1942 in Brooklyn. Attended Juilliard. Studied with Kitty Carson, Martha Graham, May O'Donnell, Antony Tudor, Gertrude Schurr. Debut with O'Donnell Co. in 1958. Has appeared in musicals, and in Donald McKayle Co. Joined Graham Co. in 1964. Artistic director Batsheva Co. 1972.

LOVE, EDWARD. Born June 29, 1950. Graduate Ohio U. Debut 1973 with Alvin Ailey Dance Theatre.

| Toni Lander | Keith Lee | Anita Littleman | Daniel Lommel | Sue Loyd |

LOVELLE, LAURA. Born May 6, 1958 in Brooklyn, NY. Studied at Dance Theatre of Harlem and made debut with company in 1973.

LOVELLE, SUSAN. Born May 22, 1954 in NYC. Attended Barnard, SUNY. Studied at Dance Theatre of Harlem, and made debut with company in 1968.

LOWSKI, WOYTEK. Born Oct. 11, 1939 in Brzesc, Poland. Studied in Warsaw and Leningrad. Debut 1958 with Warsaw Ballet, joined Bejart Ballet 1966, Cologne Ballet 1971, Roland Petit Co. in 1972; Boston Ballet 1973 as premier danseur.

LOYD, SUE. Born May 26, 1940 in Reno, Nev. Studied with Harold and Lew Christensen, Vilzak, Scolar, Danielian, Zerapse, Bruson, and Joffrey. Debut with San Francisco Ballet in 1954. Joined Joffrey Ballet in 1967. Ballet Mistress for Cincinnati Ballet; co-director Pacific Ballet.

LUBOVITCH, LAR. Born in Chicago; attended Art Inst., U. Iowa, Juilliard, ABT School, and studied with Martha Graham, Margaret Black. Debut 1962 with Pearl Lang, subsequently with Glen Tetley, John Butler, Donald McKayle, Manhattan Festival Ballet, Harkness, before forming own company. Also designs and choreographs for other companies.

LUCAS, JONATHAN. Born Aug. 14, 1922 in Sherman, Tex. Gradute of Southern Methodist U. Studied at American Ballet School. Debut 1945 in "A Lady Says Yes," followed by many Bdwy musicals. Became choreographer in 1956.

LUCCI, MICHELLE. Born Apr. 26, 1950 in Buffalo, NY. Studied at Banff School, with Joffrey, Caton, Lazowski, and Harkarvy. Debut 1968 with Royal Winnipeg Ballet. Joined Pennsylvania Ballet in 1969.

LUDERS, ADAM. Born Feb. 16, 1950 in Copenhagen, Den. Trained at Royal Danish Ballet School, and was graduated into company. Joined London Festival Ballet (1972), NYC Ballet as a principal in 1975.

LUDLOW, CONRAD. Born in Hamilton, Mont. in 1935. Began studies in San Francisco, and became member of its ballet company where he attained rank of soloist before joining N.Y.C. Ballet in 1957. Retired in 1973.

LUPPESCU, CAROLE. Born April 18, 1944 in Brooklyn. Attended Ind. U. Studied at Met Opera Ballet School. Joined Pennsylvania Ballet in 1964. Has performed with Ballet Rambert. Now retired.

LUSBY, VERNON. Born in New Orleans, La. Studied with Leila Haller, Dolin, Caron, Craske, Nijinska, Tudor. Appeared with ABT, Grands Ballets de Marquis de Cuevas, Natl. Ballet of Brazil. Also dancer and choreographer on Bdwy. Now associate director Royal Winnipeg Ballet.

LYMAN, PEGGY. Born June 28, 1950 in Cincinnati, Ohio. Studied at Stone-Camryn, Martha Graham, and Joffrey schools. Debut 1969 with NYC Opera Ballet. Joined Martha Graham Co. in 1973.

LYNN, ENID. Born in Manchester, Conn. Studied with Joseph Albano, Martha Graham, Sigurd Leeder. Director-Choreographer for Hartford Modern Dance Theatre, and Hartford Ballet.

LYNN, ROSAMOND. Born Dec. 31, 1944 in Palo Alto, Calif. Studied with Bill Griffith, Vincenzo Celli, Richard Thomas, Patricia Wilde. Debut 1964 with Philadelphia Lyric Opera, subsequently with ABT (1965), Alvin Ailey Co. (1970)

MacDONALD, BRIAN. Born May 14, 1928 in Montreal, Canada where he began choreographing for television. In 1958 became choreographer for Royal Winnepeg Ballet, and commuted to Norwegian and Royal Swedish Ballets where he held positions as director. Joined Harkness Ballet as director in 1967, left in 1968.

MacLEARY, DONALD. Born in Iverness, Scot., Aug. 22, 1937. Trained at Royal Ballet School. Joined company in 1954, became soloist in 1955 and premier danseur in 1959. Has partnered Beriosova on most of her appearances.

MacMILLAN, KENNETH. Born Dec. 11, 1930 in Scotland. Studied at Sadler's Wells and joined company (now Royal) in 1948. Debut as choreographer with Sadler's Wells Choreographers Group in 1953 with "Somnambulism." Subsequently created dances for Theatre Ballet, Royal Ballet, American Ballet Theatre, Royal Danish Stuttgart, and German Opera Ballet. Perhaps most famous are "Romeo and Juliet" and "The Invitation." Director Royal Ballet from 1970.

MADSEN, EGON. Born Aug. 24, 1944 in Copenhagen. Appeared with Pantomime Theatre and Scandinavian Ballet before joining Stuttgart Ballet in 1961. Promoted to soloist in 1963. Now principal.

MADSEN, JORN. Born Dec. 7, 1939 in Copenhagen. Studied at Royal Danish Ballet School; joined company in 1957; appointed soloist in 1961. Guest with Royal Ballet in 1965. Now retired.

MAGALLANES, NICHOLAS. Born Nov. 27 in Chihuahua, Mex. Studied at School of American Ballet. Danced with Littlefield Ballet, American Ballet Caravan, Ballet Russe de Monte Carlo. Principal dancer with N.Y.C. Ballet from its inception in 1946.

MAGNO, SUSAN. Born in 1946 in Melrose, Mass. Studied with Margaret Craske, Alice Langford, Virginia Williams. Appeared with Boston Ballet before joining Joffrey Ballet in 1965. Lar Lubovitch Co. in 1972.

MAHLER, RONI. Born in N.Y.C. in 1942. Studied with Maria Swoboda and at Ballet Russe School. Debut with Ballet Russe de Monte Carlo in 1960. Joined National Ballet in 1962 and became leading soloist in 1963. Joined ABT as soloist in 1969.

MAIORANO, ROBERT. Born Aug. 29, 1946 in Brooklyn, NY. Studied at School of American Ballet. Joined NYC Ballet in 1962.

MAKAROVA, NATALIA. Born Nov. 21, 1940 in Leningrad. Studied at Kirov School and joined company in 1959. Had triumph with her first "Giselle" in 1961. Defected in 1970 and joined ABT in 1970 as principal, making debut in "Giselle."

MALONEY, JULIE. Born in Newark, NJ. Debut 1970 with Charles Weidman. Joined Jan Wodynski company in 1972, and formed own company in 1975.

MANN, BURCH. Born in Texas: Studied with Adolph Bolm, Mordkin, and Fokine. Operates studio in Pasadena, Calif. Organized "Burch Mann Concert Group" that has become The American Folk Ballet.

MARCEAU, MARCEL. Born March 22, 1923 in Strasbourg, France. Studied with Charles Dullen and Etienne Decroux. Debut with Barrault-Renaud Co. in 1946. In 1947 formed own company, and among other works, presented "Bip" with whom he has become identified. Subsequently toured Europe, and U.S.

MARCHOWSKY, MARIE. Studied with Martha Graham: became member of company 1934-40. With own company, and as soloist, performing own choreography, has appeared in U.S. and abroad.

MARCU, REMUS. Born in Rumania where he danced with Rumanian State Opera before coming to U.S. in 1970. Has danced with Pittsburgh Ballet, Boston Ballet, Pennsylvania Ballet. Joined Eliot Feld Ballet in 1974.

MARINACCIO, GENE. Born 1931 in Newark, NJ. Studied with Bupesh Guha, Michael Brigante. Appeared with Lichine's Ballet, Petit's Ballet de Paris, Ballet Russe Monte Carlo, Ballet de Cuba. Now teaches and formed own company American Concert Ballet.

MARKO, IVAN. Born Mar. 29, 1947 in Hungary. Studied at Allami Ballet Intezet. Debut 1967 with Budapest Opera Ballet. Joined Ballet of 20th Century 1968.

MARKOVA, ALICIA. Born in London, Dec. 1, 1910. Studied with Seraphine Astafieva and Enrico Cecchetti. Appeared with Diaghilieff Ballet (1925-29), Vic-Wells Ballet (1932-5), Markova-Dolin Ballet (1935-7), Monte Carlo Ballet Russe (1938-41), prima ballerina Ballet Theatre (1941-5). Original Ballet Russe 1946, Markova-Dolin Co. (1947-8), co-founder and prima ballerina London Festival Ballet (1950-2), and has appeared as guest artist with companies throughout the world. Director of Met Opera Ballet 1963-9. Teaches at U. Cinn.

MARKS, BRUCE. Born in N.Y.C. in 1937 and studied at Met Opera School of Ballet with Tudor and Craske. Joined Met Opera Ballet in 1957, rising to rank of first dancer; joined American Ballet Theatre in 1961 as a principal dancer, and became premier danseur. Appeared as guest in 1963 with Royal Swedish Ballet, and in 1965 with London Festival Ballet. Joined Royal Danish Ballet in 1971; ABT 1974 summer season.

MARKS, J. Born in Los Angeles, Feb. 14, 1942. Founder of San Francisco Contemporary Dancers Foundation. Has choreographed over 200 works. Founder-Director of First National Nothing.

MARSICANO, MERLE. Born in Philadelphia. Studied with Ethel Phillips, Mordkin, Ruth St. Denis, Mary Wigman, Martha Graham, Louis Horst. Debut with Pennsylvania Opera. Since 1952 has presented own program of solos which she choreographs.

MARTIN, KEITH. Born June 15, 1943 in Yorkshire, Eng. Joined Royal Ballet School in 1958 and company in 1961. Appointed soloist in 1967. Joined Pa. Ballet in 1971, and now a principal.

MARTIN, YON. Born Sept. 12, 1945 in Washington, D.C. Studied with Erika Thimey, Paul Sanasardo, and at Washington School of Ballet. Debut with Dance Theatre of Wash. Joined Sanasardo Co. in 1966.

MARTINEZ, ENRIQUE. Born 1926 in Havana, Cuba where he studied with Alonso and danced with Ballet Alicia Alonso. In addition to appearing with American Ballet Theatre has created several ballets, and in 1964 served as ballet master of Bellas Artes Ballet de Mexico.

MARTINEZ, MENIA. Born Sept. 27, 1938 in Havana, Cuba. Studied at Alonso School. Made debut with Alicia Alonso Ballet in 1959; subsequently with Bolshoi (1965), Kirov (1966), and Bejart from 1969.

MARTINS, PETER. Born 1947 in Copenhagen. Trained at Royal Danish Ballet School and joined company in 1965. Granted leave to appear with N.Y.C. Ballet. Joined company in 1970 as principal.

MARTIN-VISCOUNT, BILL. Born in Winnipeg, Can. Began study at 12 with Royal Winnipeg Ballet, subsequently studied at Royal Ballet, American Ballet Theatre, and Bolshoi Schools. Joined Royal Winnipeg Ballet in 1959; took leave to appear with London Festival Ballet, and returned in 1962. Appeared with Joffrey as principal in 1969, Rio de Janeiro Ballet in 1970. In demand as guest artist with regional companies. Artistic director Memphis Ballet 1974.

MASAMI, KUNI. Born in Japan where he began career at 13. Graduate Tokyo Imperial U. Studied with Mary Wigman, Max Terpis. Has done solo recitals, taught and choreographed in many countries. Is now director of Kuni Inst. of Creative Dance in Tokyo and Los Angeles.

MASLOW, SOPHIE. Born in N.Y.C. where she studied with Blanche Talmund, and Martha Graham. Joined Graham company and became soloist. Debut as choreographer 1934. Helped Jane Dudley, William Bales to form Dudley-Maslow-Bales Trio. Helped found American Dance Festival at Conn. College. Has choreographed and appeared in many of her works. On Board of Directors and teaches for New Dance Group Studio.

MASON, KENNETH. Born April 17, 1942 in Bartford, Eng. Attended Royal Ballet School and joined company in 1959. Became principal in 1968.

MASON, MONICA. Born Sept. 6, 1941 in Johannesburg, S.A. Studied at Royal Ballet School, and joined company in 1958, rising to soloist, and principal in 1967.

MASSINE, LEONIDE. Born in Moscow, Aug. 9, 1896. Studied at Imperial Ballet School and with Domashoff Checchetti, and Legat. Discovered by Diaghilev; joined his company in 1914; became principal dancer and choreographer; Ballet de Monte Carlo 1932-41; Ballet National Theatre 1941-4, organized Ballet Russe Highlights 1945-6; subsequently appearing as guest artist and/or choreographer with almost every important company, and in films.

MASTERS, GARY. Born Oct. 17, 1948 in St.Paul, MN. Attended Juilliard, and trained with Hanya Holm. Debut 1969 with Ethel Winter company; joined Limon in 1970; promoted to soloist 1972. Also danced with Pennsylvania Ballet.

MATHEWS, FRED. Born July 10, 1945 in Pueblo, CO. Attended UCo., Bennington, Stephens Col. Joined Jose Limon Co. in 1973.

MATHIS, BONNIE. Born Sept. 8, 1942 in Milwaukee, Wisc. Attended Juilliard. Studied with Tudor and Anderson. Performed with Radio City Ballet, Paul Taylor, Norman Walker, before joining Harkness Ballet. ABT (1971) as soloist; promoted to principal in 1974.

MATTEO (VITTUCCI). Born in Utica, N.Y. Graduate of Cornell. Studied at Met Opera School, with La Meri, LaQuica, Esparsa, Azuma, Guneya, Balasaraswati. Member Met Opera Ballet (1947-51); solo debut in 1953; formed partnership with Carola Goya in 1954. Teaches, and organized Indo-American Dance Group with which he appears.

MATTHEWS, LAURENCE. Born in Hollywood, Cal. Studied with Lew and Harold Christensen, Anatole Vizak, Ted Howard, Paul Curtis, Richard Gibson, Royal Cons. Den Hag. Debut with San Francisco Ballet 1968. Joined Penn. Ballet 1973 as soloist; NYCB 1974.

MATTOX, MATT. Born Aug. 18, 1921 in Tulsa, Okla. Attended San Bernardino College; studied with Ernest Belcher, Nico Charisso, Eugene Loring, Louis Da Pron, Evelyn Bruns, Teddy Kerr, and Jack Cole. Debut 1946 in "Are You With It?," subsequently appearing in many musicals. First choreography in 1958 for "Say, Darling," followed by several Bdwy productions, and Met Opera Ballet.

MAULE, MICHAEL. Born Oct. 31, 1926 in Durban, S.Af. Studied with Vincenzo Celli and made debut in 1946 in "Annie Get Your Gun." Joined Ballet Theatre, then Ballet Alicia Alonso (1949-50),

N.Y.C. Ballet (1950-53), Ballets; U.S.A. (1959), Ballet Ensemble (1960-61). In 1964 organized own touring group. Now teaches.

MAULE, SARA. Born June 27, 1951 in Tokyo, Japan. Studied at UCal., San Francisco Ballet School. Joined SFB in 1965; became soloist 1970; Am. Ballet Theatre 1972.

MAXIMOVA, YEKATERINA. Born in Russia in 1939. Entered Bolshoi School at 10, and joined company in 1958, rising to ballerina.

MAXWELL, CARLA. Born Oct. 25, 1945 in Glendale, Calif. Juilliard graduate; debut 1965 with Limon Co. (now soloist), also appears with Louis Falco, and in concert with Clyde Morgan.

MAYBARDUK, LINDA. Born Feb. 22, 1951 in Orlando, Fla. Studied at Natl. Ballet School of Canada and graduated into company in 1969; promoted to soloist.

MAZZO, KAY. Born Jan. 17, 1947 in Chicago. Studied with Bernadene Hayes, and at School of American Ballet. In 1961 appeared with Ballets U.S.A. before joining N.Y.C. Ballet corps in 1962, became soloist in 1965, ballerina in 1969.

McBRIDE, PATRICIA. Born Aug. 23, 1942, in Teaneck, N.J., and studied at School of American Ballet. Joined N.Y.C. Ballet in 1959 and became principal dancer before leaving teens; ballerina in 1961.

McCONNELL, TEENA. Born in Montclair, NJ. Attended Columbia U. Studied at School of Am. Ballet. Joined NYCBallet in 1961; promoted to soloist in 1966.

McFALL, JOHN. Born in Kansas City, Mo.; studied at San Francisco Ballet, and joined company in 1965.

McGEHEE, HELEN. Born in Lynchburg, Va. Graduate Randolph-Macon College. Studied at Graham School and joined company; became first dancer in 1954. Among her choreographic works are "Undine," "Metamorphosis," "Nightmare," "Cassandra," and "Oresteia." Also teaches, and dances with own company.

McKAYLE, DONALD. Born in N.Y.C., July 6, 1930. Attended NYCC; studied at New Dance Group Studio, Graham School, with Nenette Charisse, Karel Shook, and Pearl Primus. Debut with New Dance Group in 1948, subsequently appeared with Dudley-Maslow-Bales, Jean Erdman, N.Y.C. Dance Theatre, Anna Sokolow, and Martha Graham. Formed own company in 1951, and in addition to choreographing, teaches.

McKENZIE, KEVIN. Born Apr. 29, 1954 in Burlington, Vt. Trained at Washington School of Ballet. Debut 1972 with National Ballet. Joined Joffrey Ballet 1974.

McLEOD, ANNE. (formerly Anne Ditson) Born Dec. 20, 1944 in Baton Rouge, La. Graduate UCLA. Studied at Louis-Nicholais School. Joined Murray Louis Co. 1970.

McKINNEY, GAYLE. Born Aug. 26, 1949 in NYC. Attended Juilliard. Made debut 1968 with Dance Theatre of Harlem.

McLERIE, ALLYN ANN. Born Dec. 1, 1926 in Grand Mere, Can. Studied with Nemchinova, Caton, De Mille, Yeichi Nimura, Holm, Graham, and Forte. First performed in ballet corps of San Carlo Opera in 1942. Bdwy debut 1943 in "One Touch of Venus" followed by many musicals. Now in films.

MEAD, ROBERT. Born April 17, 1940 in Bristol, Eng. Studied at Royal Ballet School, and joined company in 1958. Made principal dancer in 1967. Joined Hamburg Opera Ballet in 1971.

MEDEIROS, JOHN. Born June 5, 1944 in Winston Salem, N.C. Studied at Boston Cons., with Ailey, Beatty, and Segarra. Has appeared in musicals and with Alvin Ailey Co.

MEEHAN, JOHN. Born May 1, 1950 in Brisbane, Aust. Trained at Australian Ballet School and joined company in 1970.

MEEHAN, NANCY. born in San Francisco. Graduate U. Cal. Studied with Halprin, Lathrop, Graham, and Hawkins. Debut 1953 with Halprin company. Joined Erick Hawkins in 1962.

MEISTER, HANS. Born in Schaffhausen on the Rhine. Studied at Zurich Opera Ballet, Royal Ballet, Leningrad Kirov Schools. Joined Ntl. Ballet of Canada 1957; Met Opera Ballet (1962-6); Zurich Opera 1966; founder-member Swiss Chamber Ballet; principal and teacher for Finnish Natl. Opera Ballet; director Zurich Ballet 1975.

MENENDEZ, JOLINDA. Born Nov. 17, 1954 in NYC. Studied at Ntl. Academy of Ballet. Made debut with Ballet Repertory Co. Joined American Ballet Theatre 1972; promoted to soloist 1974.

MERCIER, MARGARET. Born in Montreal. Studied at Sadler's Wells School, graduating into company in 1954. Joined Les Grands Ballets Canadiens in 1958; Joffrey Ballet 1963; Harkness Ballet 1964.

MERRICK, IRIS. Born in 1915 in N.Y.C. Studied with Fokine, Fedorova, Vladimiroff Decroux, Egorova. Is now director and choreographer of Westchester Ballet Co. which she founded in 1950.

MEYER, LYNDA. Born in Texas. Studied at San Francisco Ballet School and joined company in 1962. Became principal dancer in 1966.

MILLER, BUZZ. Born in 1928 in Snowflake, Ariz. Graduate Ariz. State College. Debut 1948 in "Magdalena." In addition to Bdwy musicals, has appeared with Jack Cole Dancers, Ballets de Paris, and is choreographer.

MILLER, JANE. Born Mar. 19, 1945 in NYC. Studied at School of American Ballet. Debut 1964 with Pennsylvania Ballet; subsequently with Harkness Ballet, National Ballet as principal; Co-Director-principal with Eglevsky Ballet.

Gary Masters   **Lynda Mayburduk**   **Fred Mathews**   **Jolinda Menendez**   **Jack Moore**

MILLER, LINDA. Born Sept. 7, 1953 in Washington, DC. Attended N.C. School of Arts, School of Am. Ballet. Debut 1972 with North Carolina Dance Theatre. Joined Eliot Feld Co. in 1974.

MINAMI, ROGER. Born in Hawaii, reared in Calif. Left Long Beach State College to attend Eugene Loring's American School of Dance. Became member of Loring's Dance Players, and now teaches in Loring's school.

MITCHELL, ARTHUR. Born in N.Y.C. Mar. 27, 1934. Studied at School of American Ballet. Joined N.Y.C. Ballet in 1955 and rapidly rose to principal. Was choreographer at Spoleto, Italy, Festival for one season. Founder-director-choreographer for Dance Theatre of Harlem.

MITCHELL, JAMES. Born Feb. 29, 1920 in Sacramento, Calif. Graduate of LACC. Debut 1944 in "Bloomer Girl." Joined Ballet Theatre in 1950, subsequently danced with Met Opera, De Mille Dance Theatre, and on Bdwy.

MITCHELL, LUCINDA. Born Feb. 18, 1946 in Takoma Park, Md. Graduate Smith Col. Studied with Martha Graham. Debut 1970 with Bertram Ross Co.; Kazuko Hirabayashi Dance Theatre 1971; Martha Graham Co. 1972.

MLAKAR, VERONIKA. Born in 1935 in Zurich, Switzerland. Appeared with Roland Petit, Ruth Page, Milorad Miskovitch, Janine Charat, John Butler and Jerome Robbins before joining American Ballet Theatre in 1964.

MOCCIA, JODI. Born Oct. 24, 1954 in NYC. Trained at Am. Dance Center. Joined Alvin Ailey company in 1974.

MOFSIE, LOUIS. Born in N.Y.C., May 3, 1936. Graduate of SUNY at Buffalo. Training on Hopi and Winnebago Indian reservations. Debut at 10. In 1950, organized, directed and appeared in own group performing native Indian dances, both in N.Y.C. and on tour.

MOLINA, JOSE. Born in Madrid, Spain, Nov. 19, 1937. Studied with Pilar Monterde. Debut 1953 with Soledad Mirales Co., subsequently joined Pilar Mirales, Jose Greco, and in 1962 premiered own company in the U.S. Has since made international tours.

MONCION, FRANCISCO. Born in Dominican Republic, July 6. Studied at School of American Ballet. Danced with New Opera Co., Ballet International, Ballet Russe de Monte Carlo, and Ballet Society which became N.Y.C. Ballet. Is now a principal. First choreographic work "Pastorale" performed by company in 1957. Is also a painter.

MONK, MEREDITH. Born Nov. 20, 1943 in Lima, Peru. Graduate of Sarah Lawrence. Studied with Tarassova, Slavenska, Cunningham, Graham, Mata and Hari. Debut 1964, subsequently choreographed for herself and company.

MONTALBANO, GEORGE. Born in Bklyn. Studied with Mme. Deinitzen, Natalia Branitska., ABC. Appeared with Westchester Ballet, and in musicals, before joining Joffrey Ballet; Eliot Feld Ballet 1974.

MONTE, ELISA. Born May 23 in Brooklyn, NY. Trained with Vladimir Dokoudovsky, Maggie Black, Martha Graham. Joined Pearl Lang (1968), Baku (1971), Lar Lubovitvh (1972), Marcus Schulkino (1975), Martha Graham (1974).

MONTERO, LUIS. Born in Granada in 1939. Debut at 15 with Mariemma company. Joined Pilar Lopez, then Jose Greco, Victor Albarez. Became first dancer with Jose Molina Bailes Espanoles in 1961; also choreographs for company.

MOONEY, ELINA. Born Nov. 28, 1942 in New Orleans. Attended Sara Lawrence Col. Studied with Evelyn Davis, Weidman, Cunningham, Tamiris, Sanasardo. Debut 1961 with Tamiris-Nagrin Co., subsequently with Weidman, Marion Scott, Paul Sanasardo, Cliff Keuter, Don Redlich, and own company.

MOORE, GARY. Born Jan. 29, 1950 in Washington, D.C. Studied with Mavis Murry, Tania Rousseau, Oleg Tupine. Debut with Harkness Youth Co. in 1969, after which joined Pa. Ballet.

MOORE, JACK. Born Mar. 18, 1926 in Monticello, Ind. Graduate U. Iowa. Studied at Graham School, School of American Ballet, Conn. College, and Cunningham Studio. Debut 1951, subsequently with Nina Fonaroff, Helen McGehee, Pearl Lang, Katherine Litz, Martha Graham, Anna Sokolow, and NYC Opera, in musicals, and

his own works annually since 1957. Has taught at Conn. College, Bennington, Juilliard, UCLA, and Adelphi.

MORALES, HILDA. Born June 17, 1946 in Puerto Rico. Studied at San Juan Ballet School and American School of Ballet. Debut with N.Y.C. Ballet, then joined Penn. Ballet in 1965, becoming principal. Guest with Les Grands Ballets Canadiens, ABT 1973 as soloist.

MORAWSKI, MIECZYSLAW. Born Jan. 1, 1932 in Wilno, Poland. Studied at Warsaw Ballet School, Bolshoi and Kirov schools, and graduated as teacher. Now director of Virginia Beach Ballet.

MORDAUNT, JOANNA. Born Feb. 13, 1950 in London. Trained at Royal Ballet School; joined company in 1968; London Festival Ballet in 1970.

MORDENTE, TONY. Born in Brooklyn in 1935. Studied with Farnworth. Has appeared on Bdwy and TV, and been assistant to Gower Champion and Michael Kidd. Has also directed and choreographed musicals.

MORE, VICTORIA. Born in Los Angeles. Attended School of American Ballet. Debut with N.Y.C. Opera and joined Joffrey Ballet in 1969.

MORGAN, CLYDE. Born Jan. 30, 1940 in Cincinnati. Graduate Cleveland State Col. Studied at Bennington, Karamu House, Ballet Russe, New Dance Group. Debut 1961 with Karamu Dance Theatre; joined Limon 1965 (now soloist), also appears with Anna Sokolow, Pearl Lang, Olatunji, and in concert with Carla Maxwell.

MORGAN, EARNEST. Born Dec. 3, 1947 in Waihjwa, Hawaii. Attended Northwestern U. Studied with Jene Sugano, Gus Giordano, Ed Parish. Debut 1966 with Gus Giordano Co., subsequently in musicals before joining Paul Taylor Co. in 1969.

MORGAN, VICTORIA. Born Mar. 18, 1951 in Salt Lake City, U. Graduate UUtah with training under William Christensen. Joined Ballet West in 1970; principal since 1972.

MORISHITA, YOKO. Born in 1949 in Hiroshima, Japan. Began career at 4; attended Tachibana School, Matsuyama School. Joined Tokyo Matsyyama Ballet and rose to prima ballerina. Has been guest artist with many companies, including ABT in 1976.

MORRIS, MARNEE. Born Apr. 2, 1946 in Schenectady, N.Y. Studied with Phyllis Marmein, Cornelia Thayer, Vladimir Dokoudovsky, and at School of Am. Ballet. Joined N.Y.C. Ballet in 1961. Is now a soloist.

MORRIS, MONICA. Born Sept. 23, 1946 in Eustis, Fla. Attended Oglethorpe U. Debut 1966 with Harkness Ballet; subsequently with Martha Graham Co., Paul Taylor Co. 1972.

MOYLAN, MARY ELLEN. Born in 1926 in Cincinnati. Studied at School of American Ballet, and made debut at 16 as leading dancer in operetta "Rosalinda." In 1943 joined Ballet Russe de Monte Carlo as soloist. In 1950 became ballerina with Ballet Theatre. Retired in 1957.

MUELLER, CHRISTA. Born Dec. 20, 1950 in Cincinnati, O. Studied with Merce Cunningham, Ben Harkarvy, Harkness House. Debut 1972 with Dance Repertory Co. Joined Alvin Ailey Co. 1973.

MULLER, JENNIFER. Born Oct. 16, 1944 in Yonkers, N.Y. Graduate Juilliard. Studied with Limon, Graham, Lang, Tudor, Corvino, Craske, Horst, Sokolow. Has danced with Pearl Lang, Sophie Maslow, N.Y.C. Opera, Frances Alenikoff, Louis Falco. Member of Jose Limon Company from 1963. Teaches, and choreographs. Associate director of Falco Co.

MUMAW, BARTON. Born in 1912 in Hazelton, Pa. Studied with Ted Shawn; debut with Shawn's company in 1931 and danced with group until it disbanded. Now makes guest appearances, teaches, and appears in musicals.

MUNRO, RICHARD. Born Aug. 8, 1944, in Camberley, Eng. Trained at Hardie Ballet School. Debut with Zurich Opera Ballet, subsequently with London Festival Ballet, American Ballet Co. Now co-director of Louisville Ballet and teaches.

MURPHY, SEAMUS. Born in Hong Kong. Attended Juilliard. Appeared on Bdwy before forming own company. Also teaches.

MURRAY-WHITE, MELVA. Born May 24, 1950 in Philadelphia, Pa. Attended Md. State, Ohio State U. Studied with Marion Cuyjet, Bettye Robinson. Debut 1971 with Dance Theatre of Harlem.

MUSGROVE, TRACI. Born Feb. 7, 1948 in Carlysle, Pa. Graduate SMU. Studied with Graham, Limon, Hoving, Kuch, Yuriko. Debut 1970 with Yuriko, subsequently with Pearl Lang, Martha Graham.

MUSIL, KARL. Born Nov. 3, in Austria. Studied at Vienna State Opera School; joined company in 1953; promoted to soloist in 1958. Has appeared as guest artist with many companies.

MUSSMAN, MARJORIE. Born Feb. 19, 1943 in Columbus, O. Attended Smith College, and Sorbonne, Paris. Studied with Reznikoff, Marmein, Limon, and Joffrey. Debut with Paris Festival Ballet in 1964, and U.S. debut with Jose Limon in 1964. Member of Joffrey Ballet 1965. Currently with First Chamber Dance Co.

NAGRIN, DANIEL. Born May 22 in N.Y.C., graduate of CCNY. Studied with Graham, Tamiris, Holm, and Sokolow. Debut in 1945 in "Marianne," followed by several Bdwy musicals and choreography for Off-Bdwy productions. Now appears in solo concerts, and teaches.

NAGY, IVAN. Born Apr. 28, 1943 in Debrecen, Hungary. Studied at Budapest Opera Ballet School and joined company. Came to U.S. and National Ballet in 1965. One season with N.Y.C. Ballet; joined ABT in 1968 as soloist. Became principal in 1969.

NAHAT, DENNIS. Born Feb. 20, 1947 in Detroit, Mich. Studied at Juilliard. Debut 1965 with Joffrey Ballet. Appeared and choreographed on Bdwy before joining ABT in 1968; Soloist 1970, Principal 1973.

NAULT, FERNAND. Born Dec. 27, 1921 in Montreal, Can. Studied with Craske, Tudor, Preobrajenska, Volkova, Pereyaslavic, Leese. Debut with American Ballet Theatre in 1944, for which he has been ballet master 20 years. Artistic Director of Louisville Ballet, and associate director of Les Grands Ballets Canadiens.

NEARHOOF, PAMELA. Born May 12, 1955 in Indiana, Pa. Studied at American Ballet Center, Sulik School. Joined Joffrey Ballet 1971.

NEARY, COLLEEN. Born May 23, 1952 in Miami, FL. Trained at School of American Ballet. Joined NYC Ballet in 1969, becoming soloist in 1974.

NEARY, PATRICIA. Born Oct. 27, 1942 in Miami, Fla. Studied with Georges Milenoff and Thomas Armour, at Natl. Ballet School, School of American Ballet. From 1962 to 1968 was soloist with N.Y.C. Ballet. Now makes guest appearances. Co-director Berlin State Opera Ballet 1970. Director Le Grand Theatre du Geneve 1972.

NEELS, SANDRA. Born Sept. 21, 1942 in Las Vegas, Nev. Studied with Nicholas Vasilieff, Martha Nishitani, Richard Thomas. Debut with Merle Marsicano in 1962. Teacher at Cunningham School since 1965.

NELSON, TED. Born May 17, 1949 in San Pedro, Cal. Studied at San Francisco Ballet, School of American Ballet. Debut 1970 with San Francisco Ballet. Joined Joffrey Ballet 1973.

NERINA, NADIA. Born Oct. 21, 1927 in Cape Town, South Africa where she received training. Joined Sadler's Wells Ballet in 1946, subsequently becoming one of its leading ballerinas. Now retired.

NEUMEIR, JOHN. Born Feb. 24, 1942 in Milwaukee. Studied at Stone-Camryn, and Royal Ballet (London) schools, and with Sybil Shearer, Vera Volkova. Debut 1961 with Sybil Shearer. With Stuttgart Ballet from 1963. Director Frankfurt Opera Ballet 1969; Hamburg Opera Ballet 1973.

NIELSEN, DOUGLAS. Born June 8, 1948 in St. Paul, MN. Graduate Augburg Col. Trained with Bella Lawitsky, Donald McKayle, Mia Slavenska, Pearl Lang, Paul Sanasardo. Debut 1973 with Gus Solomons company. Has also danced with Sanasardo Co., Pearl Lang.

NIGHTINGALE, JOHN. Born Oct. 21, 1943 in Salisbury, Southern Rhodesia. Studied at London School of Contemporary Dance. Joined Paul Taylor Company in 1967.

NIKOLAIS, ALWIN. Born Nov. 25, 1912 in Southington, Conn. Studied with Graham, Humphrey, Holm, Horst, Martin, and at Bennington Summer Dance School. Professional debut 1939. Designs, composes, and choreographs for own company that tours U.S. and abroad. Was co-director of Henry St. Playhouse School of Dance and Theatre. Now co-director of Chimera Foundation for Dance.

NILES, MARY ANN. Born May 2, 1933 in N.Y.C. Studied with Nenette Charisse, Ernest Carlos, Frances Cole, and Roye Dodge. Appeared with American Dance Theatre in U.S. and Europe. Was half of Fosse-Niles dance team that toured U.S. and appeared in Bdwy musicals. Currently teaching, dancing and choreographing.

NILLO, DAVID. Born July 13, 1917 in Goldsboro. N.C. Debut with Ballet Theatre in 1940, then with Ballet Caravan and Chicago Opera Ballet before appearing in and choreographing musicals.

NIMURA, YEICHI. Born in Suwa, Japan March 25, 1908. First appeared with Operetta Taza. Soloist Manhattan Opera House 1928. Choreographed for musicals and Met Opera. Currently teaches.

NOBLE, CHERIE. Born Dec. 11, 1947 in Philadelphia. Studied with Ethel Phillips, Michael Lopuszanski, Edmund Novak, Pa. Ballet School. Debut with Novak Ballet in 1961 before joining Pennsylvania Ballet in 1962. Now artistic director Delaware Regional Ballet.

NORMAN, GARY. Born May 11, 1951 in Adelaide, Aust. Studied with Australian Ballet and joined company in 1970; National Ballet of Canada 1975.

NUCHTERN, JEANNE. Born in N.Y.C. Nov. 20, 1939. Studied with Craske, and Graham. Debut 1965 in "The King and I" followed by appearances with Martha Graham. Yuriko, Sophie Maslow, and Bertram Ross.

NUREYEV, RUDOLF. Born Mar. 17, 1938 in Russia; reared in Tartary, Bashkir. Admitted to Kirov Ballet school at 17; joined company and became premier danseur. Defected during 1961 appearance in Paris. Invited to join Royal Ballet as co-star and partner of Margot Fonteyn in 1962. Has choreographed several ballets. Considered by many as world's greatest male dancer. Has appeared with ABT, National Ballet of Canada, Australian Ballet, Paul Taylor.

O'BRIEN, SHAUN. Born Nov. 28, 1930. Studied with Fokine, Schwezoff, Diaghilev, Balanchine, School of American Ballet. Debut 1944 with Ballet International, subsequently with Ballet for America, Grand Ballet de Monte Carlo, Ballet Da Cuba, Conn. Ballet. N.Y.C. Ballet from 1949.

ODA, BONNIE. Born Sept. 15, 1951 in Honolulu, Hawaii. Graduate UHawaii. Apeared with UHawaii Dance Theater (1968–73), Ethel Winter (1971), Met. Opera Ballet (1971). Joined Martha Graham Co. 1973.

O'DONNELL, MAY. Born in Sacramento, Calif., in 1909. Debut with Estelle Reed Concert Group in San Francisco; lead dancer with Martha Graham Co. 1932–44. Formed own school and company for which she dances and choreographs.

OHARA, ORIE. Born June 18, 1945 in Tokyo. Studied at Tokyo Ballet School. Debut 1960 with Tokyo Ballet before joining Bejart Ballet.

OHMAN, FRANK. Born Jan. 7, 1939 in Los Angeles. Studied with Christensens in San Francisco, and appeared with S.F. Ballet. Joined N.Y.C. Ballet in 1962. Now soloist.

OLRICH, APRIL. Born in Zanzibar, E. Africa in 1931. Studied with Borovsky, and Tchernicheva. Joined Original Ballet Russe in 1944. Appeared on Bdwy.

O'NEAL, CHRISTINE. (formerly Christine Knoblauch) Born Feb. 25, 1949 in St. Louis, Mo. Made debut in 1966 with St. Louis Municipal Opera. Subsequently joined National Ballet, and Harkness Ballet as principal; ABT 1974.

ONSTAD, MICHAEL. Born Feb. 18, 1949 in Spokane, Wash. Studied with Robert Irwin, Anatol Joukowski, William Christensen, Gordon Paxman, Philip Keeler. Joined Ballet West as soloist in 1966.

ORIO, DIANE. Born Feb. 9, 1947 in Newark, N.J. Trained at Newark Ballet Academy, School of American Ballet, American Ballet Center. Joined Joffrey Ballet in 1968.

ORMISTON, GALE. Born April 14, 1944 in Kansas. Studied with Hanya Holm, Shirlee Dodge, and at Henry St. Playhouse. Debut 1966 with Nikolais Co. Appeared with Mimi Garrard, and formed own company in 1972.

ORR, TERRY. Born Mar. 12, 1943 in Berkeley, Calif. Studied at San Francisco Ballet School; joined company in 1959; American Ballet Theatre in 1965, became principal in 1972.

OSATO, SONO. Born Aug. 29, 1919 in Omaha, Neb. Studied with Egorova, Oboukhoff, Caton, Bolm and Bernice Holmes. Member of corps de ballet and soloist with Ballet Russe de Monte Carlo (1934–40), Ballet Theatre (1940–43), followed by Bdwy musicals.

OSSOSKY, SHELDON. Born Brooklyn, June 10, 1932. Attended Juilliard, and studied with Nikolais, Graham, Limon, Tudor, and Craske. Debut 1950, subsequently appeared in musicals and with Pearl Lang, Sophie Maslow, Fred Berke, and at Henry St. Playhouse.

OSTERGAARD, SOLVEIG. Born Jan. 7, 1939 in Denmark. Studied at Royal Danish Ballet School; joined company in 1957; appointed soloist in 1962.

OUMANSKY, VALENTINA. Born in Los Angeles; graduate of Mills College. Studied with Oumansky, de Mille, Vladimiroff, Horst, Cunningham, Graham, and Maracci. Debut with Marquis de Cuevas' Ballet International, subsequently in Bdwy musicals, before devoting full time to choreography, concert work, and teaching.

OWENS, HAYNES. Born in Montgomery, Ala. Studied with Elinor Someth, Molly Brumbly; appeared with Montgomery Civic Ballet. Attended ABC, and joined Joffrey Ballet in 1966.

OXENHAM, ANDREW. Born Oct. 12, 1945 in London, Eng. Studied with Gwenneth Lloyd, Rosella Hightower, Franchetti. Debut 1964 with Ntl. Ballet of Canada; joined Stuttgart Ballet 1969; National Ballet of Canada 1973 as soloist.

PADOW, JUDY. Born Jan. 10, 1943 in N.Y.C. Studied with Don Farnworth, Marvis Walter, Trisha Brown Schlicter, Ann Halprin. Has danced with Yvonne Rainer, and in own works.

PAGE, ANNETTE. Born Dec. 18, 1932 in Manchester, Eng. Entered Royal Ballet School in 1945, and joined company in 1950. Became ballerina in 1959. Has toured with Margot Fonteyn, and made guest appearances at Stockholm's Royal Opera. Retired in 1967.

Colleen Neary

Douglas Nielsen

Mary Ann Niles

Andrew Oxenham

Sonia Perusse

PAGE, RUTH. Born in Indianapolis, Ind. Studied with Cecchetti, Bolm, and Pavlowa. Debut 1919 with Chicago Opera Co. Toured S. America with Pavlowa, leading dancer on Bdwy, and premier danseuse with Met Opera. Danced with Diaghilev Ballet Russe, and Ballet Russe de Monte Carlo. Formed own company with Bently Stone and toured U.S., Europe, and S. America for 8 years. In Chicago, has been first dancer, choreographer, director for Allied Arts, Grand Opera Co., Federal Theatre, Ravinia Opera Festival. Currently ballet director of both Chicago Opera Ballet and Lyric Opera of Chicago, and Chicago Ballet.

PAGELS, JURGEN. Born Apr. 16, 1925 in Luebeck, Ger. Studied with Lescevskis, Harmos, Vestena, Legat, Preobrajenska, Roje, Volinin, Rausch. Debut 1946 with Luebeck Atlantic Theatre; subsequently with Dortmond Opera, Ballet Theatre, Ballet Legat, and guest artist with many companies. Now teaches at Indiana U.

PANAIEFF, MICHAEL. Born in 1913 in Novgorod, Russia. Studied with Legat, Egorova. Debut with Belgrade Royal Opera Ballet, becoming first dancer in two years; later joined Blum Ballet, Ballet Russe, and Original Ballet Russe. Now has school and performing group in Los Angeles.

PANETTA, JANET. Born Dec. 12, 1949 in NYC. Attended City Col. Studied with Margaret Craske, Antony Tudor, Alfredo Crovino. Debut 1966 with Manhattan Festival Ballet; subsequently with Met Opera Ballet, ABT, Gloria Contreras, Paul Sanasardo, Hirabayashi Dance Theatre.

PANOV, VALERY. Born in 1939 in Vilnius, Lithuania. Made debut at 15. Joined Leningrad Maly Ballet 1958; Kirov 1963 and became its lead dancer. U.S. debut 1974.

PAPA, PHYLLIS. Born Jan. 30, 1950 in Trenton, N.J. Studied at Joffrey, Harkness, and Ballet Theatre schools. Debut with Harkness Ballet in 1967. Joined ABT in 1968. Royal Danish Ballet 1970.

PAREDES, MARCOS. Born in Aguascalientes, Mex. Trained at Academia de la Danza. Danced with Ballet Contemperaneo, and Ballet Classico de Mexico before joining American Ballet Theatre in 1965. Became soloist 1968, principal 1973.

PARK, MERLE. Born Oct. 8, 1937 in Salisbury, Rhodesia. Joined Sadler's Wells (now Royal) Ballet in 1954, becoming soloist in 1958. Now a leading ballerina.

PARKER, ELLEN. Born Feb. 18 in Columbus, O. Attended N.C. School of Arts, and U. Pa. Studied with Tatiana Akinfieva, Josephine Schwarz, Oleg Briansky, Deborah Jowitt, Sonja Tyven, Job Sanders, Pauline Koner, Duncan Noble, Edward Caton. Appeared in musicals before joining Pa. First Dance Intern in Arts Admin., Consultant NYS Council on the Arts. Left in 1972.

PARKES, ROSS. Born June 17, 1940 in Sydney, Australia. Studied with Valrene Tweedie, Peggy Watson, Audrey de Vos, Martha Graham. Debut 1959 with Ballet Francais. Has danced with Ethel Winter, Bertram Ross, Helen McGehee, Martha Graham, Sophie Maslow, Glen Tetley, Mary Anthony, Carmen de Lavallade, Jeff Duncan companies. Joined Pennsylvania Ballet in 1966; Martha Graham 1973. Associate Director Mary Anthony Dance Co.

PARKINSON, GEORGINA. Born Aug. 20, 1938 in Brighton, Eng. Studied at Sadler's Wells School. Joined Royal Ballet in 1957, became soloist in 1959. Now a principal ballerina.

PARKS, JOHN E. Born Aug. 4, 1945 in the Bronx. Studied at Julliard. Teacher-dancer-choreographer for Movements Black: Dance Repertory Theatre. Joined Alvin Ailey Co. in 1970; left in 1974 for Bdwy musical.

PARRA, MARIANO. Born in Ambridge, Pa. Mar. 10, 1933. Studied with La Meri, Juan Martinez, La Quica, and Luisa Pericet in Spain. Debut 1957. Has organized and appeared with own company in N.Y.C. and on tour.

PATAROZZI, JACQUES. Born Apr. 28, 1947 in Ajallio, France. Studied with Paul Sanasardo and joined his company in 1972.

PAUL, MIMI. Born in Nashville, Tenn., Feb. 3, 1943. Studied at Washington (D.C.) School of Ballet and School of American Ballet. Debut 1960 in N.Y.C. Ballet in "Nutcracker" and became soloist in 1963. Joined ABT in 1969 as principal.

PEARSON, JERRY. Born Mar. 17, 1949 in St. Paul, Minn. At-

tended UMinn. Studied and appeared with Nancy Hauser before joining Murray Louis Co.

PEARSON, SARA. Born Apr. 22, 1949 in St. Paul, Minn. Attended UMinn. Studied and appeared with Nancy Hauser before joining Murray Louis Co.

PENNEY, JENNIFER. Born Apr. 5, 1946 in Vancouver, Can. Studied at Royal Ballet School, London, and graduated into company. Is now a principal.

PEREZ, RUDY. Born in N.Y.C. Studied with New Dance Group, Graham, Cunningham, Hawkins, Anthony, on faculty at DTW. Choreographer-Director Rudy Perez Dance Theatre, and artist-in-residence at Marymount Manhattan Col.

PERI, RIA. Born Aug. 20, 1944 in Eger, Hungary. Trained at Hungary State Ballet School, London Royal Ballet School. Debut 1964 with Royal Ballet.

PERRY, PAMARA. Born Feb. 8, 1948 in Cleveland, Ohio. Studied at School of American Ballet. Debut 1966 with Western Ballet Association of Los Angeles. With Eglevsky Ballet (1966–7), joined Joffrey Ballet in 1967. Retired in 1969.

PERRY, RONALD. Born Mar. 17, 1955 in NYC. Studied at Dance Theatre of Harlem, and made debut with company in 1969.

PERUSSE, SONIA. Born in 1954 in Longueil, Quebec, Can. Attended Ntl. Ballet School, and graduated into company in 1972. Promoted to soloist 1973.

PETERS, DELIA L. Born May 9, 1947 in N.Y.C. Attended School of American Ballet. Joined N.Y.C. Ballet in 1963.

PETERSON, CAROLYN. Born July 23, 1946 in Los Angeles. Studied with Marjorie Peterson, Irina Kosmouska, Carmelita Maracci, and at School of American Ballet. Debut 1966 with N.Y.C. Ballet.

PETERSON, STANZE. Born in Houston, Tex. Has appeared with Syvilla Fort, Edith Stephen, Charles Weidman, Eve Gentry, and Gloria Contreras. In 1963 organized Stanze Peterson Dance Theatre with which he has appeared in N.Y.C. and on tour.

PETIT, ROLAND. Born in Paris Jan. 13, 1924. Studied at Paris Opera School; became member of corps in 1939, and began choreographing. In 1945 was co-founder, ballet master, and premier danseur of Les Ballets des Champs-Elysees. In 1948 formed own company Les Ballets de Paris, for which he danced and choreographs.

PETROFF, PAUL. Born in Denmark: Studied with Katja Lindhart; Debut 1930 with Violet Fischer. Became premier danseur of de Basil's Ballet Russe; later joined Original Ballet Russe, Ballet Theatre (1943) and International Ballet. Now teaches.

PETROV, NICOLAS. Born in 1933 in Yugoslavia; studied with Ureobrajenska, Gsowsky, Massine. Appeared with Yugoslav Ntl. Theatre, Ballet de France, Theatre d'Art Ballet; lead dancer with Massine Ballet. Came to U.S. in 1967 and founded Pittsburgh Ballet Theatre in 1969 also teaches.

PHIPPS, CHARLES. Born Nov. 23, 1946 in Newton, Miss. Studied with Graham, Cunningham, and at Ballet Theatre School. Debut 1968 with Pearl Lang, subsequently with Louis Falco, Lucas Hoving.

PIERSON, ROSALIND. Born in Salt Lake City. Bennington graduate. Studied at Thomas-Fallis School, American Ballet Center. Has appeared with Ruth Currier, Charles Weidman, Ballet Concepts, Anne Wilson, DTW, Garden State Ballet.

PIKSER, ROBERTA. Born Sept. 3, 1941 in Chicago. Graduate U. Chicago. Studied with Erika Thimey, Paul Sanasardo. Debut 1951 with Dance Theatre of Washington; subsequently with Edith Stephen, Paul Sanasardo, Eleo Pomare.

PINNOCK, THOMAS. Born in Jamaica where he studied with Rex Nettleford, Eddy Thomas, Neville Black, and became principal with National Dance Theatre Co. Also studied with Martha Graham and is principal with Rod Rodgers Co. Is co-founder of Choreo-Mutations for which he choreographs.

PINCUSOFF, REVA. Born in Montreal, Can. Studied in London's Royal Ballet Sch. Has danced with Les Grands Ballets Canadiens, Pennsylvania Ballet, Eliot Feld Ballet.

PLATOFF, MARC. Born in Seattle, Wash., in 1915. Debut with de Basil's Ballet Russe; soloist with Ballet Russe de Monte Carlo 1938–42 and choreographed for them. As Marc Platt made Bdwy bow in 1943, subsequently in and choreographing for films. Was director of Radio City Ballet.

PLEVIN, MARCIA. Born Oct. 26, 1945 in Columbus, O. Graduate U. Wisc. Studied with Lang, Graham, Yuriko. Debut 1968 with Pearl Lang, subsequently with Sophie Maslow. New Dance Group, Ethel Winter.

PLISETSKAYA, MAYA. Born in Russia Nov. 20, 1925. Began studies at Moscow State School of Ballet at 8 and joined Bolshoi company in 1943, rising to premiere danseuse. Internationally famous for her "Swan Lake." Awarded Lenin Prize in 1964. In addition to dancing with Bolshoi, is now teaching. Considered one of world's greatest ballerinas.

PLUMADORE, PAUL. Born Nov. 5, 1949 in Springfield, Mass. Studied at NYU and with Kelly Holt, Jean Erdman, Nenette Charisse, Gladys Bailin. Debut 1969 with Katherine Litz, with Jean Erdman in 1970, and in concert.

POMARE, ELEO. Born in Cartagena, Colombia Oct. 22, 1937. Studied with Jose Limon, Luis Horst, Curtis James, Geoffrey Holder, and Kurt Jooss. In 1958 organized and has appeared with the Eleo Pomare Dance Co. in N.Y.C., abroad, and on tour in the U.S.

POOLE, DENNIS. Born Dec. 27, 1951 in Dallas, Tex. Trained at Harkness School, and joined company in 1968; soloist 1970; National Ballet 1971–74 as principal.

POPOVA, NINA. Born in 1922 in Russia. Studied in Paris with Preobrajenska and Egorova. Debut 1937 with Ballet de la Jeunesse. Later with Original Ballet Russe, Ballet Theatre, and Ballet Russe de Monte Carlo. Now teaches.

POSIN, KATHRYN. Born Mar. 23, 1944 in Butte, Mont. Bennington graduate. Studied with Fonaroff, Cunningham, Graham, Thomas-Fallis. Debut with Dance Theatre Workshop in 1965. Has danced with Anna Sokolow, Valerie Bettis, Lotte Goslar, American Dance Theatre, and in own works.

POURFARROKH, ALI. Born Nov. 27, 1938 in Iran. Studied at Tehran Consv. Joined ABT (1959–63), Met Opera Ballet 1963, Harkness 1964–67, 1971–72, Joffrey 1967, Frankfurt Ballet 1968, Associate Artistic Director-Ballet Master Ailey company 1973. Director Iranian National Ballet 1976.

POWELL, GRAHAM. Born in Cardiff, Wales. Aug. 2, 1948. Studied at Royal Ballet School; joined company in 1965, then Australian Ballet

POWELL, ROBERT. Born in Hawaii in 1941; graduate of HS Performing Arts. Has been featured dancer with all major American modern dance companies, and appeared with N.Y.C. Opera Ballet. Soloist with Graham Co., associate artistic director 1973.

PRICE, MARY. Born May 20, 1945 in Fort Bragg, N.C. Graduate U. Okla. Studied with Mary Anthony, Martha Graham. Debut 1970 with Mary Anthony, subsequently with Pearl Lang, Richard Gain, Larry Richardson.

PRIMUS, PEARL. Born Nov. 29, 1919 in Trinidad, B.W.I. N.Y. Debut at YMHA in 1943; first solo performance 1944. Has since choreographed and performed in West Indian, African, and primitive dances throughout the world. Also teaches.

PRINZ, JOHN. Born in Chicago May 14, 1945. Studied with Comiacoff, Allegro School, American Ballet Center, School of American Ballet. Joined N.Y.C. Ballet in 1964; Munich Ballet, then ABT in 1970. Appointed principal in 1971.

PROKOVSKY, ANDRE. Born Jan. 13, 1939 in Paris, and achieved recognition in Europe with Grand Ballet du Marquis de Cuevas and London Festival Ballet; made world tour with "Stars of the French Ballet." Joined N.Y.C. Ballet as principal dancer in 1963; London's Festival Ballet in 1967.

PROVANCHA, LEIGH. Born Mar. 22, 1953 in St. John's, Newfoundland. Studied at Wash. Ntl. School of Ballet, NC Sch. of Arts, Sch. of Am. Ballet. Debut 1972 with Ballet Repertory Co. Joined ABT 1973.

QUITMAN, CLEO. Born in Detroit. Attended Weinstein U. Studied with Martha Graham, Alfredo Corvino, Maria Nevelska. Formed N.Y. Negro Ballet Co. that toured Europe. Had appeared with Joffrey Ballet and is founder-director-choreographer of Cleo Quitman's Dance Generale.

RADIUS, ALEXANDRA. Born July 3, 1942 in Amsterdam, Holland. Studied with Benjamin Harkarvy. Debut with Nederlands Dans Theatre in 1957. Joined American Ballet Theatre in 1968 as soloist. Became principal in 1969. Joined Dutch National Ballet in 1970.

RAGOZINA, GALINA. Born in 1949 in Archangel, Russia. Joined Kirov Ballet in 1967, and rose to soloist. U.S. debut 1974.

RAIMONDO, ROBERT. Born June 18, 1945 in Jersey City, NJ. Studied at Harkness House, American Ballet Theatre School. Debut 1965 with American Festival Ballet; with Garden State Ballet (1967–70), Houston Ballet from 1972.

RAINER, YVONNE. Born in 1934 in San Francisco. Studied with Graham, Cunningham, Halprin, Stephen. Has performed with James Waring, Aileen Passloff, Beverly Schmidt, Judith Dunn. Started Judson Dance Workshop in 1962, and choreographs for own company.

RAINES, WALTER. Born Aug. 16, 1940 in Braddock, Pa. Attended Carnegie-Mellon U. Studied at Pittsburgh Playhouse, School of American Ballet, Dance Theatre of Harlem. Debut 1952 with Pittsburgh Opera Ballet; subsequently with Pennsylvania Ballet 1962, Stuttgart Ballet 1964, Dance Theatre of Harlem 1969.

RALL, TOMMY. Born Dec. 27, 1929 in Kansas City, Mo. Attended Chouinard Art Inst. Studied with Carmelita Maracci, David Lichine, and Oboukhoff of School of American Ballet. Joined Ballet Theatre in 1944, and became soloist in 1945. Has appeared in musicals, films, and choreographed for TV.

RAPP, RICHARD. Born in Milwaukee, Wisc. Studied with Adele Artinian, Ann Barzel, School of American Ballet. Joined N.Y.C. Ballet in 1958; became soloist in 1961.

RAUP, FLORITA. Born in Havana, Cuba; attended school in Springfield, O. Has studied with Holm, Limon, Humphrey, Tamiris, and Julia Berashkova. Debut in 1951. Has appeared in concert and with own group since 1953, in N.Y.C. and on tour.

REBEAUD, MICHELE. Born Jan. 24, 1948 in Paris, France. Debut 1972 with Paul Sanasardo Co.

REDLICH, DON. Born in Winona, Minn., Aug. 17, 1933. Attended U. Wisc., studied with Holm, and Humphrey. Debut in 1954 musical "The Golden Apple." Has danced with Hanya Holm, Doris Humphrey, Anna Sokolow, Murray Louis, John Butler, and in own concert program. Is teacher, choreographer, and tours with own Co.

REED, JANET. Born in Tolo, Ore., Sept. 15, 1916. Studied with William Christensen, Tudor, and Balanchine. Member of San Francisco Ballet 1937–41, Ballet Theatre 1943–6, N.Y.C. Ballet from 1949. Has been teaching since 1965.

REESE, GAIL. Born Aug. 13, 1946 in Queens, N.Y. Studied with Syvilla Fort, Hector Zaraspe, Marianne Balin. Debut with Cleo Quitman in 1967, and then with Talley Beatty, Lar Lubovitch, and Alvin Ailey from 1970.

REID, ALBERT. Born July 12, 1934 in Niagara Falls, N.Y. Graduate Stanford U. Studied with Nikolais, Cunningham, Lillian Moore, Richard Thomas, Margaret Craske. Debut 1959 with Nikolais Co., with Murray Louis, Erick Hawkins, Katherine Litz, and Yvonne Rainer.

REIN, RICHARD A. Born May 10, 1944 in N.Y.C. Attended Adelphi U. School of Am. Ballet. Debut 1965 with Atlanta Ballet, subsequently with Ruth Page's Chicago Ballet, Pa. Ballet, joined ABT in 1970, Pa. Ballet 1973.

REISER, WENDY. Born Aug. 11, 1953 in Hamilton, Can. Attended National Ballet School; joined Natl. Ballet of Canada in 1971.

REMINGTON, BARBARA. Born in 1936 in Windsor, Can. Studied with Sandra Severo, School of American Ballet, Ballet Theatre School, Royal Ballet School. Joined Royal Ballet in 1959, followed by American Ballet Theatre, Joffrey Ballet.

RENCHER, DEREK. Born June 6, 1932 in Birmingham, Eng. Studied at Royal Ballet school and joined company in 1952, rising to principal in 1969.

REVENE, NADINE. Born in N.Y.C. Studied with Helen Platova. In musicals before joining Ballet Theatre. Subsequently member of N.Y.C. Ballet, prima ballerina of Bremen Opera in Germany, and First Chamber Dance Quartet. Joined Pa. Ballet in 1970 as soloist. Now assistant ballet mistress.

REY, FRANK. Born in 1931 in Tampa, Fla. Made debut with Chicago Opera Ballet. Founder-Director Florida Dance Camp, Choreographer-in-residence for Florida Ballet Theatre. Is noted as choreographer for outdoor dramas.

REYES, RAMON DE LOS. Born in Madrid and started dancing at 9. Debut at 17 after studying with Antonio Marin. Formed own company and toured Spain, Europe, and U.S. Joined Ximenez-Vargas Co., later Roberto Iglesias Co. as leading dancer. With Maria Alba, formed Alba-Reyes Spanish Dance Co. in 1964.

REYN, JUDITH. Born Dec. 28, 1943 in Rhodesia. Studied at Royal Ballet School, London, and joined company in 1963. Member of Stuttgart Ballet since 1967; promoted to principal.

REYNOLDS, GREGORY C. Born July 18, 1952 in Washington, DC. Graduate Sarah Lawrence Col. Studied with Batya Heller, Erica Thimey, Paul Taylor. Joined Taylor company in 1973.

RHODES, CATHRYN. Born in 1958 in Westchester, NY. Studied with Iris Merrick, Don Farnworth, at Manhattan Ballet School, Manhattan School of Dance, Am. Ballet Theatre School. Joined ABT 1973.

RHODES, LAWRENCE. Born in Mt. Hope, W. Va., Nov. 24, 1939. Studied with Violette Armand. Debut with Ballet Russe de Monte Carlo. Joined Joffrey Ballet in 1960, Harkness Ballet in 1964. Became its director in 1969. Joined Netherlands National Ballet in 1970, Pa. Ballet 1972. Appeared with Eliot Feld Ballet 1974.

Ali Pourfarrokh **Wendy Reiser** **Greg Reynolds** **Judith Reyn** **Bertram Ross**

RIABOUCHINSKA, TATIANA. Born May 23, 1916 in Moscow. Studied with Alexandre Volinin, and Mathilda Kchesinska. Debut in London in 1932. With Monte Carlo Ballet Russe de Basil (1933–43), Ballet Theatre, London Festival Ballet, Theatre Colon (Buenos Aires, 1946–47). Also appeared in musicals. Now teaches.

RICHARDSON, DORENE. Born in N.Y.C., Oct. 5, 1934. Studied at NYU and Juilliard. Debut in 1953. In addition to musicals has appeared with Natanya Neumann, Sophie Maslow, Donald McKayle, and Alvin Ailey.

RICHARDSON, LARRY. Born Jan. 6, 1941 in Minerva, O. Graduate of Ohio State U. Studied with Louis Horst, Jose Limon. Has danced at Kauffman Hall, Hunter College, in musicals, and with Pearl Lang. Also choreographs and tours own company.

RIOJA, PILAR. Born Sept. 13, 1932 in Torreon, Mex. Studied with Pericet, Estampio, Ortega, Tarriba. Debut 1969 in Madrid, Spain; Carnegie Hall 1973. Tours with her own company.

RIVERA, CHITA. Born Jan. 23, in 1933 in Washington, D.C. Studied at School of American Ballet. Has become popular star of musicals, and TV.

RIVERA, LUIS. Born in Los Angeles. Studied with Michael Brigante, Martin Vargas, Luisa Triana, Mercedes & Albano, Alberto Lorca. Appeared with several companies before forming his own.

ROBBINS, JEROME. Born Oct. 11, 1918 in N.Y.C. Attended NYU. Studied with Daganova, Platova, Loring, Tudor, New Dance League, and Helen Veola. Debut in 1937 with Sandor-Sorel Co. Subsequently in musicals before joining Ballet Theater in 1940, for which he first choreographed "Fancy Free." Joined N.Y.C. Ballet in 1949 and became its associate artistic director in 1950. Formed Ballets: U.S.A. which toured Europe and U.S. (1958–1961). Has choreographed and directed many Bdwy productions and ballets.

ROBERSON, LAR. Born May 18, 1947 in Oakland, Calif. Attended Cal. State College, and Graham School. Debut 1968 with Sophie Maslow Company. Joined Graham Company in 1969. Also appeared with Pearl Lang.

ROBINSON, CHASE. Born in Panama City, Fla. Graduate of Fla. State U. Studied with Aubry Hitchins, Don Farnworth. Debut in 1956. Has since appeared with Natl. Ballet of Canada, Joffrey Ballet, Limon, Graham, Lang, Butler, Cunningham, and Hoving. Also teaches.

ROBINSON, NANCY. Born Aug. 28, 1945 in Los Angeles. Studied with Andre Tremaine, Michael Panaieff, San Francisco Ballet, joined company in 1960, became soloist in 1964. Joined American Ballet Theatre in 1967, Joffrey Co. in 1968.

RODGERS, ROD. Born in Detroit where he began his studies. Member of Erick Hawkins Dance Co., and dance supervisor of Mobilization for Youth project. Has also appeared in concert of own works and with own company for which he choreographs.

RODHAM, ROBERT. Born Sept. 2, 1939 in Pittston, Pa. Studied with Barbara Weisberger, Virginia Williams, and at School of American Ballet. Joined N.Y.C. Ballet in 1960. Ballet master, choreographer, and principal with Pennsylvania Ballet from 1963.

RODRIGUEZ, ZHANDRA. Born Mar. 17, 1947 in Caracas. Ven. Debut 1962 with Ballet National Venezuela; joined American Ballet Theatre in 1968; soloist 1970, principal 1973.

ROHAN, SHEILA. Born Nov. 20, 1947 in Staten Island, N.Y. Studied with Vincenzo Celli, Phil Black, James Truitte. Debut 1970 with Dance Theatre of Harlem.

ROMANOFF, DIMITRI. Born in Tsaritzin, Russia. Came to U.S. in 1924 to attend Stanford U. and study with Theodore Kosloff. First dancer with American Ballet Theatre when it was organized in 1940. Now directs school in San Jose, Calif.

ROMERO, RAFAEL. Born Apr. 2, 1945 in Puerto Rico. Studied at School of American Ballet, Natl. Ballet, and American Ballet Center. Has appeared with Ballets de San Juan, Westchester Ballet, Pilar Gomez, National Ballet, Joffrey Ballet, N.Y.C. Opera Ballet (1970).

RON, RACHAMIM. Born Nov. 15, 1942 in Cairo. Studied with Gertrude Kraus. Donald McKayle, Glen Tetley, Pearl Lang, Martha Graham. Debut 1963 with Batsheva Dance Co. of Israel. Joined Donald McKayle Co. in 1967 and Martha Graham in 1968. Rejoined Batsheva 1970.

ROOPE, CLOVER. Born 1937 in Bristol, Eng. Studied at Royal Ballet School and joined company in 1957. Debut as choreographer in 1958. Also appeared with Helen McGehee.

ROSARIO. Born Rosario Perez in Seville Nov. 11, 1920. Cousin of Antonio with whom she achieved international fame. Studied with Realito. With Antonio, became known as "The Kids From Seville" and toured world together until they separated in 1952. Formed own company, but changed to dance recitals. Has returned to guest star with Antonio and his Ballets de Madrid.

ROSS, BERTRAM. Born in Brooklyn, Nov. 13, 1920. Leading male dancer of the Martha Graham Co., appeared in almost every work in the active repertoire. Has appeared with own company and choreography. Now teaches.

ROSS, HERBERT. Born May 13, 1927 in Brooklyn. Studied with Doris Humphrey, Helene Platova, and Laird Leslie. Debut in "Follow the Girls" in 1944. In 1950 choreographed and appeared with Ballet Theatre in "Caprichos," subsequently choreographing for Bdwy musicals, Met Opera Ballet, American Ballet Theatre, and danced with own company in 1960.

ROSSON, KEITH. Born Jan. 24, 1937 in Birmingham, Eng. Studied at Royal Ballet School. Joined Covent Opera Ballet in 1954 and Royal Ballet in 1955. Became soloist in 1959, and principal dancer in 1964.

ROTANTE, THEODORE. Born Feb. 23, 1949 in Stamford, Conn. Studied with Nenette Charisse, Kelly Holt, Jean Erdman, Gladys Bailin, Matt Mattox, Donald McKayle. Debut in 1970 with Jean Erdman Dance Theatre.

ROTARDIER, KELVIN. Born Jan. 23, 1936 in Trinidad, W. I. Studied at London's Sigurd Leder School, Jacob's Pillow, and International School of Dance. Appeared in musicals before joining Alvin Ailey Co. in 1964.

ROTHWELL, CLINTON. Born Mar. 1, 1945 in Guildforn, Eng. Attended Royal Ballet School. Debut with Royal Opera Ballet; subsequently with San Francisco Ballet, Ntl. Ballet of Holland, and Ntl. Ballet of Canada.

ROZOW, PATRICIA. Born Feb. 18, 1947 in Brooklyn, NY. Graduate Butler U. Studied at Harkness School. Joined Ballet West in 1969. Promoted to soloist in 1971; principal in 1973.

RUDKO, DORIS. Born Oct. 18, in Milwaukee. Graduate U. Wisc. Studied with Humphrey, Weidman, Limon, Graham, Holm, Horst, Daganova, Joffrey, and Fonaroff. Debut on Bdwy 1946 in "Shooting' Star." Concert performer and choreographer since 1947. Formed own company in 1957. Is also a teacher.

RUIZ, BRUNILDA. Born in Puerto Rico June 1, 1936. Studied with Martha Melincoff, and Robert Joffrey before joining his touring group in 1955, and his company in 1961. Appeared with Philadelphia and N.Y.C. Opera companies. Joined Harkness Ballet in 1964.

RUSHING, SHIRLEY. Born in Savannah, Ga. Attended Juilliard, Bklyn Col. Studied with O'Donnell, Shurr, Bronson, Limon, Tudor, Graham. Has appeared with Eleo Pomare, Rod Rodgers, Louis Johnson, Gus Denizulu. Co-founder of Choreo-Mutations.

RUSSELL, PAUL. Born Mar. 2, 1947 in Texas. Studied at School of American Ballet, Dance Theatre of Harlem. Debut 1970 with Hartford Ballet; subsequently with Garden State Ballet, Syracuse Ballet Theatre; joined Dance Theatre of Harlem 1971.

RUDD, TOMM. Born in 1943 in Pasadena, Cal. Graduate UUtah. Studied with Willam Christensen, Bene Arnold, Gordon Paxman. Joined Ballet West 1963; made soloist 1965, principal 1969. Teaches and makes guest appearances with other companies.

RYBERG, FLEMMING. Born Nov. 24, 1940 in Copenhagen, Den. Studied at Royal Theatre in Copenhagen; made debut 1958 with Royal Danish Ballet.

Allen Sampson

Roslyn Sampson

Anthony Santiago

Christine Sarry

Marcus Schulkind

SABLE, SHERRY. Born Sept. 4, 1952 in Philadelphia. Studied at Phila. Dance Academy, Graham School. Debut 1970 with Pearl Lang, subsequently with DTW, Richard Gain.

SABLINE, OLEG. Born in 1925 in Berlin. Studied with Preobrajenska, Egorova, Colinine, Ricaus; danced with Grand Ballet de Monte Carlo, l'Opera Comique Ballet, Grand Ballet du Marquis de Cuevas. Came to U.S. in 1958. Formed and toured with own group Ballet Concertante. Currently teaches.

SADDLER, DONALD. Born Jan. 24, 1920 in Van Nys, Calif. Attended LACC. Studied with Maracci, Dolin, and Tudor. Debut in 1937, subsequently appearing with Ballet Theatre (1940–3, 1946–7), and in Bdwy musicals. First choreography "Blue Mountain Ballads" for Markova-Dolin Co. in 1948. Performed with own company in 1949. Assistant artistic director of Harkness Ballet 1964–1970. Has choreographed several Bdwy productions.

SAMPSON, ALLEN. Born Oct. 1, 1957 in NYC. Made debut with Dance Theatre of Harlem in 1972.

SAMPSON, RONDA CAROL. Born June 26, 1953 in Roanoke, Va. Made debut with Atlanta Ballet in 1968. Joined Dance Theatre of Harlem in 1969.

SAMPSON, ROSLYN. Born May 8, 1955 in Nashville, Tenn. Appeared with Atlanta Ballet; joined Dance Theatre of Harlem 1969.

SANASARDO, PAUL. Born Sept. 15, 1928 in Chicago. Attended Chicago U. Studied with Tudor, Thimey, Graham, and Slavenska. Debut in 1951 with Erika Thimey Dance Theatre; subsequently with Anna Sokolow, and Pearl Lang. In 1958 established, and directs Studio For Dance, a school for his own company that presents concerts throughout the U.S., Canada, and BWI. Choreographer and dancer on TV. Director of Modern Dance Artists (N.Y.C.), and School of Modern Dance (Saratoga, N.Y.).

SANCHEZ, MIGUEL. Born Feb. 21, 1951 in Puerto Rico. Studied at School of American Ballet, and with Anne Wooliams. Debut 1969 with Stuttgart Ballet. Is guest artist with Ballets de San Juan, P.R.

SANDERS, JOB. Born in Amsterdam in 1929. Studied with Gavrilov, and at School of American Ballet. Debut with Ballet Society. Subsequently with Ballet Russe de Monte Carlo, ABT, Ruth Page's Ballet, American Festival Ballet, Netherlands Ballet, Netherlands Dance Theatre. Began choreographing in 1956. Also teaches.

SANDONATO, BARBARA. Born July 22, 1943 in Harrison, N.Y. Studied at Lorna London School, and School of American Ballet. Debut with N.Y.C. Ballet, danced with Gloria Contreras Co., before joining Pennsylvania Ballet in 1964 and rising to principal; Canadian Ntl. Ballet 1972–3; returned to Pa. Ballet 1973.

SANTANGELO, TULY. Born May 30, 1936 in Buenos Aires. Studied at Opera Theatre, with Martha Graham, Alwin Nikolais. Debut 1956 with Brazilian Co., subsequently with Nikolais, Don Redlich (1970).

SANTIAGO, ANTHONY. Born Jan. 7, 1942 in Cartagena, Col. Studied with Craske and Tudor. Joined Les Grand Ballets Canadiens 1963–65, Met Opera Ballet 1965–72, 1974–76, Houston Ballet 1973–74.

SAPIRO, DANA. Born Jan. 2, 1952 in N.Y.C. Studied with Karin Irvin, Joffrey, and at American Ballet Center. Debut 1970 with Joffrey Ballet. Joined Alvin Ailey company 1972.

SAPPINGTON, MARGO. Born in Baytown, Tex., July 30, 1947. Studied with Camille Hill, Matt Mattox, and at American Ballet Center. Debut with Joffrey Ballet in 1965. Also appeared in musicals, and choreographs.

SARRY, CHRISTINE. Born in Long Beach, Calif. in 1947. Studied with Silver, Howard, Maracci, Oumansky, Fallis, Thomas. Joined Joffrey Ballet in 1963. American Ballet Theatre in 1964. American Ballet Co. (1969), rejoined ABT as soloist in 1971; Eliot Feld Ballet 1974.

SARSTADT, MARIAN. Born July 11, 1942 in Amsterdam. Studied at Scapino School, with Mme. Nora, Audrey de Vos. Debut in 1958 with Scapino Ballet. Joined de Cuevas Co. in 1960. Netherlands Dance Theatre in 1962.

SATINOFF, JEFF. Born Nov. 6, 1954 in Philadelphia, Pa. Attended N.C. School of Arts. Debut 1972 with North Carolina Dance Theatre. Joined Eliot Feld Co. 1974.

SATO, SHOZO. Born May 18, 1933 in Kobe, Japan. Graduate Tokyo U. Debut with Classical Ballet in 1948. Has appeared around the world in concert and lecture demonstrations since 1964.

SAUL, PETER. Born Feb. 10, 1936 in N.Y.C. Studied with Craske, Tudor, and Cunningham. Appeared with Met Opera Ballet 1956–7, International Ballet 1960–61, American Ballet Theatre 1962–4, Les Grands Ballets Canadien 1964–5, Merce Cunningham 1966–7.

SCHANNE, MARGRETHE. Born in Copenhagen Nov. 21, 1921. Graduate of Royal Danish Ballet school; joined company, in mid-1940's, rapidly rising to premiere danseuse and the epitome of the Bournonville style. Briefly joined Petit's Ballets des Champs-Elysses in Paris and in 1947 made London debut with it before returning to Royal Danish Ballet where she became synonymous with "La Sylphide." Made N.Y. debut in it in 1956, and danced it for farewell performance in N.Y. and in Copenhagen in 1966. Now teaches.

SCHEEPERS, MARTIN. Born in 1933 in Arnheim, Holland. Studied with Georgi, Adret, Crofton, Lifar, Gsovsky, Kiss. Debut in 1948 with Amsterdam Opera. Joined Champs-Elysses and London Festival Ballets before American Ballet Theatre in 1960.

SCHORER, SUKI. Born in Cambridge, Mass. Attended U. Cal. Studied at San Francisco Ballet School and joined company. In 1959 joined N.Y.C. Ballet, becoming soloist in 1963, ballerina in 1969. Retired in 1971 and teaches.

SCHRAMEK, TOMAS. Born in Bratislave, Czech. Began training at 9. Graduate Musical and Theatrical Academy. Joined Slovak Character Dance Co. 1959, rising to principal. Left Czech. in 1968 to join National Ballet of Canada. Promoted to principal 1973.

SCHULKIND, MARCUS. Born Feb. 21, 1948 in N.Y.C. Graduate Goddard Col. Studied at Juilliard. Debut 1968 with Pearl Lang, then with Norman Walker, Felix Fibich; joined Batsheva in 1970.

SCOTT, MARION. Born July 24, 1922 in Chicago. Studied with Graham, Humphrey, Weidman, Horst, Tamiris, and Slavenska. Debut with Humphrey-Weidman Co. in 1942. Danced with Tamiris, and in 1964 formed own company for which she choreographs. Also teaches.

SCOTT, WILLIAM. Born Nov. 3, 1950 in N.Y.C. Studied with Martha Graham, Harkness House, Richard Thomas. Debut 1968 with Harkness Youth Co. Joined Dance Theatre of Harlem in 1970. Is also ballet master and teacher.

SEGARRA, RAMON. Born Nov. 26, 1939 in Mayaguez, P.R. Studied with Chafee, Malinka, Moore, Pereyaslavec, Vilzak, Oboukoff, Vladimiroff, Eglevsky, and Zaraspe. Debut 1954 with Ballet Chafee, subsequently appearing as soloist with May O'Donnell Co. (1956–8), Ballet Russe de Monte Carlo (1958–61), N.Y.C. Ballet (1961–4), and ballet master of Ailey Co. from 1970. Ballet Master Hamburg Stage Opera Ballet 1972; Ballet Hispanico 1972.

SEIGENFELD, BILLY. Born Oct. 15, 1948 in Mt. Vernon, N.Y. Graduate Brown U. Studied with Nikolais. Debut 1970 with Don Redlich Co., subsequently with Elina Mooney.

SEKIL, YAROSLAV. Born in Ukrania in 1930. Entered Bolshoi School in 1949, and joined company in 1951. Became one of leading character dancers.

SELF, KEVIN. Born Apr. 21, 1955 in Denton, Tex. Attended NC School of Arts. Debut 1973 with Agnes DeMille Heritage Dance Theatre. Joined ABT 1974.

SELLERS, JOAN. Born Sept. 21, 1937 in N.Y.C. Studied with Graham, Cunningham, Thomas, Fallis, Farnworth. Debut 1960 with Dance Theatre, subsequently with DTW, James Cunningham Co.

SERAVALLI, ROSANNA. Born March 9, 1943 in Florence, Italy. Trained and performed in Italy before joining American Ballet Theatre in 1963.

Ruby Shang

Eddie Shellman

Kirsten Simone

Earle Sieveling

Trinette Singleton

SERGAVA, KATHERINE. Born in Tiflis, Russia. Studied with Kehessinska, Fokine, Kyasht, Mendes. Danced with Mordkin Ballet, Ballet Theatre (1940), Original Ballet Russe. More recently appeared in musicals.

SERRANO, LUPE. Born Dec. 7, 1930 in Santiago, Chile. Studied in Mexico City with Dambre and joined Mexico City Ballet Co. Organized Mexican Academy of Modern Dance. After studying with Celli and Tudor, performed with Ballet Russe, and Ballet Theatre (since 1953).

SERRANO, RAYMOND. Born Apr. 19, 1950 in Vieques, P.R. Studied at Thalia Mann Sch., Sch. of Am. Ballet. Debut 1968 with National Ballet. Appeared with Eglevsky Co., Ballet Concerto, Ballet Repertory Co. before joining ABT 1975.

SETTERFIELD, VALDA. Born Sept. 17, 1934 in Margate, Eng. Studied with Rambert, Karsavina, Waring, Cunningham. Debut with Ballet Rambert in 1955. Since, with James Waring, Aileen Pasloff, Katherine Litz, David Gordon, Merce Cunningham.

SEYMOUR, LYNN. Born in 1939 in Wainwright, Alberta, Canada. Studied at Royal Ballet School, London graduating into company. Besides appearing as dramatic ballerina with Royal Ballet, has made guest appearances with Stuttgart, and Canadian National Ballet. Guest artist with Ailey Co. 1970–71. Rejoined Royal Ballet 1970.

SHANG, RUBY. Born Nov. 16, 1948 in Tokyo where she began studies at 6. Attended Pembroke Col. Studied with Julie Strandberg, Martha Graham, Iehige Reiko. Joined Paul Taylor Co. in 1971.

SHANKAR, UDAY. Born in Udayapur, India, in 1902. Had such success helping his father produce Hindu plays and ballets, that Anna Pavlova requested his help, and he appeared with her in "Radha-Krishna." At her insistence, pursued dance career. Organized own company and toured U.S. in 1931, 1952, 1962, and 1968. Has been more responsible than any other dancer for arousing interest in Indian dance.

SHAW, BRIAN. Born June 28, 1928 in Golear, Yorkshire, Eng. At 14 entered Sadler's Wells School, and joined company 2 years later, becoming one of Royal Ballet's outstanding principal dancers.

SHEARER, MOIRA. Born in Dunfermline, Scotland. Jan. 17, 1926. Studied with Legat and Preobrajenska; joined International Ballet at 15, transferring to Sadler's Wells and became ballerina in 1944. More recently has appeared on stage and films.

SHEARER, SYBIL. Born in Toronto, Can. Studied in France and Eng. Before forming and choreographing for own group, appeared with Humphrey Weidman Co., and Theatre Dance Co. Also teaches.

SHELLMAN, EDDIE. Born May 10, 1956 in Tampa, FL. Studied with Herbert Lehman, Alvin Ailey, NY Sch. of Ballet. Debut 1975 with Dance Theatre of Harlem.

SHELTON, SARA. Born Dec. 17, 1943. Studied at Henry St. Playhouse. Debut 1966 with Bill Frank Co., subsequently with Nikolais, Louis Murray, Mimi Garrard, Raymond Johnson. Also teaches and choreographs.

SHERMAN, HOPE (a.k.a. Asha Devi, Antonia Esperanza, Sha'Ana). Born in 1944 in Leonia, NJ. Studied at Met Opera School, in India, Japan, Spain, Columbia U. Gives solo concerts and teaches.

SHERWOOD, GARY. Born Sept. 24, 1941, in Swindon, Eng. Studied at Royal Ballet School; joined company in 1961; Western Theatre Ballet 1965; London's Festival Ballet 1966; returned to Royal Ballet in 1967.

SHIMIN, TONIA. Born Sept. 16, 1942 in N.Y.C. Attended Met Opera Ballet, Royal Ballet, Graham schools. Debut 1965 with Martha Graham, subsequently with Pearl Lang, Gus Solomons, Anna Sokolow, Mary Anthony. Joined Jose Limon Co. 1975.

SHIMOFF, KAREL. Born in Los Angeles where she began studies with Irina Kosmovska. Appeared with L.A. Junior Ballet and N.Y.C. Ballet's "Nutcracker" in L.A. in 1961. Studied at School of American Ballet, and joined N.Y.C. Ballet for 2 years, before returning as principal dancer with Ballet of Los Angeles.

SHULER, ARLENE. Born Oct. 18, 1947 in Cleveland, O. Studied at School of American Ballet, and American Ballet Center. Debut with N.Y.C. Ballet in 1960, and joined Joffrey Ballet in 1965.

SHURR, GERTRUDE. Born in Riga, Latvia. Studied at Denishawn, and with Humphrey, Weidman, and Graham. Has appeared with Denishawn Co., Humphrey-Weidman Concert Co., and Martha Graham. Now teaches.

SIBLEY, ANTOINETTE. Born in Bromley, Eng., Feb. 27, 1939. Studied at Royal Ballet School, and made debut with them in 1956, becoming soloist in 1959, principal in 1960.

SIDIMUS, JOYSANNE. Born June 21 in NYC. Attended Barnard Col., School of Am. Ballet, Joffrey School. Debut 1958 with NYC-Ballet. Subsequently with London Festival Ballet, National Ballet of Canada, Pennsylvania Ballet. Ballet Mistress Grands Ballets de Geneve (1971), Ballet Repertory Co. from 1973. Also teaches.

SIMMONS, DANIEL. Born in Edinburg, Tex. Studied at Pan American U., San Francisco Ballet School. Debut with SF Ballet 1967.

SIMON, VICTORIA. Born in 1939 in N.Y.C. Studied at School of American Ballet, American Ballet Center, Ballet Theatre School. Joined N.Y.C. Ballet in 1958, promoted to soloist in 1963.

SIMONE, KIRSTEN. Born July 1, 1934 in Copenhagen. Studied at School of Royal Theatre; made debut with Royal Danish Ballet in 1952, subsequently becoming principal dancer. Has appeared with Ruth Page Opera Ballet, Royal Winnipeg Ballet, Royal Swedish Ballet.

SIMONEN-SVANSTROM, SEIJA. Born in Helsinki, Finland, Sept. 7, 1935. Studied at Finnish Natl. Opera Ballet School, and with Nikitina, Baltazcheva, Semjonowa, Lopuchkina, Karnakoski, Stahlberg, Northcote, Franzel, and Craske. Debut 1952 with Helsinki Natl. Opera. Has appeared with Finnish Natl. Ballet, and London Festival Ballet.

SINGLETON, SARAH. Born Apr. 21, 1951 in Morgantown, WVa. Graduate Stephens Col. Studied with Susan Abbey, Rebecca Harris, Karel Shook, Paul Sanasardo. Debut 1972 with Sanasardo Dance Co.

SINGLETON, TRINETTE. Born in Beverly, Mass., Nov. 20, 1945. Studied with Harriet James, and at American Ballet Center. Debut with Joffrey Ballet in 1965.

SIZOVA, ALLA. Born in Moscow in 1939. Studied at Leningrad Ballet School. Joined Kirov Co. in 1958, and became its youngest ballerina.

SKIBINE, GEORGE. Born Jan. 17, 1920 in Russia. Studied with Preobrajenska, and Oboukhoff. Debut with Ballet de Monte Carlo in 1937, and with company until 1939. Original Ballet Russe (1939–40). American Ballet Theatre (1940–1942). Marquis de Cuevas Grand Ballet (1947–56), Theatre National de Opera Paris (1956–64), artistic director of Harkness Ballet 1964–66. Currently works with regional companies. Director Dallas Civic Ballet.

SLAVENSKA, MIA. Born in 1916 in Yugoslavia. At 12 made debut and toured Europe with Anton Vyanc, subsequently with Lifar and Dolin, and prima ballerina with Ballet Russe de Monte Carlo, before forming own company Ballet Variant that toured Americas and Europe. Has worked with many regional companies, toured with Slavinska-Franklin Co. Currently teaches at UCLA.

SLAYTON, JEFF. Born Sept. 5, 1945 in Richmond, Va. Attended Adelphi U. Studied with Merce Cunningham and made debut with his company in 1968. Appears with Viola Farber Co.

SLEEP, WAYNE. Born July 17, 1948 in Plymouth, England. Attended Royal Ballet School, and was graduated into the company in 1966.

SMALL, ROBERT. Born Dec. 19, 1949 in Moline, Ill. UCLA graduate. Studied with Gloria Newman. Murray Louis, Nikolais, and at Am. School of Ballet. Debut in 1971 with Murray Louis Co.

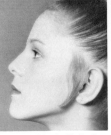

Gus Solomons **Cristina Stirling** **Sergiu Stefanschi** **Carol-Marie Strizak** **Jan Stripling**

SMALLS, SAMUEL. Born Feb. 17, 1951 in N.Y.C. Attended CCNY. Studied with Lester Wilson, Jamie Rodgers, Harkness House. Debut 1969 with Dance Theatre of Harlem.

SMUIN, MICHAEL. Born Oct. 13, 1929 in Missoula, Mont. Studied with Christensen brothers, William Dollar and Richard Thomas. Joined San Francisco Ballet in 1957, and made choreographic debut in 1961. Has choreographed for Harkness and Ballet Theatre. A principal with American Ballet Theatre since 1969. Associated director San Francisco Ballet 1973.

SOKOLOW, ANNA. Born in 1912 in Hartford, Conn. Studied with Graham and Horst. Became member of Graham Co. but left to form own in 1938. Internationally known as choreographer, and her works include many modern classics. Formed Lyric Theatre Co. in Israel in 1962. Has taught at major studios and universities, and choreographed for Broadway, TV, and opera.

SOLINO, LOUIS. Born Feb. 7, 1942 in Philadelphia. Studied with Graham, O'Donnell, Schurr, Walker, Anthony, Farnworth. Has performed with Glen Tetley, Mary Anthony, Sophie Maslow, Norman Walker, Arthur Bauman, Seamus Murphy, and Jose Limon.

SOLOMON, ROBERT. Born Feb. 13, 1945 in The Bronx. Studied at Henry Street Playhouse. Has appeared with Henry Street Playhouse Company, and Nikolais.

SOLOMON, RUTH. Born June 10, 1936 in N.Y.C. Studied with Jean Erdman and joined company in 1957, still appears with her between teaching. Now head of Dance-Theatre program at U. Cal. at Santa Cruz.

SOLOMONS, GUS, Jr. Born in Boston where he studied with Jan Veen and Robert Cohan. Danced with Donald McKayle, Joyce Trisler, Pearl Lang, Martha Graham, Merce Cunningham. Formed own company in 1971.

SOLOV, ZACHARY. Born in 1923 in Philadelphia. Studied with Littlefield, Preobrajenska, Carlos, Holm, and Humphrey and at American Ballet School. Debut with Catherine Littlefield Ballet Co. Later joined American Ballet, New Opera Co., Loring Dance Players, and Ballet Theatre. In 1951 became choreographer for Met Opera Ballet. Toured own company 1961-1962. Also appeared on Bdwy and with regional companies.

SOLOVYOV, YURI. Born Aug. 10, 1940. Graduated from Leningrad Ballet School and into Kirov Co. in 1958. Has become one of its leading soloists.

SOMBERT, CLAIRE. Born in 1935 in Courbevoie, France. A pupil of Brieux, made debut in 1950. Has appeared with Ballets de Paris. Ballets Jean Babilee, Miskovitch Co. Toured U.S. with Michel Bruel.

SOMES, MICHAEL. Born Sept. 28, 1917 in Horsley, Eng. Attended Sadler's Wells School; joined company (now Royal) in 1937, and became lead dancer in 1938. For many years, partner for Margot Fonteyn, and creator of many famous roles. In 1962 appointed assistant director of company, and still performs character roles.

SOWINSKI, JOHN. Born in Scranton, PA. Began studies at 5. Has danced with NYC Ballet, Pennsylvania Ballet, ABT (1965-69), American Ballet Co., Eliot Feld Ballet (1974-   ).

SORKIN, NAOMI. Born Oct. 23, 1948 in Chicago. Studied at Stone-Camryn School. Debut with Chicago Lyric Opera Ballet in 1963. Joined ABT in 1966; promoted to soloist in 1971. Joined San Francisco Ballet 1973; Eliot Feld Ballet 1974.

SPASSOFF, BOJAN. Born in Oslo, Norway. Appeared with Ntl. Ballet of Holland, Royal Danish Ballet, ABT, and joined San Francisco Ballet 1973.

SPIZZO, CHRISTINE. Born Apr. 3, 1953 in Belleville, Ill. Attended N.C. School of Arts, San Francisco Ballet Sch., Sch. of Am. Ballet. Debut 1971 with National Ballet; joined ABT 1974.

SPOHR, ARNOLD. Born in Saskatchewan, Can. Joined Winnipeg company in 1945, rising to leading dancer, and appeared in England partnering Markova. Began choreographing in 1950. In 1958 was appointed director of Royal Winnipeg Ballet for which he choreographs.

SPURLOCK, ESTELLE. Born May 9, 1949 in Jersey City, N.J. Graduate Boston Cons. Studied with Sonia Wilson, Lar Lubovitch, James Truitte. Debut 1971 with Alvin Ailey Co.

STACKHOUSE, SARAH. (formerly Sally). Born in Chicago, Graduate U. Wisc. Studied with Arrby Blinn, Steffi Nossen, Perry-Mansfield School, John Begg, Limon, Graham, and Nagrin. Joined Limon company in 1959. Also appeared with Alvin Ailey Co. Teaches at Juilliard and Conn. College.

STARBUCK, JAMES. Born in Albuquerque, New Mex. Attended College of Pacific. Debut 1934 with Ballet Modern, subsequently appearing with San Francisco Opera Ballet. Ballet Russe de Monte Carlo (1939-44). On Bdwy in musicals before first choreography for "Fanny." Has since choreographed and directed for theatre and TV.

STEELE, MICHAEL. Born in Roanoke, Va. Studied at American Ballet School, and made debut with N.Y.C. Ballet.

STEELE, ROBERT. Born June 22, 1946 in Erie, Pa. Attended Boston Cons. Studied with Statia Sublette, Virginia Williams, Stanley Williams, Vera Volkova. Debut 1974 with Boston Ballet; subsequently with Pennsylvania Ballet 1964, American Festival Ballet 1965, Royal Danish Ballet 1966, Boston Ballet 1968.

STEFANSCHI, SERGIU. Born Mar. 2, 1941 in Roumania. Graduate of Academie Ballet. Debut 1962 with Bucharest Opera Ballet; subsequently with Theatre Francais de la Dance, National Ballet of Canada 1971 as principal.

STEPHEN, EDITH. Born in Salamanca, N.Y. Studied with Doris Humphrey, Jose Limon, Mary Wigman, Rudolf Laban. Debut in 1962 with own company and choreography. Has toured U.S. and Europe.

STEVENSON, BEN. Born April 4 in Portsmouth, Eng. Was principal dancer for many years with London's Festival Ballet. Retired to teach but makes guest appearances. Directed Harkness Youth Co., National Ballet, Chicago Ballet, Houston Ballet (1975).

STEWART, DELIA WEDDINGTON. Born in Meridian, Miss. Studied at Ballet Arts Center, Ballet Theatre, and International Dance Schools. Appeared in Bdwy musicals. Director of Dixie Darling Dance Group. In 1963 became artistic director of Mississippi Coast Ballet.

STIRLING, CRISTINA. Born May 22, 1940 in London. Trained at Audrey de Vos and Andrew Hardie School. Debut with Sadler's Wells Opera Ballet. Subsequently with Netherlands Ballet, London Festival Ballet, American Ballet Co. Now co-director of Louisville Ballet and teacher.

STOCK, GAILENE. Born Jan. 28, 1946 in Ballarat, Aust. Studied with Paul Hammond, Rosella Hightower, and at London's Royal Ballet School. Debut 1962 with Australian Ballet; subsequently with Grande Ballet Classique de France (1963), Teatro del Balletto di Roma (1964), Ntl. Ballet of Canada (1973).

STONE, BENTLEY. Born in Plankinston, S.Dak. Studied with Severn, Caskey, Albertier. Novikoff, and Rambert. After dancing in musicals joined Chicago Civic Opera, becoming premier danseur. Also danced with Ballet Rambert, Ballet Russe, and Page-Stone Ballet for which he choreographed many works.

STRICKLER, ILENE. Born July 5, 1952 in NYC. Studied at Met Opera Ballet School. Debut 1969 with Manhattan Festival Ballet; subsequently with Yuriko Co., Boston Ballet 1973.

STRIPLING, JAN. Born Sept 27, 1947 in Essen, Ger. Studied with Volkova, Tudor, Jooss, Hoving, and Jean Lebron. Joined Stuttgart Ballet in 1963; promoted to principal.

STRIZAK, CAROL-MARIE. Born Jan. 8, 1957 in Chicago, IL. Studied at School of American Ballet. Made debut 1974 with NYC Ballet.

STROGANOVA, NINA. Born in Copenhagen, and studied at Royal Danish Ballet with Preobrajenska and Dokoudovsky. Appeared with Ballet de L'Opera Comique Paris, Mordkin Ballet, National Ballet Theatre, de Basil's Original Ballet Russe, Ballet Russe de Monte Carlo, and Danish Royal Ballet. Was co-director and ballerina of Dokoudovsky-Stroganova Ballet. Is now a teacher.

STRUCHKOVA, RAISSA. Born in 1925 in Moscow; graduate of Bolshoi School in 1944. Became soloist in 1946 with company; now a prima ballerina. Has appeared in almost every ballet performed in Bolshoi repertoire.

| Britt Swanson | Russell Sultzbach | Veronica Tennant | Paul Taylor | Maria Tallchief |

SUKANYA. Born Nov. 14, 1946 in Calcutta, India. Trained with Deva Prasad Das, Raja Reddy, and at Pan Dan Allur School. Tours in solo concerts.

SULTZBACH, RUSSELL. Born in Gainesville, Fla. Studied at Royal School, and American Ballet Center. Debut 1972 with Joffrey Ballet.

SUMNER, CAROL. Born Feb. 24, 1940 in Brooklyn. Studied with Eileen O'Connor and at School of American Ballet. Joined N.Y.C. Ballet, becoming soloist in 1963.

SURMEYAN, HAZAROS. Born Jan. 21, 1943 in Skopje, Yugo. Began training at 13. Made debut with Skopje Opera Ballet; subsequently with Belgrade Opera Ballet, Mannheim Opera Ballet, Cologne Opera Ballet. Joined National Ballet of Canada in 1966. Is now a principal and teacher.

SUTHERLAND, DAVID. Born Sept. 18, 1941 in Santa Ana, Cal. Studied with Michel Panaieff, Aaron Girard. Debut 1959 with Ballet de Cuba. Joined Stuttgart Ballet in 1965; promoted to principal.

SUTHERLAND, PAUL. Born in 1935 in Louisville, Ky. Joined Ballet Theatre in 1957, subsequently dancing with Royal Winnipeg Ballet, and Joffrey Ballet. Rejoined American Ballet Theatre as soloist in 1964; promoted principal 1966; Harkness in 1969, Joffrey 1971.

SUTOWSKI, THOR. Born in Trenton, NJ. in Jan. 1945. Studied with Rosella Hightower, Franchette, Williams, Franklin, Tupine, Pereyaslavec. Debut with San Diego Ballet; then with San Francisco Ballet, National Ballet, Hamburg Opera Ballet, Norwegian Opera Ballet where he became premier soloist. Now co-director of San Diego Ballet.

SUZUKI, DAWN. Born in Slocan, B.C., Can. Graduate U. Toronto; studied at Canadian Royal Academy of Dance, Banff and Martha Graham Schools. Debut with Yuriko in 1967, followed by performances with Pearl Lang. Joined Graham Co. in 1968.

SVETLOVA, MARINA. Born May 3, 1922 in Paris. Studied with Trefilova, Egorova, and Vilzak. With Original Ballet Russe (1939–41). Ballet Theatre (1942), prima ballerina Met Opera Ballet (1943–50), N.Y.C. Opera (1950–52), own concert group (1944–58), and as guest with most important European companies, Artistic Director of Dallas Civic Ballet; choreographer for Dallas, Seattle, and Houston Operas; Teaches at Indiana U.

SWANSON, BRITT. Born June 6, 1947 in Fargo, N.Dak. Studied at S.F. Ballet Sch., N.Y. School of Ballet. Debut 1963 with Chicago Opera Ballet, subsequently with S.F. Ballet, on Bdwy, with Paul Sanasardo, Paul Taylor (1969).

SWAYZE, PATRICK. Born in Houston, TX. Studied at Harkness House. Joined Eliot Feld Ballet 1975.

TALIAFERRO, CLAY. Born Apr. 5, 1940 in Lynchburg, Va. Attended Boston Consv. Debut 1964 with Emily Frankel Co. Has appeared with companies of Donald McKayle, Sophie Maslow, Buzz Miller, Stuart Hodes, Jose Limon.

TALLCHIEF, MARIA. Born Jan. 24, 1925 in Fairfax, Okla. After studying with Nijinska, joined Ballet Russe de Monte Carlo in 1942, and became leading dancer. In 1948 joined N.Y.C. Ballet as prima ballerina, and excelled in classic roles. Has appeared as guest artist with Paris Opera and other European companies. Retired in 1965.

TALLCHIEF, MARJORIE. Born Oct. 19, 1927 on Indian reservation in Oklahoma. Studied with Nijinska, and Lichine. Debut with American Ballet Theatre in 1945, subsequently with Marquis de Cuevas Ballet (1947–56), Theatre National Opera de Paris (1956–54), Bolshoi (1964), and Harkness Ballet in 1964. Resigned in 1966. Now teaches. Associate director Dallas Civic Ballet.

TALMAGE, ROBERT. Born June 24, 1943 in Washington, D.C. Attended S.F. State Col. Studied with Eugene Loring. Appeared with Atlanta Ballet, in musicals, before joining Joffrey Ballet in 1968.

TANNER, RICHARD. Born Oct. 28, 1949 in Phoenix, Ariz. Graduate U. Utah. Studied at School of Am. Ballet. Made debut with N.Y.C. Ballet in 1968.

TARAS, JOHN. Born in N.Y.C. Apr. 18, 1919. Studied with Fokine, Vilzak, Shollar, and at School of American Ballet. Appeared in musicals and with Ballet Caravan, Littlefield Ballet, American

Ballet, and Ballet Theatre with which he became soloist, ballet master, and choreographed first ballet "Graziana" in 1945. Joined Marquis de Cuevas' Grand Ballet in 1948. Returned to N.Y.C. Ballet in 1959 as assistant to Balanchine. Has created and staged ballets for companies throughout the world.

TAVERNER, SONIA. Born in Byfleet, Eng., in 1936. Studied at Sadler's Wells, and joined company before moving to Canada where she became member of Royal Winnipeg Ballet, developing into its premiere danseuse. Joined Pa. Ballet as principal in 1971; left in 1972.

TAYLOR, BURTON. Born Aug. 19, 1943 in White Plains, N.Y. Studied with Danielian, and at Ballet Theatre School. Debut with Eglevsky Ballet in 1959 before joining American Ballet Theatre, Joffrey Co. in 1969.

TAYLOR, JUNE. Born in 1918 in Chicago. Studied with Merriel Abbott. Debut in "George White's Scandals of 1931." Choreographer for June Taylor Dancers and director of own school.

TAYLOR, PAUL. Born in Allegheny County, Pa., July 29, 1930. Attended Syracuse U., Juilliard, Met Opera Ballet, and Graham Schools. Studied with Craske and Tudor. Member of Graham Co. for 6 years, and appeared with Merce Cunningham, Pearl Lang, Anna Sokolow, and N.Y.C. Ballet. In 1960 formed and choreographs for own company that tours U.S. and Europe annually.

TCHERINA, LUDMILLA. Born in Paris in 1925. Trained with d'Allesandri, Clustine, Preobrajenska. Has appeared with Monte Carlo Opera, Ballets des Champs-Elysees, Nouveau Ballet de Monte Carlo. Toured with own company, and now appears in films.

TCHERKASSKY, MARIANNA. Born 1953 in Glen Cove, N.Y. Studied with her mother Lillian Tcherkassky; made debut with Eglevsky Ballet; joined ABT in 1970; soloist in 1972; principal 1976.

TENNANT, VERONICA. Born Jan. 15, 1947 in London, Eng. Studied in Eng., and Ntl. Ballet School of Canada. Debut 1964 with Ntl. Ballet of Canada, and rapidly rose to principal.

TETLEY, GLEN. Born Feb. 3, 1926 in Cleveland, Ohio. Attended Franklin and Marshall College, and NYU graduate. Studied with Holm, Graham, Tudor, and Craske. Debut in 1946 in "On The Town," subsequently with Hanya Holm (1946–9), John Butler (1951–9), N.Y.C. Opera (1951–66), Robert Joffrey (1955–6), Martha Graham (1957–60). American Ballet Theatre (1958–60), Ballets; U.S.A. (1960–1), Nederlands Dans Theatre (1962–5). Formed own company in 1961, and choreographs. Director of Stuttgart Ballet 1974.

THARP, TWYLA. Born in Portland, IN. in 1941. Graduate Barnard College. Studied with Collonette, Schwetzoff, Farnworth, Louis, Mattox, Graham, Nikolais, Taylor, and Cunningham. Debut with Paul Taylor in 1965. Has organized, choreographed, and appeared with own company in N.Y.C. and on tour.

THOMAS, RICHARD. Born in Paintsville, KY. Studied with Bronislava Nijinska. After appearing on Bdwy, joined Ballet Theatre in 1946. With his wife, former ballerina Barbara Fallis, operates NY School of Ballet.

THOMAS, ROBERT. Born Mar. 5, 1948 in Iowa City. Studied with Anne Kirksen, and at Harkness School. Joined Harkness Ballet in 1968. Joffrey Ballet 1970.

THOMPSON, BASIL. Born in Newcasle-on-Tyne, Eng. Studied at Sadler's Wells. Joined Covent Garden Ballet in 1954, the Royal Ballet, ABT in 1960. Currently ballet master of Joffrey Ballet.

THOMPSON, CLIVE. Born in Kingston, Jamaica, B.W.I., Oct. 20. Studied with and joined Ivy Baxter's Dance Co. Attended Soohih School of Classical Dance, and University College of West Indies. In 1958 represented Jamaica at Federal Festival of Arts. Won Jamaican award for choreography and contribution to dance. Came to U.S. in 1960, studied with Graham, and joined company in 1961. Also with Talley Beatty, Pearl Lang, Yuriko, Geoffrey Holder, and Alvin Ailey.

THORESEN, TERJE. Born in 1945 in Stockholm. Debut in 1959. Appeared with Royal Dramatic Theatre, Stockholm Dance Theatre, Syvilla Fort African Dance Group.

TIMOFEYEVA, NINA. Born in 1935 in Russia. Entered Leningrad Ballet School and graduated into Kirov Co. in 1953. Joined Bolshoi in 1956 and is a principal ballerina.

TIPPET, CLARK. Born Oct. 5, 1954 in Parsons, Kan. Trained at National Academy of Ballet. Made debut with American Ballet Theatre 1972; principal 1976.

TODD, CAROLINE A. Born Mar. 29, 1944 in Savannah, GA. Trained at School of Am. Ballet, Am. Ballet Theatre, Am. Ballet Center. Debut 1965 with Am. Ballet Theatre; joined NYC Ballet 1967.

TOMASSON, HELGI. Born Oct. 8, in Reykjavik, Iceland. Studied with Sigidur Arman, Erik Bidsted, Vera Volkova, and American Ballet School. Debut in Copenhagen's Pantomine Theatre in 1958. In 1961 joined Joffrey Ballet; Harkness Ballet in 1964; N.Y.C. Ballet in 1970, becoming principal.

TOMLINSON, MEL A. Born Jan. 3, 1954 in Raleigh, NC. Attended NC School of Arts, Dance Theatre of Harlem. Debut 1973 with Agnes deMille's Heritage Dance Theatre. Joined Dance Theatre of Harlem 1974.

TORRES, JULIO. Born in Ponce, PR. Attended NY High School of Performing Arts. Appeared with Jose Greco, Carmen Amaya, Vienna Volksopera, Pilar Lopez. Founder-Director-Choreographer of Puerto Rican Dance Theatre.

TOTH, EDRA. Born in 1952 in Budapest, Hungary. Trained with Alda Marova, E. Virginia Williams. Joined Boston Ballet in 1965, rising to principal.

TOUMANOVA, TAMARA. Born in 1919. Protege of Pavlowa; danced first leading role with Paris Opera at 10; ballerina with Ballet Russe de Monte Carlo at 16. Joined Rene Blum Co. in 1939; returned to Paris Opera in 1947, and to London with de Cuevas Ballet in 1949. More recently in films.

TRACY, PAULA. Born Feb. 25 in San Francisco where she studied with Lew and Harold Christensen. Debut with San Francisco Ballet in 1956. Joined American Ballet Theatre in 1967, San Francisco Ballet 1973.

TRISLER, JOYCE. Born in Los Angeles in 1934. Graduate of Juilliard. Studied with Horton, Maracci, Tudor, Holm, Joffrey, Caton. Debut with Horton Co. in 1951. Became member of Juilliard Dance Theater, and performed with own group, for which she choreographed. Has also choreographed for musicals and operas. Now teaches.

TROUNSON, MARILYN. Born Sept. 30, 1947 in San Francisco. Graduated from Royal Ballet School and joined company in 1966. Joined Stuttgart as principal.

TUDOR, ANTONY. Born Aug. 4, 1908 in London. Studied with Marie Rambert, and made debut with her in 1930, when he also choreographed his first work. Joined Vic-Wells Ballet (1933–5), and became choreographer. Formed own company, London Ballet, in N.Y. in 1938. In 1940 joined American Ballet Theatre as soloist and choreographer. Has produced ballets for N.Y.C. Ballet, Theatre Colon, Deutsche Opera, and Komaki Ballet. Was in charge of Met Opera Ballet School (1957–63); artistic director Royal Swedish Ballet 1963–64. Considered one of world's greatest choreographers. Associate director Am. Ballet Theatre 1974.

TUNE, TOMMY. Born Feb. 28, 1939 in Wichita Falls, Tex. Graduate UTex. Has been featured dancer in films and on Bdwy.

TUPINE, OLEG. Born in 1920 aboard ship off Istanbul. Studied with Egorova and made debut with her company. Joined Original Ballet Russe in 1938, Markova-Dolin Co. in 1947. Ballet Russe de Monte Carlo in 1951, then formed own company. Now teaches.

TURKO, PATRICIA. Born May 22, 1942 in Pittsburgh. Studied at School of American Ballet. Danced with Pittsburgh and Philadelphia Opera companies and in musicals before joining Pennsylvania Ballet in 1964. Now retired.

TURNEY, MATT. Born in Americus, Ga. Joined Martha Graham Co. in 1951. Also danced with Donald McKayle, Alvin Ailey, Paul Taylor, and Pearl Lang.

TUROFF, CAROL. Born Jan. 14, 1947 in New Jersey. NYU graduate; studied with Jean Erdman, Erick Hawkins. Debut 1968 with Hawkins Co., subsequently appearing with Jean Erdman, and in concert.

TUZER, TANJU. Born May 17, 1944 in Istanbul, Turkey. Trained at State Conservatory. Made debut with Turkish State Ballet 1961. Joined Hamburg State Opera Ballet 1969, Harkness Ballet 1972.

UCHIDA, CHRISTINE. Born in Chicago, Ill. Studied with Vincenzo Celli, School of American Ballet, American Ballet Center. Debut 1972 with Joffrey Ballet.

UCHIYAMA, AYAKO. Born in Hokkaido, Japan in 1925. Began studies in Tokyo with Masami Kuni, Aiko Yuzaki and Takaya Eguchi. In 1950 organized Uchiyama Art Dance School. Awarded scholarship to study in U.S. with Graham, Horst, Limon, Cunningham, Joffrey, Ballet Russe School, and Luigi's Jazz Center. Has given many concerts and recitals in Japan, and U.S. under sponsorship of Japan and Asia Societies.

ULANOVA, GALINA. Born in Russia, Jan. 8, 1910. Studied with Vagonova. Graduate of Leningrad State School of Ballet. Joined Bolshoi Company and became Russia's greatest lyric ballerina. Now in retirement, but coaches for Bolshoi.

ULLATE, VICTOR. Born in Spain. Studied with Rosella Hightower, Maria de Avila. Debut with Antonio. At 18 joined Bejart Ballet.

URIS, VICTORIA. Born Nov. 28, 1949 in NYC. Graduate NYU. Studied with May O'Donnell, Viola Farber, Martha Graham, Nenette Charisse. Debut 1971 with Norman Walker company, and subsequently with NY Dance Collective, Sandra Neels, Rosalind Newman, Paul Taylor Dance Co. (1975).

UTHOFF, MICHAEL. Born in Santiago, Chile, Nov. 5, 1943. Graduate of U. Chile. Studied at Juilliard, School of American Ballet, American Ballet Center, and with Tudor, and Limon. Debut with Limon's company in 1964. Appeared with American Dance Theatre before he joined Joffrey Ballet in 1965, First Chamber Dance Co. (1969). Since 1972 artistic director of Hartford Ballet, and teacher at SUNY in Purchase N.Y.

VALDOR, ANTONY. Began career with Marquis de Cuevas Company, subsequently appearing with Jose Torres' Ballet Espagnol, Opera de Marseille, Theatre du Chatelet, Theatre Massimo de Palermo. Currently ballet master of San Francisco Ballet.

VALENTINE, PAUL. Born March 23, 1919 in N.Y.C. Began career at 14 with Ballet Russe de Monte Carlo, subsequently as Val Valentinoff with Fokine Ballet, and Mordkin Ballet. Since 1937 has appeared in theatre, TV, and night clubs.

VAN DYKE, JAN. Born April 15, 1941, in Washington, D.C. Studied with Ethel Butler, Martha Graham, Merce Cunningham, and at Conn. College, Henry St. Playhouse. Dancer-choreographer-director of Church St. Dance Co., and appeared with DTW.

VAN HAMEL, MARTINE. Born Nov. 16, 1945 in Brussels. Attended Natl. Ballet School of Canada. Debut 1963 with Natl. Ballet of Can. Guest with Royal Swedish Ballet, Royal Winnipeg Ballet, Joffrey Ballet, before joining ABT. Became soloist in 1971, principal 1973.

VARDI, YAIR. Born May 29, 1948 in Israel. Studied at Batsheva Dance Studio, and joined Batsheva Dance Co.

VARGAS, GEORGE. Born Apr. 19, 1949 in Barranquilla, Col. Studied with Thomas Armour, School of American Ballet. Debut 1968 with Eglevsky Ballet; joined Boston Ballet 1969.

VASSILIEV, VLADIMIR. Born in Russia in 1940. Studied at Bolshoi School and joined company in 1958, becoming soloist in 1959, then principal.

VEGA, ANTONIO. Born in Huelva, Spain. Studied with Pericet and Antonio Marin. Has danced with Jose Molina, Luisillo, Marienna, Antonio, and Jose Greco. Joined Ballet Granada in 1968 as soloist.

VERNON, GWEN. Born Jan. 13, 1926 in Culver City, CA. Studied with Ernest Belcher, Carmelita Maracci. Danced with Aida Broadbent, Jack Cole companies. Became assistant to Cole, before becoming star of Bdwy musicals.

VERDY, VIOLETTE. Born in Brittany, Dec. 1, 1933. Debut in 1944 with Roland Petit. Danced with Royal Ballet, Paris Opera Ballet before joining ABT in 1957. Joined NYC Ballet as principal in 1958.

VERE, DIANA. Born Sept. 29, 1942 in Trinidad. Studied at Royal Ballet School and joined company in 1962; promoted to soloist in 1968, principal 1970.

VERED, AVNER. Born Feb. 3, 1938 in Israel. Debut 1965 with Bertram Ross, subsequently with Jose Limon, Pearl Lang.

VERSO, EDWARD. Born Oct. 25, 1941 in N.Y.C. Studied with Vincenzo Celli. Appeared on Bdwy and with Ballets U.S.A., before joining American Ballet Theatre in 1962, Joffrey Ballet in 1969. Directs his own school, and Festival Dance Theatre in N.J.

VESAK, NORBERT. Born Oct. 22, 1936 in Vancouver, Can. Studied at Royal Acad., with Craske, Shawn, Volkova, Cunningham, Koner, La Meri. Director San Francisco Opera Ballet 1971–74. Guest choreographer for many companies. Director-choreographer Met Opera Ballet 1976.

VEST, VANE. Born in Vienna. Studied with Larry Boyette. Debut with Denver Civic Ballet; subsequently with Ballet Theatre Players, ABT 1968, San Francisco Ballet 1972.

VETRA, VIJA. Born Feb. 6 in Latvia. Studied in Vienna, and India. Debut 1945 in Burgertheatre, Vienna. Since 1955 has toured world in solo concerts, and teaches in own N.Y. studio.

VIKULOV, SERGEI. Trained at Leningrad Ballet School. Joined Kirov Company in 1956.

VILLELLA, EDWARD. Born Oct. 1, 1936, in Bayside, Queens, N.Y. Began studies at School of American Ballet at 10. Graduate of Maritime College. Joined N.Y.C. Ballet in 1957, and rapidly rose to leading dancer. First male guest artist to appear with Royal Danish Ballet. Appeared in N.Y.C. Center productions of "Brigadoon," and on TV. Recently choreographed for N.Y.C. Ballet and own ensemble.

VODEHNAL, ANDREA. Born in 1938 in Oak Park, Ill. Studied at Ballet Russe School, and School of American Ballet, and with Semenova and Danilova. Joined Ballet Russe de Monte Carlo in 1957, and became soloist in 1961. Joined National Ballet in 1962 as ballerina.

VOLLMAR, JOCELYN. Entered native San Francisco Ballet School at 12 and joined company at 17 in 1943. Later with N.Y.C.

Caroline Todd

Michael Uthoff

Karin von Aroldingen

Norbert Vesak

Kerry Williams

Ballet, American Ballet Theatre, de Cuevas Ballet, and Borovansky Australian Ballet. Rejoined S.F. Ballet in 1957, and has choreographed several ballets.

VON AROLDINGEN, KARIN. Born July 9, 1941 in Germany. Studied with Edwardova, Gsovsky. Debut 1958 in Frankfurt. Joined N.Y.C. Ballet in 1961, soloist 1967, principal 1972.

VONDERSAAR, JEANETTE. Born May 17, 1951 in Indianapolis, Ind. Trained at Harkness School, and made debut with company in 1969.

WAGNER, RICHARD. Born Jan. 30, 1939 in Atlantic City, N.J. Studied with Antony Tudor. Debut with Ballet Russe de Monte Carlo in 1957; joined American Ballet Theatre in 1960, and Harkness Ballet in 1964 as dancer and choreographer.

WAGONER, DAN. Born July 13, 1932 in Springfield, W.Va. Attended U.W.Va. Studied with Ethel Butler, Martha Graham. Debut 1958 with Graham, subsequently with Merce Cunningham, Paul Taylor, and in own choreography and concerts.

WALKER, DAVID HATCH. Born Mar. 14, 1949 in Edmonton, Can. Studied at Natl. Ballet School, Toronto Dance Theatre, Martha Graham. Debut 1968 with Ballet Rambert, London, subsequently with Donald McKayle, Lar Lubovitch, Martha Graham.

WALKER, NORMAN. Born in N.Y.C. in 1934. Studied at HS Performing Arts. Appeared with May O'Donnell, Yuriko, Pauline Koner, and Pearl Lang. Began choreographing while in army, and afterward taught at Utah State U., Choreographed for musicals and festivals throughout U.S. Now appears with own company, and choreographs for it as well as others. Also teaches, and was artistic director of Batsheva Co., and Jacob's Pillow.

WALL, DAVID. Born in London, March 15, 1946. Attended Royal Ballet School, and made debut with company in 1962. Now a principal.

WALLSTROM, GAY. Born Mar. 9, 1949 in Beaumont, Tex. Studied at American Ballet Center and joined Joffrey Ballet in 1968.

WARD, CHARLES. Born Oct. 24, 1952 in Los Angeles, Cal. Studied with Audrey Share, Stanley Holden, Michael Lland, Ballet Theatre School, Gene Marinaccio. Debut 1970 with Houston Ballet; joined ABT 1972; promoted to soloist 1974; principal 1976.

WARDELL, MARCIA. Born Dec. 22, 1948 in Lansing, Mich. Studied with Elizabeth Wiel Bergmann, Betty Jones, Ethel Winter, Alfredo Corvino, Murray Louis, Nikolais, Gladys Bailin. Debut in 1971 with Murray Louis Co.

WARNER, DENISE. Born Mar. 24, 1951 in Meriden, Conn. Studied with Vera Nikitins, American Ballet Theatre School. Debut 1968 with Hartford Ballet; joined ABT 1972.

WARREN, GRETCHEN. Born Apr. 7, 1945 in Princeton, N.J. Attended Aparri School, School of Ballet, Royal Ballet, and National Ballet Schools. Debut in 1964 with Covent Garden Opera Ballet; subsequently with Icelandic Natl. Opera Ballet, National Ballet (1964–5), Pa. Ballet from 1965. Made soloist in 1968.

WARREN, VINCENT. Born Aug. 31, 1938 in Jacksonville, Fla. Studied at Ballet Theatre School. Debut 1957 with Met Opera Ballet, subsequently with Santa Fe Opera, James Waring, Aileen Pasloff, Guatemala Natl. Ballet, Penn. Ballet, Cologne Opera Ballet, Les Grands Ballets Canadiens.

WATANABE, MIYOKO. Born in Japan and began training at 6. Joined all-girls Kabuki Troupe and became one of its leading performers. Came to U.S. in 1960 as announcer-interpreter for Kabuki troupe, and remained to perform in concert and teach classic Japanese dances.

WATTS, JONATHAN. Born in 1933 in Cheyenne, Wyo. Studied with Joffrey, Shurr, and O'Donnell. Debut with Joffrey before joining N.Y.C. Ballet in 1954, Australian Ballet 1962, and Cologne Opera Ballet as premier danseur in 1965. Now director Am. Ballet Center.

WAYNE, DENNIS. Born July 19, 1945 in St. Petersburg, Fla. Debut 1962 with Norman Walker Co.; subsequently with Harkness Ballet 1963, Joffrey Ballet 1970; ABT as soloist 1974. Resigned 1975 to form own company.

WEBER, DIANA. Born Jan. 16, in Passaic, N.J. Studied at Ballet Theatre School. Joined ABT in 1962; became soloist in 1966; San Francisco Ballet 1973.

WEISS, JEROME. Born in Florida; graduate Juilliard. Debut with Miami Ballet; subsequently with Atlanta Ballet, Netherlands Dans Theatre 1968, Harkness Ballet 1971, San Francisco Ballet 1973.

WEISS, ROBERT. Born Mar. 1, 1949 in NYC. Studied at School of Am. Ballet. Joined NYC Ballet in 1966; promoted to soloist in 1972.

WELCH, GARTH. Born Apr. 14, 1936 in Brisbane, Aust. Studied with Phyllis Danaher, Victor Gzovsky, Anna Northcote, Zaraspe, Martha Graham. Debut 1955 with Borovansky Ballet, subsequently with Western Theatre Ballet, Marquis de Cuevas Ballet, Australian Ballet (1962).

WELLS, BRUCE. Born Jan. 17, 1950 in Tacoma, Wash. Studied with Patricia Cairns, Banff School, School of American Ballet. Joined N.Y.C. Ballet in 1967, dancing soloist and principal roles since 1969.

WELLS, DORREN. Born June 25, 1937 in London. Studied at Royal Ballet School and made debut with company in 1955, rising to ballerina.

WENGERD, TIM. Born Jan. 4, 1945 in Boston. Graduate U. Utah. Studied with Elizabeth Waters, Yuriko, Ethel Winter, Merce Cunningham, Viola Farber, Donald McKayle. Debut in 1966 with Ririe-Woodbury Co. Dancer-choreographer with Repertory Dance Theatre from 1966. Joined Graham Co. 1972.

WESCHE, PATRICIA. Born Oct. 13, 1952 in West Islip, N.Y. Attended American Ballet Theatre School. Debut 1969 with ABT.

WESLOW, WILLIAM. Born Mar. 20, 1925 in Seattle, Wash. Studied with Mary Ann Wells. Appeared on Bdwy and TV before joining Ballet Theatre in 1949. Joined N.Y.C. Ballet in 1958.

WHELAN, SUSAN. Born Feb. 26, 1948 in N.Y.C. Studied with Eglevsky, at Ballet Theatre, and Harkness schools. Joined Harkness Ballet in 1966, ABT 1971.

WHITE, FRANKLIN. Born in 1924 in Shoreham, Kent, Eng. After 3 years with Ballet Rambert, joined Royal Ballet in 1942. Is also well known as lecturer on ballet.

WHITE, GLENN. Born Aug. 6, 1949 in Pittsburg, Calif. Studied at Norfolk Ballet Academy. American Ballet Center, Debut 1968 with N.Y.C. Opera, joined Joffrey Company in 1969.

WHITE, ONNA. Born in 1925 in Cape Breton Island, Nova Scotia. Debut with San Francisco Opera Ballet Co. Became assistant choreographer to Michael Kidd, and subsequently choreographer for Bdwy, Hollywood, and London productions.

WHITENER, WILLIAM. Born Aug. 17, 1951 in Seattle, Wash. Studied with Karen Irvin, Mary Staton, Hector Zaraspe, Perry Brunson. Debut 1969 with City Center Joffrey Ballet.

WILDE, PATRICIA. Born in Ottawa, Can. July 16, 1928 where she studied before joining Marquis de Cuevas' Ballet International and continuing studies at School of American Ballet. Joined N.Y.C. Ballet in 1950 and became one of its leading ballerinas, having danced almost every role in the company's repertoire. Director of Harkness School. Now teaches. Ballet mistress for ABT.

WILLIAMS, ANTHONY. Born June 11, 1946 in Naples, Italy. Studied with Virginia Williams and Joffrey. Debut 1964 with Boston Ballet. Joined Joffrey company 1968; rejoined Boston Ballet in 1969. Soloist with Royal Winnipeg Ballet.

WILLIAMS, DANIEL. Born in 1943 in San Francisco. Studied with Welland Lathrop, Gloria Unti, May O'Donnell, Gertrude Shurr, Nina Fonaroff, Wishmary Hunt, Paul Taylor. Joined Taylor's company in 1963 and appears in most of his repertoire.

WILLIAMS, DEREK. Born Dec. 14, 1945 in Jamaica, WI. Studied at Harkness House, Martha Graham School. Debut with Jamaican Ntl. Dance Co. Joined Dance Theatre of Harlem 1968.

WILLIAMS, DUDLEY. Born in N.Y.C. where he began dance lessons at 6. Studied with Shook, O'Donnell, Tudor, Graham, and at Juilliard. Has appeared with May O'Donnell, Martha Graham, Donald McKayle, Talley Beatty, and Alvin Ailey from 1964.

WILLIAMS, KERRY. Born in Philadelphia; studied at San Francisco Ballet School, and made debut with company. Joined American Ballet Co., and returned to SF Ballet in 1972.

Paul Wilson **Anne Wilson** **Joe Wyatt** **Yuriko** **Karoly Zsedenyi**

WILLIAMS, STANLEY. Born in 1925 in Chappel, Eng. Studied at Royal Danish Ballet and joined company in 1943. Became soloist in 1949. Teacher and guest artist since 1950. Ballet master and leading dancer with Ballet Comique (1953–4). Knighted by King of Denmark. Since 1964, on staff of School of Am Ballet.

WILSON, ANNE. Born in Philadelphia. Graduate of U. of Chicago. Studied with Fokine, Tudor, Weidman, Elizabeth Anderson, Etienne Decroux, and Heinz Poll. Debut 1940 with American Ballet Theatre. Also with Weidman, and in 1964 formed own co. Noted for solo concert-lecture "The Ballet Story" which she has toured extensively.

WILSON, JOHN. Born in 1927 in Los Angeles. Studied with Katherine Dunham. Toured with Harriette Ann Gray, appeared in concert with own group, and Joyce Trisler. Joined Joffrey Ballet in 1956, Harkness Ballet in 1964.

WILSON, PAUL. Born Oct. 19, 1949 in Carbondale, Pa. Studied with Barbara Doerffer, Charles Weidman, Zena Rommett. Joined Weidman Co. 1971. Also danced with Jan Wodynski, Jeff Duncan, Xoregos Co. Formed Theatredance Asylum 1975. Also teaches.

WILSON, SALLIE. Born Apr. 18, 1932 in Ft. Worth, Tex. Studied with Tudor and Craske. Joined American Ballet Theatre in 1959, and in 1963 became principal dancer. Has also appeared with Met Opera and N.Y.C. Ballets.

WILSON, ZANE. Born Feb. 25, 1951 in Elkton, Md. Attended UMd. Trained at Harkness School and joined Harkness Ballet in 1970.

WINTER, ETHEL. Born in Wrentham, Mass., June 18, 1924. Graduate of Bennington College, Soloist with Martha Graham Co. since 1964. Has taught Graham Method in various schools in Eng. and appeared as lecture-demonstrator. Her own choreography has received recognition, and is included in repertoire of Batsheva Co. Also appeared with N.Y.C. Opera, and Sophie Maslow.

WOLENSKI, CHESTER. Born Nov. 16, 1931 in New Jersey. Attended Juilliard, and American School of Ballet. Debut 1956 with Jose Limon, subsequently with Anna Sokolow, Donald McKayle, John Butler, American Dance Theatre, Juilliard Dance Theatre, Jack Moore, Bill Frank and Ruth Currier. Also appeared in musicals.

WONG, MEL. Born Dec. 2, 1938 in Oakland, Cal. Graduate UCLA. Studied at Academy of Ballet. SF Ballet School, School of Am. Ballet, Cunningham Studio. Debut in 1968 with Merce Cunningham Co.

WOOD, DONNA. Born Nov. 21, 1954 in NYC. Joined Alvin Ailey Dance Theatre 1972.

WOODIN, PETER. Born in Tucson, Ariz. Graduate Wesleyan U. Debut 1971 with Lucas Hoving Co.; subsequently with Utah Repertory Dance Theatre, Gus Solomons, Chamber Arts Dance Players, Alvin Ailey Dance Theatre 1973.

WRIGHT, KAREN. Born Oct. 25, 1956 in Denver, CO. Studied at Dance Theatre of Harlem and joined company in 1975.

WRIGHT, REBECCA. Born Dec. 5, 1947 in Springfield, Ohio. Studied with David McLain and Josephine Schwarz. Joined Joffrey Ballet in 1966; ABT 1975 as soloist.

WYATT, JOSEPH. Born Jan. 23, 1950 in Trinidad, WI. Attended State U. of NY. Joined Dance Theatre of Harlem in 1973.

YOHN, ROBERT. Born Sept. 23, 1943 in Fresno, Calif. Studied at Fresno State Col., New Dance Group, and with Charles Kelley, Perry Brunson. Has appeared with New Dance Group, Bruce King, and joined Erick Hawkins Company in 1968.

YOUNG, CYNTHIA. Born Dec. 16, 1954 in Salt Lake City, U. Studied with Carol Reed, Ben Lokey, William Christensen, Anatole Vilzak, Gordon Paxman. Joined Ballet West in 1970; promoted to soloist 1973; principal 1974.

YOUNG, GAYLE. Born Nov. 7, in Lexington, Ky. Began study with Dorothy Pring at U. Calif. Studied at Ballet Theatre School, and joined Joffrey Ballet. Appeared on Bdwy and with N.Y.C. Ballet before joining American Ballet Theatre in 1960. Became principal in 1964.

YOURTH, LINDA. Born in Maplewood, N.J. in 1944. Studied at Sch. of Am. Ballet. At 14 joined Eglevsky's Ballet; NYCB at 16, rising to soloist. Joined Ballet du Grand Theatre de Geneve (1968–71). Returned to NYCB in 1971.

YOUSKEVITCH, IGOR. Born in Moscow, Mar. 13, 1912. Studied with Preobrajenska. Debut in Paris with Nijinska company; joined De Basil's Ballet, then, Ballet Russe de Monte Carlo. In 1946 became premier danseur with Ballet Theatre. Currently operating own school in N.Y.C.

YOUSKEVITCH, MARIA. Born Dec. 11, 1945 in N.Y.C. Studied with father, Igor Youskevitch, and made debut with his company in 1963. Appeared with Met Opera Ballet before joining American Ballet Theatre in 1967. Promoted to soloist 1973.

YUAN, TINA. Born Oct. 9, 1947 in Shanghai, China. Attended Juilliard, Martha Graham School. Debut 1969 with Pearl Lang; subsequently Yuriko 1970, Chinese Dance Co. 1972, Alvin Ailey Co. 1972.

YUDENICH, ALEXEI. Born July 5, 1943 in Sarajevo, Yugoslavia. Studied at Sarajevo Opera Ballet School, and made debut with company. Guest artist with Sagreb Opera Ballet before joining Pennsylvania Ballet in 1964 as principal dancer; retired in 1973 and now teaches.

YURIKO. Born Feb. 2, 1920 in San Jose, Calif. Began professional career at 6 with group that toured Japan for 7 years. Studied with Martha Graham, and joined company in 1944, becoming soloist and choreographer. Formed own company in 1948 with which she has appeared in N.Y. and on tour. Also appeared in musicals.

ZAMIR, BATYA. Studied with Alwin Nikolais, Gladys Bailin, Phyllis Lamhut, Murray Louis, Mimi Garrard, Rachel Fibish, Joy Boutilier, and in own concerts and choreography. Also teaches.

ZHDANOV, YURI. Born in Moscow in 1925. Began career at 12 before attending Bolshoi School. Joined Company in 1944, became Ulanova's partner in 1951. Is now retired.

ZIDE, ROCHELLE. Born in Boston, Ap. 21, 1938. Studied with Hoctor, Williams, Pereyaslavec, Joffrey, Danielian, and at Ballet Russe School. Debut in 1954 with Ballet Russe de Monte Carlo, subsequently appearing with Joffrey Ballet (1958), Ballets U.S.A. (1961), American Dances (1963), N.Y.C. Opera Ballet (1958–63), Ballet Spectaculars (1963), and became ballet mistress of Joffrey Ballet in 1965.

ZIMMERMANN, GERDA. Born Mar. 26, in Cuxhaven, Ger. Studied with Georgi, Wigman, Horst, Zena Rommett. Soloist with Landestheater Hannover 1959–62. Choreographer from 1967. Solo recitals in U.S. from 1967 and in Ger. Formed Kammertanz Theatre. Teaches.

ZITO, DOROTHY. Born in Jersey City, N.J. Attended Juilliard. Studied at Graham, Harkness schools, and N.Y. School of Ballet. Debut 1969 with New Dance Group, subsequently with Pearl Lang.

ZOMPAKOS, STANLEY. Born in N.Y.C. May 12, 1925. Studied with Balanchine and at School of American Ballet. Debut 1942 with New Opera Co. In Bdwy musicals, with Ballet Russe de Monte Carlo (1954–6), and became artistic director of Charleston, S.C., Civic Ballet.

ZORINA, VERA. Born Jan. 2, 1917 in Berlin, Ger. Studied with Edwardova, Tatiana and Victor Gsovsky, Dolin, and Legat. Debut 1930 in Berlin. Toured with Ballet Russe de Monte Carlo (1934–6). Made N.Y.C. debut in "I Married An Angel" in 1938. Joined Ballet Theatre in 1943. Subsequently, appeared in Bdwy productions, films.

ZORITCH, GEORGE. Born in Moscow June 6, 1919. Studied in Lithuania, Paris, and N.Y., with Preobrajenska, Vilzak, Vladimiroff, and Oboukhoff. Debut 1933 with Ida Rubenstein Co. in Paris. Joined de Basil Ballet Russe 1936. Ballet Russe de Monte Carlo 1938, Grand Ballet de Marquis de Cuevas (1951–8), Marina Svetlova Co (1961), then formed own company. A favorite teacher and choreographer for regional ballet companies. Head of UAriz. dance dept

ZSEDENYI, KAROLY. Born in Hungary; studied in Paris with Lubov Egorova. Made debut with Royal Opera Ballet of Budapest becoming first dancer, and later director. 1948 became director of Royal Opera Houses Ballets in Brussels and Antwerp. In 1951 organized Ballet Experimental in Chile. Came to NYC in 1964 and started his school and the Zsedenyi Ballet.

OBITUARIES

CYRIL WILLIAM BEAUMONT, 85, historian and bookseller, died in London, May 24, 1976. At 19 he opened his own bookshop, and soon, C. W. Beaumont & Co. became the recognized center for dance publications in England. In 1922 he co-founded the Cecchetti Society with Enrico Cecchetti. His collected dance criticism is found in "Dancers under My Lens." His principal contribution to dance history is "The Complete Book of Ballets," first issued in 1937 with several later updated editions. His honors included the Legion of Honor in 1950 and the Order of the British Empire in 1962. His total published works of more than 60 volumes included his 1974 memoirs "Bookseller at the Ballet." No reported survivors.

BUSBY BERKELEY, nee William Berkeley Enos, 80, choreographer, died March 14, 1976, in his home in Palm Springs, CA. Began his career as a Broadway dancer. In the 1930's he went to Hollywood to choreograph for films. Some of his best known movies are "42nd Street," "Ziegfeld Girls," and "Gold Diggers of 1935." His sixth wife survives.

DAVID BLAIR, nee David Butterfield, 43, dancer-choreographer, and at the time of his death in London on Apr. 1, 1976, he was director-designate of the Norwegian Ballet. A scholarship student at Sadler's Wells School, he later joined the company which became the Royal Ballet. In 1961 he became Margot Fonteyn's official partner. Surviving are his widow, ballerina Maryon Lane, and twin daughters.

HEINZ BOSL, 28, first soloist of the Munich State Opera Ballet, died of cancer on June 12, 1975. In recent years he had partnered Dame Margot Fonteyn on several of her world-wide tours. No reported survivors.

HILDA BUTSOVA, nee Hilda Boots, 78, died of a heart attack March 21, 1976, in White Plains, NY, where she was visiting. From 1912-1925 she was with the Pavlova company, and after that with Michael Mordkin. English-born Butsova had been living in NY since her retirement in 1932. Surviving are her husband Harry Mills who was manager of the Pavlova company when they were married in 1925, and a son.

LISA DUNCAN, 76, one of six adopted daughters of Isadora Duncan, died Jan. 24, 1976, in Dresden, Ger. In the 1920's and 1930's she danced with the Isadorables, and later taught in Paris. No reported survivors.

DEBORAH KAYE, 83, nee Deborah Goldfarb, dancer, died May 4, 1976, in NYC. Her Broadway shows included "Blossom Time" and "Diamond Lil" with Mae West, and later with her husband, tap dancer Murray Evans, she ran dancing schools in the Bronx. Two sisters and a brother survive.

EDITH JANE FAULKNER, 81, former dancer, died July 29, 1975 in Los Angeles, after a brief illness. In 1929 she began operating the Falcon Dance Studios in Hollywood, in partnership with her husband, Ralph Faulkner, who survives.

SYVILLA FORT, 58, dancer-teacher, and pioneer in black dance, died of cancer on November 8, 1975, in NYC. As a teacher she provided a spiritual home together with training and inspiration for three generations of black artists at her Manhattan studio, and for eight years before that she was with the Teachers College of Columbia University. From 1948 to 1955 she was dance director at the Catherine Dunham School. Her unique style of Afro-Caribbean dance is recognized as being the foundation for modern black dance. She had been a soloist with the Dunham dancers and appeared with them in the film, "Stormy Weather". Born in Seattle, she was the widow of dancer, Buddy Phillips. Surviving are two brothers and a stepson.

David Blair

BARBARA FROME, 54, former Broadway and club dancer, died of cancer on March 17, 1976, in Hollywood. Her many credits included "George White's Scandals" and "Earl Carroll's Vanities". Her husband and son survive.

ELIZAVETA PAVLOVNA GERDT, 84, Soviet ballerina and teacher, died in November of 1975 in the USSR. She had danced with Nijinski, and was well known as a teacher of a generation of Soviet dancers. From 1908 to 1928 she created works for Folkine as well as dancing the roles of Aurora, Odette-Odile, Giselle, and Raymonda. After her retirement she became a leading teacher for Kirov and Bolshoi. No reported survivors.

FERNANDO GRAHAL, 32, nee Fernando Felix Grajales, dancer-choreographer, was killed by an armed fugitive on September 4, 1975, in San Juan, P.R. He appeared in several Broadway musicals, and choreographed the Jacques Brel production of "Man of La Mancha" in Brussels and Paris. He is survived by his mother, brother, and a sister.

FIORELLA KEANE, reported in her 40's, ballet mistress of ABT, died June 9, 1976, in NYC after a brief illness. She began her professional career as a dancer with the Royal Ballet, later becoming a teacher with the Juilliard School and ballet mistress of Alvin Ailey's Dance Theatre. Surviving are her parents and two sons.

BORIS KNIASEFF, 75, dancer-teacher, died October 6, 1975, in Paris after a brief illness. In 1932 he was named ballet master at the Opera Comique, and later choreographed for Ballet Russe, Roland Petite, and the Rome Opera. No reported survivors.

JOHN KRIZA, 56, dancer and former star of ABT, was drowned in the Gulf of Mexico on August 18, 1975, while visiting his sister. A pioneer of American Ballet, he joined ABT at its founding in 1940, and for more than twenty years was one of its principal dancers. He was best known for his roles in "Billy the Kid", "Fancy Free", and "Rodeo", as well as many classics. After retirement in 1966 he served as assistant director of ABT and was guest teacher throughout the country. He is survived by his sister.

ALEKSANDR LAPAURI, 49, dancer-choreographer, died in a car crash August 8, 1975. Formerly one of the Bolshoi Ballet's leading dramatic dancers, he was often teamed with his wife, Raissa Struchkova, thrilling audiences with their athletic feats. He joined the Bolshoi in 1944 and later choreographed two Ballets for them as well as teaching for their school since 1946. In 1955, the Government awarded him title of Honored Artist of the Russian Soviet Federated Socialist Republic. His wife survives.

TILLY LOSCH, 70, international exotic dancer of the 1920's and 30's, died of cancer on December 24, 1975, in NYC. Acclaimed by critics for her "superb grace", "brilliant technique", and "personal charm", she made her debut at 6 at the Royal Opera House in Vienna. With her sensational first solo appearance in "Schlagobers" in 1924 she became a prima-ballerina overnight. Max Reinhardt then starred her in his Salzburg Festival for two seasons. Later she starred with Lotte Lenya in Ballanchine's, "The Seven Deadly Sins", and with the Astaires in "The Bandwagon". She choreographed and danced in the revues, "This Year of Grace" and "Wake Up and Dream". She also acted in the films, "The Garden of Allah", "Duel in the Sun", and "The Good Earth". She was married twice, and left no immediate survivors.

MARIA MAKAROVA, 90, ballerina, died in November, 1975, in Rio de Janeiro, Brazil. She danced with Pavlova in 1910, and married Vladimir Dranichnikoff in 1920. Her chief successes were "Une Nuit d'Egypte", "Salome", and "La Bayadere". She was made an honorary Artist of the Republic in 1934, and later taught in Paris and Rio until her death. No reported survivors.

MARGARET McGONIGLE, 66, nee Margaret M. Frost, dancer, died August 27, 1975 in Philadelphia. One of the original 1925 Roxyettes at New York's Roxy Theatre, she began dancing with the Gertrude Hoffman girls when she was 16. Surviving are her husband, mother, and sister.

JO MIELZINER, 74, stage designer, died on March 15, 1976, in NYC. Although best known for his theatrical work, he was also an outstanding ballet designer, creating sets for Tudor's, "Pillars of Fire", Ballanchine's, "Who Cares?", and "Slaughter on Tenth Avenue", as well as many Broadway musicals with a strong balletic element. He is survived by two sons and a daughter.

SARAH OSNATH-HALEVY, 62, dancer-singer-mime, died October 12, 1975, of lung cancer in NYC. She was first brought to the U.S. by S. Hurok in the mid-1930's for a concert tour. She performed Hebrew, Yemenite, Persian, and Russian songs and dances. No reported survivors.

DMITRI SHOSTAKOVITCH, 68, internationally acclaimed composer, died near Moscow August 9, 1975, of a heart ailment. He was the most famous and publicized of contemporary Soviet composers, and contributed works for a number of ballets including "The Golden Age", "The Bolt", and "The Stream". Leonide Massine used his "Symphony No. 1" for "Rouge et Noir" in 1939, and the first movement of "Symphony No. 7" was used by Kirov's Igor Belsky for a ballet. Surviving are his widow, a son, and a daughter.

LUBOV TCHERNICHEVA, 85, former ballerina for Diaghilev and Massine, died in March, 1976, in London. She became a soloist with Diaghilev's Ballet Russe in 1913 and remained with the company until 1929. She later danced leading roles in Massine's, "Les Femmes de Bonne Humeur", Nijinska's, "Les Noces", Ballanchine's, "Apollo", and in Cranko's, "Romeo and Juliet" which was her last stage appearance in 1959. No reported survivors.

PAVEL VIRSKY, 70, leading Soviet choreographer, died July 8, 1975, in USSR. He was, with Moiseyev, one of the great pioneers of the folk ensemble, and from 1937 until his death he was artistic director and principal choreographer of the Ukrainian Dance Company. Early in his career he served as ballet master in many parts of the Soviet Union. In 1936 he was principal dancer and choreographer of the Kiev Opera Ballet. In 1962, his Ukrainian company made its debut at the Met to unanimous raves. No reported survivors.

John Kriza
as Billy the Kid

JAMES WARING, 53, choreographer-dancer, died December 1975, of cancer in NYC. He was a leader of a generation of choreographers that flowered in the early 1960's, remarkable for his originality and sense of style. He used this knowledge to the fullest in such works as "Imperceptible Elongation No. 1", "At the Cafe Fleurette", "Tomato Expose", "Phrases", and "Amoretti". Both the Pennsylvania Ballet and the Netherlands Dance Theatre were among the companies to perform his works. No survivors were reported.

PRINCESS WHITE, 95, jazz dancer-singer, collapsed and died March 20, 1976, in Mamaroneck, N.Y. after a performance. She was a headliner in the South in the era when Jazz and blues were taking shape. She also wrote several compositions. Surviving are a daughter, three adopted daughters, and an adopted son.

LEONID YAKOBSON, 71, Soviet ballet master, died in October 1975, in Moscow. He had been with the Bolshoi and Kirov Theatres creating solos and small ensemble works for which he was best known in the West. As a choreographer in 1930 he created an acrobatic solo for Ulanova in "The Golden Age", and later gained importance with Strauss's, "Til Eulenspiegel". His best known ballets were "Spartacus", "Shuraleah", and the solo, "Vestris" for Baryshnikov. In 1961 he was awarded the gold medal of the Dance Academy in Paris, and in 1970 founded the Choreographic Miniature Ensemble. He also staged operas and films, his last work being the Soviet-American film, "The Bluebird". His wife survives.

ALEXEI YERMOLEYEV, 65, Soviet dancer-teacher-choreographer, died of a heart attack in December, 1975, in Moscow. As long time partner of Ulanova, he was a principal dancer with Kirov and the Bolshoi. In 1940 he was artistic director of the Riga Opera and Ballet Theatre. His staged works include "The Nightingale" and "Flames of the Heart". A dancer of heroic style, his best known roles were in "Romeo and Juliet", "The Bronze Horseman", "The Red Flowers", and "Giselle". Following his retirement he taught at the Bolshoi School. No reported survivors.

CHRISTL ZIMMERL, 37, dancer, died March 19, 1976, of cancer in Vienna. A leading dancer with the Vienna Opera since 1956, best roles were caractere and demicaractere. Her husband and children survive.

INDEX

207

209

210

213

218